GENDER AND THE POLITICS
OF WELFARE REFORM

WOMEN IN CULTURE AND SOCIETY
A series edited by Catharine R. Stimpson

GENDER AND THE
POLITICS
OF WELFARE REFORM

Mothers' Pensions in Chicago, 1911–1929

JOANNE L. GOODWIN

THE UNIVERSITY OF CHICAGO PRESS
Chicago and London

JOANNE L. GOODWIN is assistant professor of history at the University of Nevada, Las Vegas.

THE UNIVERSITY OF CHICAGO PRESS, CHICAGO 60637
THE UNIVERSITY OF CHICAGO PRESS, LTD., LONDON

© 1997 by The University of Chicago
All rights reserved. Published 1997
Printed in the United States of America

06 05 04 03 02 01 00 99 98 97   1 2 3 4 5

ISBN: 0–226–30392–6 (cloth)
ISBN: 0–226–30393–4 (paper)

Library of Congress Cataloging-in-Publication Data

Goodwin, Joanne L.
    Gender and the politics of welfare reform : mothers' pensions in Chicago, 1911–1929 / Joanne L. Goodwin.
        p.   cm. — (Women in culture and society)
    Includes bibliographical references and index.
        ISBN 0-226-30392-6 (cloth : alk. paper). — ISBN 0-226-30393-4 (paper : alk. paper)
        1. Mothers' pensions—Illinois—Chicago—History. 2. Women heads of households—Government policy—Illinois—Chicago—History. I. Title. II. Series.
    HV699.4.C48G66   1997
    362.83'82'0977311—dc21   96-47158
                                                                                                   CIP

To Roy J. Goodwin and Laurie R. Lytel

Contents

Tables

Foreword

Catharine R. Stimpson

In 1996, the U.S. government passed legislation to end "welfare as we know it." Helping this to happen was a collective delusion that we, the citizens of the United States, knew what we were ending. We did not. Preferring ideology to reality, ignorance to awareness, half-truths to complexity, we instead ended welfare as many people wished to know it.

This mixture of errors triumphant and political will occurred despite the best efforts of scholars such as Linda Gordon, Mark H. Leff, Patrick D. Moynihan, and Theda Skocpol to write responsible if varying accounts of welfare. Fortunately, their work comprises a vital repository of knowledge to use as we design welfare's post–"end it as we know it" future. Joanne L. Goodwin joins their company with her notable first book.

The focus of *Gender and the Politics of Welfare Reform*—the mothers' pension in Chicago between 1900 and 1930—is crucial. For the mothers' pension was the first social welfare policy for women in the United States; Chicago, the "city of . . . wind lifting people,"[1] the home of reformers and social scientists, was a pioneer in establishing this policy; and the period from 1900 to 1930 was one of reform and debate about American citizenship and the government's responsibility for its citizens, including poor and vulnerable ones.

Goodwin's careful, resonant narrative makes three persuasive arguments. First, the mothers' pension was a policy about women and gender. Not until the 1920s did the justification for such state spending shift to the support of children. Claiming the role of citizen, women helped to shape this policy, but it emerged only after wrenching contests about women's nature and status. Goodwin is correctly attentive to the importance of class, racial, and ethnic divergences among women. The well-educated, middle-class reformer living in a settlement house tended to respond to the mothers' pension differently than an ill-educated, working-class, immigrant widow living in a tenement with several children to bring up. Foreshadowing the 1996 welfare legislation, such a woman was to lose her county-supplied funds in 1913 because her family was "alien."

Goodwin's second argument is that there was a political struggle, not only to create policy, but to control the jobs and funding that accompanied the mothers' pension program. She draws on archival sources to dramatize a ferocious struggle among political parties, participants in civil society, and the new government bureaucracies whose existence was and still is questioned. Third, Goodwin analyzes the economic roles that pensioned women were required to play. Even as the state recognized their service as mothers, it demanded "self-support and fiscal responsibility" (p. 157). A forerunner of contemporary workfare accompanied the founding of welfare. African-American women, culturally banned by virulent racism as potentially fit "mothers of the race," were then racially stereotyped as fit members of the labor force.

Significantly but not surprisingly, the last part of *Gender and the Politics of Welfare Reform* offers a "political lesson": "While the problems of economic security for mother-only families cannot be solved outside the context of these larger transitions in our political economy, opportunities exist to find universal solutions. Single-mother families share many of the same problems as working-poor families. Policies directed at those areas of shared need would have a greater chance for political support. Americans are unlikely to reduce their expectations of their government, but how far the public will go to expand social provision for the poor remains to be seen" (pp. 196–97). Goodwin's account offers activists the complicating but clarifying knowledge we can derive from history—if we have the realism to do so.

Acknowledgments

This book began as a dissertation at the University of Michigan and has been shaped by several individuals who helped me formulate the original questions and design of the study. Louise Tilly first drew my attention to the importance of examining gender in the process of state formation and set me on this worthwhile path. Mary Corcoran, Carol Karlsen, and Maris Vinovskis grounded this work with their own respective insights on poverty, gender, and policy history. I am most indebted to Terry McDonald, whose questions gave structure to my ideas, whose intellectual challenges made the work stronger, and whose wit and wisdom greatly enhanced the entire process. My career in academia began in the Women's History Program at Sarah Lawrence College under the able guidance of Amy Swerdlow. Her help and the intellectual stimulation of the college changed the direction of my professional life and formed the scholarly foundation for this work.

I am deeply appreciative of the financial support contributed toward the research and writing of this book by the American Council of Learned Societies, National Endowment for the Humanities Summer Stipend Program, American Historical Association's Albert J. Beveridge Grant for Research in the History of the Western Hemisphere, and the University of Michigan. A faculty development leave from the University of Nevada, Las Vegas, provided much needed time as I completed this book.

One of the most valued resources available to researchers is the able and willing assistance of librarians and archivists. I have benefited much from the aid of those associated with the Chicago Historical Society, Newberry Library, Library of Congress, National Archives, and the University of Chicago Library. Mary Ann Bamberger at the University Library of the University of Illinois at Chicago offered special assistance on my research questions over several years. I also want to thank the librarians at the University of Nevada, Las Vegas who helped considerably in the last round of manuscript preparation.

I am grateful to Blackwell Publishers for allowing me to reprint some of the material in chapters 1, 2, and 5 of this book, which previously appeared in "An American Experiment in Paid Motherhood: The Implementation of Mothers' Pensions in Early Twentieth Century Chicago," *Gender and History* 4:3

(Autumn 1992): 323–343. The *Journal of Social History* has allowed me to publish in the Conclusion parts of my article, "'Employable Mothers' and 'Suitable Work': A Re-evaluation of Welfare and Wage-earning for Women in the Twentieth-Century United States," which appeared during winter 1995.

I have benefited from many lively conversations and debates with scholars of gender and the welfare state over the course of several years. The ideas in this book developed out of and in response to comments on my research by Eileen Boris, Linda Gordon, Molly Ladd-Taylor, Sybil Lipschultz, Sonya Michel, Barbara Nelson, Ann Orloff, James Patterson, and Theda Skocpol. In particular, many friends and colleagues gave generously of their time to read and comment on all or part of the manuscript. Paula Baker, Julie Greene, Alice Kessler-Harris, and Rickie Solinger provided helpful support and important criticisms at an early stage of revision. Eileen Boris, Miriam Cohen, Elizabeth Faue, and Robyn Muncy read the entire manuscript and provided useful suggestions.

Special thanks are owed to Karen Wilson. She was a wonderful editor, who guided me through the process with friendly advice. Carol Saller improved the book with her valuable questions and copyediting.

Friends have made the completion of this project more pleasurable. Jan Denali, Odessa DeGrieck Denali, LeAnn Fields, Melanie Hawthorne, and Diane Meisenhelter offered support, friendship, and invaluable advice along the way. Laurie Lytel deserves much credit for helping me to keep things in perspective. Her humor and constant support made the writing of this book more enjoyable.

"Let the Progressive Twins Do Your Work," political cartoon, October 1914. Photo courtesy of the Newberry Library.

Introduction

In 1913, Illinois women celebrated the victory of their suffrage campaign. Catherine Waugh McCulloch, a lawyer who had played a major role in the campaign, called it women's "biggest victory" to date and encouraged women to use their new voting power on "everything that affects our lives and our homes and our health and our happiness."[1] Chicago social reformers Harriet Vittum and Mary McDowell wasted no time in exercising their new powers. They ran for the office of Cook County commissioner. As a political cartoon published in the *Chicago Daily Tribune* illustrated, they appealed to the era's hybrid image of women in politics. The candidates, armed with a broom and a brush, chased two male characterizations of political corruption. "If we are elected," the caption read, "we will begin to scrub and sweep at once to clean up the county board."[2] Their campaigns ended abruptly when the state Supreme Court limited the franchise victory and excluded county offices, but other women entered campaigns for eligible offices such as Chicago's "alderwomanic" positions in 1914. Candidates frequently used domestic slogans, such as cleaning up politics, putting the public house in order, and extending social welfare as a way to appeal to women voters. Many reform women were well-positioned to capitalize on the new opportunities of citizenship presented by the vote.[3]

During the same period in another part of Chicago, an Italian immigrant family negotiated a different set of challenges. Seven years earlier, the Capri family immigrated to the United States from Sicily. Although the father soon began his own barber shop in Chicago, repeated illnesses kept him from earning a steady living. When he died in 1912, the family had no life insurance and no family network to help them through the transition. Mrs. Capri found herself ill prepared to support a family of five children, having never worked for wages, but despite the fact that she spoke only a little English, she began to take small jobs sewing or washing. The Capris soon made the acquaintance of a network of private Chicago agencies, including the Visiting Nurses Association, the Municipal Tuberculosis Sanitarium, the United Charities, and the Vocational Bureau, which provided scholarships for two of the children. They had left the Roman Catholic church, but a Protestant church contributed three dollars a week over a period of seven years for their aid. The family also received a county-funded mothers' pension for a brief period of time, but amendments to the policy in 1913 disqualified them on the basis of citizenship. Mrs. Capri represented the prototypical "dependent mother." Through no fault of her own she must raise her family alone, but do so while she earned wages too low to support one, let alone six people. In addition, she faced particular legal liabilities. Her status as the wife of a nonresident immigrant man limited her claim to public aid as well as to the vote.[4]

These Chicago stories illustrate two of the most challenging issues of the twentieth century—the shifting boundaries of citizenship and Americans' increased expectations of their government. American politics underwent a major transformation during the first decades of the twentieth century as Americans realigned their views on the question of political citizenship. On one hand, women struggled for and won the right to vote in all the states by 1920, while at the same time southern African Americans lost this right and others through Jim Crow laws. The changes in politics extended beyond voting to the structure of politics and ideas about government. The system of courts and parties that had operated during the nineteenth century proved inadequate to address the problems and mediate the conflicting interests of an increasingly complex society. Interest-group politics emerged as a force in a political world of party organizations; liberalism challenged the distribution of power and resources; and the government began to take a more active role in Americans' lives. Although the public sector remained small in comparison to its development by midcentury, these years saw the expansion of government bureaucracy as well as greater demands for measures of social provision. Americans' involvement in debates on citizenship and the role of government took place not on the distant level of national government but on the local level—in cities and in states.[5]

Organized women played a significant role in the transition from a limited government to one that expanded its responsibility for social provision. Working through voluntary associations and civic organizations, they lobbied their elected officials to place a greater share of the costs and operation of services for the ill, aged, youth, and indigent in the public sector. This "domestication of politics," which Paula Baker identified, relied upon a shift in the role of political parties as well as the organization of middle-class women. By the Progressive Era, hundreds of thousands of women organized through local branches of national organizations, trade unions, voluntary associations, and settlement houses used claims of maternity, equality, and social justice to legitimate their agenda in politics. The period marked what Kathryn Kish Sklar called "the maturation of political culture of middle class women." Despite wide variations in philosophy and even politics, their mobilization served as an early model for interest-group politics.[6]

Yet, as historians of women have shown, no homogeneous group called "women" ever existed. The two scenes that opened this book reflect the enormous distance between impoverished women and middle-class women in social experience, economic opportunity, and political access. These groups had significantly different interactions with the public sector—one group petitioning for services within the political system and the other campaigning to govern, or at least shape, the system. Variations in education, employment, and cultural mobility while not static did shape different class experiences. Race also influenced strategies for public activism. The African American clubwomen of Chicago worked within a political context characterized by significant skepticism about the degree to which the public sector might directly benefit their community, but they were persistent in their efforts to gain representation. Women also took diverse stands on partisan politics. Even among the relatively homogeneous Chicago Woman's City Club, a group organized to provide a reform agenda in city politics, political differences unmistakably emerged following the limited suffrage in 1913. These local examples of differences were replicated across the nation in what historians have identified as the end of suffrage unity. The era produced a range of political discourses and strategies which shifted over time in relation to each other as well as to other political forces. Some became submerged within dominant political organizations.[7]

This book explores the issues of citizenship, gender, and government responsibility with an analysis of a major component of the modern state—public welfare—and the first policy created specifically for mother-only families: mothers' pensions. This experiment in social provision captured the concerns of a wide array of groups with promises to honor motherhood, to subsidize domestic labor, and to stop juvenile delinquency. Within ten years, forty states and the territories of Alaska and Hawaii had passed some form of legislation for impoverished mother-only families. While others have explored the origins of the policy from a national perspective, this is the first study to discuss the policy as it evolved in the context of local politics. It examines the political strategies of women's activism in relation to politicians, courts, and charities. The study begins in 1911 with Illinois' passage of the first state-wide bill and traces its evolution to the eve of the Great Depression.[8]

Three arguments are developed within these chapters. First, the mothers' pension, which has been discussed as a child welfare measure, initially had as one of its goals the expansion of married women's rights. This perspective has been overlooked because the supporters themselves shifted their discourse from women to children and because the policy became a measure of welfare, not a maternal endowment. Mothers' pensions evolved during a unique reform moment in American history during which time women's rights were in the foreground and women became increasingly self-conscious of themselves as political actors. Wage-earning women organized to improve their conditions first through unions, then through legislation. African American women organized for suffrage, but also for basic civil rights in campaigns against lynching and Jim Crow laws. Middle-class white women, who had long been active in the voluntary sector, reinvigorated their claims to public citizenship and became the driving force in campaigns for suffrage and what have been called "maternalist" policies—those that protected home and family. The majority of organized women may have agreed upon the pursuit of the vote, but they disagreed on how it would be used to further the status of women. Women's roles and "mother-work" were debated, and exceptions to the rule of domesticity were implicitly established on the basis of class or race. Consequently, policies like mothers' pensions, which were entrenched in social expectations of women in general and mothers specifically, were riddled with contradictions.[9]

Examining the development of mothers' pensions as a component of women's rights illuminates the larger issue at stake during the period—the reconfiguration of citizenship to include women. Some women reformers focused on expanding the definition of citizenship to include voting rights and industrial democracy, but they also struggled with the question of reinterpreting the parameters of citizenship to embrace the conditions of women's lives. How would the public sector confer full rights and duties of citizenship to women—a group previously considered dependents? Would women receive equal treatment in all respects, or would sex differences shape rights and responsibilities? These somewhat philosophical issues became concrete when addressing the problem of how to deal with the extreme poverty of mother-only families.

Through the nineteenth century, married women's legal and political status had been framed within familial relations. Their political representation as well as their economic security fell under the domain of the male head of household. As Linda Kerber has shown for an earlier era, the domestic prescriptions of womanhood could be blended with a nationalist political agenda, as in the ideology of Republican Motherhood. The question for the early twentieth century was how changing opportunities would fit with traditional expectations. Citizenship had evolved around the ideal of independence. The definition of a male citizen included characteristics of virility, productivity, and self-sufficiency in all realms. Men who did not meet these criteria, the poor for example, found themselves labeled as effeminate, weak, or unproductive. Women who followed societal prescriptions would not strive to fill the standards set for men. What then would a woman citizen be? In the early twentieth century, the movement for women's rights had expanded the definition; yet a majority of organized women continued to see women's greatest potential in traditional terms—as wife and mother. Those who linked mothers' pensions to maternal service shared this view and focused on a woman's ability to rear good citizens.[10]

The gendered delineation of citizenship exposes one of the central puzzles of mothers' pensions—how could economic security for mother-only families be achieved? If the tenet of the marriage contract placed legal responsibility for support with the husband (and the principle of economic equity had little foundation in practice), on what basis should the government be asked to assume this private responsibility for a woman with dependent children? Initially, some advocates argued that mothers had a right to be insured against life's insecurities, as either a measure of social justice or on the basis of maternal citizenship, but this view confronted a tradition of self-support. Women's organizations that had supported the enactment of mothers' pension legislation in several states came to disagree on these questions. The uniform rhetorical commitment to "protect motherhood" faltered on the criteria for support. By the mid-1930s, as social planners and politicians hammered out the design of the Social Security Act, considerable ambiguity remained concerning society's understanding of women as mothers, workers, and citizens.

The second argument addresses the politics of welfare reform. If consensus characterized the push for mothers' pension laws, as Mark Leff and Theda Skocpol have argued, it was political conflict that characterized the program after its passage.[11] By politics, I mean the contest for power and authority to control the policy; conflicting agendas of political actors—both partisan and nonpartisan; and different levels of access by groups to political parties, state structures, and public finances at the time. The mothers' pension program tested the limits of Americans' willingness to experiment with universal social provision. It also revealed the challenges of restructuring the local state. In Chicago, officials tried to maintain their control over the jobs and appropriations designated for public welfare, but the new program's location in the juvenile court provided an opportunity to limit patronage appointments. Conflicts emerged over the expansion of the policy, and the elected officials, regardless of their party, attempted to limit the growth of the program.

In her national study of the passage of mothers' pension laws, Theda

Skocpol credited women's civic associations like the General Federation of Women's Clubs and the National Congress of Mothers for the groundswell of support for mothers' pensions. She found little evidence to support the prominent role given by historians to activist settlement workers or women's organizations such as the Women's Trade Union League or the National Consumers' League. This assessment raises the question: what happened to that mass support after passage of the laws? Skocpol argues that mothers' pensions became weak programs because the network of local-based politics lent itself to passage of laws, rather than the "drawn-out and varied, locality-by-locality, state-by-state struggles" of implementation. The Chicago evidence suggests a different conclusion.[12]

Two distinct strategies emerged in Chicago to meet the resistance at the local level. One strategy came from representatives of women's clubs who acted as an interest group—lobbying, writing legislation, and forming political alliances. They served as an effective counterbalance and may be credited with the expansion of the appropriations in the years after World War I. A second political strategy can be found in the work of Chicago social reformers Edith Abbott, Sophonisba Breckinridge, and Julia Lathrop. Together they shared a plan to use mothers' pensions as a model to enlarge the "positive" role of government. They wanted social provision extended more broadly to Americans without what they believed to be the preexisting necessity to trade political allegiance for public aid. They wanted to use state capacity to develop an alternate route to political authority. These three used the term "social politics" to describe what amounted to a direct challenge to political patronage. Support for an activist state also represented advocacy for an interventionist and regulatory state. With little apparent reflection upon the biases in their perspectives, they legitimated such action on the basis that unregulated affairs had created a system in which certain individuals, political institutions, and business organizations had obtained such power in American society that it threatened the existence of not only social institutions and social values, but democracy itself. If women's rights were to be protected and expanded, these reformers believed government offered the greatest resources to move their agenda forward.[13]

In addition to the organized strategies, women who applied for pensions presented a third source of pressure on the county administration. The thousands of women who applied for aid often waited months or longer because of inadequate appropriations. Across the nation, as in Chicago, women appealed to public agencies. Although they remained unorganized, they created a tremendous symbol of a constituency ignored by politicians. Advocates for mothers' pensions used this symbol to gain support for an enlarged program.[14]

There is a threefold significance to the political actions and the contest for control over mothers' pensions in Chicago. They redirect our attention to the interest-group politics practiced by some organized reform women that succeeded in gaining support for the new policy. They underscore the success of these actions in redistributing public funds toward impoverished women and their families during a period when social policies met with constraints. Finally, they highlight the development of an infrastructure that transferred the provision of services from political parties to administrative state agencies.

Finally, this book challenges the perception that mothers' pensions paid mothers to stay home and rear their children. Instead, the story that emerges from these sources is one in which wage-earning and welfare were enmeshed and the pension served as a wage subsidy, not replacement. Supporters of the policy spoke in terms of an endowment for "mother-work," yet in practice women faced earning requirements as forcefully applied as maternalist ideals. The policy succeeded in keeping families together and prevented the removal of children to orphanages, but it never supported mothers to stay home and rear their children, because contemporary values of self-support and fiscal constraints worked against that goal and created a policy that put mothers in the workforce. The situation for impoverished mothers was further complicated because the expectation to earn coexisted with the emerging characterization of mothers as "unemployables" in social policy.

Gender analyses of mothers' pensions have focused more on the regulatory aspects of women's reproductive and domestic activities and have given less attention to the demands for wage-earning.[15] For example, feminist scholars' understanding of mothers' pensions and aid to dependent children revolves around the historical construction of the "family wage" ideal. The family wage idealized social relationships within the family with a model of male breadwinners and female homemakers. Drafted into social insurance provisions, it led to an unequal system of benefits for male-headed and female-headed families. Proponents of the family wage analysis need to go beyond policy intent, however, and explain variant practices. For example, how can the family wage model account for the practice of requiring earning from mothers who were accepted for mothers' aid? The case can be made that rather than restrict women's enterprise to the home, the outcome of mothers' pensions encouraged women to earn without giving them the resources to do so.[16]

The discovery that wage-earning was a central component of mothers' pensions in Chicago and across the nation recasts the pioneer policy as one that clearly linked families, markets, and politics as it combined the roles of caregiver and wage-earner for over one-half of the women. Similarly, understanding the centrality of wage-earning clarifies the way in which moral and racial ideologies worked in concert with earning requirements. Programs routinely excluded groups like deserted women on the basis that they could be self-supporting. Dominant views of race insinuated themselves into ideals of self-support by assuming that African American women had always earned and were therefore "more able" to work. Finally, the recognition of expectations of wage-earning brings to the forefront the politics of public spending and its impact on the shape of the program. By focusing on the manner in which local politics and fiscal constraints worked with gender and race ideology to construct a dual role for mothers who received aid, one gains a clearer understanding of welfare policies as they developed for mother-only families throughout the twentieth century.

§

Much of the scholarly debate on the range of women's political experience and the gendered construction of citizenship in the United States has revolved around two models of postsuffrage politics—organized women who based their political agenda on the goal of equality of treatment under the law, and women who incorporated sexual differences into their analyses. The field has moved beyond William O'Neill's distinction between social feminism and hard-core feminism, to the analyses of equality and difference arguments, to the most recent distinctions between feminist, womanist, and maternalist politics. Nevertheless, new interpretations continue to use these two models as reference points. What may appear at first to be academic hairsplitting has a much larger and significant purpose; that is, to understand the theoretical as well as strategic differences among different groups of women in the twentieth century and the ramifications of those choices.[17]

Concerned about the undifferentiated use of the term "feminism" to describe a wide range of public activism, Nancy Cott persuasively argued for a more precise definition of the term. Building upon Linda Gordon's work, Cott defined feminism as an "opposition to sex hierarchy," a recognition that "women's condition is socially constructed," and an identification with the concerns of the larger group—women. Feminist political action could be distinguished from other gender-specific actions of organized women in that the former sought to balance power between the sexes in all aspects of life. Despite the advantages of Cott's more limited definition, historians continue to use broader definitions of feminism to describe a range of agency from women's rights to domestic authority.[18]

The second model of women's activism focused on sexual difference as the basis for women's public claims. Two notable examples are studies of protective labor legislation and more recent research on maternalism. Maternalist politics attracted considerable attention because it defined the mass mobilization of women who, although not committed to feminist principles of sexual equality, nevertheless used gender-specific ideas to expand political participation. Their civic maternalism drew broad-based support to suffrage campaigns as well as programs like mothers' pensions and maternity-infant health care. The women involved identified politically as mothers and used that identity as the basis for their claims as citizens. Family relations, not feminists' individual rights, distinguished maternalist political strategies.[19]

While these models enable us to categorize some actors within each group—National Woman's Party feminists and National Congress of Mothers maternalists, for example—a large and significant middle ground of politically active women fit less neatly. African American women's activism has been called "womanist" to distinguish its agenda of race and sex politics, but it has been difficult to clearly differentiate other groups. One indication of the problem historians are having is the practice of combining terms to identify positions such as "sentimental maternalists" and "maternalist feminists." The former idealized maternity and made global assumptions about caring for "other people's children." The latter promoted family-centered social policy designed to improve women's condition, but nevertheless based their ideas upon assumptions of sexual difference. The problem of distinguishing groups of actors is not simple because, as Nancy Cott has argued, human beings do not fit neatly into the categories scholars make.[20]

Feminism and maternalism are invaluable frameworks for U.S. women's political activism, but they remain inadequate to capture the range of significant politics during an era of contested social relations and changing political dynamics. They conceal the "crossover" element by which individual women supported organizations with different agendas; they obscure the broader arena of social justice work undertaken by some progressive reformers; they sidestep the context and actions of African American women reformers; and they leave us wondering about working-class women's positions.

The problem of definition manifests itself in understanding the women reformers who are central to this study, Edith Abbott and Sophonisba Breckin-ridge. They have been called social feminists, progressive maternalists, mater-nalist feminists, and social democrats. Their extensive research and writing illustrates that they stand in between those who would maintain Victorian-style, biologically based sexual differences and feminist advocates of the equal rights amendment. They analyzed the social politics of gender differently from both feminists, as defined above, and maternalists. They applied their ground-breaking research to both organizational and political strategies to create social policy that they believed would expand the rights for women. In Wendy Sar-vasy's words, they were interested in exposing "how unequal power relations turned biological differences into socially-constructed, substantive gender in-equalities"; and they spent much of their professional lives attempting to rem-edy the situation. They challenged gender norms by the careers they chose and the professional lives they lived, as historian Ellen Fitzpatrick has noted. Fi-nally, they saw women's rights as part of the larger campaign for social justice which included expanded opportunities for the poor, laborers, and blacks.[21]

A more accurate definition of these activists is as "social justice femi-nists." The phrase captures their commitment to women's rights principles de-spite the conflicts over the equal rights amendment beginning in the 1920s. It also separates them from the simple characterization as "social mothers." Con-temporaries frequently depicted the social politics agenda as an extension of family roles, but that phrase minimizes the efforts of these women to achieve so-cial independence. It perpetuates a limited vision of their work, relevant only to the realm of family. Social welfare went beyond measures for mothers and chil-dren for these women. They linked economic systems with politics and social relations. The definition of these reformers as social justice feminists captures the breadth of that vision.[22]

The maternalist and feminist interpretations also do not adequately cap-ture the dynamics of race and gender politics.[23] Race problematizes maternal-ism's universalist assumptions and feminism's focus on sex equity. Equality had a different text and meaning for African Americans. The history of reform women illuminates the difference through their focus on education, anti-lynching, and anti–Jim Crow campaigns. None of the questions on women's status, labor, and relation to the state can be discussed substantively without considering race. These issues arose during one of the most racially virulent eras of modern history, when race defined women's status, the arena and type of work one performed, and a family's access to public and private services. Similarly, while African Americans shared some meanings of the term "moth-erhood" with white women, the term held distinctly different meanings for them, as well. Working mothers did not produce the same degree of anxiety among the National Association of Colored Women, for example, as they did among the General Federation of Women's Clubs or the National Congress of Mothers. Child protection for African Americans carried within it lessons of survival in a segregated society. Scholars of African American women's history have used the term "womanist" to capture the distinctive elements of political action and to distinguish the reform politics and movements from those of middle-class white women.[24]

Finally, the existing frameworks for interpreting women's politics raise questions about working-class women. In which model, for example, would we find a position that supported expanded employment opportunities for women, while at the same time recognizing women's value within the family economy? Studies have made clear that working-class women saw themselves in both worlds of market and home. Perhaps the distinction in political strategies rests less with support for or opposition to the family wage than with differences between those who trusted in private solutions and those who looked to the public sector to liberalize and equitably distribute resources despite conservative political opposition. One of the goals of the mothers' pension for its progressive advocates was to reduce the economic penalties of married life for impoverished women and to gain for the working-class wife the type of security achieved for the middle-class wife through private insurance.[25]

In order to better understand the varied politics of the early twentieth century and the forces surrounding their development, we will need to tolerate the complexity of several categories until a synthesis evolves. The gendered analyses of social provision, however, have made one point clear: legislation based on separate treatment always carried a penalty in the long term. By linking women's citizenship rights to potential or actual motherhood in a world where male citizenship was based on individual claims, equality of treatment for women remained out of reach.

§

Chicago offers a premier case study to explore the politics of implementation that changed the shape of mothers' pension policy. Illinois passed the first statewide enabling legislation in 1911, and Cook County had the largest program in the state. The prestige of Chicago's reform community, in particular its progressive settlements and its juvenile court, drew national attention to the policy. Chicago's most renowned settlement house, Hull House, supported the work of female professionals active in the development of mothers' pensions. As Chicago struggled to shape its program, the efforts became the subject of commentary and criticism as well as a model for other states and municipalities considering similar legislation. Chicago's significant industries, large immigrant population, social and labor activities, and political life all highlight the conflicts involved in the process of expanding the local state.[26]

Chicago embodied all the potential and problems of a rapidly expanding American city at the turn of the century. Its economy flourished from the prosperous grain, lumber, and livestock industries as well as from the city's development as a manufacturing center in the last quarter of the nineteenth century. Chicago was home to some of the nation's wealthiest capitalists and the scene of some of labor's most historic disputes. The population nearly doubled, from approximately 1.7 million to 3.4 million, between 1900 and 1930.[27]

Not only did the metropolitan population grow, but it became more heterogeneous. One-third of the city's new residents in the first decade arrived from Europe. Around World War I, European immigration waned and African American southern migration increased. The newcomers moved into neighborhoods established by their countrymen and women. Jane Addams's description of the area around Hull House and west of the downtown loop captured the diversity of the city in the early 1890s.

> Between Halsted Street and the river live about ten thousand Italians: Neapolitans, Sicilians, and Calabrians, with an occasional Lombard or Venetian. To the south on Twelfth Street are many Germans, and side streets are given over almost entirely to Polish and Russian Jews. Still farther south, these Jewish colonies merge into a huge Bohemian colony, so vast that Chicago ranks as the third Bohemian city in the world. To the northwest are many Canadian-French, clannish in spite of their long residence in America, and to the north are many Irish and first-generation Americans. On the streets directly west and farther north are well-to-do English-speaking families, many of whom own their houses and have lived in the neighborhood for years.[28]

To the south of the downtown loop lay Chicago's Black Metropolis. Over 200,000 African Americans migrated to Chicago between 1900 and 1930, the majority attracted by economic opportunities unheard of in the South. According to sociologist E. Franklin Frazier, the residents nearest the loop had recently arrived from the South and lived in "decaying residences," but as one traveled further south the residents had better incomes and held a greater number of service and professional jobs. Allan Spear and James Grossman have described the historical process of residential segregation that characterized the development of Chicago's South Side. Unable to move up and disperse throughout the city as other newcomers did, African Americans of all economic strata lived in the area and gave birth to a wide range of local economic, religious, cultural, and civic institutions.[29]

The poorer areas in Chicago lay close to the city's center, its industries and businesses. These areas had twice the population density of the city at large, with some households housing up to sixteen people. As one Chicago historian noted, "within one room, entire families had a noisome abode, a place of women's work by day and sleep by night."[30] Overcrowding and poor sanitation came to characterize the slums and ghettos. But overcrowding helped save money for families on precarious incomes. The economic security of workers' families depended upon regular employment at a "living wage"; yet its existence remained a rarity among the majority of semiskilled and unskilled workers. Unpredictable business cycles, unregulated industries, and low wages commonly associated with unorganized labor characterized their economic environment. Families relied on the composite income of all members. Only a small percentage of all married women worked, but that figure increased dramatically among families headed by women and among African American families. Children also supplied a portion of the family income.

Working-class families had little interest in charity. When disaster struck, they turned to relatives, self-help groups, mutual aid societies, fraternal organizations, and churches. Jane Addams found that "working people live in the same streets with those in need of charity, but they themselves, so long as they have health and good wages, require and want none of it."[31] Historian Lizabeth Cohen also described the reluctance of working-class families to rely on relief; they turned instead to private sources until the crisis of the Great Depression made that impossible. Both depictions obscure the fact that although they disliked relief, the working class used both public and private charity. Regular periods of unemployment left workers in vulnerable economic circumstances, but major downturns such as those that occurred in 1893–1894, 1908, and 1913–1914 created massive problems for unemployed men and women who flooded public relief offices. In addition, the self-sufficient system of mutual aid wore thin for those with long-term needs. After several months, the ill, deserted, or widowed often found themselves with no recourse but private and public charity.[32]

The crises of massive unemployment, desertion, and transiency which accompanied the industrial depression of 1893 brought the public's attention to the issue of inadequate public services. Private relief agencies had been taxed beyond their limits and the public relief offices, controlled by the County Board of Commissioners and its appointed county agent of poor relief, showed little interest in increasing expenditures to meet the crises. Instead, the County Board focused on better methods to organize industry and stabilize employment for male workers. The absence of direction from elected officials created an opening for Chicago's reform community to intervene.[33]

Hull House, founded by Jane Addams and Ellen Gates Starr in 1889, played a significant role in expanding public provision. Chicago had thirty-four settlements in 1911, but none was more notable than Hull House as a center for community outreach, research, investigation, and political activity.[34] Three of the early residents—Julia Lathrop, Edith Abbott, and Sophonisba Breckinridge—became pioneers in the fields of social investigation and social welfare. Lathrop joined Graham Taylor, director of the Chicago Commons settlement, to begin Chicago's first school for social work education. The School of Civics and Philanthropy trained the first generation of social work professionals and conducted some of the early studies on housing, the juvenile court, and employment in Chicago. Abbott and Breckinridge directed the social investigation department and eventually succeeded in getting the professional school affiliated with the University of Chicago. They produced the earliest social research that justified mothers' pensions and helped to shape the policy at the local and national levels.[35]

These settlement workers attempted to bring the resources of the local state to bear on neighborhood problems through the use of social science research. Higher standards of living for Chicago's working families included better wages and workplace conditions, but they also included improved municipal provisions in health, sanitation, housing, education, and welfare. The settlement workers' efforts to improve the general welfare necessitated political intervention and challenged the status quo of charity societies. They also reflected an emerging philosophy among progressive intellectuals which favored using state powers for social change. Abbott described the combination of social research and political action that she and her colleagues engaged in as "social politics."[36]

As urban life became more complex, organized women became active in negotiating the distribution of resources toward projects identified with their specific agendas. The Chicago Woman's Club had a long history of reform and had been closely tied to the formation of the juvenile court. The Chicago Woman's City Club took an active role in promoting social welfare and fostered women's political participation through ward organization. The membership included women who had previous political experience in suffrage or settlements, as well as women who preferred the educational aspects of club work over activism. Like clubwomen across the country, these reform women sought state action to rectify specific ills. Protective labor legislation, anti–child labor laws, minimum wage bills, and mothers' pensions were promoted as a means to rectify gender inequities at home and in the marketplace. With partial suffrage in 1913, the club increased its educational forums on voting and citizenship. It also developed a city welfare reform agenda.[37] During the 1920s, the reform momentum slowed in a context of postwar conservatism, but in Illinois, the state-level gains of social legislation provided evidence that the use of centralized state actions could more equitably distribute benefits to citizens.[38]

The Illinois Federation of Colored Women's Clubs addressed these civic issues while it also worked to relieve race-specific needs. The nearly sixty clubs that belonged to the federation by 1921 spent much of their energy fundraising to provide direct relief to families and to help support organizations and institutions. The clubs supported homes for working women, day nurseries, homes for the aged, and industrial schools in addition to their suffrage and race-equity work. While white women's clubs struggled with the issue of working mothers, African American clubwomen recognized wage-earning as a necessity rather than a flaw in female identity. Chicago clubwoman Elizabeth Davis noted that a majority of African American women "supplemented their husbands small salaries in their ambitious efforts to give their children superior advantages." Davis refuted the idea that wage-earning negatively impacted women's character, and described working women as "resplendent and triumphant rejoicing in a pure and noble womanhood." As suffrage became imminent, candidates attempted to secure the loyalty of black clubwomen. Ida B. Wells-Barnett described her work with the Alpha Suffrage League and the Second Ward political organization during the 1910s as double-edged. African American women had demonstrated their ability to get the vote out for candidates who promised to bring benefits back to the community, but their candidates failed to act upon their promises for the predominantly black Second Ward.[39]

The development of the mothers' pension program in Chicago has unique characteristics that distinguish it from similar movements in other major cities. As the first major program, it withstood tremendous national attention. Similarly, the degree of involvement of educated professional women in the expansion of the policy arose from their unique relationship to both social welfare and women's political networks. It would be a mistake, however, to view the program, and therefore this study, as an aberration. The politics of welfare reform, evaluated here through an analysis of the structure of social provision, the opportunities for political action, the diverse strategies of organized women reformers, and the forms of political resistance, provide a framework for comparative studies.

§

The book begins by laying out the varied discourses on "dependent motherhood" as they developed on the national level at the turn of the century. Supporters of mothers' pensions agreed that impoverished women had special needs that differed from those of male heads of families, but they had different perspectives on the justification for mothers' aid. This survey of a range of positions, both mainstream and alternative, provides the background from which to understand the competing interests in favor of and in opposition to the idea of aid to mother-only families. Included are the mainstream positions of the National Conference of Charities and Correction, the professional body that served as a clearinghouse for both traditional and reform ideas; the National Congress of Mothers, whose commitment to the privatization of child rearing and domestic life led them to strongly promote a maternal pension for service to the state; and social justice feminists, who saw mothers' pensions as a measure to balance gender inequities and expand married women's rights. The alternative views of the National Association of Colored Women, socialists, feminists, and advocates of social insurance complete the spectrum of ideas proposed to address this critical issue.

Chapter 2 describes the terrain of public welfare as it existed prior to and alongside of mothers' pensions. In particular, it describes how poor relief was used and by whom. The poor relief system exhibited gendered practices in that male-headed families received support only under conditions of extreme economic distress due to illness, permanent disability, or periods of unemployment. Women with dependent children, on the other hand, were expected to earn, but they were also acknowledged as having long-term periods of need because of the presence of young children in the family. The foreign-born predominated on the public relief rolls through the mid-1920s, by which time African Americans proportionately became the largest constituency on county relief. As this change took place, however, the county expanded new programs for the poor, specifically for mother-only families, and reduced the budget for poor relief. In the process, Chicago developed a system of public provision that provided distinctly different benefits to different types of poor families.

Chicago's active reform and social science community created abundant social survey data used to support demands for mothers' pensions. Edith Abbott, Sophonisba Breckinridge, and Julia Lathrop used their research in conjunction with private-sector organizing to promote the idea of pensions. Active at the national level as progressive voices in the National Conference of Charities and Correction, they also worked to write legislation and shape new state structures at the local level. Chapter 3 traces the development of their social politics agenda within the context of emerging ideas of liberalism and an activist state. The government alone had the authority to centralize administration, regulate hiring, and pool revenues. Abbott, Breckinridge, and Lathrop believed that if these processes could be removed from partisan control and directed by a neutral or progressive administration, great gains could be made in social provision. Although they did not propose the initial mothers' pension legislation in Illinois, they conducted research that led to its promotion and supported the policy in state and national forums.

Authorship of the original legislation was contested, but the scurry to claim control of the policy is well documented. Chapter 4 assesses the prolonged power struggles between the juvenile court, county government, and private sector for the control of jobs and funding that accompanied the mothers' pension program. The efforts of Chicago's white clubwomen created a countervailing force to politicians' resistance. Abbott and Breckinridge saw the opportunity presented by mothers' pensions to centralize welfare services and to replace the influence of party politicians with that of social work professionals through the administrative control of welfare. While they hoped to achieve more equitable treatment for impoverished women, they also wanted to create a political vehicle that served as an alternative to local organization politics. Despite the political conservatism of the 1920s, a group of Chicago clubwomen succeeded in mounting sufficient political pressure to expand a public program for mother-only families. Using interest-group tactics, representatives of Chicago's reform clubs lobbied the state legislature to expand the revenue base and pressured county officials to allocate the maximum funds to the program. Their success in these areas promoted a pension program that by the 1920s grew at a rate far exceeding other social programs. Scholarly criticism of the mothers' pension program which evaluated it as a small program reaching only an elite group with meager stipends overlooked the fact that the policy also represented a tremendous expansion in fiscal expenditures, a significant accomplishment for its supporters.

The program's implementation was not one of simple progressive achievement, however. In fact, the outcomes of this proposed endowment for motherhood belied its promise. Chapter 5 describes the impact of the politics of implementation on pensioned families during the first sixteen years. It examines the characteristics of pensioned families and their family economy, and it documents the extent to which economic considerations related to wage-earning served to restrict the distribution of pensions. The political pressure to limit the expansion of the program led to exclusionary criteria and an expectation that women would earn part of their support. Despite the fact that the fiscal growth of the policy surpassed that of other public aid by the mid-1920s, annual appropriations remained well below demand. Women's entrance to or exit from the program turned on administrators' ideas about their ability to earn.

Several factors contributed to a crisis in the mothers' pension program at the onset of the depression. Political conservatism, diverse political directions of postsuffrage women's groups, and fiscal deficits debilitated the social experiment in aid to dependent families. Recognizing the deteriorating conditions of reform, advocates abandoned their justification of the policy as "justice for mothers" and focused more exclusively on the benefits of child welfare for most of the 1920s. Neither this ideological shift nor the screening process of applicants prevented the damage that resulted from declining fiscal revenues. On the eve of the depression, over 10,000 eligible women in Chicago were unable to receive benefits, a problem lessened only by federal intervention of the New Deal.

The mothers' pension policy illuminates the transition in the relations between women and the public sector as mothers, workers, and citizens. Women's appeals to the public sector for financial support and the government's acceptance of some measure of fiscal responsibility for poor women, regardless how meager, represented a new direction in Americans' ideas about their government. Similarly, the development of new agencies in local and state government changed the distribution of public resources from one based in political parties and private agencies to one based in expanding public bureaucracies. Acting on principles embedded in ideas of gender, women collaborated in the construction of the policy; but a variety of competing perspectives engaged with local politics to shape a compromised mothers' pension program. The criteria upon which the state qualified its aid to poor women replicated the power differentials of society. Under the facade of universal provision, the program maintained the dual role of provider and caretaker for some working-poor women, while it excluded others altogether based on their earning potential. While the economic stability of mothers' pension families improved relative to their contemporaries on poor relief, the economic viability of mother-only families remained little changed. As mothers, a few received subsidies. As workers, women received little support from either unions or social insurance advocates, and debatable "protection" through legislation. As citizens, impoverished working mothers had a marginal political identity. Those women who sought to create a new system of provision and an alternative route to political authority did not succeed in separating politics from welfare, but the system of welfare was indeed transformed. To the extent that patronage existed in the delivery of public aid services, that system was challenged and changed. Their failures were not theirs alone, but rather speak to the politics of the welfare state and the rise and decline of American's commitment to activist state principles.

Case worker visiting a mother and child. Chicago Historical Society.

O N E

Defining the Problems of "Dependent Motherhood"

How shall we make the child an active contributor to the wealth, comfort, and happiness of the community, and how shall we most economically care for those who must be a public burden?
                    —Hastings H. Hart, "The Economic Aspect of the Child Problem"

These friendless mothers are our especial responsibility. They grew up to believe in marriage and home-building. Now is it fair that we let them find it a tragedy?
                    —Mrs. G. H. Robertson, "The State's Duty to Fatherless Children"

A woman whose wages are fixed on the basis of individual subsistence, who is quite unable to earn a family wage, is still held by a legal obligation to support her children, with a desperate penalty of forfeiture if she fails.
                    —Jane Addams, "Charity and Social Justice"

"Dependent motherhood" drew the attention of charities, women's organizations, child welfare advocates, and social planners during the first decades of the twentieth century.[1] Yet, as the three views quoted above suggest, no consensus existed on the precise constitution of the problem, or as important, its solution. Despite the dominance of maternalist ideals and plans to protect motherhood, a survey of the debate on dependent motherhood exposes a multiplicity of views on the expectations placed upon the impoverished mother. It also reveals the degree to which the shifting terrain of race and motherhood shaped women's citizenship. Why did this discussion about dependent motherhood arise when it did? The Progressive Era produced major changes in social relations between men and women, husbands and wives, blacks and whites, and workers and employers. An expression of these tensions arose in debates over and challenges to ascribed social hierarchies and corresponding social roles. This chapter explores the breadth of the debate on dependent mothers from the views of traditionalist child savers of the charity organization societies to those of the maternalists of the National Congress of Mothers, feminists, labor, social insurance advocates, and social justice feminists. How did they define the problem of dependent motherhood? What solutions did they present? To what degree did they think the public sector had a role in addressing the issue? These groups did not have an equal influence in shaping the policy, but understanding the range of positions articulated at the time and their relative power helps to explain the policy that developed and its limits.

One position in the debate, child-saving, sought the most effective and efficient care for impoverished children. Steeped in nineteenth-century charity views of personal responsibility for poverty and failure, this tradition asked: how could children of the poor best be socialized to be productive citizens? As Hastings Hart's statement illustrates, many child-savers believed that the successful ordering of society depended upon families raising children to be productive and independent citizens who would contribute to the health and wealth of the state. The father had a responsibility to support the family as an independent wage-earner, and the mother had a responsibility to raise their children into self-sufficient citizens. Child-savers feared that poor families would fail to complete this cycle, thereby fostering dependency, weakening society, and creating a drain on the public economy.

Maternalists shared a belief in the functional relationship between the family and citizenship, but they elevated the value of the maternal role. As Robertson's appeal for "friendless mothers" indicates, maternalists sought to protect women within the structure of the family. The condition of impoverished mothers revealed the nightmarish alternative. Traditionalist women's organizations, such as the National Congress of Mothers, utilized gender-specific arguments based on what they defined as the universalizing experience of motherhood. They stressed the importance of the mother in child-rearing, in shaping the "lives of future citizens," and promoted the idea of a pension for indigent mothers as a payment for service to the state. This argument retained the functional relationship between family, citizenship, and society, and exalted the position and status of the mother in this process.

In the first decades of the twentieth century, the increased political activism of women and their organization for political equality and social justice added new perspectives to the definition of the problem of dependent motherhood. Feminists identified the problem as one of economic dependence, and social justice feminists attempted to ameliorate the structural causes of women's poverty. Both groups agreed that low wages, occupational segregation, and women's caregiving role shaped and limited women's opportunities. Both supported mothers' pension laws during the 1910s. Unlike the National Congress of Mothers, however, they framed pensions within the larger issue of expanded social democracy and saw the potential of public aid as a step toward economic independence for women. Although their proposals differed on issues of protection or equality, they challenged the structural inequities and the dual burdens faced by working-poor women.[2]

Race altered Americans' perception of both dependency and motherhood.[3] This is evident in the relative silence on race within mainstream discussions, the identity of the African American mother who was frequently a worker as well as a mother, and the different terms in which African American women reformers discussed dependency. Not only did the broader reform community express little interest in integrated policies, but it assumed that the care of dependent African American children would be handled privately. An infrequent panel at the National Conference of Charities and Correction discussed the problems of African Americans and the methods of care for dependent "colored" children, but the majority of social work organizations followed the segregationist mandate of *Plessy v. Ferguson,* that these issues would be addressed separately.[4] African American clubwomen did not denigrate mothers who combined wage-earning with family life. They hoped to improve the economic prospects of all African American families, but they also viewed a mother's earnings as a sacrifice for and commitment to a stronger family. Women were not defined as dependents, even when they had young children.

During the 1910s, initial plans to protect workers' families through social insurance began to be discussed. These plans held the potential for a universal program of social provision. But the decision to base benefits on workers' contributions, and the ideology of the planners to support the breadwinner ideal, severely limited women's participation. Standing between charity and social insurance, advocates for a policy for dependent mothers endorsed a policy alternatively called mothers' pensions, mothers' aid, or aid to dependent children. A review of the national dialogue sets the stage for understanding the tensions and contradictions present in the policy.[5]

THE NATIONAL CONFERENCE OF CHARITIES AND CORRECTION

The National Conference of Charities and Correction (NCCC), an organization of representatives from public and private charities, voluntary associations, courts, settlement houses, and child welfare agencies, actively debated new alternatives for the care of dependent families at the turn of the century. The problem of dependent motherhood was a problem of family relief for the majority of members in the NCCC. Before 1910, the debate took place between those who saw the problem as one of personal responsibility and those who saw broader structural explanations for poverty which demanded a public response. The conference had significance within the national discussion of policies for dependent mothers, because it acted as an informal clearinghouse for social welfare policies and because its members were instrumental in the delivery of services. The NCCC's organizational structure allowed for information and policy recommendations to be easily disseminated through its national and state-level conferences. A consensus on the provision of care gradually developed between the 1890s and the 1910s. The NCCC opposed the previous model of institutional care offered by orphanages and poorhouses and promoted a policy of "family-based" care. The latter (which also included an early form of foster care) incorporated the idea of subsidies to mothers to keep their dependent children at home. Members never came to an agreement on the causes of poverty, and this failure undermined the coherence of mothers' pension plans in discussions about the wage-earning responsibilities of poor mothers.[6]

A few states created a precedent for aid to children in their own homes during the nineteenth century. The California legislature authorized state subsidies to local poor relief agencies in 1880 to help indigent mothers keep their children at home, but this resource remained inactive until 1904, when relief officials discovered that two-thirds of the state's 5,000 institutionalized children were half-orphans. Franklin Sanborn of Massachusetts raised the idea of aid to dependent families at the 1890 National Conference of Charities and Correction meeting, but the influential Josephine Shaw Lowell of New York's Charity Organization Society firmly denounced it. Lowell argued that such policies encouraged desertion, eliminated the work ethic, and destabilized families. The Charity Organization Society used its powerful influence again in 1898 when it effectively stopped the implementation of a New York State bill to provide widows an allowance equal to that paid to institutions for the care of dependent children. The bill never went into effect because the mayor of New York City, pressured by private charities, persuaded the governor not to implement it. Other states initiated policies that addressed the problem of support for poor, mother-only families. For example, Oklahoma and Michigan passed legislation in 1908 and 1911 respectively that authorized publicly funded school scholarships to poor families as a means to reduce the need for children's wages. These early precedents illustrate the powerful influence of the charity organization societies and their child-saving strategies, as well as the incremental measures taken to move toward public funding.[7]

The child-saving movement focused on eliminating "poverty and vice" in the lives of indigent children by changing the behavior of their parents and, ultimately, the child. The impetus for the movement came from the belief that poverty raised unique problems for society, because the poor were less able to demonstrate their citizenship through appropriate moral responsibility and its resultant public economy. A secure family life provided the foundation for a strong nation by producing independent and capable citizens. "Good citizenship is the measure of the wealth and power of a nation," the Child-Saving Committee of the National Conference of Charities and Correction reported in 1897. "Because of this truth the rescue of child-life from the depressing conditions of unfortunate heredity or degrading environment exemplifies in government the fundamental law of self-preservation, and justifies the proposition that the welfare of the child is the concern of the State."[8]

Public economy and good citizenship were two tightly interwoven themes in child-savers' view of a solution. They supported the move to family-centered care partially because institutional care was an "expensive and complicated form of machinery." And they linked the effectiveness of child-rearing to the ability of individuals eventually to support themselves. Take, for example, the following presentation on "the child problem" from the 1891 meeting of the National Conference of Charities and Correction. Parents must teach their children that they "ought not to be wards of the State, county, or city, to be fed, housed, and clothed without labor. They must be taught that society does not owe them a living unless they are willing to work for it. The children must be trained to be industrious, and to prepare for taking care of themselves in the future and to provide for those who are dependent upon them."[9] Child-savers gave a nod to environmental and structural effects, but primarily focused on the parents' failure to fulfill "their moral obligations to their children."[10]

Despite the language and gestures directed toward children, parents proved to be the target of the child-saving agenda. Discussion focused on the need to enforce paternal responsibility for economic support and encourage maternal responsibility for child-rearing. Children would be "saved" from repeating the patterns of their parents and subsequently would save public and private treasuries from the need to support them. This view of the failings of the impoverished family had particular impact upon mother-only families. Dependency was stigmatized and public aid seen as an opportunity for "parents and relatives to relieve themselves of the responsibilities of their children."[11] Such views left those associated with charity societies unlikely to support subsidies for impoverished mothers.

There were a few voices within the conference before the 1910s who described the problems of poverty and dependent mothers as the result of capitalism's structural weaknesses. They rejected the arguments that behavior could fully explain the problems of the poor and that impoverished parents were less capable to raise their children than parents with greater means. "If the laboring classes as a whole got their rights in existing wealth," claimed Reverend S. S. Craig, "there would be little or no poverty among them."[12] Craig's solution involved the public seizure of private property and the redistribution of wealth. While such proposals did not gain much headway among conference participants, a structural analysis of poverty became the dominant position during the 1910s, as did the call for a greater role for government in addressing the failures of the economic system to meet the needs of workers and their families.[13]

The special circumstances of mother-only families received attention within the conference during the first years of the twentieth century. The "charity framework," which drove standard relief-giving practices, is captured in the following discussion from 1901 entitled "Needy Families in Their Homes":

> In the case of a widow with a number of small children, charity workers generally agree that the home should be preserved if possible, that the mother should do some work to support the family, and that, where she cannot earn sufficient (as in most cases), her earnings should be supplemented by relief. As a rule, the amount of relief given is small and irregularly granted.[14]

The three themes evident in this discussion—family maintenance, the significance of a mothers' care of children, and the necessity of wage-earning—dominated the NCCC discussions. Gender had little impact upon the requirement for able-bodied adults to earn. Commentators raised the particular problems associated with wage-work for women outside the home, including the poor availability of day nurseries, lack of supervision of children at home in the absence of the mother, and the low wages for women's labor, but the values of self-support and the disinclination to acquire public expenses reinforced the need for a mother to earn.

Over the next several years, proposals for the problems of dependent mothers continued to run between those who viewed personal behavior as the primary cause and cure and those who saw the economic and legal relations of the family as treating women unfairly. Among the former group, Harry McCormack, director of Cook County, Illinois, poor relief, referred to poverty as a disease and advocated restrictions on marriage among the poor.[15] Others worried that aid to dependent families would give absent husbands the wrong message, that they could refuse their legal obligation to support their families.

They suggested, therefore, that the wife and children should be allowed to suffer in poverty to serve as a "moral lesson" to the nonsupporting man. Many believed that the only aid given to a family should be in the form of job-hunting. "Relief should be given only in the form of work wherever the wife is able to work," one participant noted.[16]

On the other side of the debate, advocates highlighted the injustice perpetrated against impoverished mothers. Sherman Kingsley, of Chicago's Relief and Aid Society, criticized a policy that promoted the physical deterioration of women through overwork and low wages. "I believe that every city allows the sacrifice of good mothers," he told the conference, by creating a system that encourages women to "work themselves to death trying to support their children." Why should the NCCC continue to endorse a practice in which private child-caring institutions received funds for the care of dependent children, but a child's natural parent could not? Kingsley's colleague, Julian Mack, judge of Chicago's juvenile court, suggested that women could better attend to their children's needs and subsequently reduce juvenile delinquency if they received a pension. Florence Kelley, director of the National Consumers' League and former Hull House resident, sharply criticized the federal government for providing more care for young lobsters in Maine than for the children of dead or disabled workers. She took the opportunity to advocate school stipends as a policy to counteract the need for child labor in poor families.[17]

The forum on family subsidies held at the National Conference of Charities and Correction included disparate views in the early years of the century, but the majority accepted home care over institutions and advocated self-support for the able-bodied. They discussed the policy followed by some private agencies to subsidize poor mothers' earnings, but the strength of the charity organization societies' views reflected little acceptance for a universal provision for dependent motherhood. Others entirely ignored the absence of services for impoverished women and believed that "the wife ought not to be a wage worker at any period of her conjugal existence."[18] The problem had been identified, but before 1910 no clear consensus on public aid had been achieved. Another national organization, the National Congress of Mothers, took the lead and formulated a distinctly maternalist argument for public support of mothers in poverty—a maternal pension for service to the state.

NATIONAL CONGRESS OF MOTHERS

Unlike the NCCC, the National Congress of Mothers (NCM) did not see relief-giving as its central purpose. Rather, it formed to raise the standards of child-rearing, home life, and the mother's role in society. Impoverished mothers and their children became a focus for the organization as it expanded its mission to bring "mother-love" into public affairs. The existence of the charity-seeking widow or deserted mother provided for NCM members a shocking example of the failed promise of marriage and the degradation of motherhood. According to Theda Skocpol, the NCM became the country's greatest advocate for a maternal pension for child-rearing service to the state.

Alice McLellan Birney, a native of Georgia, made the call for a national "gathering of mothers" during a mothers' meeting in New York in 1895. Birney educated herself as a young mother, reading the works of G. Stanley Hall, Friedrich Froebel, and Herbert Spencer, but she realized the greater need that existed for child-rearing materials and the potential of a mobilized organization of mothers. The first annual congress met in Washington, D.C., two years later, at which time the members agreed to improve the condition of child-rearing in the country through child study, child welfare work, and parent-teacher cooperation. State and local groups formed mothers' clubs and child study clubs to share the latest scientific and psychological research on child development. To improve conditions for all children, the membership was encouraged "to carry the mother-love and mother-thought into all that concerns or touches childhood in Home, School, Church, State or Legislation." Under the leadership of Hannah Kent Schoff, founder of the Pennsylvania Congress of Mothers and vice president of the national organization, the NCM sponsored legislation that it believed furthered the welfare of the country's children.[19]

Members of the NCM united around a set of ideals. They believed that all mothers shared a common bond because they all experienced childbirth and child-rearing. They believed that nature endowed women with innate characteristics and created distinct differences between the sexes. They believed that men and women must use their different talents to serve society, not in competition but through recognition of and value for their different contributions. Women's skills revolved around the family and child-rearing. By elevating child-rearing and its significance in the process of child development, the NCM wanted to revitalize women's traditional role in the home and reassert their value within contemporary society.

Membership grew rapidly in the organization. Two thousand women attended the first meeting in 1897, but by 1899 membership reached 50,000 and by 1920 it had grown to 190,000. Most of the members were white, middle-class mothers who met in mothers' clubs for self-education and mutual support, but the NCM also had the support of economic and political elites. Phoebe A.

Hearst, mother of newspaper publisher William Randolph Hearst and wife of California Senator George Hearst, financed the organization in its early years. Theodore Roosevelt sat on the Advisory Council and sympathetically supported the organization's work. According to Molly Ladd-Taylor, the NCM attracted so many women because of its focus on traditional family values and its elevation of women's role. In a period of shifting social relations, smaller families, greater educational opportunities for women, and increased workforce participation by women, middle-class women feared the diminishing importance of their role as mothers. The NCM sought to expand women's traditional role without challenging familial or social relations.[20]

The leaders and supporters of this organization adhered to the belief in the central relationship of family life to social order, but the NCM interjected a specifically maternalist component to this idea. Mothers had the power to affect the direction of their children's lives, and thus held significant potential for social change. They sought to endow women with the authority to create and shape social forces beyond the nursery. Hannah Schoff believed that specific social problems such as poverty, alcoholism, and delinquency could be overcome through proper education and training in the home. Judge Ben Lindsey, who became the chair of the Juvenile Court Committee, articulated this position when he stated that "the home is the basis of society and all civil, social, and physical betterment must be reached through intelligent efforts to raise the standards of home-life—of marriage—of motherhood—of fatherhood—and of citizenship." President Theodore Roosevelt linked the actions of mothers to national security when he told the annual meeting, "In the last analysis the welfare of the State depends absolutely upon whether or not the average family, the average man and woman and their children, represent the kind of citizenship fit for the foundation of a great nation." The resolution or persistence of social ills, according to the NCM, rested upon the success or failure of a mother's efforts. This perspective, which enhanced the position and authority of mothers, also reduced the process of change to individual actions and gave little import to economic or structural factors in the creation of social problems.[21]

In addition to giving attention to the value of women's work within the home, the leadership of the NCM saw the merit of extending that domestic role to reform the public sector.[22] They established committees to promote legislation for the "child and the home," because they viewed it as the best way to improve the welfare of the greatest number of people in a short time. In 1903, Josephine Hart of Chicago presided as the chair of the Committee on Dependent, Defective and Delinquent Children, formed to investigate and influence legislation on the treatment of juveniles. In 1904, the NCM formed a Committee on Child Labor. Florence Kelley, general secretary of the National Consumers' League and coorganizer of the National Child Labor Committee, assumed the chair of this committee until 1906, when she resigned for health reasons. In 1905, Hannah Schoff asked Judge Ben Lindsey of Denver's juvenile court to head the Committee of Juvenile Court and Probation Work.[23] The NCM also used its influence in the U.S. Congress. Florence Kelley succeeded in gaining the organization's support for the Senate bill to create the first national investigation of the labor conditions of child and women workers. The NCM supported the idea of a federal children's bureau, first in 1908 with a convention resolution, and again in 1912 with an endorsement as national momentum for the bureau increased.[24]

The NCM membership tended to view the state as a projection of harmonious and benevolent familial relations. Consider the following depiction of maternal activism presented to the national conference. "The state is a parent, and, as a wise and gentle and kind and loving parent, should beam down upon each child alike. . . . We the mothers of the land, should go in a body and make the appeal for what we wish; then our desires expressed—just gifts given by a loving Father, received equally by the children."[25] In 1905, "the mothers of the nation" took part in a historic meeting with educators, government officials, and the president of the United States at the Ninth National Congress of Mothers. The women came "not as theorists, but as mothers, with the mother heart developed" to address the needs of children. Speaking to the Congress of Mothers, Theodore Roosevelt highlighted the maternalist vision by elevating the value of women's work within the home when compared to the work of statesmen. "All the problems that we deal with as public men, all the questions of the tariff, of finance, of foreign policy, sink into absolute insignificance compared with the great problem of securing and keeping a proper home life in the average family of the average citizen of this Republic."[26] Roosevelt reinforced the traditional values held by NCM members when he asserted "certain old truths . . . which no amount of progress can alter," that men were meant to support their families and women were meant to maintain the home and raise the children.[27]

In its fullest manifestation, maternalism promoted the idea of "universal mothering" and led members to move beyond their own families to work for others. Calls for work on behalf of the "less fortunate" frequently appeared in their publications. In 1905, Hannah Schoff captured the essence of this sentiment in her address to the Ninth National Congress. "There is a broader motherhood than the motherhood that mothers one's own; there is the spirit of the

Lord that is in the mother that mothers all children, and it is because the world has lacked that, that the conditions of the children of this country have not been better."[28] Schoff's address went beyond a call for volunteerism. She placed the actions of these middle-class mothers in the context of a social mission—one essential for the security of the nation.

All relations were not equal in the actions of the mothers' congresses, however. Just as the NCM did not challenge social relations between the sexes, so too did it maintain the status quo in race relations. The ideal of an organization of mothers based in the universal experience of child-rearing fell short in practice. African American women's interest in mothers' clubs and in the NCM was met with the recommendation to organize separately. The board recorded its policy on racially mixed groups by stating that "the National Congress of Mothers, embracing as it does all the states, and having consulted with those who are most interested in the welfare of the colored people . . . recommends colored mothers have an organization of their own, and all circles of colored mothers clubs be advised to affiliate with such an organization." In this case, racial bias and politics superseded the spirit of "universal mothering."[29]

The leadership of the NCM encouraged women's traditional roles of mothering and child-rearing and used them as a justification for greater involvement in public issues. Their ideology located power in individual action. Mothers could have an impact on social problems through child development practice. Their emphasis on individual action and the centrality of the privatized family did not preclude appeals to the state, however. The vitality of family life held such importance for social and political stability that the state could legitimately intervene to ensure social control.

NATIONAL ASSOCIATION OF COLORED WOMEN

Traditions within the African American community as well as the racism of American society contributed to the creation of separate streams of reform work by African Americans. Racism also fostered different definitions of womanhood, motherhood, and dependency. White America had a contradictory view of the African American woman's abilities to mother. She was eulogized with rapturous praise as a "mammy" when employed by whites, as W. E. B. Du Bois reminded us. Yet, under her own roof, caring for her own children, she was called "thriftless and stupid" and condemned for rearing a child to reach "beyond her station." Organized women, therefore, had to define their own agenda as well as counteract the perceptions of a dominant society. Women's clubs added to their goals of "racial progress and uplift" a challenge to the insidious attacks on the character of women. Whether one looks at Josephine St. Pierre

Ruffin, who called African American women together in a national meeting to
organize a better plan for the future of their children, then living under the "peculiar conditions" caused by virulent race ideologies; or Mary Church Terrell's
description of the different life chances faced by African American children; or
the countless clubwomen who created and sustained day nurseries and Phyllis
Wheatley Homes around the country, they "redress[ed] the harsh consequences
of black economic discrimination, political subordination, and white su-
premacy," in Darlene Clark Hine's words.[30]

Founded in 1896 from the combined efforts of the National Federation of
Afro-American Women and the National League of Colored Women, the National Association of Colored Women (NACW) became the national umbrella
organization for state, regional, and city clubs. They had a broad agenda and
divided their efforts through several national committees. By World War I,
membership had reached 100,000 and the organization's influence became recognized politically. During the mid-1920s, the "Seven Plank Platform of the
NACW" outlined the organization's central concerns: education, industry,
thrift, citizenship, racial solidarity, interracial relations, and social service.[31]

The first convention of the NACW in 1897 laid out a "platform of racial
self-defense," in Dorothy Salem's words, and demonstrated the pivotal role
women must play.[32] Members believed that women found their greatest authority in the home and promoted women's domestic role. Between its founding and
World War I, these views of women's importance in the home peppered the
pages of the *National Notes*. "All the best thought now agree that woman is man's
equal intellectually, and that she deserves and should receive a liberal education." Nevertheless, her most important work resided with the family. "Now, let
us place this ideal woman where her work begins as queen and mother. . . . The
heart of the home is this queenly woman."[33] Referring to a movement for mothers' clubs in the South, another writer hoped it would foster race progress in that
"the surest method of elevating any people is to instil true womanly principles
into the homes; . . . from pure womanhood must necessarily follow pure homes"
and from that will come "a people strong in intellect, morals, and religion."[34]
Using language similar to the maternalists in the NCM, the members were told
that "it is the woman's duty to add to the refinement, culture, and beauty of the
home, by keeping the human picture beautiful, educational, and uplifting."[35]

Leaders used maternalist ideals to promote women's activities within the
home and family, and to reinforce a legacy of community work. No contradic-
tion existed in expanding upon one's skills within the larger community. In her
inaugural presidential address to the NACW, Mary Church Terrell raised fa-

miliar maternalist themes on the power of domestic authority and women's ability to expand their maternal role to change the direction of social progress.

> Believing that it is only through the home that a people can become really good and truly great, the N.A.C.W. shall enter that sacred domain to inculcate right principles of living and correct false views of life . . . So long as the majority of people call that place home in which the air is foul, the manners bad and the morals worse, just so long is this so called home a menace to health, a breeder of vice, and the abode of crime.[36]

But Terrell also pointed out the special challenges faced by African American mothers and the way in which racism made their goals different from other mothers.

> As parents, teachers and guardians, we teach our children to be honest and industrious, to cultivate their minds, to become skilled workmen, to be energetic and then to be hopeful. . . . But how bitter is the contrast between the feelings of joy and hope which thrill the heart of the white mother and those which stir the soul of her colored sister. . . . For before her babe she sees the thorny path of prejudice and proscription his little feet must tread.[37]

Other African American leaders called for the use of maternal authority in the resolution of community problems. Fannie Barrier Williams asked women to "become the civic mothers of the race by establishing a sort of special relationship between those who help and those who need help."[38] Nannie Burroughs expressed a form of cross-class maternalism in her statement that "every mother can become a benefactor to the race. It matters not how poor the mother if she possesses a character in which sobriety, honor and integrity, and every other wholesome virtue hold sway."[39] NACW leaders believed in the individual power represented by maternal care, but they also understood the need to organize against larger structures of power.

This focus on idealized motherhood and a woman's function to maintain order in the home differed in important ways from that expressed in the white women's club movement. According to Evelyn Brooks Higginbotham, "Racist representations of black women as unclean, disease-carrying, and promiscuous conjoined with representations of black households as dirty, pathological, and disorderly." A woman's duty to home and family came with increased responsibilities to the race. Her "failure" at mothering or homemaking "left black mothers ultimately accountable for *contributing* lives to the 'bad' and for 'every discrimination we suffer.'"[40] Racism gave a different meaning to otherwise typical women's club work. Kindergartens and mothers' clubs went beyond child education to help teach self-respect and pride as a survival tool for children who would face the "indignities" and "cruel prejudice" of racism.[41]

Women's work as mothers and civic mothers did not preclude their work for wages. In contrast to white reform women's discomfort with wage-earning mothers, many African American women reformers viewed women's earning as a necessity within their community. As early as 1898, *National Notes* published articles that recognized the parallel value of women's work as wage-earners and as mothers. One article encouraged readers to "have more race pride, and remember that every young colored woman who succeeds along any industrial line, helps the whole race to advance."[42] Club members, who were themselves among the middle-class, associated the need to earn with those less fortunate, but nevertheless praised the work of the homemaker at the same time that they called for expanded areas of available work for women. "A woman's greatest and most beneficent work has always been, and must always be, in the home. . . . Out of nothing our women have created homes and made respectability." But, the article continued, greater efforts must also be applied to expand areas of work, cooperatives, and businesses that could help women's job prospects.[43] Race shaped the message in this area as well. In the words of Mary Church Terrell, one woman's efforts reflected on the prospects for the race: "It is the duty of every wage-earning colored woman to become thoroughly proficient in whatever work she engages, so that she may render the best service of which she is capable and thus do her part toward establishing a reputation for excellent workmanship among colored women."[44] A distinctive piece on women's economic independence published by Laura Drake Gill, president of the College for Women in Sewanee, Tennessee, stated that every woman should have a "skilled occupation" from which she could support herself. Although marriage would interrupt her career, Gill argued that women should arrange with their husbands "some equitable division of the family income" to avoid dependence and return to work when the children were raised.[45] Rather than oppose work for women, single or married, the leadership of the NACW recognized the need for many earners in a majority of families and developed lines of reform that would aid working women, such as professional training and day nurseries. During the 1930s, when resources dwindled, the organization maintained its commitment to two central committees—Better Homes, and Women and Industry. When policies limited employment for married women during the depression, the *National Notes* expressed concern that this plan would exacerbate the problems for African American women and their families.[46]

Dependency also had a different meaning within the public forums of the NACW. The incidence of poverty, female headship, and working mothers did not produce an outcry about dependent mothers as it did within the white reform community. Instead, women were understood to be both mothers and workers; thus the category of dependency applied to those unable to earn—the aged, children, the unemployed, or the ill. The organization's broader agenda included programs aimed to encourage economic independence—education, nurses training, kindergartens, day nurseries, and civil rights. Local chapters of the NACW organized "rescue" work for "fallen women and girls," and "friendly visiting" for families whose "demoralizing influences" potentially "endangered" their children.[47] The NACW defined the problems of impoverished women in terms of employment opportunity; consequently one finds very little discussion of either mothers' pensions or general relief. The best aid for poor mothers, in their view, consisted of eliminating barriers to work and providing support services such as child care. In this vein, Terrell called upon each chapter to provide a day nursery. Such community work would help the children and demonstrate an "interest in our sisters, whose lot is harder than our own."[48]

African Americans developed private, not public services, for several reasons. First, the African American community had a long tradition of self-help. At the turn of the century, both Booker T. Washington and W. E. B. Du Bois, whose disagreements on race progress are well-documented, agreed that self-help gave communities autonomy, economic control, and self-determination. In his 1909 assessment of social betterment for African Americans, Du Bois sought public funding for only one area—education.[49] In her study of Baptist women, Evelyn Brooks Higginbotham described the theme of personal responsibility espoused by the churchwomen as a "politics of respectability." This personal politics "emphasized reform of individual behavior and attitudes both as a goal in itself and as a strategy for reform of the entire structural system of American race relations."[50] The NACW recognized the church and the state as "the two great agencies of human improvement," but their efforts needed to be supplemented by voluntarism. The state could provide education as a vehicle for development; the church was overwhelmed in meeting its own obligations; and the only agencies left to assist those in need were organized charities that could work with both church and school.[51] African Americans, like all Americans, relied on the private, voluntary sector for social services. As the expectations for greater public provision increased among some groups at the turn of the century, African Americans appear to have taken a more limited approach in appeals for public intervention.

A second explanation for the reliance on private sources rests in the repressive nature of race politics. Blacks had less access to local political organization and fewer representatives in parties and governing bodies. They found the public sector less generous in the distribution of resources than other groups. This does not indicate a rejection of the state, however. The African American community sought action from the state, as the legislative agenda of the early twentieth century makes clear. Men and women mobilized at the local and national levels to change lynching, segregation, and peonage laws. Moreover, the effects of segregation were not always predictable. In some cities like Atlanta, segregation created a system whereby black agencies received public support to provide services to the black community. In other cities, like Chicago, segregation resulted in fewer public services and more reliance on the private sector.[52]

In contrast to the language of needs or special protection frequently found in the white women's reform agenda, African American women in the NACW used a language of equality. "Seeking no favors because of our color, nor patronage because of our needs," Mary Church Terrell wrote in 1901, "we knock at the bar of Justice and ask for an equal chance." Solutions to the problems of mother-only families would be resolved by granting civil rights and employment opportunity, as well as building strong homes.[53]

THE 1909 WHITE HOUSE CONFERENCE

The issues of citizenship, family responsibility, and dependent motherhood came to a point of national focus in January 1909 when Theodore Roosevelt agreed to sponsor the White House Conference on the Care of Dependent Children. The conference resolutions emphasized the essential role of the mother in the process of child development and advocated a subsidy for mothers who had lost the support of the family's father. Representatives from a wide range of child welfare organizations, juvenile courts, charity societies, settlements, and public institutions participated in the landmark event. Many were closely allied with the National Conference of Charities and Correction and the National Congress of Mothers and reflected the points of view discussed in those meetings. On the other hand, only a few representatives of the African American community appear on the invited list. White Chicagoans were well represented at the conference and on the Committee on Resolutions. Julian Mack, by then a circuit court judge, and Hastings Hart were part of the five-member committee that compiled the resolutions. Other Chicago participants included Jane Addams, Louise de Koven Bowen and Josephine (Mrs. Hastings)

Hart of the Juvenile Court Committee; Charles Henderson; Sherman Kingsley; Julia Lathrop, Illinois Board of Public Charities; Merritt Pinckney, juvenile court judge; Julius Rosenwald, of various Jewish charities; and Henry Thurston, chief probation officer of the juvenile court.[54]

The White House conference confirmed two directions within child welfare policy. The first accepted an expanded role for the public sector in measures for dependent children through protective, regulatory, or social insurance legislation. The second direction promoted the "family setting" and rejected institutional care for poor children. While the majority of policy proposals applied directly to states, the conference attendees implicitly recognized the responsibility of the federal government for the promotion of child welfare by holding the conference in the nation's capital and by endorsing the idea of a federal children's bureau.

The principal of home care for dependent children ranked first on the list of conference resolutions submitted by Theodore Roosevelt to the U.S. Congress. The statement contained several significant assumptions about family life, the mother's role, and the primacy of local jurisdiction, all of which shaped the policy for mother-only families.

> Home life is the highest and finest product of civilization. It is the great molding force of mind and of character. Children should not be deprived of it except for urgent and compelling reasons. Children of parents of worthy character, suffering from temporary misfortune and children of reasonably efficient and deserving mothers who are without the support of the normal breadwinner, should, as a rule, be kept with their parents, such aid being given as may be necessary to maintain suitable homes for the rearing of the children. This aid should be given by such methods and from such sources as may be determined by the general relief policy of each community, preferably in the form of private charity, rather than of public relief. Except in unusual circumstances, the home should not be broken up for reasons of poverty, but only for considerations of inefficiency or immorality.[55]

The emphasis on home care reflected concerns expressed earlier in the National Conference of Charities and Correction—that children kept at home cost the public less in the short term than institutional care. It also reified the benefits of home life in the development of citizens, which offered long-term economic benefits as well.

Specific assumptions about the role of the mother in child-rearing and the significance of that role to society lie at the heart of the discussion on home care.

Rabbi Emil Hirsch, president of the National Conference of Jewish Charities and a member of the Illinois Board of Public Charities, described the relationship of motherhood to social well-being in terms of rights and obligations. "She has rendered to society a service by becoming a mother, and she continues to render a social service if she devotes herself to her child and brings her child up to good citizenship. Then society is morally bound to help the mother discharge that purpose." Hirsch suggested that an obligatory relationship existed between the state and its maternal citizens based on the services a mother provided to society. In addition, he spoke of a woman's right to expect such support from the state: "It is her right to expect compensation at the hand of society that ultimately . . . is the gainer by her maternal devotion." Despite such language, the awards of service were not automatic; they hinged upon the woman meeting ambiguous criteria reiterated in phrases such as "worthy character," "deserving mothers," and "suitable homes." Maternal service alone did not form the basis for an entitlement; it was performance of that work according to a set of standards defined and evaluated by others.[56]

Some advocated a more expansive view of pensions. Julian Mack advocated the extension of aid to mothers with children born out of wedlock. Charles Henderson, University of Chicago sociology professor, past president of the National Conference of Charities and Correction, and future member of the American Association for Labor Legislation's Social Insurance Committee, advocated support without insisting on the labor of either children or mothers. "It may be that her best service for society, as well as to the children," Henderson argued, "is in that employment in which she alone can render the best help . . . the care of the children." Denver juvenile court judge Ben Lindsey linked the rights of children and provision for their care to the broader issues of social justice.[57]

The White House conference did not have the authority to set national policy. It recognized the rights of states and localities to determine the details of policies, in particular whether assistance should come from public or private funds. Nevertheless, the conference reflected a significant trend in welfare thought, one which met strong resistance. The charity organization societies launched the greatest attack upon the idea of mothers' aid on the basis of ideological disagreements and self-interest. They argued that public aid demoralized the poor, provided a disincentive to work, and contributed to a decline in familial responsibility, particularly on the part of fathers toward their families. Public aid, in the view of the charity societies, led to a "corruption" of the character of the poor. But the poor were not the only ones corrupted by public relief in the view of charities. They also used "corruption" to refer to the political mis-use of funds which had led some eastern states to eliminate public assistance in the nineteenth century. The "bottomless trough" of public funds and the in-effective public administration of relief so inadequately served the interests of both the poor and society that private control of relief policy through charities remained the only viable recourse from the perspective of the charity organiza-tion societies. Some societies supported the principle of aid to dependent chil-dren, but only under conditions in which they controlled the mechanisms of provision. It would be difficult to imagine that the charity organization societies were not concerned that the rise of public subsidies would negatively impact the influence they held.[58] Despite opposition, the momentum for some form of provision for dependent mothers accelerated after the 1909 conference.

MOTHERS' PENSION ALTERNATIVES AND PROPOSALS

Socialists and feminists contributed to the debate on mothers' pensions both in theory and practical politics. Their position focused on securing economic in-dependence for women and in challenging the domestic claim on women's labor. Two specific contributions can be found in the analysis of women's eco-nomic position developed by Charlotte Perkins Gilman and in the European-inspired plan for a maternal endowment.[59]

The burden of working-class women's "double day" filled commentaries of progressive reform, but the clearest and most radical analysis had come years earlier from Charlotte Perkins Gilman. Her 1898 treatise, *Women and Econom-ics*, carefully defined the liabilities of the sexual division of labor and the ways in which it fostered and perpetuated women's dependent status. Gilman por-trayed the "fiction" of marriage's domestic partnership as a trap because "women's work," particularly in bearing and rearing children, left them entirely unfit for wage work and economically dependent upon their husbands. The idea that marriage offered a partnership of equals, each person providing different resources, obscured the fact that men could purchase homemaking services, while women could rarely hope to replace men's wages. Rather than reward women's housekeeping and child-rearing services as labor, it was viewed as a "duty" to the family. This duty had economic consequences, however, in that it circumscribed their ability to enter the labor force. The majority of women earned only a minimal income, and thus could not expect to support themselves or their children if necessary.[60] For Gilman, women's independence balanced on the separation of the biological act of reproduction from the social act of child-rearing. In contrast to maternalist ideas, Gilman rejected idealizations of motherhood as essentialist and ill founded. She believed that women would be better served with socialized housework, collectivized kitchens, and group child care. These ideas led her to speak critically of the maternal endowment, because the plan would reinforce women's role as primary caretakers and institutionalize women's inferiority.[61]

The early advocates of maternal endowments shared much of Gilman's analysis, but differed in their solutions. Like Gilman, endowment supporters in Britain and the United States located the source of women's economic dependence in the gender system that left a woman's services in the home unpaid and her compensation as an implied share of her husband's wage. They also agreed that this system fostered a marginal status for women in the labor force. However, rather than change the social relations of home and market, the endowment proposed a universal stipend to cover the costs of child-rearing. The British drew upon their precedents for subsidizing nonproducers, such as the aged or disabled, and argued that children also should be considered nonproducers and thus eligible for such provision.[62]

In 1906, British socialist H. G. Wells explored the issue of state support for families and the maternal endowment in two articles published in the United States. In one, he criticized the manifestations of private ownership evident in families and the idea that men controlled certain aspects of the lives of their wives and children. Wells proposed that a more enlightened view would consider parenting as a form of "social service" which, if performed well, should receive compensation. "People rear children for the State and the future," he wrote. "If they do that well they do the whole world a service, and deserve payment just as much as if they built a bridge or raised a crop of wheat." An endowment would equalize opportunities for children's development regardless of the family income. But Wells's plan contained weaknesses. It assumed that women would be the primary caretakers and suggested that the endowment be subject to the merit of parental performance. This would necessitate a regulatory body and preclude universal coverage. He also restricted the application of his idea to "legitimate" children and those who were "healthy and successful."[63] Gilman criticized the endowment proposals and Wells in particular for assuming that women alone would bear the responsibility for child-rearing. Rather than reinforce the limitations of gender based on biological function, Gilman challenged Wells and other socialists to further the equality of men and women by providing support for child care.[64]

The idea for a maternal endowment received support in the United States from feminists such as Crystal Eastman, Harriet Stanton Blatch, and Katharine Anthony. In it they saw the opportunity to acknowledge women's choice to parent, but also to secure some measure of economic security. Eastman believed that the only way to guarantee that motherhood would not create dependency was to ensure an endowment for service to the state. In her preface to the U.S. publication of *Endowment for Motherhood*, Anthony emphasized that such a plan would provide for all Americans what was now available only to the rich.[65] Women's economic independence remained at the center of feminists' arguments for an endowment during the 1910s. In sharp contrast to those who defended the privatized family and traditional family relations, including maternalists, feminists sought to reconstruct those relations based on principles of equity. A woman's claim to citizenship must rest upon the same foundation as that of a man, and not be derived exclusively from family relations. To tie women's citizenship to familial relations, feminists argued, created the foundation for sexual inequality in law, economics, and politics.

Although never seriously debated by U.S. policy makers, problems existed with the endowment. Some plans contained aspects of pronatalist nationalism and classist eugenics, when, for example, proponents argued that the status of women was inextricably linked to the status of motherhood and used fears of foreign elements to make the case. "Unless the system is altered the nation will continue to be recruited, in an ever growing proportion, from the ranks of those who are physically and mentally the least fit," Rathbone argued for the British case. Also, rather than separating reproduction from parenting as Gilman had proposed, most endowment plans continued to position women as caregivers. Finally, plans for maternal endowments, while never spelling out the specifics, implied that good parenting would necessitate some form of regulation of behavior.[66]

A definitive example of socialist involvement in the debate on mothers' aid appears in Sherry Katz's study of California.[67] Katz found a difference in the type of advocacy by socialists from that of progressives in that the former called for a widespread system of social provision, a form of social insurance, or a "right of the poor" to public aid. Socialist women used terms of sexual differentiation to promote their agenda, but the broader discourse advanced female independence, Katz found. At the same time that socialist women supported mothers' aid in California, they also endorsed wage and hour legislation and labor unionization as measures to improve the economic position of working-class women. Interestingly, the 1913 California legislature passed a minimum wage law, but the proposals for mothers' aid were reduced to a restrictive and limited provision. Opposition to the more inclusive bills was articulated in one case as the fear that "it would be like laying the foundation for a new social order."[68] The radical critique of gender relations and domestic economy offered by socialists and feminists had a marginal influence in the outcome of California policy. While this does not diminish the theoretical contributions made, it is informative about the structure of political opportunity at the time. The principles of sexual equality and universal coverage were inconsistent with the agenda of charities and maternalists. Those groups were vital to the political coalitions that passed mothers' pensions.

Feminists and socialists continued to work for women's economic independence in a variety of ways—many of which overlapped with the tactics of social justice feminists. Wage supports such as the minimum wage, wage subsidies such as pensions, and private or social insurance provided a broad forum for economic advancement. The divergence in strategies between feminists and social justice feminists became too great during the 1920s, when feminists within the National Woman's Party pursued the equal rights amendment as the single best method for sex equality and moved to secure the blanket amendment in 1923. Social justice feminists chose wage supports for employed women, pensions for those with young children, and inclusion within social insurance plans. They believed such policies provided an incremental step toward "substantive equality."

The National Congress of Mothers' leadership also found a measure of gender injustice in a system that enhanced women's economic insecurity simply because they made a commitment to raise children. Inspired by the White House conference, the NCM stepped up its program for the protection of American families and home life through its legislative agenda for mothers' pensions. They believed pensions would serve as a measure of family insurance for those unable to purchase private policies. Pensions could also prevent the rise of greater social ills such as crime and family disruption. "The greatest asset in [the] life of man or woman is to have a mother's care during infancy and childhood. To deny children a mother's care because of poverty . . . is an injustice to the state." Mothers' pension legislation made the link between the instrumental role of the mother in the family and the well-being of family, community, and state.[69]

The first specific mention of aid to mothers with dependent children within the NCM occurred in an article in the *National Congress of Mothers Magazine* a month after the White House Conference on the Care of Dependent Children. Edwin D. Solenberger, general secretary of the Philadelphia Children's Aid Society, condemned the relief practice of breaking up families when the father died or deserted. In place of this policy, Solenberger advocated "that a regular pension ought to be provided to supplement [a mother's] earnings until some of her children are old enough to leave school and to help support the family." The pension would be available to all mothers regardless of their marital status. This idea reflected the general principle of care for dependent children developed during the White House conference.[70]

The "strongest talk in favor of mothers' pensions" took place at the Second International Congress of Child Welfare sponsored by the NCM in April 1911. Mrs. G. H. Robertson addressed the gathering on "The State's Duty to Fatherless Children" and linked the experience of motherhood with the social responsibility of the state. "Mothers are bound together," she said, "by a tie closer than blood. We (no matter whether we live in a palace or hovel) have felt the same physical and mental anguish that belongs alone to motherhood." Women in the NCM, she added, had a special obligation to those women whose misfortune lay in the fact that their husbands had died or deserted them. "These friendless mothers are our especial responsibility," Robertson continued. "They grew up to believe in marriage and home-building. Now is it fair that we let them find it a tragedy?" She wanted to see a national commission and appropriations for mother-only families, including deserted wives and never-married women along with widows with young children. As a result of this address, the NCM passed a conference resolution calling for state-level support that would enable mothers to continue to care for their children. It also authorized all state congresses to work for passage of pension legislation. The *Child Welfare Magazine* consistently provided positive coverage of the mothers' pension movement after 1911.[71]

Not surprisingly, the initial arguments in favor of pensions within the NCM endorsed the aid as a form of payment for service to the state. A woman who had "divided her body by creating other lives for the good of the state, one who has contributed to citizenship" should not under any conditions be classified as a pauper. Her years spent nurturing children into healthy citizens provided a service equally as valuable as the soldier who defended the nation. One newspaper that covered the International Congress of Child Welfare in 1911 applauded the move to protect motherhood from poverty and linked the action to the declining birthrate. "It is inevitable that the day will come when the supreme service of the mothers of the nation will be publicly honored, when the strongest claim that a woman can make to social distinction will be the number of healthy children she had contributed to its citizenship. . . . When that time comes every mother will have the pledge of the state that her reward for bearing children shall not be a struggle against poverty, but that every child she brings into the world will have guarantee against want until it has arrived at an age when it can earn its own living." The pension-for-service argument stressed that state support of mother-only families provided a better value to the state.

Not only was the provision less expensive than institutional care, but the children were more likely to result in better citizens when raised within their own families.[72]

Within a few years, the discussion of pensions within the NCM shifted from an adulatory recognition of the work of mothers to a social policy for the control of social ills. As implementation of mothers' pension policy began, class-based fears of inappropriate family structure and changing roles of motherhood replaced earlier articulations of maternal solidarity. In 1914, the NCM adopted a resolution that recommended a universal system of pension laws because it offered "the most effective method of checking truancy and child labor." President Hannah Schoff linked fears about criminal activity to the working mother's absence from the home and noted that pensions could help reduce juvenile crime. This argument still recognized the social value of women's work as mothers, despite the shift from entitlement to regulatory language. However, the leadership of the NCM abandoned its rhetoric of universal maternal bonding, and poor mothers increasingly became objects of their fear. Members received notice to be cautious of a policy that could "relieve fathers of the legal duty of providing for children." The most profound reversal occurred in December 1914 when Hannah Schoff wrote that "the mother's pension then is for the benefit of the children and the State, and not the mother" at all.[73]

Other mothers' pension promoters noted the wariness with which the NCM lent its support. In a letter to Hannah Schoff, Ben Lindsey of Denver's juvenile court wrote of the cool reception the policy received from NCM members, particularly when compared to the endorsement of working-class women. Lindsey wrote:

> While I haven't any doubt that the great majority of the members of the Woman's Club, and the Mothers' Congress are on my side, still, it is rather interesting to note that the bitter warfare provoked by a real attack against the fundamental causes of poverty and crime has seemed to so intimidate these organizations, that it seems to be impossible to address either the Mothers' Congress or the Woman's Club in Denver on this subject; although outside of Denver . . . I am always a very welcome guest to discuss the problem. . . . The only women's organizations that pass resolutions in my favor and stand by me in the public fight is [*sic*] just the ordinary mothers, and the garment workers and women in the trades and industries, who know nothing about the Mothers' Congress and the Woman's Club. . . . The labor people and the labor unions, the poor and the lowly and those whom we helped, have never hesitated to come promptly to my rescue in such emergencies.[74]

Hannah Schoff's response to Lindsey acknowledged the difficulty of maintaining support from the local Congress of Mothers clubs in the face of political opposition. Schoff wrote:

> The situation is easily understood by me. Both organizations have as members women whose husbands are allied in business ways with the political organizations which you are fighting. It is their bread and butter. The organizations, by taking up such fights, bring difficulty into their ranks and they find opposition in their own membership to any movement which is radical. . . . In my work for the Juvenile Court here [Philadelphia] I had good help until the work came up against organizations which had been in existence for years and with which the new work seemed in some ways to conflict.[75]

Once on the ground, the idea of "paid motherhood" ran afoul of other interests. Some private charities opposed removing women from the workforce and objected to publicly funded programs. Some politicians saw this new arena of public spending as a challenge to their domain in distributing public goods. These forms of resistance proved more difficult than the earlier stages of promoting universal claims to benefit motherhood.

The NCM promoted mothers' pensions across the states with its appeals to the value of good mothering for individual families and society as a whole. Its goals coincided with other nationalist concerns about the decline in family size, fear of "race suicide," and threats from social problems perceived to be caused by immigration, expansion of cities, and the unregulated cycles of industrial capitalism. The functional justification for a woman's role at home— raising citizens—offered a stabilizing component in a period of great social change. The white, predominantly middle-class members of the NCM viewed mothers' pensions as an opportunity to secure family life among that sector of society that they believed experienced the greatest vulnerability and provided the greatest threat—the poor. As localities began to put the law into practice, however, the universalism that had characterized their earlier support became tempered by local politics. Although the NCM continued to support pension legislation, its endorsement shifted from an entitlement for maternity to a measure of control for social problems.

A third gender-specific perspective on dependent mothers emerged with an agenda situated between socialists and maternalists. Social justice feminists, many of whom had started in settlement work, attempted to place women's rights at the center of talks on social provision and industrial justice. They understood the problem of poor mother-only families as a systematic problem which included the structure of the labor market, limited opportunities in education and training, and the division of labor within the family. However, unlike some socialists and feminists, they did not confront family relations. Rather they sought ameliorative solutions that they thought would expand women's opportunities. They supported the minimum wage, mothers' pensions, and social insurance plans for women.[76]

In 1910, Edith Abbott published *Women in Industry,* an unprecedented assessment of the condition of women wage-earners. The book was a landmark for its depiction of occupational segregation and gendered wage structures. In it she underscored the reality that unskilled working women could never work their way to economic independence because their wages prohibited it. Furthermore, Abbott pointed out that the "woman movement" had benefited educated women most while working-class women found their opportunities little changed. The working-class woman "has undoubtedly been wronged in the past," she wrote, owing to "the pseudo-democratic refusal to recognize class distinctions in discussions of the woman question." Her study and her subsequent research aimed to help rectify that situation. Also in 1910, Sophonisba Breckinridge raised as a policy issue the need for a form of insurance that would provide to working-class mothers and wives the same measure of security that economically privileged workers provided their families through private insurance. Jane Addams gave authority to the ideas of her Hull House colleagues when she assumed the presidency of the National Conference of Charities and Correction in 1910. Her presidential address drew attention to the role of welfare workers in "making a new state" through their efforts for greater regulation of industry and protective legislation for workers and dependents. Her address called attention to the special needs of mother-only families. She chastised existing social policy that refused assistance to women with young children in an effort to enforce the work ethic of relief policy, pointing out that women's wages could not support one person, let alone a family. Addams stressed the inequity of forcing mothers to "perform the offices of two parents" and advocated public support for both family subsidies and the minimum wage. Addams did not assume a leadership role in the movement for mothers' pensions either nationally or in Chicago, yet her Hull House associates kept her informed of the new research and policy directions.[77]

The work of social justice feminists overlapped at times with organized women's labor, particularly on protective legislation. Although the American Federation of Labor attempted to raise workers' living standards through collective bargaining, women workers addressed the issue of dependency and wage standards through minimum wage campaigns. Initially, the minimum wage represented a measure of "industrial justice" that would enable the working woman to support not only herself, but her dependents. It was part of a larger critique of industrial capitalism and the unregulated power it had amassed. The Women's Trade Union League (WTUL), which made minimum wages for women one of its goals as early as 1907, did not shy from a serious criticism of capital when it challenged the "monopoly rights" afforded to corporations to set wages below any decent living standard and called for an end to "subsidies" for industry produced by a disorganized system.[78] The American Federation of Labor rejected legislative solutions for its members before the 1920s, but it supported a minimum wage law for women, hoping that it would prevent a lowering of wages overall.[79] Several states set up minimum wage boards in the 1910s and Massachusetts passed the first minimum wage law in 1917 with a dozen other states following over the next five years. The social insurance movement rejected this legislation as part of its proposals (as it did mothers' pensions), but in a rare admission of the value of minimum wage laws, Irene Osgood Andrews, assistant secretary of the American Association for Labor Legislation, acknowledged that such legislation could be a significant benefit for women workers who were irregularly employed.[80] Florence Kelley of the National Consumers' League and Felix Frankfurter of Harvard Law School succeeded in getting a model minimum wage bill passed for the District of Columbia in 1918. They hoped that state legislatures would adopt a version of this law, but the Supreme Court dashed those plans in 1923 when it rejected the legal premise of the legislation in *Adkins v. Children's Hospital*.[81]

Private philanthropies and governmental bodies also undertook research on the situation of mother-only families. These studies sought to discover the particular characteristics of poverty among widowed and deserted families as well as to supply evidence that could be used in the mothers' pension policy debates. The Children's Bureau sponsored several informative studies, including a review of Illinois' progress with mothers' pensions. New York, Wisconsin, and Massachusetts created state commissions to investigate mothers' pensions during the 1910s. The problem of impoverished widows consumed much of the attention; however, the studies also investigated the issue of minimum wages and the problem of support for deserted women and children. They confirmed earlier findings reported by Abbott, the Department of Labor study on child and woman workers, and reports to the NCCC that women who assumed the dual role of support and child-rearing suffered from overwork and deteriorating health. They also confirmed that the high proportion of unskilled women workers made it improbable that they could ever achieve self-support. Many mother-only families relied on children's wages for subsistence. To achieve a basic standard of health and well-being, these families would need some form of income supplement. In general, the studies stated that the policy of pensioning families would work only in cases of effective supervision and administration. Similarly, those who supported a mothers' pension recommended that deserted women be excluded despite their need or "worthiness" because of fears that such support would encourage men's irresponsibility toward their families. The strength of the charity organization societies and their ability to influence the direction of pension policy may have accounted for this development.[82]

The discussions on aid to dependent families frequently turned to the balance between public aid and wage-work for the mother, and it is useful to summarize the range of positions. On one end of the spectrum rested advocates of maternal endowments who argued that the value of a woman's labor justified a public expenditure—an endowment—to sustain her and her children. These advocates could vary from the maternalists of the NCM, who sought to elevate motherhood and reinforce family relations, to the socialist feminists, who supported a universal plan as a measure to eliminate wage inequity. Despite these great differences, they shared a focus on the value of women's labor within the home.

At the opposite end of the spectrum were representatives of charities, like Edward T. Devine, who resolutely held the position that women, when able-bodied, should earn. Government would interfere if it provided public funds; thus the only appropriate government function was to improve the availability of work. In his criticism of the mothers' pension idea, Devine wrote:

> To the mothers themselves it seems natural, inevitable, and appropriate that they should work. Most of them have worked before marriage, many of them have worked during their married life, and that as widows they should earn a living for themselves and children is simply in the course of nature, an obvious and unquestionable obligation. What they feel is that the mother should work—not of course if she is nursing an infant in arms, or about to be confined, or if she is seriously ill, or if there is some extraordinary demand upon her in the home, such as an invalid child demanding constant attention, or a large number of very young children, and no older person in the family to look after them. Working mothers have real hardships and grievances, but that an able-bodied woman under forty, with one or two children, should be expected to earn a large part or all of her support, is not one of them. Even when there are three or four children

the mother would generally scout the idea that she could not earn their living if she is given a fair chance. Not the necessity of earning, however, but the difficulty of finding work is what is more apt to cause her anxiety.[83]

The charity organization view followed the tradition of poor relief in that it insisted that all able-bodied adults work for their self-support regardless of their sex or their child-rearing responsibilities.

Some representatives of public and private charities attempted to justify a middle ground for pensions as actual wage subsidies. Consider for example, two agents from Boston's Associated Charities who recognized the contributions made by women in the home, but found greater advantages in their subsidized earning. Private agencies had success promoting wage-earning along with grants because it gave "the mother a stronger influence with her children and calls forth a special loyalty from them." Work also helped the mother, they suggested, by breaking up her routine. "A day or two of work a week outside was really better for the mother than to keep her always at home, for life can be too dull some times, even in a tenement, and except where there is a young baby."[84] However, many reformers who wanted improvements in both social provision and labor conditions viewed wage subsidies as a mistake.

A few progressive reformers presented a different perspective on wage-earning, one that recognized the value of women's domestic labor as well as the relationship between women's poverty and their limited wage-earning opportunities. They frequently linked mothers' pensions to the issue of better work conditions and minimum wage campaigns, because they understood that women's vulnerable economic status developed as a result of inequities and industrial resistance to women workers. Anna Garlin Spencer told the National Conference of Charities and Correction that the poverty of widows and deserted women was "caused, or terribly increased by the inability of women to get suitable work or sufficient wages when left widowed or deserted." She said that poverty "can never be treated intelligently by the charitable public until the factor of the mother's economic power and adaptability is given its proper place."[85] Mary Van Kleeck found the relation between relief and wage-earning a "transitory service measure" and advocated the "recognition of the right of women to be trained for their work" and an insistence upon living wages for women.[86] Edith Abbott and Sophonisba Breckinridge criticized the "well-meaning persons of other classes, who, accepting the 'sphere of woman' doctrine, would limit the activities of women of all classes to the bearing and rearing of children" and insisted upon the "right of women" to a place in industry.[87] Issues of education and training for women, employment opportunities, and a living or minimum wage became a part of the long-term solution to the problem.

Poor single mothers left some indication of their ideas about their double day in their comments to caseworkers and letters to the Children's Bureau. One woman confided to a caseworker her distress over trying to be both a homemaker and wage-earner. "What can I do for my children, when I am away working every day? I have no time to look after them, to mend their clothes, to care for the house, to know what they are doing."[88] Numerous letters to the Children's Bureau from women across the country echoed a similar theme and the need for aid. From Montana, a woman asked for "a pension to help a mother and child to keep her from working her self to death . . . and she not feel humiliated as a pauper." From Mississippi, a widow who had been sick for five months told the Children's Bureau, "I got three little childrens to suport and I want the goverment to help me." Another request, which was addressed to "Oncle Sam" from a mother of thirteen children, asked, "Wil you pleas help me raise my family."[89]

Recognizing impoverished women's handicap in wage-earning, some social justice feminists, including Abbott, Breckinridge, and Kelley, came to the conclusion that the greatest benefits might be found in working for the minimum wage while also promoting mothers' pensions. This combination had the support of many in women's labor circles. In testimony to the New York State Commission on Relief for Widowed Mothers, Abbott and Breckinridge took the opposite stance of Edward Devine, and suggested that he made unrealistic demands to expect a woman "to succeed in her duties of keeping her home and children while she uses up in earning money, time and strength, all of which are needed to discharge the more fundamental duty." Rather than insist on earning, rather than place more unskilled women workers in the workforce, and rather than run the risk of lowering wages, they wanted a form of insurance for mothers.[90]

During the 1920s, after ten years of experience with mothers' pension laws, some of the best-informed commentators on the policy recognized that it operated as a wage subsidy program. Sophonisba Breckinridge wrote in 1923, in the midst of the equal rights debate and around the time of the minimum wage defeat in the Supreme Court, that working mothers who received mothers' pensions would create a downward pressure on wages unless they received either an equal wage or family wage. A few years later, Leila Houghteling, a colleague of Breckinridge, wrote that those considering minimum wage rates must realize that women supported families as did men and that the policy to subsidize their wages with public or private charity would never resolve the issue adequately.[91]

Social insurance offered another potential policy for universal social provision, but the construction of a policy based on labor force contributions severely limited its potential for the majority of working-class mother-only families. In the early 1900s, reformers, businessmen, labor leaders, and academics debated proposals for social insurance, both for the aged and as remedies for the problems created by industrial life—in particular, disability, death, and unemployment. Economically advantaged families could protect themselves through private forms of insurance, but standard-of-living studies pointed to the grim fact that the majority of working-class families could not meet the basic costs of living, let alone set aside sufficient savings to cover illness, injury, or death. Furthermore, working-class men under forty-five years of age had a high death rate, but among the workers in unskilled and service occupations those rates increased. Social insurance would extend the benefits of insurance to those who could not otherwise afford it through pooled resources and cost-sharing between the worker, employer, and government.[92]

Proponents shared certain assumptions. They believed that the state served as a positive vehicle for social well-being; that social insurance movements, like those initiated in Europe, represented a move toward modernization; and that all plans would need to be adapted to the U.S. context. These ideas gained increased prominence within professional organizations like the NCCC as a measure against the insecurity of life for working-class families. Just a few years after Florence Kelley and Jane Addams emphasized the need for better wages for working women and a system of aid for mother-only families, calls for workingmen's insurance and social justice filled the presidential addresses of this organization. Graham Taylor pointed out that a transition in public care was already underway as local governments assumed a larger share of aid for the aged, widows with children, and the ill than private agencies. Between 1912 and 1914, the presidents of the conference challenged laissez-faire doctrines that restricted state intervention. It was time for a change in policy and support for "the right to work," "protection against unemployment," and "the right to old age, reasonably free from care and anxiety."[93] While many reformers supported parts of those views, one group came to be identified with social insurance policies—the American Association for Labor Legislation (AALL).

John Commons and Richard Ely launched the AALL in 1906 at the University of Wisconsin. They operated on a volunteer staff for three years, then hired John B. Andrews, a student of Commons, to run the organization. The AALL attracted economists, political scientists, social workers, and labor leaders who wanted to liberalize labor laws by providing the best social science research available on select topics to legislators and groups already organized for legislative reform work.[94] Criticizing existent models of charity as outmoded, unresponsive, and inadequate, the AALL members sought new policies to address the negative impact of industrial capitalism on the wage-earner. Early social insurance investigations focused on workmen's compensation, sickness insurance, old-age benefits, and measures for the unemployed. The organization's first efforts with workmen's compensation drew upon principles of private insurance and European models of workers' social insurance. Some state legislatures passed workmen's compensation at the same time as mothers' pension laws, establishing the right of workers to compensation if hurt on the job.[95]

What provisions did the social insurance advocates develop to address the needs of the impoverished single mother? They defined the problems associated with mother-only families (by which they meant widows) as child labor, poor employment opportunities for women, and the resulting poverty. However, unlike their female reform counterparts, the AALL did not examine women's problems independently from those of the male-headed family. Their discussions on women's economic dependency included two provisions: assistance for workers' widows and orphans, and maternity insurance as a component of health insurance. Some members recognized the limited programs in the United States. While European workers' dependents received a form of nationalized life insurance, U.S. workmen's compensation laws paid so little in injury and death benefits that women and children needed to work. The AALL's remedy was an increase in benefits, extension of benefits for the entire period of disability or widowhood, and an extension of benefits for children until they reached the age of sixteen years. The AALL discussed the minimum wage and mothers' pensions, but it decided that these policies did not fall within the scope of their social insurance agenda.[96]

In fact, mothers' pensions received a negative reception from the group. "Its essential features," Isaac Rubinow wrote in 1913, "are those of a system of public relief rather than insurance." He referred to the elements of supervision, moral regulation, and means testing which surrounded the policies and its discussions. Edward T. Devine thought that a combination of personal responsibility and widows' insurance would solve the problems of dependent mothers. Mothers' pensions represented "a backward step," and women who were deserted, unmarried, or married to men in uncovered industries could always apply to relief, according to Devine. The AALL proposals were limited by their commitment to a system of contributory insurance and the idea that married women were not a permanent part of the workforce. The result was a policy that benefited a small portion of workers' families.[97]

Many supporters of mothers' pensions wanted women included in these plans. They agreed that mothers' pensions had limits, but they would not accept the exclusion of mother-only family issues from the social insurance agenda. William Hard, an editor and former head of the Northwestern University settlement, challenged Edward Devine in the pages of the *American Labor Legislation Review*. "Social insurance, in any competent totality of operation, remains a future ideal." What, he asked, would social insurance advocates propose for impoverished working mothers in the interim?[98] A few years later, Edith Abbott and Sherman Kingsley made a similar point at a conference on social insurance in Washington, D.C. Abbott told the assembled that mothers' pension legislation held no "final measure of social justice to the wage earner" but it served a constituency left outside current social insurance proposals. The majority of families who received mothers' pensions at that time could not receive benefits from social insurance because casual and unskilled jobs were not covered. Until the time social insurance expanded its coverage to include general workplace accidents, occupational diseases, death, unemployment, and maternity benefits, an intermediate policy such as mothers' pensions served poor women. Abbott did not address the central criticisms regarding regulation and income testing.[99]

The AALL did attempt to include a provision for maternity benefits in its health insurance bills. Although they were unsuccessful, the measures proposed that wives of insured men and working women who were themselves insured would receive sick pay for time missed owing to childbirth. Bills were sent to legislatures in New York and Massachusetts. Labor women in New York encouraged the bill's passage. Julia Lathrop, representing the Children's Bureau, supported the idea of a paid leave as a health and welfare issue. Mary Conynton of the Bureau of Labor Statistics said women were in the workforce to stay and needed consideration in these policies, and she sharply criticized ideas that represented married women's workforce participation as inconsistent with American standards. The view "that only the wives of negroes, non-English-speaking aliens, and defectives and delinquents work for wages in this country" was not only bigoted, but inaccurate and held back much needed resources for working women in the United States. But there were also concerns about the measure. Florence Kelley wanted the contributory measure dropped for low-wage workers. Lathrop and Grace Abbott (second director of the U.S. Children's Bureau and Edith Abbott's sister) wanted coverage for all women workers, not only those married to an insured man or who had themselves been "taxed to provide the benefit." The bills were defeated in the state legislatures.[100]

The movement for mothers' pensions and the movement for social insurance never merged to create the universal coverage advocated by Abbott. Rather, the AALL limited its plans to families of insured workers. Two branches of social provision for mother-only families emerged, each determined by the workplace participation of the male wage-earner. The widows of men who worked in selected industries became eligible for survivors' benefits (expanded in the Social Security Act amendment of 1939). Women whose husbands worked outside these covered industries, or who were without a husband, found their social justice in mothers' pensions or poor relief.

§

The early twentieth century witnessed a wide-ranging discussion on the problems of and solutions for impoverished mother-only families. A consensus emerged on the need for a subsidy, but other fundamental disagreements remained. Would the program be universal or selective? Should public or private agencies administer the policy? Under what conditions should women and children earn wages? To what degree did earning offer benefits or detriments to mothers? The diverse views of "dependency" and "motherhood" expressed in these debates made visible the contradictions of social categories in the definition of woman as citizen in modern society, and highlighted the tensions surrounding a woman's roles as mother, worker, and citizen. The variety of positions reflects not only different social goals but disparate political possibilities.

The mobilization of organized women played an important role in drawing the public's attention to the issues of women's poverty. Most understood working-class women's dependence as both political and economic. Others saw the primary objective as securing the family and woman's maternal role within it. In general, organized women initially agreed that most mother-only families should receive aid. But among the supporters of mothers' pensions, important differences existed. Traditionalists, such as members of the National Congress of Mothers, wanted to heighten the social value of mothers and their mother-work. Their claim for pensions rested upon maternal service to the state through parenting. Feminists and socialists also valued women's domestic labor but endorsed an endowment as a means toward economic independence. They saw universal payment to mothers as the only way to counteract inequities caused by the division of labor. Social justice feminists supported economic independence, but believed it to be a practical impossibility for working-poor mothers in light of existing labor practices, cultural traditions, and familial relations. Their proposals sought incremental change through protective labor laws and social welfare measures. These varied arguments came together to gain passage of mothers' pension laws, and thus succeeded in establishing the precedent of public aid to mother-only families despite different views about women's claims as citizens.

But women's organizations did not operate within a policy vacuum. Aside from their own differences, they faced competing views of social provision from the charity organization societies and those promoting social insurance. Despite an emerging consensus among professional social work organizations that the home offered the most effective and efficient place to care for dependent children, any proposal that endorsed a more activist state had to contend with a tradition of personal responsibility as well as great distrust of government intervention. The charity view of dependency offered few alternatives for the working-poor mother. She should earn her way to self-sufficiency. Social insurance would have been a likely foundation for dependent-family policy, but the AALL chose a strategy that relied upon contributions from workers and employers and prioritized women's homemaking role. Mothers' pension bills passed state legislatures to face an uncertain future in the local arena.

The debates on the national level attested to the strength of interest generated by the new policy, but the actual operation would unfold at the local level. As the mothers' pension program unfolded in Chicago, it interacted with an established and structured system of public aid.

Cook County officials distribute Christmas baskets, 1916. Chicago Historical Society.

The Structure of Public Provision: Gender and Race in Chicago's Welfare System

The problem of poverty in American cities received critical attention from urban reformers between 1890 and 1910. Intent on moving beyond nineteenth-century notions and practices, and inspired by British social surveys and new "social scientific" methods, Americans began to collect facts on urban working conditions, housing, and poverty. Chicago became the subject of one of the earliest surveys when Congress authorized a study of urban poverty in four cities in 1892. Florence Kelley, then a resident at Hull House, became the Department of Labor's "special agent" for the neighborhood surrounding the city's most famous settlement. In addition to the statistical tabulations presented in the government volume, Kelley and several other contributors used the research as a basis for further study of their neighbors and presented it in the more accessible publication *Hull House Maps and Papers*. This book detailed the variety and patterns of residents' lives in the area described as "the poorest and probably the most crowded section of Chicago."[1]

> Rear tenements and alleys form the core of the district, and it is there that the densest crowds of the most wretched and destitute congregate. Little idea can be given of the filthy and rotten tenements, the dingy courts and tumble down sheds, the foul stables and dilapidated outhouses, the broken sewer pipes, the piles of garbage fairly alive with diseased odors.[2]

The volume hoped to gain the public's support for changes in the conditions that contributed to poverty. Employment and family income, in addition to the obvious focus on health and housing, took center stage in this and other early studies.

The ability to work one's way out of poverty and the structural impediments to self-support proved one central theme. Many studies focused on the importance of raising the father's wage in families. Citing myriads of standard-of-living studies, reformers argued that while he was not the sole earner in the family, his wages usually provided the primary income and the first line of defense for the family's survival. The focus on adult male wages and male employment fit within a broader social framework of family roles, a gendered division of labor, and an economic structure that privileged male earners.[3] Yet, this focus did little to assist adult women in poverty. Women's poverty usually resulted from the absence of the adult male earner, and labor or social reforms directed at employment for a male-headed family made little sense for the mother-only family. The sole responsibility for young children and barriers to self-support created a different set of obstacles. When women went out to work, they faced limited wage-earning opportunities, their wages were a fraction of their male peers, and they had the additional task of long-term child care. Children's wage-earning reduced the dual burden of mother-only families as did charity and public relief. However, an improvement in the economic cycle had less effect upon the structural problems of lower wages and part-time work for unskilled working women.

Unlike many early works on poverty, the Hull House volume introduced family relations as an element to incorporate into an analysis of poverty.[4] Not only low-paid jobs, but intermittent work led to the extent of poverty found in the area. Families responded to those economic conditions by sending many members to earn.

> In this neighborhood, generally a wife and children are sources of income as well as avenues of expense. . . . women wash, do "home finishing" on ready-made clothing, or pick and sell rags; boys run errands and "shine"; the girls work in factories, get places as cash-girls, or sell papers on the streets; and the very babies sew buttons on knee-pants and shirt waists, each bringing in a trifle to fill out the scanty income. The theory that "every man supports his own family" is as idle in a district like this as the fiction that "everyone can get work if he wants it."[5]

Women experienced particular and distinct problems that needed to be addressed, as Julia Lathrop noted in her contribution to this volume. "Here amongst all, save the Italians, flourishes the masculine expedient of temporary disappearance in the face of nonemployment or domestic complexity, or both; paradoxically enough the intermittent husband is a constant factor in the economic problem of many a household."[6] As reformers conducted these early social surveys on the causes and extent of poverty in the United States, they compiled information that would confront, challenge, and in some cases, change the existent ideas about poverty and the structures of social provision.

This chapter explores the urban services for the city's poor and traces the patterns of public poor relief use by Chicagoans. It explores the structures and systems of public aid and sets a context for the discussion of the mothers' pension program. This chapter reveals a set of social assumptions underlying the distribution of public poor relief that guided social policy. The most pervasive of these assumptions was the idea that able-bodied adults should be self-supporting. This measure of employability applied most rigidly to men, who for the most part received aid only for brief periods and in lieu of work opportunities. A slightly more flexible measure applied to some women with young children. They could receive relief for extended periods of time in recognition of their child-rearing responsibilities; however, they too were expected to earn part-time as ideals of domesticity collided with those of self-support. Great variations applied to women, however, and race, marital status, or the number of children could influence decisions about aid. The "unemployables," those exempt from the expectation of self-support, comprised the aged, permanently disabled, and children under the legal working age (once that was established). The ill or partially disabled received a temporary respite from the duty to earn. Public ambivalence about the degree to which citizens ought to receive public aid was tightly interwoven with ideas about private responsibility, race, and concerns about public expenditures.

The period under study in Chicago witnessed a transformation in the development of public aid. At the beginning of the century, the county public welfare system consisted of a poorhouse, hospitals, mental institution, juvenile court, and a program of poor relief. These structures of provision provided different levels and types of aid to individuals and families. By the end of the 1920s, local government had made a significant investment of public funds and added two new programs directed specifically at mother-only families. The expansion of programs continued the pattern of providing categorical aid, exacerbated the problem of disproportionate benefits particularly for African Americans, and maintained the gendered construction of policies.

Although this study focuses on the rise of public programs, early-twentieth-century poor relief is a story of coordinated benefits between public and private agencies. Public aid developed alongside a diverse assortment of private relief agencies that at the end of the nineteenth century provided the bulk of services to the poor. Divided by ethnic, religious, or national affiliations, the majority of private charities provided for "their own" to the extent that their resources allowed them. In fact, the wide variations in funding and the outright exclusion of benefits to some groups provided one of the motivations for expanding public aid. Social justice reformers frequently made their arguments for expanded public provision in terms of citizenship rights or democratic principles. The close relationship between public and private charities is important to this analysis for two reasons. It reminds us of the tradition of segregated systems of provision on the basis of race and religion during the period. Furthermore, it highlights the transfer of costs from private organizations to the public sector for long-term care, specifically of mother-only families.[7]

Reformers also hoped to challenge the politicization of welfare while at the same time asserting their professional expertise as administrators of public welfare. Politicians sympathetically objectified the ill, widowed, and aged in campaign rhetoric, but they also appealed to an undoubtedly larger group of constituents with promises to reduce spending and cut off "welfare cheats." Not only did no significant increase in poor relief appropriations occur over time, but this segment of provision declined relative to new forms of public aid. Politicians used the county welfare offices as sites for patronage during campaign cycles, which led reformers to push for merit-based hiring. With the creation of mothers' pensions, local partisans faced a direct challenge by pension advocates. Who would control the new branch of local government, its jobs, and the money appropriated? Advocates of new methods and liberal state agendas competed with proponents of existing measures of charity and public welfare.

The chapter begins with an account of the structures of public aid and the families who used poor relief in Cook County. I then turn to a comparison of the two predominant groups, two-parent and mother-only families, and the policy initiatives directed toward them. The chapter ends with a discussion of poor relief appropriations.

THE STRUCTURES AND POPULATIONS OF POOR RELIEF

In Chicago, as across the United States at the turn of the century, the provision of public aid to the poor resided with county government. The Cook County Board of Commissioners oversaw the management of several institutions that provided a system of aid and it appropriated funds for their operation.[8] Three institutions—the poorhouse, the juvenile court, and "outdoor" poor relief—provide the background for understanding the development of mothers' pensions.

The poorhouse, officially called the Infirmary, was located twenty miles southwest of Chicago at Oak Forest at the time. Several populations used the poorhouse, but the aged poor were most numerous during the first two decades of the twentieth century. Nearly half the residents were over sixty years of age and 67 percent were over fifty (see table 1). The number of residents swelled during the winter months as male laborers or tradesmen sought refuge during industrial downturns or inclement weather. Male residents outnumbered female residents three to one. Widowed women, most of whom listed their previous occupation as "housework," made up a significant size group. Their age, loss of

TABLE 1 Infirmary Residents by Age Group, 1918

Age Group	Number	Percentage
Over 40	2,542	81
Over 50	2,103	67
Over 60	1,412	45

Note: These percentages are representative of the aged population at the infirmary during the first two decades of the century.
Source: Cook County, IL, Board of County Commissioners, *Charity Service Reports*, Infirmary (1918).

family support, or lack of training for employment all contributed to their arrival at the poorhouse. Children made up a small minority of poorhouse residents and yet the public outcry over the presence of children in the poorhouse led to a new state structure designed to protect them—the juvenile court.[9]

In 1899, Chicago became the first city in the nation to establish a juvenile court. Prior to its creation, the state treated children the same as adults for criminal offenses and dispatched poor children to one of three places: state industrial schools, another family's home through the "placing out" system, or the poorhouse. The presence of poor and orphaned children in poorhouses caught the attention of women's organizations and some social welfare workers who thought the state could provide better opportunities for youth. The movement combined interests in children's rights and in the social control of juvenile delinquency. Julia Lathrop made the first point in a speech to the Illinois Conference of Charities and Corrections in 1897. The protection children received from the state should not be determined by their economic status. If the state protected the health and well-being of children of means through guardianship and inheritance laws, Lathrop argued, it should similarly protect children without the advantages of wealth.

> As it [the state] now says to the rich child, "You are under the protection of the State" . . . so we want the State to say to the poor child and the neglected child needing such supervision all the more because without fortune, "You are the ward of the State; your interests shall be constantly in mind. . . . the State will not forget you nor forget to know all the time that you have a proper home, a genuine education and as fair a chance in life as possible."[10]

Motivated by social justice or social regulation, organized women played a central role in the juvenile court movement in Chicago.

The Chicago Woman's Club drafted a juvenile court law in 1895 but never submitted it to the legislature because of questions regarding its constitutionality. Three years later the idea of a juvenile court law arose again and the Chicago Woman's Club joined with the State Board of Public Charities, the Illinois Federation of Women's Clubs, the Chicago Bar Association, and the State Conference of Charities and Corrections to pass the new bill through the legislature. Club members Julia Lathrop, Louise de Koven Bowen, Lucy Flower, Jane Addams, and Hannah Soloman supported the court legislation, and played an instrumental role in financing the probation officers of the court.[11]

Child dependency cases accounted for over one-half of all those heard by the Chicago Juvenile Court. A large percentage of those cases resulted from the death or desertion of one or both parents. For example, in 1912, 40.6 percent of the dependent children who appeared before the court did so because one or both of their parents had died (see table 2). An additional 21.6 percent of the cases came to the court owing to desertion. Other factors of parental "unfit-

TABLE 2 Causes of Child Dependency, 1912

Cause		Percentage
Mother dead	13.6	
Father dead	21.4	
Both dead	5.6	
Parent(s) dead		40.6
Father deserted	15.4	
Mother deserted	3.2	
Both parents deserted	3.0	
Parent(s) deserted		21.6
One or both drunk	6.0	
One or both immoral	6.0	
One or both ill	3.8	
One or both insane	3.9	
Parent(s) unfit		19.7
Parents separated		7.6
Lack of care		6.0
Other		4.5
Total		100.0

Source: Cook County, IL, Board of County Commissioners, Charity Service Reports, Juvenile Court (1912).

ness" that resulted in dependency included drunkenness, immorality, illness, and insanity.[12] Widowed and deserted mothers brought the majority of dependent cases to the court and frequently requested aid from public or private agencies. The juvenile court referred those families to private and public charities or, at times, sent children to training or industrial schools.

The juvenile court had additional significance for political and institutional reasons. It weakened county politicians' direct influence over child welfare as it located authority in a new apparatus of local government. Prior to the establishment of the juvenile court, county officials appointed probation officers. The new law transferred that authority to the judge of the juvenile court, who appointed a staff of probation officers and encouraged the assistance of civic groups. The new law did not provide funding for officers' salaries, however, and women's clubs, settlement workers, and private welfare agencies filled the gap by raising funds to pay probation officers. This resulted in close relations between the court and these groups. They forged an alliance with the juvenile court's administration, encouraged hiring by merit, and consequently challenged a source of patronage. Friction between the Chicago Juvenile Court and Cook County officials periodically surfaced over the control of dependent-child policy.

Poor relief offered the third form of public aid, and for those who qualified, an alternative to the poorhouse or the juvenile court. Following the conventions of nineteenth-century charity, the poor relief office closely regulated recipients and discouraged income transfers. A family who applied for aid soon had a visit from an "examining agent," the purpose of which was to verify the information in the application and report on the condition of the home. The final decision rested with the county agent, who had a legal obligation to follow the "Pauper Law."[13] If approved, the family returned to the poor relief office to receive their goods—a bag of groceries, pair of shoes, order of coal, or medical care. During the 1893 depression, Julia Lathrop described those seeking relief in the neighborhood surrounding Hull House as "a solid, pressing crowd of hundreds of shabby men and shawled or hooded women, coming from all parts of a great city . . . standing hour after hour with market-baskets high above their heads . . . having the common language of their persistency, their weariness, their chill and hunger."[14] Poor relief provided the last resort to families of the "submerged tenth," who came only after all other efforts failed.[15]

Several eastern cities had eliminated public aid or "outdoor" relief because of fears that it would lead to political corruption and dependence. These cities turned over relief services to private charity organization societies. Cook

County maintained its public agencies, and relief workers cooperated to create a system of provision. The county office of poor relief and its director, the poor relief agent, reported to the Board of County Commissioners. At times, the County Board president and the relief agent worked hand in hand to reduce expenditures or, conversely, to increase temporary employment positions. Settlement workers frequently criticized the political motivations of elected officials who they believed used the program for political gain. Although social workers had made an inroad into the juvenile court, the county agent's poor relief office defended its operations from outsiders.

OVERVIEW OF FAMILIES ON POOR RELIEF

As the population of Chicago increased (it more than doubled between 1900 and 1930), so too did the idea that an expanding population drew greater resources from the public relief system. In his 1906 report to the county commissioners, relief agent John W. Belmont linked the increase in the demands on the poor relief office to the expansion of population in Chicago and Cook County. He explained that the portion of "defectives, old and infirm, widows with small children, [and] deserted families" who were unable to support themselves increased as the city grew.[16] Yet, a comparison of population to public relief figures between 1910 and 1930 demonstrates the fallacy of that projection. Expressed as a ratio of relief families to the population, 37.3 families were on relief for every 10,000 Chicagoans in 1910; 17.6 families in 1920; and 38.5 families for 1927. Every year the number of families on poor relief rose and fell with no correlation to overall population growth.[17]

Yet, it was not the population as a whole that concerned the relief offices as much as those groups—immigrants and migrants—perceived most likely to become dependent on public aid. The foreign-born made up one-third of the total metropolitan population in 1900 and 1910. After two decades of declining immigration figures due to World War I and immigration restrictions, those Chicagoans born abroad still made up one-quarter of all residents in 1930. In addition, the Great Migration of southern African Americans to Chicago changed the city's population. Leaving repressive southern Jim Crow laws to seek better jobs and lives in the North, between 50,000 and 70,000 African Americans arrived in Chicago between 1916 and 1920, and an estimated 100,000 more during the next decade. The ratio of African Americans in the population increased from 2 percent in 1900 to 7 percent in 1930.[18] Julia Lathrop's description of the foreign-born residents living near Hull House in 1893 could as easily describe families ten years later. "Here is a foreign population, living in every sort of mal-adjustment,—rural Italians, in shambling wooden tenements; Russian

Jews, whose two main resources are tailoring and peddling, quite incapable in general of applying themselves to severe manual labor or skilled trades, and hopelessly unemployed in hard times; here are Germans and Irish, largely of that type which is reduced by drink to a squalor it is otherwise far above."[19] Lathrop's description, while relying too easily on stereotypic characterizations, tried to capture both cultural and structural impediments to prosperity.

The foreign-born population dominated public relief until the mid-1920s, when African Americans' use of public relief increased rapidly. Concerns about the problems associated with urban growth, and relief administrators' interest in what they believed might be a potential correlation between one's racial or national background and poverty, led to extensive data collection on Chicago's large foreign-born population, and with the Great Migration, on African Americans.[20] The poor relief office recorded twenty-seven national and racial groups that received assistance between 1904 and 1920, and added two categories in 1921. Table 3 illustrates the proportion of families in the general population compared to the proportion of those on relief. Native-born relief recipients comprised 26 percent of all relief families in 1910, yet when divided into racial and national categories, native-born whites made up the single largest group of all recipients before World War I. African Americans made up a small group on relief (6 percent) even though they were overrepresented relative to their population, as were many immigrants.[21]

TABLE 3 Percentage of Families in the General Population and among Poor Relief Families by Race and Nativity, 1910–1930

	1910		1920		1930	
	Pop.	Relief	Pop.	Relief	Pop.	Relief
European American	62	20	66	24	67	30
African American	2	6	4	8	7	31
Total native-born	64	26	70	32	74	61
Germans	7	11	4	8	3	4
Irish	3	10	2	5	2	2
Italian	2	8	2	11	2	8
Polish	6	19	5	19	4	11
Other	18	26	17	25	15	14
Total foreign-born	36	74	30	68	26	39
Total	100	100	100	100	100	100

Sources: Chicago population figures from *Thirteenth Census, 1910: Population; Fourteenth Census, 1920: Population; Fifteenth Census, 1930: Population*. For data on foreign-born families, see the *Fourteenth Census: 1920*, vol. 2: 739. For relief figures, see Cook County, IL, Board of County Commissioners, *Charity Service Reports*, 1910, 1920, 1927.

Four nationalities made up the largest groups among the foreign-born on relief: Polish, German, Irish, and Italian. Through World War I, Polish families made up the largest segment (19 percent) and German families followed with an average of 10 percent of all relief families. Irish families made up 10 percent of those on relief until 1913, when the rate began to decline. Italians, on the other hand, increased their participation from 8 percent in 1910 to 10 percent in 1918 and 11 percent by 1920. After World War I, Polish families remained a significant relief constituency but declined from 19 percent of all families in 1920 to 11 percent by the end of the decade. Italian families kept between 8 and 11 percent during the 1920s. Foreign-born German and Irish families continued to decrease public relief use and by the end of the decade, these groups made up only 4 percent and 2 percent of all families, respectively. A comparison of populations on relief to those in the census confirms these trends. European immigrants had the highest ratio of relief receipt, although it dropped over two decades from 27.45 to 15.06 per 10,000 persons. Both native-born European Americans and African Americans increased their receipt of relief. By the end of the 1920s, black and white Americans each had slightly over 11 persons on relief per 10,000 in the population. The emphasis on trends in relief use by racial and national groups should not overshadow the fact that, at any one point in time, very few citizens used public relief.[22]

During the 1920s, the populations on relief shifted. Chicago experienced an economic boom as business and building expanded and the prosperity reached an array of workers: immigrant and native-born, white and black. The improved economy led St. Clair Drake and Horace R. Cayton to call the second half of the 1920s "the most prosperous" yet for the city's black citizens.[23] In contrast to the employment picture described by contemporaries, a gradual increase in the use of public poor relief began by mid-decade and continued to the eve of the depression. Furthermore, different groups relied on poor relief. The foreign-born, who had consistently outnumbered native-born families on public relief, declined in number while the native-born took an increasingly larger share. Immigration restrictions no doubt played a part in the reduction; nevertheless, the rise in relief use by native-born Americans from 32 percent in 1920 to 61 percent in 1930 warrants further examination.

The greatest change in native-born Americans' use of public relief occurred among African Americans. Their participation increased from 7 percent of all public relief families in 1900 to 24 percent in 1921 and remained between 20 and 30 percent for the second half of the decade. By 1927, one-half of all native-born Americans, and one-third of all families using poor relief in

Chicago were African American (see tables 3 and 4). This shift may be partially explained by several interrelated trends. First, the relative populations on relief adjusted to two trends in the 1920s. Immigration declined and the children of European immigrants became incorporated into the category of "Americans." Second, as economic opportunities improved throughout the decade, some groups had greater advantage in taking and keeping jobs. Conversely, the second wave of the migration placed additional pressures upon the black community, and by 1928 several organizations, including the Chicago Urban League, noted higher rates of unemployment among African Americans as layoffs increased. Third, although some historians have explained the limited use of charities by blacks as either overt racism or self-selected resistance to white charities, the Chicago race riot of 1919 may have also played a part. One of the issues at the center of the riot was African Americans' right to access of public services. Heightened expectations within the black community could explain a part of the increased demands upon public relief. Fourth, the African American community developed a system of private agencies that worked in conjunction with the city's other agencies. As the infrastructure within the black community developed, so too did information and access to public poor relief during the 1920s.[24]

Social services remained largely segregated in Chicago as the majority of private providers refused to accept African Americans and the state facilities accepted few, if any.[25] An active reform community established a range of institutions from the Provident Hospital to the Phyllis Wheatley Home, the YMCA, and independent homes for the care of dependent children. Settlements like the Wendell Phillips settlement on the West Side and the Frederick Douglass Cen-

TABLE 4 Number and Percentage of Native-born American Families on Poor Relief, 1920–1927

	European American		African American		All Relief Families
Year	Number	%	Number	%	Number
1920	1,165	24	391	8	4,798
1921	2,003	23	2,022	24	8,601
1922	2,710	31	874	10	8,664
1923	1,945	36	317	6	5,432
1924	1,933	25	1,884	24	7,755
1925	2,787	28	2,758	28	10,018
1926	2,903	30	2,262	24	9,571
1927	3,714	30	3,787	31	12,315

Source: Cook County, IL, Board of County Commissioners, "Tabulated Record of the Department of Poor Relief," Charity Service Reports (1920–1927).

ter on the South Side attempted to address an array of social welfare issues. Women's clubs, churches, and mutual aid societies raised funds for assistance to the poor. But the community stretched its financial resources to the limit in an attempt to establish separate structures of social service and address widespread poverty exacerbated by the second wave of migration in the 1920s. Despite the wide array of community efforts, they remained independent of each other until 1917, when the Chicago Urban League became the central clearinghouse for services within the black community. The Urban League reiterated that it was not a relief agency and focused on employment opportunities, as its motto "Not Alms but Opportunity" suggested. The organization identified its role as a co-ordinator of social services to the city's African American population and worked with agencies to widen employment opportunities for men and women.[26]

While much more exploration is needed on the relations between public and private relief and the African American community, two themes are clear. Community institutions such as the Chicago *Defender* and the Urban League emphasized self-support measures and viewed charity as an instrument of dependency to be avoided whenever possible. At the same time, the 1920s saw greater organization and professionalization of African American social work and an increased use of poor relief by the city's African Americans. They did so, however, at a time when state structures rapidly expanded and public poor relief shrank relative to total public funding.

In addition to national origins and race, poor relief officials closely followed the degree to which family status influenced the number of families receiving aid. They knew that the majority of male-headed families on relief came on and off the rolls, but female-headed families represented longer-term care. Two-parent families' use of public relief fluctuated markedly with periods of rapid increase during cycles of unemployment (1908, 1915, and 1921–1922), followed by sharp declines as the employment picture improved. This pattern remained constant until the mid-1920s, when two-parent families steadily increased their numbers on relief (see table 5). Compared to the distinct fluctuations of two-parent families, relief use by widows and deserted women showed less variation throughout the period. The number of female-headed families using relief increased to 1911, declined through the mid-1920s, and then began to increase steadily through the end of the decade. From 1904 through 1915, female-headed families had the highest rates of participation, averaging 19.52 per 10,000 population. After World War I, the rate declined to 9.7 per 10,000 until the mid-1920s, at which time the ratio began to increase again. When a subset of female-headed families with children under the legal working age is examined,

TABLE 5 Number of Families on Public Poor Relief by Family Status, 1905–1927

Year	Married	Female-headed	Other	Total
1905	3,039	3,828	169	7,036
1907	1,973	3,303	155	5,431
1909	4,633	4,463	207	9,303
1911	5,246	5,103	305	10,654
1913	4,913	4,325	249	9,487
1915	12,399	4,468	386	17,253
1917	4,557	3,697	275	8,529
1919	2,598	2,908	191	5,697
1921	5,624	2,672	305	8,601
1923	2,698	2,498	236	5,432
1925	5,835	3,805	378	10,018
1927	7,531	4,318	466	12,315

Source: Cook County, IL, Board of County Commissioners, *Charity Service Reports* (1905–1927).

the pattern is repeated. Participation peaked in 1912 with 18.14 families per 10,000 population, then gradually declined through the 1910s and into the early 1920s. By 1924, the trend reversed and the number of women with dependent children using poor relief again began to increase. The introduction of mothers' pensions in 1911 accounts for some of the decline of relief use by these families.[27]

Contemporaries attributed different causes to the economic need of two-parent families and those headed by a woman. In particular, the poverty of "dependent mothers" drew widespread attention not only for ideological reasons, but because these families represented greater costs for the public treasury. Distinct differences existed between these families and the policies developed for them.

Unemployment and Male-headed Families

The provision of relief for male heads of families could be justified for two reasons: extreme but temporary need and long-term dependency. Relief agents carefully constructed policies to ensure that men who received aid because of transitory need did not become a permanent member of the dependent class. Men had to be temporarily unemployed but essentially employable, or they must have a condition that rendered them virtually unable to work and therefore eligible for long-term aid. Men most frequently named temporary unemployment as the cause that brought them to apply for aid; but disability, illness, and old age provided other reasons.

Yet it is unemployment during periods of economic dislocation that most dramatically correlates with the annual fluctuations in two-parent families' poor relief use in Chicago. Twelve thousand families received county relief in 1908, the vast majority of whom were unemployed owing to the "industrial depressions" that followed the financial panic of October 1907. The "disastrous financial effects of the European war," which sent "workingmen and small tradesmen to want and destitution" in the winter of 1914–1915, set a precedent in appeals for aid, according to the county's *Charity Service Report*. The numbers of unemployed families declined substantially over the next five years (1916 to 1920) as employment opportunities expanded with wartime production. Robert S. Abbott, editor of the Chicago *Defender*, remarked upon the oportunities in employment for African Americans in Chicago. The business upturn "has meant that the thousands who a year ago were dependents upon charity are today employed making a comfortable living for themselves and their families." The Cook County Board president, Peter Reinberg, noted a 20 percent drop in outdoor relief use in 1918 "owing to favorable industrial conditions which produced a demand for the labor." But in 1921, when massive unemployment again hit Chicago, the county poor relief agent remarked that the scarcity of jobs made it very difficult to help families find work, and the number of families who received aid increased 63 percent. In 1927, another economic downturn increased the demands upon public relief and led one observer to remark: "Our whole community life is affected by these periods of unemployment. The whole subject is one to which the nation shall have to give more attention in the future." This premonitory remark not only called attention to the public sector's responsibility to citizens during an industrial downturn, but highlighted the downturn's deleterious effect upon workers' families.[28]

One such family was that of Marcus Jackson. The Jacksons moved to Chicago in 1917 from their home in Fayette County, Mississippi. He had steady work as a manual laborer earning three dollars a day until 1921, when the downturn made it difficult to find jobs. Mrs. Jackson, who cared for their seven children, was pregnant again and unable to earn. Their oldest daughter, who was sixteen years old, did not attend school but her physical weakness made it difficult for her to find employment. When the poor relief office became aware of the family, the mother was ill, the father had irregular work, and the children were not attending school because they did not have adequate clothing. The poor relief office gave the Jackson family food relief on two occasions and shoes for the children. The services provided by the public poor relief office were small in quantity, short in duration, and based upon their assessment that the family would be able to support themselves.[29]

Unemployed workers wanted the municipal government to intervene on their behalf, but to create jobs rather than increase poor relief. The unemployment crises of 1908 and 1915 brought masses of workers to the county commissioner meetings with calls for "wages not welfare" and "jobs not charity." Each period of widespread layoffs corresponded with intense periods of labor organization and discontent. As the European war created problems for industry in the United States and the ranks of unemployed homeless men swelled in Chicago, labor groups pressured the city to take action to provide employment.

In January 1914, the Committee on Unemployed of the International Brotherhood Welfare Association (based at Hull House) directed a letter to the county commissioners seeking "useful work" for the city's unemployed men. The county's Finance Committee rejected the idea. The unemployment crisis worsened in 1915 and workers whose small savings had been depleted jammed the poor relief offices. In January 1915, those who took part in the March of the Unemployed called for "Jobs not Charity" but they were answered with police arrest.[30] Public relief remained a last resort and only a small number of all the unemployed turned to it. Several years later, during the postwar depression, one relief worker noted that of the 50,000 unemployed workers in March 1921, fewer than 1 percent had applied for public or private aid.[31]

Elected officials and private organizations coordinated the public policy response to the crisis of unemployment, which, in the case of adult male workers, revolved around expanded employment opportunities. In 1908, county agent John Belmont asked the County Board to consider some measure of responsibility for the citizens affected by the industrial downturns. "Since the margin between unemployment and dependency is small," he argued, "it may well be asked what steps, if any, should be taken by the State to prevent many of these people from being pushed into the ranks of dependents." Belmont's comment synthesized a conventional fear regarding economic dependency in society. He advocated a federal plan for unemployment but at the local level he suggested that the state employment office coordinate their work with the poor relief office. By 1909, branches of the Illinois Free Employment Office were located in district relief offices.[32]

Chicago took additional steps to mediate adult male unemployment by appointing the Municipal Markets Commission in 1914. The commission's report is significant for its recognition of the structural causes of unemployment and for its delineation of a new policy option quite different from poor relief. The report asserted a citizen's right to employment, defined a "citizen" as male, and found that government had a responsibility to intervene when business failed to provide work. In a shift from the past, the report did not blame individuals for unemployment but rather found it to be a negative by-product of the industrial system. The vicissitudes of local industry and its demand for labor remained unregulated and produced severe consequences for the thousands of able-bodied workers unable to find jobs. This situation created tremendous economic waste and the report called on the city to protect its citizens' "right to expect that our city officials will endeavour to procure employment for those who are unemployed through no fault of their own." The city had a policy for the impoverished, the report noted, but none for the "employable unemployed." The right of a citizen to employment "should be addressed to men who are heads of families." Other families in which the male breadwinner was absent, ill, or incapacitated should be ineligible for these unemployment policies and cared for by relief agencies. The commission's proposals clearly distinguished work programs from relief. Finally, the Municipal Markets Commission proposed public unemployment insurance, the creation of short-term public works projects, and a reorganization of public employment offices. The city's major document on unemployment policy advocated a dual track of provision for families. Those with able-bodied men at the head should receive job-specific benefits, while female-headed families remained classified as unemployable, their employment needs ignored, and their benefits determined by poor relief. In such plans, we see the antecedents of a gendered social provision separating benefits on the basis of sex and associating benefits with those determined to be employable or unemployable.[33]

These recommendations did not cover all men equally, but followed the patterns of labor segmentation. The city's African American population had serious difficulty finding jobs during downturns and the Chicago Urban League dedicated much of its service to finding people work. During the postwar depression, the Urban League organized employment bureaus where men could register for work and receive a ticket for a night's lodging and a meal. Efforts to place black workers in jobs often fell behind those for white workers, however, and as one United Charities worker commented in May 1921, the situation for blacks was "becoming worse rather than better."[34]

Poor relief administrators viewed the influx of unemployed families as a specialized problem—a result of the disorganization of industry which would be relieved with a change in the economic cycle. Until the economy stabilized, public and private agencies combined their efforts to mediate the economic need with charity and to coordinate work through employment offices. Both working-class and middle-class proponents of unemployment programs conceived of a divide between policies for those understood to be employable and those viewed as unemployable. They rejected the idea that women might be primary wage-earners and directed working-poor, single mothers to the poor relief office. The job policies, although weakly designed and complicit with racial segregation, also reinforced a double dependency for poor women: one within the family and one within the workforce.

Mother-Only Families

The majority of female-headed families on public relief had two characteristics that distinguished them from two-parent families: low-paying jobs combined with the sole care of young children. Both predicted long-term need for these families. Few working-class families earned enough to save for emergencies. Many of those who had death benefits from insurance exhausted them within a few months. Consequently, women left without resources soon began wage-earning to help support their children. The poor relief records frequently refer to women's wage-earning. The relief agent called the widows with small children who supported themselves soon after the loss of their husbands symbols of the "Chicago spirit of self-dependence." But wage-earning did not provide a panacea for poverty or a measure of economic independence. The problem for these women was not the absence of a job, but the inability to work full-time and receive a living wage. While men most frequently listed unemployment as their reason for seeking relief, women most often listed low wages.[35]

In addition, the responsibility for the care of young children set these families apart. Over 75 percent of all women on poor relief (widowed, deserted, or divorced) provided the sole care for children under fourteen years of age. A woman with two or three children could expect to provide child support over a period of twenty to twenty-four years. In response, many mothers worked part-time and relied upon relief to subsidize the family income. When children reached the legal age to work, they no longer received dependent status and their earnings became a part of the family resources used to evaluate a family's need.[36]

Widows like Marya Kruszka shared many characteristics of families who received public aid. She became the sole support of her family when her husband died from a shooting during a family fight. Their four children ranged in age from eighteen months to eleven years, all too young to work legally. The family's insurance paid for the funeral and covered household expenses for several months. Five months later, Marya Kruszka's sister and aunt appealed to a local agency for assistance on her behalf. The caseworker suggested that she apply for day work such as domestic service, dishwashing, homework, or factory work. At first, she worked in a box factory for ten hours a day while her sister looked after her children. Then she tried making brushes at home. At the end of six days, she had made six brushes for a total wage of 75 cents and was ready to quit homework. But Kruszka hated "the thought of going back to the box factory and begging a new person each day to keep her baby." Despite the fact that she did not want to seek charity, within the month Marya Kruszka had accepted a Thanksgiving basket, coal from the county relief agent, and a coupon for milk for one month. The caseworker helped her apply for a mothers' pension, but the case was rejected because of a forthcoming benefit from a relative's will. One year after her husband's death, Marya Kruszka found "satisfactory work" in a restaurant, although "she deplore[d] the fact that during the next five or six years when supervision will mean so much to the children, she will be unable to oversee them." The county poor relief continued medical care for the children.[37]

In contrast to "right to work" initiatives for male-headed families, the linkage between low wages, economic dependency, and the care of children in mother-only families did not occupy the attention of elected officials prior to the passage of mothers' pensions. The local discussion of these issues occurred within Chicago's progressive settlements and the Women's Trade Union League. In 1905, three Chicago settlement workers, Edith Abbott, Sophonisba Breckinridge, and Mary McDowell, led a national campaign for a federal investigation into the conditions of working women and children. Women were in the workforce to stay, they argued, and information about their situation would prove essential to understanding the industrial situation and addressing its associated problems. "However earnestly we may deplore the fact that women are in factories instead of homes," Mary McDowell wrote, "we must squarely face conditions as they exist."[38] The proposal for an investigation received the support of the Women's Trade Union League, the General Federation of Women's Clubs, and the American Federation of Labor. President Theodore Roosevelt signed the bill into law in 1907.[39]

The minimum wage movement also linked wages to women's poverty. The discussion frequently focused on single women workers, yet concerns about working mothers also appeared. Contemporaries recognized the debilitating effect of the "double day" and the high incidence of poverty among mother-only families. As early as 1906, "representatives of every union in Chicago which had women within its ranks" conducted a symposium on "a living wage for working women" at Hull House. A few years later, Agnes Nestor led the Women's Trade Union League in a legislative campaign for the minimum wage in Illinois. Middle-class women of the Chicago Woman's Club lent their support to the movement by holding a conference on minimum wage in 1912 and calling for a state minimum-wage commission in 1913. Both working-class and middle-class reform women recognized that women's poverty could not be eliminated without attacking their low wages; and yet, minimum wage was one of the last reforms to be enacted.[40]

Child care, or day nurseries as they were called, remained entirely a private-sector enterprise. Despite the relative silence about day nurseries from pension advocates, Chicago had several dozen centers founded by churches, settlements, women's clubs, and community agencies, which cared for children of working parents during the 1910s and 1920s. The Chicago Council of Social Agencies recognized the need for day care for those children "who for social or economic reasons cannot receive parental care" and whose mothers worked because they were the only breadwinners, or because of "the inadequate earnings of the regular breadwinner."[41] Most of the children who used the centers lived with both parents. They were entirely privately funded and subject to the restrictions imposed by their sponsors. Several charged a small fee. The Chicago Association of Day Nurseries (later called the Day Nursery Section of the Chicago Council of Social Agencies) attempted to centralize information and set standards for child care during the 1920s. In 1929, the Chicago Department of Public Welfare noted the "great need for the free day nursery" to accommodate working widows and deserted or unmarried mothers.[42]

In contrast to the silence on working women's rights in the 1914 Municipal Markets Commission Report, several agencies recognized the need for women to earn. The Chicago Department of Public Welfare and the Chicago Urban League ran employment bureaus for women. Although not directly tied to the poor relief office, agencies attempted to coordinate services, and case records like that of Marya Kruszka note the efforts to place mothers in jobs. The city department promoted itself as a placement service for women's jobs in stores and businesses as well as in factory, domestic, or service work. However, placement figures indicate that many more jobs existed in service than in the higher paying areas. Contrary to the protective sentiment against night work, this department also made efforts to accommodate women's schedules. In response to a letter advertising the services of the employment bureau, several women wrote inquiring about evening work. "They had children and could not leave home during the day, but wished to do something to add to the family income." The department connected them to employers. At the Chicago Urban League, women made up nearly one-half of the applicants for jobs in 1922–1923, but filled only one-third of the positions. Clerical and typing jobs were featured here, too, but again more placements occurred in service. Three-quarters of women's job placements from the Urban League were in laundry or domestic work in 1926. Two years later, the Urban League reported that job placements had declined overall, and the situation for domestic workers was particularly poor. Wage rates had dropped to approximately half the previous year's wage, or $2.50 a day.[43] Although never specifically promoted as a solution to poverty in mother-only families, and in spite of the fact that social workers challenged this as the best policy for unskilled mothers, women's wage-earning became a part of family income for those on relief.

The reform legislation that did win the support of reformers, charity organizations, and juvenile court administrators retained an ambiguity about their wage-earning role. Before I discuss the new initiatives for mother-only families, a closer examination of the differences within this group is needed.

MOTHER-ONLY FAMILIES ON POOR RELIEF: CHARACTERISTICS AND COMPARISONS

Despite their shared characteristics, differences of family status and race separated the available services for mother-only families. Relative to family status, much has been written about the availability of public provision for "worthy" widows. Indeed the largest group of women on relief were widows, approximately 38 percent of all relief families between 1904 and 1911. The proportion of widowed families fell slightly throughout the period with the exception of the years surrounding World War I. The decline may be explained in part by the introduction of additional public programs in which widows participated, specifically the mothers' pension program and perhaps workmen's compensation benefits.[44] While deserted women made up approximately 15 percent of all the families receiving relief over the entire period, they comprised nearly half of the mother-only families with dependent children (see table 6). In fact, a comparison of mother-only families with children under age fourteen in the home shows that widows and deserted women shared the public benefits provided through poor relief. Consequently, a policy for mother-only families would need to address the issues of both widows and deserted women to reduce the numbers of dependent children significantly. Divorced women and never-married women with children received relief, but their portion of cases remained negligible. Divorced women comprised at the most 1 percent of families on aid, and never-married women less than one-half percent. Compared to the general population, widows were overrepresented among relief families, while divorced women were slightly underrepresented.[45]

TABLE 6 Number and Percentage of Female-headed Families on Poor Relief by Marital Status, 1905–1927

Year	Widowed Number	%	Deserted Number	%	Divorced Number	%	Total
1905	2,859	41	939	13	30	1	3,828
1907	2,405	44	855	16	43	1	3,303
1909	3,088	33	1,290	14	85	1	4,463
1911	3,446	32	1,566	15	91	1	5,103
1913	2,754	29	1,492	16	79	1	4,325
1915	2,791	16	1,592	9	85	1	4,468
1917	2,213	26	1,387	16	97	1	3,697
1919	1,982	35	878	15	48	1	2,908
1921	1,709	20	883	10	80	1	2,672
1923	1,568	29	859	16	71	1	2,498
1925	2,242	22	1,474	15	89	1	3,805
1927	2,336	19	1,870	15	112	1	4,318

Source: Cook County, IL, Board of County Commissioners, Charity Service Reports (1905–1927).

It is more difficult to compare the differences between mother-only families on the basis of race and nationality. The county did not keep data on mother-only families with dependent children by race or national origin. However, the census may provide an indication of probable degree of need by examining the percentage of female-headed families by age groups. In table 7, the percentage of all female-headed families in Chicago is compared to a subset of women between the ages of fifteen and forty-four. The subset reflects an assumption that the majority of childbearing occurred between these years. If female headship and the presence of young children are two indicators of economic need for families, then this can serve to identify those groups most likely to need relief services. Significant differences between the groups are evident.[46]

TABLE 7 Percentage of Female-headed Families in Chicago by Nativity, Race, and Age

	1900 All ages	15–44 yrs	1910 All ages	15–44 yrs	1920 All ages	15–44 yrs
All Chicago families	18	6	17	5	19	7
European American	10	5	11	4	10	3
African American	41	23	43	22	35	18
Foreign-Born	30	7	27	5	18	3

Source: Figures for 1900 and 1910 are from the Thirteenth Census, 1910: Population, vol. 1, 643. Figures for nativity and age are from the Fourteenth Census, 1920: Population, vol. 2, 473; ibid., vol. 3, 248; and the Fifteenth Census, 1930: Population, vol. 6, "Families," 367.

Native-born European American families had the lowest incidence of female headship in the younger age group, with nearly 5 percent in 1900 and 3 percent in 1920. Foreign-born women had higher rates overall, but the majority of these women were aged widows with no dependent children. The younger group more closely approximated native-born European American women, with 7 percent in 1900 and 3 percent in 1920. Figures for African American women differed. First, nearly half of the families headed by women were in the younger age group, a distinctly different pattern from that of the other two groups. Second, female headship occurred more often than in the other groups: 23 percent in 1900 and 18 percent in 1920. These figures raise two important points relative to poor relief and populations in need. Nearly one-fifth of Chicago's African American women were potentially responsible for both child care and wage-earning, indicators widely held to predict economic need. In addition, if access to and attitudes toward using relief were similar across groups, one would expect to find a significant representation of African American women on poor relief. Instead, as the earlier discussion illustrated, some of the foreign-born groups had far greater representation on relief until the mid-1920s, when the participation of African Americans increased.

The differences among mother-only families became most significant as local government created new structures to address dependent mothers. As we saw in chapter 1, mothers in poverty with the care of young children raised the spectre of declining American standards and the collateral issue of the appropriate location of women's work. In developing proposals, reformers recognized that mothers with young children had to earn within a structure of low-paying work as well as provide care for young children. But local relief agencies had their own concerns about the problems of child dependency and working mothers. Nonsupporting husbands and widowed families meant tremendous additional expenditures for the public sector. Although the ideal of maternal domesticity prevailed, so too did ideas about self-support. When the two collided, as they did in the formulation of new programs, some women were perceived to be more able to work than others, producing a system that provided different levels of aid to different groups of poor mothers.

In 1911, Cook County initiated two new policies for mother-only families: mothers' pensions and a Court of Domestic Relations for deserted or abandoned women. Both programs were housed in the courts, administered by judges and social workers, and received public funds for their operations. As I noted above, deserted families made up between one-third and one-half of all mother-only families on relief. A contemporary study found that women between thirty and thirty-five years old headed the majority of deserted families

(63 percent), and nearly half of these families (48 percent) had between three and four children. A Chicago Department of Public Welfare study for the years 1909 to 1915 found that while desertion occurred in all groups, it was higher among the poor, providing a "poor man's divorce," or what Julia Lathrop had referred to as the "masculine expedient of temporary disappearance" in her review of Chicago poverty in 1893. Desertion particularly hit the African American community. E. Franklin Frazier found that African American women were overrepresented among deserted families who applied for poor relief (21 percent) and among desertion cases that came to the Court of Domestic Relations (15.6 percent). The category "deserted" may have included couples who were separated or never married, Frazier pointed out.[47]

Contemporaries struggled to define the causes of desertion. Many reformers, like Lathrop, preferred the structural explanations of employment cycles. Others, like the relief agent, "advanced the theory that bad cooking, etc., on the part of the woman is the cause, and that the proper training of girls in domestic science, etc., will do away with it to a considerable extent."[48] Despite the wide range of analyses of the problem, local government created a new division to address the problems of these families. Its provision differed radically from mothers' pensions and, because of the large number of African Americans, resulted in fewer resources for those Chicagoans.

In April 1911, the new Court of Domestic Relations opened within the Cook County Municipal Court. The judges agreed to establish this court to hear "all cases involving wrongs against women and children," but two-thirds of the cases heard during its early years concerned abandonment and nonsupport. Women who were separated from their husbands, who had children out of marriage, or whose husbands had deserted them could apply for assistance from this court if they were willing to press charges against their children's father. Administrators recognized the hardship this requirement placed upon deserted mothers, but they argued that it was essential in order to combat the public perception that public spending would not encourage deserting husbands.

> The desertion of wife and children by the male breadwinner is a continuing and baffling problem. The ineffective legislation under which desertion is a misdemeanour only, the lack of uniform federal law, the difficulty of enforcement of such legislation as exists, results in an unjust burden upon the deserted mothers and a shifting of parental responsibility upon the public.[49]

The Court of Domestic Relations offered no material aid to families, but it served as a clearinghouse. It received applications, pursued parties deemed legally responsible, disbursed funds if they were retrieved, and referred women to other agencies when appropriate. If the family was impoverished, they would most likely be referred back to the poor relief department.

Public provision for "dependent mothers" expanded during the 1910s in Chicago, but with uneven distributive benefits. In addition to existing poor relief and the new mothers' pension program, the nonsupport division of the Court of Domestic Relations sought to retrieve remuneration from husbands and relatives. This division of social services channeled deserted and abandoned women who sought aid from the state through this court and reserved mothers' pensions for widows predominantly, until 1921.

FISCAL POLITICS AND POOR RELIEF

One of the ways to measure the status of public provision is to consider the degree to which it received support with funds from the public treasury. This aspect of social welfare history has received relatively little attention from historians for the early twentieth century.[50] The generosity of the ward boss—his use of informal patronage to gain political support—is one of the oldest narratives in urban politics. A Thanksgiving basket, an admittance to the County Hospital, help for a family member with the police or courts, all helped build the base of support for the ward boss through personal contact and aid. Yet few studies have examined how and whether politicians supported public welfare formally. The following discussion examines the degree to which politicians funded welfare by comparing the Cook County Board of Commissioners appropriations over nearly two decades. A comparison between the total budget and that section restricted to relief supplies provides a relative measure of the expansion and contraction of the public sector. The findings illustrate that per capita appropriations declined in both the general account and the relief budget when adjusted for inflation. In other words, for those people who were eligible only to receive poor relief, the real value of that part of the county budget decreased over time.[51]

County officials consistently complained about too little revenue to pay for new public services. The state legislature set a specific tax rate for general appropriations and Cook County collected additional revenues through property assessments and departmental fees. But the cost to maintain county departments increased dramatically at points. For example, between 1902 and 1907 the budget increased 40 percent and created a county deficit of $1,500,000. Each administration passed the deficit along to its successor from the 1890s through the 1920s, and presidents of the County Board of Commissioners repeatedly appealed to the state legislature to increase their revenue base. As late as 1930, County Board president Anton Cermak noted that tax collection delays and a loss of revenue from property reassessments had depleted the county treasury and made it impossible to carry on public services. To what degree the short-comings existed because of demands for new services or as a result of patron-age abuse is not entirely clear. The county's population continued to increase between 1900 and 1930 and the state legislature did expand the county's respon-sibilities without making corresponding tax increases. Regardless of cause, the expenses of previous political administrations and charges of misappropriated funds frequently peppered campaigns, as did charges of graft and corruption. The tensions between funding, politics, and expanded municipal obligations were felt by the general public as well as by the recipients of poor relief.[52]

Appropriations for the County Board of Commissioners did increase over these years. Between 1911 and 1926, county appropriations grew by 151.8 percent, but inflation eroded that amount to a much smaller increase of 37.5 per-cent. Table 8 compares the county appropriations to those of poor relief in both current value and inflation-adjusted (real) value. The pattern is similar on a population basis. The county commissioners increased appropriations per 100 residents by 71.9 percent, but when inflation is accounted for, the budget actu-ally declined by 6.3 percent. The average appropriation per 100 county residents dropped 22 percent throughout the 1910s and then rose through the 1920s.

Relief appropriations fared worse. The budget for relief supplies, that is the amount spent directly on material aid to the poor exclusive of adminis-trative costs, did not keep pace with the total county expenditures. The supply budget increased 62.5 percent between 1911 and 1926, but when adjusted for in-flation, this apparent gain becomes an actual decline in value of 11 percent. Ad-justing for variations in population, the relief figures become even smaller. Although the appropriation increased 16.8 percent in current value, its real value showed an actual decline of 36.2 percent in the level of welfare funding for direct aid.[53]

One explanation for the decline lies in local relief politics. Relief admin-istrators felt political pressure to minimize expenses and did so by freezing new cases, a strategy that produced waiting lists of several hundred people at times. In addition, public and private agencies transferred families to each other. In the years preceding World War I, the public transfer of cases to private agencies oc-curred most frequently, but by the 1920s local agencies made arrangements with public agencies to accept long-term cases, thus allowing private charities to fo-cus on short-term services. By 1928, public relief in Cook County surpassed pri-

Table 8 County Budget and Relief Appropriations: Current and Inflation-Adjusted Value, 1911–1926

	1911	1912	1913	1915	1916	1917	1918
	Appropriations in thousands of dollars						
County budget							
Current	13,503.6	13,961.8	15,295.1	11,017.3	13,182.5	12,477.3	12,038.1
Inflation-adjusted	14,214.3	14,543.6	15,449.6	11,242.1	12,320.1	9,672.3	7,667.6
Relief supplies							
Current	200.0	274.5	229.5	270.0	240.0	215.0	235.9
Inflation-adjusted	210.5	285.9	231.8	275.5	224.2	166.6	150.2
	Appropriations per 100 residents						
County budget							
Current	545.9	549.3	586.1	401.2	468.4	432.9	408.0
Inflation-adjusted	574.7	572.2	592.0	409.4	437.8	335.6	259.9
Poor relief supplies							
Current	8.8	11.9	9.7	10.9	9.5	8.3	9.0
Inflation-adjusted	9.3	12.4	9.8	11.1	8.9	6.4	5.7

	1919	1920	1921	1922	1923	1924	1925	1926
Appropriations in thousands of dollars								
County budget								
Current	12,007.8	20,547.7	19,602.2	23,482.7	19,742.4	20,619.9	30,227.6	34,011.1
Inflation-adjusted	6,745.9	9,974.6	11,074.7	14,231.9	11,751.4	12,201.1	17,472.6	19,546.6
Poor relief supplies								
Current	180.0	200.0	215.0	247.0	225.0	175.0	250.0	325.0
Inflation-adjusted	101.1	97.0	121.4	149.6	133.9	103.0	144.5	186.7
Comparative appropriations per 100 residents								
County budget								
Current	397.8	665.7	617.2	719.1	588.4	598.6	855.2	938.5
Inflation-adjusted	223.5	323.1	348.7	435.8	350.2	354.2	494.3	539.3
Poor relief supplies								
Current	6.7	7.3	7.7	8.7	7.7	5.9	8.3	10.4
Inflation-adjusted	3.7	3.6	4.3	5.3	4.6	3.5	4.8	6.0

Sources: Cook County, IL, County Board of Commissioners, *Proceedings*, Appropriations, as finally adopted (1911–1926); *Report of the Department of Health of the City of Chicago for the Years 1926 to 1930* (Chicago: Chicago Department of Health, 1931); Paul Douglas, *Real Wages in the United States, 1890-1926* (Boston: Houghton Mifflin, Co., 1930), 40-42, 60-61.

Notes: Appropriations are in thousands of dollars, except in population comparisons. Douglas's Index of Relative Living Costs used 1914 = 100. The amount used for poor relief appropriations refers only to that segment of the budget used for material aid. The per capita figures for relief supplies used city population figures that elevated slightly the per capita figure. No consistent data were available for 1914.

vate relief. Nearly two-thirds (63.7 percent) of the money spent in the county on welfare was distributed through the Bureau of Public Welfare and mothers' pensions.[54]

During the campaigns for the Board of County Commissioners, the candidates for president pledged to care for those unable to care for themselves. They promised to fulfill their duties as the head of Cook County government by reducing the number of "cheaters" while also providing better services to those who needed them. Unlike the campaign rhetoric, the figures of poor relief appropriations demonstrate that they were a very low priority on the County Board's agenda. Families with able-bodied workers received a minimum of benefits. This practice not only maintained the tenet of self-support derived from the pauper law, but it also provided a rationale for limiting appropriations.

§

From the vantage point of the late 1920s looking back to the depression of 1893, much had changed in the structure and organization of public welfare. Where once the only institutional supports for women with dependent children were the poorhouse and public or private charities, in the 1920s new programs housed in the courts attempted to mediate the social and economic problems of mothers with young children. Social workers received more training and worked in expanded public and private agencies. Social survey research produced more information than ever before on the living standards and economic needs of working-class families. The public sector worked closely with private agencies, but this expansion came with additional costs, and government adopted a greater share of the expense of welfare services. The United Charities of Chicago served short-term cases of need and the county served the long-term poor. Periodically, the county would try to dodge its obligation and shift cases to the private sector, particularly during economic downturns or fiscal crises, but overall the trend toward increased public spending continued.

Both the use of poor relief benefits and the creation of new programs demonstrate the relevance of gender in the poverty programs. Men and women who headed families used poor relief differently. During periods of high unemployment and correspondingly great relief demand, local policy measures focused on employment (albeit ineffectively) as a solution to the problems of dependency for men. Arguments for "a citizen's right to work" gained political legitimacy, particularly during severe depressions. Poverty in mother-only families received more ambiguous attention. Women's responsibility for the care of young children and their marginalization within the labor market made them less able to rebound from poverty through employment and higher wages when the economy improved. Public and private agencies endorsed women's caretaking role by providing some of these families with relief for a longer period of time. Nevertheless, wage-earning was not only necessary but expected for both older children and mothers to maintain family support. This problem of gender-specific liabilities for dependent mothers formed the impetus for changing welfare to provide greater protections for mother-only families.

The expansion of the system of welfare institutionalized different benefits for impoverished mothers, however. Families accepted for mothers' pensions received greater benefits than poor relief offered. Those groups relegated to the office of poor relief, like deserted and unmarried women, a disproportionate group of which were African American, received only in-kind benefits. The effect of that separation of services was compounded when politicians reduced their already meager support for poor relief, and families received a relatively shrinking piece of public aid over time.

How these new programs for working-poor mothers evolved, and the degree to which they enhanced women's opportunities or continued to reinforce gender relations that inhibited women's economic independence, is a story that includes not only social reformers' views, but also political opportunities, existing structures, and social ideals. The beginning of mothers' pension policy, in Illinois and in the nation, was part of a larger effort in American social reform to reshape politics and develop an activist state.

Sophonisba Breckinridge (*right*), Edith Abbott (*left*), and Julia Lathrop (*bottom*). The University of Illinois at Chicago, The University Library, Department of Special Collections, Jane Addams Memorial Collection.

THREE

Gender and Social Policy: The Origins
of Mothers' Pension Policy in Illinois

The first publicly funded subsidy for mother-only families passed the state legislature with little obvious political organization in Illinois. No public commissions studied the ramifications of the proposal prior to its passage. No public campaigns or mass demonstrations drew attention to the need for such a program. The bill had no legal model to follow. The discussion that preceded the bill largely confined itself to associations of social workers and child welfare workers. Progressive social workers in Chicago had begun a process of advocating public support for dependent children in mother-only families based on their social research. Yet the first state law that authorized voluntary public funding to families with dependent children slipped into existence without their consultation. Historians have discussed the role of organized women's clubs, social workers, and juvenile court judges in the development of mothers' pensions nationally, but none have pursued the specific link between plans for a "new state," policy research, and the politics of implementation.

This chapter examines the connection between emerging ideas of an enlarged, activist state and the origins of Illinois' mothers' pension law through the work of three individuals who played a central role in the creation of the policy—Julia Lathrop, Sophonisba Breckinridge, and Edith Abbott. Although their contributions to the development of social work are well-known, little has been written on the evolution of their ideas on social policy for single mothers. Their ideas about restructuring the public sector, their research, which aimed to promote social legislation, and their work as social justice reformers place them firmly within that segment of Progressive Era reform that sought to limit monopolies of power, regulate industry, and expand the power of social groups. These women were among that group of early-twentieth-century professional women for whom political, social, and economic equality was a personal as well as political goal. Their writings reveal that equality for women was a central issue. Despite differences between them, they shared an understanding that the early twentieth century was women's moment—an important stage in a process of gradual democratization of American society. In a climate defined by private voluntarism and market forces, they attempted to expand the boundaries of citizenship and opportunities for women. Although they presented their agenda as nonpartisan, this obscured the inherently political character of their reforms, as well as the legacy of political activity in their personal lives. They called their work "social politics," they challenged the patronage system directly, and they worked to expand an activist state.[1]

Conversely, their reform agenda and practices share the criticisms lodged against progressivism and welfare state policies. The elitism of professional policy makers, the contradictions of expanding democracy through creating bureaucracies, the pursuit of gender equality through measures of protection, the greater regulation of impoverished women's lives through policies intended to improve them, all point to serious contradictions that evolved from their measures. This chapter focuses on the evolution of social thought produced by these reformers; ideas that changed over time within a political context that also changed. Situated between traditions of voluntarism, laissez-faire economics, and social democracy, they negotiated a political system of policy making. The chapter concludes with an account of the dispute over the origins of the first state law for mothers' pensions.

SETTLEMENTS, SURVEYS, AND SOCIAL POLITICS

Chicago was home to several settlements in the early twentieth century, but none as renowned as Hull House. Founded by Jane Addams and Ellen Gates Starr in 1889, Hull House modeled itself after London's Toynbee Hall by replicating a blend of social research with social services.[2] Residents participated in the federal study on urban slums in 1893 and collected data on the working and living conditions of several Chicago immigrant communities in the surrounding neighborhoods. They updated a study on nationalities in the area in 1905 and 1906, as well as a housing survey based on the 1901 Chicago Homes Association study.[3] Situated between the collectivist ideas of socialists and the laissez-faire ideals of charity organization societies, Hull House reformers used survey methods to create a new way of thinking about the problems and solutions to urban poverty. In their capacities as research investigators, factory inspectors, labor union advocates, juvenile court probation officers, or public and private relief visitors, the residents identified areas in which local government failed to provide community services. The research led to their involvement in politics. Social science methods of survey work provided them, as Kathryn Kish Sklar has argued, "a crucial means of overturning the fundamental premises of the liberal, laissez-faire state."[4]

The provision of welfare sat at the center of the reform critique of municipal political corruption, and Jane Addams's formulation of urban politics is one of the best known. The machine system was inefficient, corrupt, and inequitable in its distribution of public resources, she claimed. Nevertheless, people supported the ward boss because he offered them individual acts of kindness. Attending weddings, bailing out drunks, getting minor charges dropped, or delivering food baskets to the needy demonstrated shared values and created a loyalty that bound voters to the political organization. "The Alderman is really elected because he is a good friend and neighbor," Addams wrote. Her view of municipal politics undoubtedly influenced many who worked with her at Hull House and may have contributed to new strategies of gaining political power. Regardless of the extent to which bosses provided actual goods in the ward or precinct, both reformers and bosses understood that the government had a role in providing public services and that control over these services was the issue.[5]

The health of democracy depended upon its extension into industrial and social life for the women featured in this chapter. When direct intervention into local politics failed to achieve the desired results, they turned to the legal system, the courts, and new administrative bureaus of government. This route to political authority did not replace suffrage and parties, but added an alternative path, another method to influence the functions and structure of government. Central to their strategy was an abounding, if somewhat unexplained, faith in the state. When obstacles thwarted the progress of "detached groups," those outside the mainstream of partisan politics, they formed coalitions and sought redress from the government. These political lessons became part of the legacy of Hull House reform.

Julia Lathrop was the first of the three to move to Hull House and enter reform work. The daughter of parents who supported women's rights, Julia Lathrop achieved distinction as the first director of the United States Children's Bureau. She grew up around law and politics with her father, William Lathrop, a lawyer who served one term in the Illinois state legislature and one term in the United States Congress; and her mother, Sarah Potter Lathrop, who was described as "an ardent suffragist." Both parents "thought women should have equal opportunities with men and told [their] daughters over and over again they could do anything they wanted to."[6] After attending Rockford College for one year, she transferred to Vassar, where she received a degree in 1880. Her interest in women's rights and the humane treatment of dependent persons found a focus when she heard Jane Addams and Ellen Gates Starr speak at Rockford

College about their plans to establish a settlement house in Chicago. Impressed and interested by what she heard, Lathrop, at the age of thirty-two, moved to Hull House in 1890, where she lived for the next twenty years.[7]

Over the next few years, Lathrop matured from a practitioner of benevolent reform to an advocate of social welfare utilizing social research methods. During the depression of 1893, she volunteered to investigate relief cases for the county agent in the neighborhood surrounding Hull House.[8] Her account of that work, published in *Hull House Maps and Papers*, strongly criticized the charity view of self-help as a solution to poverty. She described her neighbors as having "an average wage-rate so low as to render thrift, even if it existed, an ineffective insurance against emergencies." Initially an advocate of self-reliance, Lathrop reexamined her views in the face of severe economic crisis and remarked that such poverty led one "at once to inquire what happens when the power of self-help is lost."[9] The work with the county also led her to dedicate herself to professionalization of the field. It was no surprise that the poor viewed county assistance as the last resort, despite their desperate condition, when one witnessed the poor relief office's processes and erratic administration. "The methods of this office, with its records kept as each changing administration chooses, its doles subject to every sort of small political influence, and its failure to co-operate with private charities," Lathrop wrote, "are not such as science can approve."[10] Trained personnel and the elimination of politics from welfare administration provided the best solution for these problems, she thought.[11] Lathrop soon had two opportunities to shape the policies she criticized, as a member of the State Public Charities Commission and as the director of the department of social investigation at the Chicago School of Civics and Philanthropy.

In 1893, Governor John P. Altgeld appointed her to the Illinois Board of Public Charities, the first woman to hold the post. This position gave her an intimate view of the needs of the state's institutional population and she campaigned for separate facilities for children, improved care of the insane, expanded services for African American children, and an end to political interference in welfare administration. At the same time, Lathrop worked with others to create the Illinois Conference of Charities and Corrections to generate greater public awareness about necessary reforms. The Juvenile Court Law was an early success.[12] Lathrop also used her position on the Board of Public Charities to publicize her views on merit appointments and civil service reform: the demand for better trained personnel and hiring on the basis of ability, not spoils.

In 1901, Lathrop resigned her position in a highly publicized protest of what she regarded as Governor Richard Yates's patronage appointments, this despite his campaign promises to end political intervention.[13] Governor Charles Deneen reappointed her in 1905. Lathrop advocated an increase in public social services because she saw in it the potential to raise the "professional standards" of social welfare and the possibility to provide both "comprehensive" and "continuous" services.[14]

While detached from her position on the State Board, Lathrop joined Graham Taylor, director of Chicago Commons settlement, to develop a series of courses designed to train social workers in the expanding field of social service. Taylor began a series of lectures on social problems in 1895 at the Chicago Commons and within a few years had shaped this program to meet the educational and training needs of social workers. By 1903, Taylor succeeded in attracting the support of William R. Harper, the University of Chicago's president, who provided a small grant and classroom space for Taylor's Social Science Center for Practical Training in Philanthropic and Social Work. The following year in 1904, Lathrop joined Taylor, Charles Henderson of the sociology department of the University of Chicago, and Robert Hunter, author of *Poverty* and the study of Chicago housing, on the faculty of the Chicago Institute of Social Science.[15] She lectured on public institutions and the juvenile court movement and in 1907 became the first director of its department of social investigation.[16] When funding from the Russell Sage Foundation provided the opportunity to expand the research department, Julia Lathrop hired a new Hull House resident, Sophonisba Preston Breckinridge, to assist in the work. With graduate training in law and political economy, Breckinridge had already published on women's legal and economic concerns when Lathrop recruited her.

Breckinridge came from a distinguished Kentucky family with deep roots in public life. Her great-grandfather, John Breckinridge, held the offices of U.S. senator and attorney general for Thomas Jefferson. Her father, William Breckinridge, served as a U.S. congressman and a Lexington lawyer. Her brother Desha operated the *Lexington Herald*, and her sister-in-law, Madeline McDowell Breckinridge, was a social reformer in Lexington. The Breckinridge family expressed greater ambivalence about female ambition than the Lathrops, although they did support education for women.[17] Breckinridge graduated from Wellesley in 1888, and like other women of her background and generation, she knew she wanted to utilize her skills, yet wandered for some time seeking her direction.

After a brief period teaching in the District of Columbia, she returned to Lexington to assume the family responsibilities left when her mother died. She studied law in her father's office and became the first woman to pass the Kentucky bar in 1894. Despite this accomplishment, Breckinridge never developed a legal practice and received little support from her family to do so.

The discouragement that characterized the years after college ended in 1895 when a friend from Wellesley, May Estelle Cook, encouraged Breckinridge to live with her in the Chicago suburb of Oak Park. Cook introduced Breckinridge to Marion Talbot, dean of women and head of the department of household administration at the University of Chicago. Talbot offered Breckinridge employment and suggested that she accept a scholarship that would allow her to pursue a doctorate in political science. Breckinridge later referred to Talbot as the one who "rescued her."

At the University of Chicago, Breckinridge pursued her interest in law and politics with two distinctly different mentors. During her first year, she studied with Ernst Freund and wrote her Master's essay on Kentucky's judicial system. Freund, a recent arrival to Chicago, was deeply involved in his own exploration of a set of ideas about activist government and the use of legal and political systems for "enlightened legislation and reform." Freund was particularly intrigued by the balance between the protection of individual rights and the use of state power to counteract economic inequities produced by industry. In his 1904 book, *The Police Power*, he developed a definition for the authority of government action as "the power of promoting the public welfare by restraining and regulating the use of liberty and property."[18] Breckinridge continued a professional and personal association with Freund over several years, working on such issues as wages and hours, rights for children born out of wedlock, and welfare law. Later in her career, Freund's ideas on the expansion of state authority were evident in her work on welfare and public administration. In 1897, however, Breckinridge began doctoral work with J. Laurence Laughlin, a political economy professor with different ideas. Mary Furner described Laughlin's career as "ultraconservative" and the man as one whose ideas "made it impossible for him to condone a positive role for the state in economic or social affairs."[19] At the same time, Laughlin had the reputation of supporting and encouraging women students in their studies. The dissertation took a conservative view on monetary policy but retained qualities from her work with Freund. In 1901, Breckinridge became the first woman to receive a doctorate in political science from the University of Chicago, and in 1904 she again achieved the status of pioneer as the first woman to receive a law degree from the school.

Her accomplishments did not lead to professional opportunities immediately, however. Women in political science or economics rarely received faculty appointments at that time. Breckinridge compared her options to those of her male colleagues in her unpublished autobiography. "Although I was given the PhD degree magna cum laude," she wrote, "no position in political science or economics was offered me. The men in the two departments, Boyd and Millis and Fertig and Wesley Mitchell and others went off to positions in college and university faculties."[20] Marion Talbot assisted her friend once again by hiring her as an assistant professor in the department of household administration and offering her the position of assistant dean of women.

Breckinridge's interest in the legal aspects of reform, particularly legislation that affected women, rapidly became evident in her teaching and research. Her courses entitled the "Legal and Economic Position of Women," "Modern Aspects of the Household," and "Consumption" focused on the economic aspects of women's domestic roles. She added the "Legal Aspects of Labor" the following year, 1905–1906, to explore the position of women wage-earners. Edith Abbott attended Breckinridge's classes, and within a few years the two published a series of articles that presented a critique of occupational segregation, domestic ideology, and the lack of equal pay for equal work.

Women's rights as individuals took center stage in two early articles that explored the undervalued position of women in the economy and the limits of protectionism. Breckinridge focused on the conflicts between issues of equality and policies for working women in a 1906 article, "Legislative Control of Women's Work." In this piece, she argued that social policy for women workers went beyond the minimum standard of health and safety and defined differential treatment for male and female workers. "It has been declared a matter of public concern," she wrote, "that no group of its women workers should be allowed to unfit themselves by excessive hours of work . . . for the burden of motherhood which each of them should be able to assume."[21] She criticized the limitation of women's opportunities for employment because of "mediaeval" thinking about social intercourse between the sexes, and she faulted the goals of so-called protective legislation, which she warned was "not enacted exclusively, or even primarily, for the benefit of women themselves."[22] Rather, such legislation placed the "well-being of the community," defined by its interest in the potential maternity of working women, ahead of the individual rights of women workers to bargain in the workplace. Breckinridge urged employers to negotiate with organized women for shorter hours, and argued that such action would produce "a higher grade of labor" worth the investment. In a second article, written with Edith Abbott, Breckinridge again criticized the limitation of women's right to work. The article challenged those "well-meaning persons of other classes who accepting the 'sphere of woman' doctrine, would limit the activities of women of all classes to the bearing and rearing of children, and to making home comfortable under circumstances determined by the amount of the man's wages rather than by the woman's energy or peculiar ability."[23] In later years, Breckinridge's work also addressed women's inequitable treatment as unemployed workers. She criticized unemployment studies, which frequently overlooked women and created a policy vacuum regarding poor and under-employed women and their families.[24] The significance of these articles rests in their explicit delineation of her early positions on equality and protectionism, views that would be qualified in her later work. They also reveal areas in which Breckinridge legitimated the use of state authority to define minimum standards of labor.

Through her work at the University of Chicago, Breckinridge eventually met Jane Addams, Grace Abbott, and Agnes Nestor, women with whom she would work closely in Chicago's reform community. She initiated with Mary McDowell of the University settlement the federal investigation of woman and child wage-earners.[25] In 1907, she joined the Women's Trade Union League, became a member of the Municipal Suffrage for Women, and became a resident of Hull House while on a break from the University of Chicago.[26] Hull House also offered the forum through which Breckinridge met Graham Taylor and Julia Lathrop and learned of their school for training people in the field of social work. Julia Lathrop sought Breckinridge's assistance in writing the Russell Sage Foundation grant to develop a social research department, and when the project received funding, Breckinridge agreed to assist Lathrop in developing the program.[27] As director of the research department in 1908, Breckinridge continued to work on a wide range of social issues, including anti–child labor laws, housing, immigrant rights, equity for African Americans, and women's rights. Her collaborator and friend, Edith Abbott, whom she had first met as a student in one of her classes, joined her as assistant director.

Edith Abbott's name is synonymous with the field of social work, but in 1908 she had not fully embraced the idea of publicly funded welfare. Her work with Hull House reformers and on mothers' pension policy would convince her of that need. According to her writings, her parents instilled a deep respect for social justice and individual rights as well as an ethic of voluntarism.[28] About her mother, Elizabeth Abbott, she wrote "in mother's Quaker family, the rights of women belonged with the rights of the Indian and the rights of the Negro. Everyone must be free and equal and every one should be dealt with on the basis of 'equity and justice.'"[29] Othman Abbott, her father, spent his life in law and politics in Nebraska, served in the Senate, and became the first lieutenant governor of the state. Both Edith and her sister, Grace, spent hours in the courthouse listening to their father argue cases. These early experiences and values influenced both women's choices to use law and politics in the service of social reform.

Abbott's parents supported education for women, but the depression of 1893 temporarily stalled her career. She graduated from high school that year, but the family had suffered an economic setback and Edith went to work as a teacher rather than proceed directly to college. Eight years later she graduated from the University of Nebraska. The following year, 1902, she took summer courses with J. Laurence Laughlin and Thorstein Veblen at the University of Chicago, which led to a fellowship in political economy at the university. As a full-time student, she focused entirely on the social sciences, fields dominated entirely by men. Abbott's interests in the legal and economic concerns of women were peaked in Breckinridge's course. In fact, Breckinridge liked to say that Abbott formulated the topic for *Women in Industry* while studying with her. Abbott completed her dissertation, "A Statistical Study of the Wages of Unskilled Labor in the United States, 1830–1900," in 1905 under Laughlin.[30]

In the years immediately following graduate school, Abbott pursued her research on women's economic status and worked for the Women's Trade Union League in Boston and the Carnegie Institution's study on women's employment. She published several articles from her research in the *Journal of Political Economy* between 1906 and 1907, but her monograph, *Women in Industry*, remains a classic in the field. Published in 1910, reviews recognized it as "a valuable contribution to economic history" and a groundbreaking study of sex differences in the workforce participation of women. It raised significant questions about occupational segregation, wage disparity, and what Abbott referred to as the "industrial dependence" of unskilled women workers. Furthermore, the study linked the poverty of women to the low-wage structure in which they worked.[31]

In the fall of 1906, Abbott's thoughts on the relationship between poverty and state policy were influenced by her studies in England with Beatrice Webb and Sidney Webb at the London School of Economics and Political Science. She immersed herself in a setting of "intensified exposure to socialist thought, the practicalities of London's municipal politics, and the ferment building up within the newly appointed Royal Commission on the Poor Law." Beatrice Webb was at the time a member of the Royal Commission on the Poor Laws and Relief of Distress, and engaged in serious critique of the country's relief system which she later elaborated in her minority report. Abbott had the opportunity to hear conservative views of Poor Law proponents, as well as the Fabian and Labour positions. Abbott's biographer, Lela Costin, found that Abbott rejected economic arguments for state-controlled industry, but more readily accepted the political and social goals of the Fabians; that is, the extension of government responsibility to its citizens. Ellen Fitzpatrick characterized this period as one of "intellectual turmoil" for Abbott. In retrospect, it may have been the ideas of universalized benefits and centralized administration that most strongly influenced Abbott. She returned to them in later years in both teaching and writing when she used European examples to emphasize the need for alternative methods of social provision in the United States.[32]

Perhaps one of the most interesting contributions from this period was Abbott's analysis of the connection between London's employment programs and women's restricted employment opportunities. Using data collected from municipal programs for the unemployed, Abbott found that working men and women experienced the hardship of depressions similarly; and that both would prefer to provide for themselves rather than rely on public provisions. An important distinction between the sexes did exist however, in what Abbott called the "industrial inefficiency" of women's labor force participation. Men who used the employment services were totally without work, while women had one job and tried to augment it with another. That is, women who worked partial hours as charwomen, laundry workers, and office cleaners used London's employment programs to make additional money through other part-time work. This practice revealed the marginality of women workers and the need to raise the value of women's labor through job training, Abbott argued. Her suggestion focused entirely on the wage-earning aspect of women's lives and found a definite role for the government.[33]

Abbott's ideas at this point blended her early views of self-reliance with her newer views of state responsibility. Government had the legitimate authority to intervene to correct the failures of economic systems—in particular, when the flaws of industrial organization created poverty and unemployment. At the same time, she understood that working people chose self-support over reliance on relief and she believed that social policy ought to enhance opportunities for independence. Relief was never intended as the "final measure of social justice for the wage-earner," she remarked several years later. "The final remedy of course is such a lifting of the wage levels as shall make it possible for the wage-earner to provide for his own wife and children after his own death, without leaving them to be investigated and supervised by any relief agency, public or private."[34] The family ideology present in this statement obscured Abbott's belief in broader values. Society had a responsibility to provide work for all who were able to work: immigrants, the unemployed, and single mothers could attain a higher standard of living with an improved economy. However, when the economy failed to provide a decent standard of living, the government had the responsibility to provide unstigmatized universal measures of assistance for health, education, and welfare.[35]

Abbott returned to the United States in the fall of 1907 and taught for one year at Wellesley College. During this period, Breckinridge corresponded with her and requested her advice on issues. She wrote Abbott in the summer about the prospect of directing the research for a study on the Chicago Juvenile Court. "I have had a great problem on my mind for the last six weeks due to the fact that Miss Addams offers me the job in connection with the juvenile court work of the city," Breckinridge wrote. "I have not yet decided what I am going to do about it; but I suppose as Miss Talbot thinks that I am of more use here than there, I will probably take her judgement rather than Miss Addmas [sic] still I dont know."[36] Breckinridge did undertake the study, and by the fall she sent Abbott a draft of the survey schedule for her comments. Early in 1908, Breckinridge, Grace Abbott, and Julia Lathrop all lived at Hull House and they conspired to bring Edith back to Chicago. She had been dissatisfied at Wellesley, so when Grace encouraged Edith to join her at Hull House, and when Breckinridge offered her the job of assistant director of social investigation at the School of Civics and Philanthropy, Edith Abbott returned to Chicago.

Social Research

The first major study of the new research division evaluated the "Juvenile Court of Chicago and Its Wards—Delinquent, Truant, Dependent." The juvenile court system was still relatively new, and child welfare workers wanted to evaluate the effectiveness of the court's work as well as to explore the opportunities for research provided by the case records. Julia Lathrop, who had worked with the Chicago Woman's Club to secure the legislation that created the nation's first juvenile court in Chicago, proposed the study to the Russell

Sage Foundation. She put Sophonisba Breckinridge, who had been promoted to director of the department of social investigation at the School of Civics and Philanthropy, in charge of the study while Lathrop assumed other duties as vice president and trustee of the school. The first stage of research, on delinquency, conducted between 1907 and 1909, analyzed 14,099 cases of children brought before the court during the first ten years of its existence and attempted to discover the patterns and causes of delinquency among youth. The second stage of research, on truancy, conducted between 1910 and 1912, evaluated additional records of the public schools, municipal court, and the compulsory education department.[37]

The juvenile court studies dramatically revealed the relationship between poverty, crime, and mother-only families. The demands of both earning wages and caring for children placed great hardships on women, with the result that large numbers of children from mother-only families ended up in the juvenile court. Criminal behavior existed among all classes; however, the poor were more frequently brought into the court for their offenses. Ninety-two percent of the young women and 77 percent of the young men who appeared in the juvenile court came from families that the study classified as "poor" or "very poor." In the group of "poor" families, the father lived at home and continued to provide the main economic support of the family, although he was usually unskilled and worked irregularly. In the group of "very poor" families, the father had either died, deserted, or become ill and the mother assumed the task of earning, but her lack of employment experience and her responsibilities at home led her to take marginal jobs like cleaning or scrubbing. This group of very poor accounted for 68 percent of the young women and 37 percent of the young men whose cases came into court. Abbott and Breckinridge argued, however, that the cause of juvenile crime did not rest in the individual flaws of the child or the mother, but rather emerged from larger social and environmental problems involving neighborhoods, education, job opportunities, and poverty.[38]

In 1910, Breckinridge published "Neglected Widowhood," an article based on the juvenile court research which attempted to make a legal case for the public support of mother-only families. Breckinridge reasoned that the existence of dower rights and nonsupport laws demonstrated Americans' acceptance of the legal premise of support and maintenance for widows and children in the event of the loss of the husband. However, this legal premise proved most operative when significant property was involved. "When the husband is the owner of property there is now a fairly substantial guaranty furnished to the woman who becomes a wife and mother that she is putting her hand to a task in which the community feels deep concern, for which reasonable support and maintenance will be supplied." For a working-poor family, that guarantee of support had inadequate legal provision, with the result that indigent single mothers carried a dual role as wage-earners and homemakers.[39] Their wage-earning remained severely limited by the lack of occupational skill, and their efforts to maintain the family were compromised. Breckinridge described the difficult circumstances in which "the unsupported mother undertakes to carry the double burden of earning the support and of performing the domestic duties which, under our present habits of thinking, are inextricably intertwined with her maternal duties."[40] The result in many mother-only families was a high rate of poverty. Breckinridge attempted to argue that society's acceptance of the *right to support* should take precedence over society's ideal that family support remain a private responsibility.

Central to her argument was an evaluation of the economic "risk" taken by a woman in the marriage contract. In exchange for economic support, she offered her husband and children the value of her reproductive and domestic labor. Society had an investment in upholding the terms of support in the marriage contract and had enforced legal obligations that recognized a widow's right to an inheritance and a wife's right to support. However, while meant broadly, the laws in fact applied narrowly to those of means. The article posed the question: Does the state not have a binding responsibility to ensure the rights of support to all wives regardless of their economic means? In doing so, Breckinridge placed the issue of support within the context of married women's rights and sought a legal foundation that could equitably serve women of all classes. The proposal shared elements found in maternalist arguments for pensions, that is, the concern for the economic protection of wives and mothers based upon their service to the family. Yet Breckinridge pushed the issue of a woman's rights within the marriage contract much further, hoping to establish a premise that could justify coverage from social insurance.[41]

The problems of mother-only families took center stage in the juvenile court studies.[42] The authors emphasized the extreme hardship placed upon women, the difficulties of carrying two roles, and the undesirability of continuing a policy that separated children from parents because of poverty. Notes from case records illustrated their points. In one family with four children in which the father died eight years before they appeared in court, "the mother has gone out washing ever since. She is now working in a laundry, earning from seven to eight dollars a week, and is away from home all day."[43] Another widow remarried and then lost her second husband. She also supported her family by washing. "The mother goes out to wash while the grandmother stays at home and takes care of the house, which is kept neat and pleasant," the case record reported. "The mother and grandmother are very nice women who have struggled hard to keep independent. They take one lodger."[44] A family headed by a woman was not, in itself, the cause of delinquency, Breckinridge argued. The family had the capability to provide adequate home care, but poverty prevented them from doing so. The analysis of the first stage of court studies tried to shift the focus of existing policy. Despite their good intentions and hard labor, Abbott and Breckinridge argued, these women simply could not provide supervision to their children when they were out to work.

In the 1910 article by Breckinridge and the volumes coauthored with Abbott, a direct call for a guarantee of support for poor mothers emerged. "Whether it be termed a pension for the mother, or 'adequate aliment on condition of caring for her children,' [as suggested in the minority report of the Royal Commission on the Poor Law] or pay for her services as agent of the court, or a grant in aid of family life," Breckinridge wrote, "it should be available, sufficient in amount, regular in payment, dignifying in its assurance of the community's concern for the well-being of her group."[45] Not all mothers would benefit equally from a subsidy plan, and Breckinridge categorized the mothers into three groups. The first included women who, except for poverty, were fully capable of keeping their homes together and who would benefit from assistance. The second group she characterized as "incompetent," but capable of change. This group included, for example, a woman whose home might be "dirty," but who supported her children by leaving home to wash each day. It also included a woman who had supported herself and three children for seven years by factory work, but who had recently become a "drunkard" and lived in an "old shack" but who it was believed could break her habit. In these, and other cases, Breckinridge argued that a "wiser and kinder policy, if only undertaken at an earlier period" could have stopped the negative effects on family life. The third group, which she noted was small in number, comprised those who were hopelessly unable to maintain family life. The responsibility for a policy of family aid would eventually be assumed by the public sector, Breckinridge thought, but until that time the best method would develop in cooperation between the juvenile court and private agencies.[46]

Over the next decade, Breckinridge outlined a justification for the extension of state power in relation to issues of child welfare. In line with contemporary arguments used in anti–child labor legislation and married women's guardianship rights, Breckinridge rejected the father's claim to "do what he will with his own" and similar attitudes that treated family members as property. She believed that a father "was never more than a trustee holding title for the equitable owner, the true beneficiary—the community—who is now in a position to demand an accounting." Her statement reflected little concern for the potentially negative consequences of ascribing powers to state agencies. Rather, she believed that the government exercised legitimate authority when it established certain standards for the health and well-being of children, particularly when parents failed to do so.[47]

THE APPLICATION OF RESEARCH TO POLICY

Chicago reformers frequently cited the juvenile court study and its findings in both the local and national arenas in an effort to generate public support for its proposals. Julia Lathrop referred to it in two papers delivered before the Illinois State Conference of Charities and Corrections in 1908. "Perhaps no single neglect of private philanthropy is to-day more flagrant than the failure to initiate dignified methods of so pensioning families in which a good competent mother is now compelled to be the breadwinner, that the children shall have the normal amount of care from that mother, a care for which the state itself can well afford to pay and which in time it will not fear to guarantee."[48] Lathrop criticized the charity organization societies' rejection of outdoor aid and cited several examples of European social insurance as evidence of satisfactory alternative methods of public policy. Large numbers of children of working mothers came to the juvenile court, but rather than blame the mother, Lathrop stated, the problems of single mothers needed a new social policy. "Philanthropists go to law as their forebears went to mill and to meeting—to provide for the acknowledged demands of material and moral comfort."[49] Poor relief could not address the economic crisis faced by families of the working poor, and certain "dangers" beset mother-only families, such as child labor, juvenile delinquency, and family dissolution. "Why should we fear any method of dignified and adequate support as much as we should fear the consequences of our present neglect?" Lathrop asked.[50] The time had come for a new evaluation of the issue of social insurance—one that utilized new social research and evidence from Europe. The time had come to rely on government as "the organ of the governed," she concluded.[51]

Breckinridge presented the policy recommendations of the juvenile court study to the 1910 Illinois State Conference of Charities and Corrections and called for the compensation of women's labor in child rearing. The recommendations of the paper departed radically from previous ideas of poor relief. She recommended a national minimum standard of child welfare and public aid for single mothers. "If we allow the mother who is deprived of her natural support to assume the burden of support, as well as the duties of nurture and care, we are not saving the pittance she earns—we are wasting the skill she might use in caring for her children." As a model, Breckinridge referred to the Jewish Charities of Chicago, who had developed a plan to pension single mothers. Cooperation between public and private agencies would be necessary until the public sector assumed full coordination of child welfare services. "Ultimately, of course the hope of a universal plan will be realized in accordance with which the mother will be constituted the express and recognized agent of the community in caring for its young as she is now its tacitly recognized servant." She did not persuade that year's conference to recommend legislative action on behalf of mothers' pensions, but it is noteworthy that Breckinridge proposed the plan in terms of social insurance and redefined the undervalued role of servant to one of agent in legitimating a claim to insurance.[52]

Jane Addams used the platform of her presidential address to the National Conference of Charities and Correction in May 1910 to call for the state's care for mothers with dependent children. Sections of her address drew heavily from Breckinridge's work as she argued that women were barely able to support themselves on the wages they received let alone support their young children. On a more local venue, Addams repeated this message to a Mothers' Day meeting at Chicago's Neighborhood House. Instead of taking children out of families and institutionalizing them, she proposed a pension to the mother. Speaking of its benefits for children and its socializing impact on women, she told her audience, "It would allow her to lessen her work just enough to give them the needed attention, it would keep them under the healthful mother influence and it would make her a better woman." Addams also noted that more day nurseries and shorter work hours would also improve women's condition.[53]

In addition to the public advocacy of Hull House reformers, Chicago's juvenile court judges Julian Mack and Merritt Pinckney utilized the research.[54] The court, particularly under Mack and Pinckney, supported the direction of progressive reform suggested by the research efforts of Breckinridge and Abbott. Mack first became acquainted with Breckinridge and Abbott while on the law faculty at the University of Chicago, and his involvement with Chicago's United Jewish Charities and the problems of Jewish immigrants involved him in several activities that overlapped with Hull House projects. In 1903, his appointment to the juvenile court gave him an opportunity to broaden his commitment to child welfare issues. He worked with Addams and Breckinridge on the board of directors of the Juvenile Protective Association and served on the organizing committee for the White House Conference on the Care of Dependent Children in 1909. His 1912 presidential address to the National Conference of Charities and Correction in which he called for broad measures of social justice for working-class families promoted the ideas advocated in the juvenile court study, including a pension for mothers.

> The child's right to a healthy normal family life is to be met, not merely by forbidding child labor and by destroying the pest-breeding hovels of the slums, but also by maintaining the integrity of the family through freeing the wage-earner from unnecessary and avoidable industrial accidents and diseases threatening his premature death, through making it possible for the widowed mother to remain at home and devote herself to the nurture and training of her children.[55]

Although Mack ended his term in the juvenile court in 1905, he continued to work on issues of single mothers and dependent children through his efforts in the private sector.

Three years later, the Chicago Juvenile Court had another vocal advocate in the person of Judge Merritt Pinckney. He participated in both the National Conference of Charities and Correction and the 1909 White House conference and became very well-informed on the debates within the field of child dependency. Pinckney presided as judge of the Chicago Juvenile Court during the research project conducted by Breckinridge and Abbott. He frequently said that his support for the idea of mothers' pensions evolved from his experiences with impoverished families who appeared before the court. When the effort to investigate dependent family cases became too large, Pinckney and chief probation officer John Witter developed an informal policy to handle cases out of court and place children in their homes rather than in institutions. They relied on the aid of private charity organizations to supplement the family's earnings with a small stipend.

Breckinridge and Abbott used the research from the juvenile court study to change social policy for a small group of families headed by working mothers who were extremely poor. They focused not only on the criminal activity of the child, but on the environmental context of poverty as a cause of family distress. They influenced the discussion on the causes of juvenile delinquency by focusing less on the individual's behavior and more on the structural problems faced by single mothers. At the same time, the authors did not adopt a universal approach to such reform. Their proposal did not call for a minimum standard of living for all mothers in poverty, but rather applied it only to those with whom the greatest measure of family rehabilitation would be achieved—or, as Breckinridge put it, those mothers who had the ability "to keep a clean and decent home." Working with the knowledge of women's limited employment opportunities and the recognition of society's support for women's traditional child-rearing role, they succeeded in shifting ideas within the reform community and creating a context amenable to a new policy, while adhering to the type of regulation found in charity societies.

THE CONTEST OF ORIGINS OF THE MOTHERS' PENSION POLICY

The legislative session had been marked by intense reform activity. Organized groups of women unionists, suffragists, and the State Federation of Labor lobbied in Springfield for their legislative bills during the spring of 1911. Agnes Nestor of the Women's Trade Union League worked around the clock for the passage of the ten-hour law for women in manufacturing and mercantile trades. Woman suffrage activists such as Catherine Waugh McCulloch pushed the voting bill in the state capitol. The State Federation of Labor negotiated for labor's position on a compromise to the employer liability bill and the workmen's compensation act.

The same week that bills for women's suffrage and the ten-hour workday were discussed in the state legislature, Carl Lundberg, a Republican state senator from Chicago, introduced the Funds to Parents bill as an amendment to the Juvenile Court Act of 1907. The original bill read:

> If the parent or parents of such dependent or neglected child are poor and unable to properly care for the said child, but are otherwise proper guardians and it is for the welfare of such child to remain at home, the court may enter an order finding such facts and fixing the amount of money necessary to enable the parent or parents to properly care for such child, and thereupon it shall be the duty of the County Board through its County Agent or otherwise, to pay to such parent or parents or to such other person for them as the court may direct at such times as said order may designate the amount so specified for the care of such dependent or neglected child until the further order of the Court.[56]

The Funds to Parents bill authorized the court to use public funds for children who were placed on probation in their homes, and allowed either parent to receive aid. The Senate and House discussed the bill throughout the spring, made one revision, and passed it without opposition. It received the governor's approval on 5 June 1911.[57]

The law signaled an increase in public responsibility toward dependent children. Not only did it make public resources available where primarily private resources had existed, but it also directed those funds toward subsidized home care rather than institutionalization. The legislation also suggested that a minimum standard of living existed under which no family should fall and proposed a cash, not in-kind, contribution toward meeting that standard.[58] In its original form, either parent could receive aid. The legislation was also significant in its attempt to separate the policy from the political and administrative structure of poor relief. The County Board of Commissioners and its appointee, the county agent, were responsible for the funding and administration of all public welfare. The new policy for dependent families was attached to the juvenile court, however, and an entirely separate structure created for its administration within the court. This gave the juvenile court judge unprecedented authority in distributing funds to poor families. Despite vague language that did not specify how these goals were to be administered, the new legislation held the potential for a new form of social support.

Conflicting information on the origins of the bill makes it difficult to determine its authorship. Springfield and Chicago newspapers covered the suffrage and labor bills, their opponents, and their supporters, but the Funds to Parents bill received no coverage. This may be because a eugenics measure introduced by Senator Edmund Beal of Alton, Illinois, overshadowed Lundberg's proposal. Beal called his plan an "anti-race suicide bill," which would pay a birth subsidy of $100 for each child born to women within the first two years of marriage. He referred to the allegedly low birthrates in the "rich wards" and the high birthrates in "poorer districts" to gain support for the bill, which he hoped would encourage middle-class and wealthy people to bear more children. Belle Squire, a columnist for the *Chicago Tribune* women's section, took Beal's bill to task. She challenged the ideas behind the race suicide argument, and wrote that no one had the right to determine the number of children for anyone else. Without making a reference to the bill just proposed in Springfield, Squire suggested that poor mothers would have greater need for public support than those of the middle class.[59]

The day after Lundberg introduced the Funds to Parents bill, Timothy

Hurley, one of the original framers of the juvenile court law, called attention to the need for a new policy for dependent care.[60] He criticized the court's methods for dealing with dependent children, which included separating children from working-poor parents. "No courts or institutions can take care of the children as well as their parents," he said. While not explicitly endorsing the Funds to Parents Act, Hurley aired one of the popular reasons to support it. Possibly in response to Hurley's charge, the *Chicago Tribune* ran a story on the positive aspect of the court's work a few days later. The story described the family of Mrs. Annie Bachaus, a widow with five children, who had appeared before Judge Pinckney of the Chicago Juvenile Court and requested support for her children. Although employed, she could not earn enough to support her family. Rather than send her children away to institutions at a cost to the county of $50 per month, Mrs. Bachaus asked the court for $20 a month in a pension. This plan, she argued, would save the court $30 per month. Pinckney complied with the request.[61]

In addition, three major news stories preceded the legislation that may have alerted the general public to the need for some form of aid for single-mother families. In January 1910, a terrible mining disaster in Cherry, Illinois, left approximately 100 women and 442 children without any means of support.[62] The following fall, 25,000 Chicago garment workers went on a four-month strike that highlighted the lack of a living wage in one of Chicago's largest industries.[63] Both events were widely covered in Chicago's newspapers and both stressed the desperate situation for workers and their families. A study of Chicago schools in 1908 found a great number of mothers trying to support several children on less than three dollars a week. The study, which found 15,000 starving children in school, drew attention to the need for some type of policy. Industrial accidents, low wages, and the lack of provision for workers' families in case of accident or death all contributed to an increase in family poverty.[64]

Although clearly linked to labor conditions, the Funds to Parents law did not arise from organized labor's agenda. Its efforts in the state legislature in the spring of 1911 focused on ensuring that the employer liability, workmen's compensation, and ten-hour bills reflected labor's interests. Wages and hours issues, not welfare, preoccupied labor, including the Women's Trade Union League. Socialists also did not push for this program, but viewed reforms as concessions. For example, Robert Hunter told the readers of the *Chicago Daily Socialist* that reform "helped them to win by begging what they might have won by their own manhood."[65] Mothers' pensions, while supported after the fact by both groups, were viewed as an extension of charity and thus were not on the agenda of these organizations.

A few of Chicago's women's clubs took credit for the passage of the law. The Children's Day Association had regularly attended the dependency hearings in the juvenile court since 1908. When it became apparent that a woman could be separated from her children because of poverty, a representative of the organization provided the family with money to keep it intact. This spontaneous charity developed into long-term pensioning for some families. The Children's Day Association claimed that it "persistently urged [mothers' pension] legislation at Springfield." The club's president said she discussed the idea of public support to widows with Governor Deneen in February 1911; however, the organization recorded no such activity in its legislative agenda in Chicago's newspapers.[66]

One might expect that the state chapter of the National Congress of Mothers would have been active in the lobbying because the national organization had been an early proponent of endowed motherhood.[67] The Illinois Congress of Mothers reported its activities to the national organization but made no reference to a mothers' pension law previous to its passage. Ten thousand women attended the 1910 annual meeting in Rockford to discuss "means for bettering their own and other people's children," but aid to dependent children did not have a place on the agenda.[68] At the annual state meeting in May 1911, at the height of the legislative session, the ICM chapter discussed a legislative agenda that included child labor and child mortality, but mothers' pensions were not among the issues.[69] The first reference to the Illinois mothers' pension law in NCM literature appeared shortly after its passage, noting that a member of the Illinois Congress of Mothers had been appointed to a citizen's board overseeing the policy.[70] The first substantive notice appeared in December 1911. It emphasized the need to limit the eligibility of applicants and force mothers to "demonstrate their capability as household managers."[71] The state organization did not record its full advocacy of the policy until 1915, when the annual meeting endorsed a program to enact mothers' pensions in every county of the state.[72]

The Chicago Woman's Club also recorded no involvement in the passage of the bill, despite its work for the juvenile court and dependent children. In the year leading up to the Funds to Parents Act, the Legislative Committee of the Chicago Woman's Club recorded efforts on behalf of the national pure food law, a state-level ten-hour law for working women, anti–child labor legislation, and a municipal lodging house for women. No discussion of aid to dependent families took place, however. The Woman's City Club, organized in 1910 to educate women about public affairs and "to assist in arousing an increased sense of social responsibility for the safeguarding of the home, the maintenance of good government, and the ennobling of that larger home of all—the city," was the most politically active of Chicago's women's clubs. The leadership of this club drew heavily from the city's settlements, and while generally concerned with welfare issues, it did not take up a campaign for mothers' pensions until the end of the 1910s.[73]

At the 1914 State Conference of Charities and Corrections, a representative of the Illinois Federation of Women's Clubs stated that "the Federation was active in working for the passage of a Mothers' Pension bill."[74] Despite such claims, there is little public record of any activity for passage. At the end of 1911, the *Chicago Tribune* published a year-end retrospective of the accomplishments of Chicago's women's clubs. Many listed their charity enterprises and legislative activities, but none referred to the mothers' pensions law.[75] While little evidence exists to confirm women's clubs' claims to have lobbied for the measure initially, they became a strong pressure group for expanding eligibility and benefits in subsequent revisions of the law.

Henry Neil, an Oak Park resident and justice of the peace who claimed to have passed the Funds to Parents Act through the state legislature, became a visible proponent of the legislation by writing articles in newspapers and journals, speaking at local clubs, and eventually organizing mothers' pension leagues in several states.[76] In 1909, Neil and municipal court judge McKenzie Cleland formed the Chicago-based National Probation League. The league's main objective promoted an adult probation system for first offenders as an alternative to imprisonment. Cleland had developed such a plan while he served as judge of the Maxwell Street Court, and argued that adult probation allowed a man to "support his family while being reformed." In the course of their work, Neil and Cleland became aware of the desperate situation faced by women who were responsible for the support of their families. In the spring of 1911, Neil and Cleland were in Springfield to lobby for their adult probation legislation. The state legislature passed an adult probation bill, but not the one proposed by the National Probation League. Nevertheless, both men claimed that they had pushed through the "mothers' pension" bill.[77]

In contrast to the relative absence of coverage on lobbying efforts for this legislation, Neil conducted a publicity campaign in the Chicago press following its passage in which he promoted the policy and claimed the title of "father of mothers' pensions." Neil relied on a popular argument to promote the policy: poverty should not contribute to the separation of families. He stressed the overwhelming difficulty of the dual role for poor mothers and criticized relief agencies' policy of enforced work for mothers and older children. The state, he argued, would enjoy a savings by paying mothers to raise their children at home rather than sending them to institutions. But Neil went beyond the familiar, with his plan for Mothers' Pensions Leagues. The leagues consisted of pension advocates who would survey districts for needy families, assist them in the application and court hearing process, and provide the court with accurate information on the costs of "proper care" for children. He offered "efficient women" five dollars a day if they secured ten new memberships in the league. In addition to organizing the leagues, Neil criticized the operations of charity agencies and argued that they continued to break up families rather than assist them to stay together. The combination of Neil's program to publicize the new state program for single mothers, and his critique of the existing structure proved too much for some among the charity elite.[78]

Chicago's social-work community, the charity establishment, and the national reform network assigned credit for the Funds to Parents Act to Merritt Pinckney, while leaving the precise authorship of the bill vague. Pinckney consistently supported the policy, but he never claimed to be its author, and the social-work community criticized the bill for its broad scope and indefinite terms. Historians, citing these sources, have generally credited Pinckney with passage of the act. Pinckney and his chief probation officer, John Witter, had established an informal policy of pensioning families with private aid to avoid breaking up poor families headed by women. In 1910, the juvenile court report to the Cook County Board of Commissioners, written by Witter, specifically advocated that the informal policy of support of dependent children in their own homes be expanded. He wrote:

> Purely a lack of funds for support should never be reason enough to separate mother and child; to rob a child of that which no institution can render a proper substitute—a mother's love. Were we to consider this from the standpoint of expense alone, private organizations have proved, in a limited way, that the ordinary parent can, by keeping the family together, provide for the child with less money than it costs the state to care for the child in an institution.[79]

This proposal corresponded with those made in the policy recommendations of the Abbott and Breckinridge studies on dependency and delinquency.

Yet in none of these documents do any of the actors discuss writing such legislation. In fact, most social-work commentators bemoaned the fact that they were not consulted on the bill. In their review of the pension legislation, Abbott and Breckinridge inferred that Pinckney and Witter had previewed the legislation for the Funds to Parents Act before the legislature discussed it, but they did not outright credit them with its authorship. Regardless, accounts of the act in contemporary social welfare literature singularly credit Pinckney with transforming a loosely defined act into a working policy.[80]

Neil's high-profile promotion of the new policy and the Chicago charity establishment's desire to control the policy created a sensational conflict. The latter conducted a campaign in both the local Chicago press and national social-work publications to discredit Neil and denounce his claim to authorship of the Funds to Parents bill. Just two months after Cook County implemented the pension policy, Louise de Koven Bowen (benefactor, philanthropist, and director of the Juvenile Protective Association) and municipal court judge Harry Olson challenged Neil and Cleland's claims to authorship and charged them with soliciting funds under false pretenses. They argued that Neil was not the "real father" of mothers' pension legislation as he had claimed in his literature, and Bowen warned women's clubs that his solicitation of funds for "humanitarian legislation" supported his organization rather than poor families.[81] Neil and Cleland counterattacked by charging that the "professional charities" of Chicago used contributions "to line the pockets of persons who are not objects of charity."[82] They claimed that the Juvenile Protective Association's budget for 1911 spent 80 percent of the funds on salaries, and charged that attacks like Bowen's were motivated by a fear that private charity donations would decrease as public programs expanded.

The public debate over the program's origins and the censure of Neil continued for at least one more year. Neil criticized both the juvenile court's administration as "too cautious" in its application of the law following legislative restrictions, and the role of charities in the revision of the law that had "broken up tens of thousands of homes by compelling the dependent mothers to work at the wash tubs in some one else's basement six days a week when they should stay at home and give their own children proper care."[83] The board of directors of the United Charities of Chicago discussed Neil's latest round of charges and decided to pursue a counterpublicity campaign.[84] In February and March of 1913, the *Survey*, a national publication for social workers and charity organizations, ran three short notices about Neil. The notices referred to him as a "promoter" who traveled widely advertising his "scheme" of organizing leagues to promote pension legislation. They charged him with profiteering from membership collections and promoting false and inaccurate pension information. Neil responded to the *Survey*, but a second article discredited him by pointing out a series of errors he had made.[85]

A master's essay, written shortly after the passage of the new law, corroborated Neil's claims. Ruth Newberry argued that McKenzie Cleland wrote the Funds to Parents Act after learning of a similar assistance policy in New Zealand. Henry Neil took the bill to Springfield and persuaded Carl Lundberg to introduce it.[86] Years later, Grace Abbott clarified the dispute that took place in Chicago. She said that while Neil "may have written and had introduced into the legislature the very badly drawn statute which was enacted in 1911," the law would never have received attention had not Pinckney and others created an atmosphere receptive to the idea. It took the administrative structure of the juvenile court and the cooperation of social agencies, Abbott insisted, to put the policy in place. The struggle over attribution of the bill's origins provides early indication of the interests that would later emerge to control the new policy.[87]

The settlement workers who had initiated the research on the need for a new policy did not attend the final days of the legislative session in Springfield. Breckinridge and others at the School of Civics and Philanthropy were involved in the Child Welfare Exhibit, a massive exhibition to educate the public on the need for better social policy. New York had sponsored a similar exhibit, and members of the philanthropic community, including Julius Rosenwald and Mrs. Emmons Blaine, approached the school to coordinate a similar show in Chicago.[88] It lasted two weeks and attracted 416,848 visitors. The *Chicago Daily Tribune* called the exhibit "ruthless." "It drags motherhood from its veil of sweet scented sanctity," the notice read, "and shows it as a plain, important function, taking place frequently among filthy surroundings under the guidance of ignorant midwives."[89] One of the themes that could be found in the exhibit and the accompanying lectures was the need for greater government involvement in the provision of social welfare services. Despite the long history and "good intentions" of private agencies, speaker after speaker pointed out that the need far outweighed the capacity of private agencies to respond.[90]

Many made a plea for aid to dependent children in their homes. Judge Julian Mack, previously of the Chicago Juvenile Court, called for municipal pensions for widows with small children at the opening proceedings: "Call this Socialism if you will. Don't be afraid of words. To me it is not Socialism. It is the duty of the state to support the decent poor out of the public funds."[91] The *Chicago Daily Tribune* did not interpret Mack's recommendation as socialist but agreed the time had come to end the policy that separated working-class mothers from their children.[92] Judge Pinckney, in his description of the court's work, called the system for dependent children "entirely inadequate" and noted the court's inability to provide any public aid for mothers with young children. He proposed that "when a child is kept at home with the mother, the state of Illinois ought to give the same financial assistance for the support and maintenance of the child that it does when the child is sent to an institution." He announced that a bill had recently passed the Senate and was now under consideration in the House. "The speaker of the House and influential members of that body have been written to and urged to put that bill through."[93] Later, Pinckney defended the expenditure of public funds for mothers' pensions. "The motherhood it honors, the child it protects, the home it preserves, are worthy objects of a people's solicitude and of a state's benefactions."[94] While Pinckney agreed that social insurance policies offered the best measure of prevention against causes of poverty for mother-only families, he asked: "must deserving motherhood, the sacredness of home life and the welfare of children await the slow evolution of our social, industrial and political life?"[95]

§

Lathrop, Breckinridge and Abbott played a unique role in establishing a rationale for public funding of mothers' pensions. Their view of the positive potential of the state and their perception of the legal and economic vulnerabilities of single-mother families led them to use their research in service to social policy. The social surveys of Chicago's juvenile court conducted by Breckinridge and Abbott were widely discussed in reform circles and their recommendations were often repeated. The researchers' network of reformers helped provide a wide audience for the idea of mothers' aid. Despite their interest, they did not propose the initial legislation, but as the following chapter explains, they played an important advocacy role in shaping it.

Lathrop's contribution included the research context she constructed at the School of Civics and Philanthropy, her impact on the Illinois Board of Public Charities, and her federal role. While Jane Addams noted that Lathrop played an active role in securing the legislation, she offered no details, and Lathrop herself made no mention of any involvement with the Funds to Parents Act.[96] In the spring of 1911, Lathrop worked on a revision to the placing-out section of the Juvenile Court Law. She had the opportunity to extend her vision of cooperation between government and civil society in 1912 when President Taft appointed her the first head of the newly formed U.S. Children's Bureau within the Department of Labor. From this position, she continued to blend social research with social policy. Studies of infant mortality, child labor, juvenile courts, and mothers' pensions frequently relied on the research capabilities of her friends and associates in Chicago. She used the resources of the federal government to provide the funding for research on policy issues for which she hoped state and federal action might be taken. Years later, Lathrop pointed to the mothers' pension program as an example of social policy that held the principle, if not the practice, of eliminating poverty. "It [poverty] is at the basis of our social problem. I believe that within fifty years we can make a start toward abolishing poverty. . . . An illustration of this is . . . the principle that cash allowances or pensions from public funds made to mothers struggling with extreme poverty are the most economical way to prevent the neglect and ruin of children."[97] The state was central to the plan of eliminating poverty.

Breckinridge followed her mentor Ernst Freund's interest in the administrative state. Only the government had the authority to centralize administration, control hiring through civil service, and pool tax revenues to provide a broad source of funding. In the 1910s, county politicians controlled these processes, and both Breckinridge and Abbott thought they could work around partisan influence by creating administrative sectors of government. Breckinridge placed the claim for public support of single mothers within the larger context of women's rights. She wanted to extend married women's rights by establishing a legal foundation for support, regardless of one's means. Mothers' pensions took the first step toward social insurance for mother-only families. She also wanted to secure better working conditions for women. Aware that women workers had weak bargaining power, she supported legislative reforms to improve conditions, partly by providing education and training to raise the labor value of women workers. Her support for mothers' pensions fit within "the program of emancipation" for women in that it would remove the "nonindustrial" worker from wage competition and help to reduce the practice of lowering wage standards.[98] Throughout her career, Breckinridge joined political rights with economic rights for women. Poverty, infant mortality, dependency, and maternal death rates could all be reduced, she argued, through policies that raised the standard of living.[99] In 1931, she pushed for legislation that would put poor relief on a state contributory basis, and cited mothers' pensions as a successful example of this plan.[100] Later in her life, Breckinridge looked back at the 1910s and sharply criticized the United States for its "travesty on American family experience" through the free use of the term "American standard of living." The government had the opportunity to give meaning to the phrase when a national minimum standard of living had been discussed, but it did not do so. Breckinridge found even the work of the Economic Security Act to be inadequate in its provision.[101]

Edith Abbott's views on public provision shifted significantly from her days as a graduate student through her first decade in social research. Frequently using European models of social insurance to bolster her arguments, she became a firm advocate of universal programs over contributory plans throughout her career.[102] In her 1917 review of the Illinois mothers' pension law, Abbott pilloried local politicians for the inadequacy of grants, inconsistencies in eligibility decisions, and other failings of their administration.[103] "Local responsibility leads directly to irresponsibility," she said. No welfare system that depended on local politicians could ever produce effective social policy.[104] She wanted the state system restructured to include centralized funding, and cited the British Royal Commission on the Poor Laws as a precedent. She developed this perspective in the courses she taught at the School of Civics and Philanthropy and later at the University of Chicago. Such views, while contentious within relief communities at large, were similar to the views of other progressives on the organization of the modern state. Abbott's interest in mothers' pensions continued well through the depression and into the formulation of New Deal policies. She served on the Advisory Committee on Public Employment and Public Assistance to the President's Committee on Economic Security in 1934 and consistently opposed the continuation of relief measures like the means test, while advocating the principles of pensions and social insurance. "Social Security is still not social security if we give only to those who can prove that they are destitute," she wrote. Mothers' pensions, which had been replaced with a federal policy of categorical aid to dependent children, should be replaced, Abbott argued, with a universal child's allowance.[105]

The nation's first state-level law for public aid to dependent children in their own homes, the Funds to Parents Act, passed the legislature with more than 70 percent of the vote. In a session with over 700 House bills alone, and one that ran almost a day and a half beyond its closing deadline, the legislation faced no immediate resistance.[106] Did this easy passage signify great support for new social legislation or simply the lack of any major opposition? Contemporary observers stressed the latter point. Abbott believed that the program's popularity could be attributed to the fact that "mothers' pensions do not interfere with any great vested interests, and they do not even interfere with the taxpayers' interests, since the laws are largely optional and local authorities are not required to appropriate for them or may make their appropriations as niggardly as they please."[107] Although faced with little political opposition initially, the new policy met immediate and significant contests for control at the point of implementation—county government. The expansion of public expenditure to one sector of local government for mothers' pensions sharply defined political interests and forced pension advocates to clarify their social politics agenda.

Women's political activism was frequently represented by images of domestic activity.
University of Illinois at Chicago, The University Library, Department of Special
Collections, Woman's Civic Magazine Collection.

The Politics of Welfare Reform

Chicago residents first heard about the new policy of mothers' pensions through their churches and newspapers. In early October, Chicago's clergy devoted a part of their sermons to praise the new law. "It is humane and reasonable. It is a protection to the home, the basis of all our institutions," said one minister. "Many will think first of the dollar and cents that this law will cost the taxpayers of Cook County," warned another, "but the humanitarian consideration should come first."[1] Press coverage expanded around Thanksgiving 1911. Families had received pensions for a little more than one month, but the seasonal holiday provided a sentimental opportunity for newspapers to highlight the humanitarian aspects of the policy.[2] The city's major papers ran stories similar to the one below.

> There was Widow Smith, for example, with her little family of four, their father dead these six months.
>
> In the kitchen stove a fire burned brightly thanks to Johnny Smith's agility in corralling coal dropped by the engines "down by the yards" while the watchman's back was turned. Around the stove the children huddled, munching dry bits of bread and warming frost-pinched fingers and toes. They chattered gayly in childhood's irrepressible fashion between bites, while the mother sat far back, silently digesting the truth of their utter destitution and its consequences.
>
> To let them run about in the fall half hungry and with feet almost on the ground just to have them with her, was one thing. But to permit them to be cold and hungry without flannels, warm stockings or blankets in weather like this was unforgivable selfishness. More than that, it meant sickness—croup, pneumonia, maybe death. Almost as bad, it meant doctor's bills. Tomorrow she would end it all and do as she had been told, give the children to "the sisters" and go her way alone. . . .
>
> But a new and beautiful tomorrow dawned for the Widow Smith . . . Riding on the wings of the terrific snowstorm and the most drastic fall in temperature in a short time that Chicago has ever experienced, came the order from somebody in authority to somebody else in authority . . . "Put the 'mothers' pension' act into effect."
>
> Behold, therefore, all that week, one Mrs. Smith after another, whose

only crime has been to lose her husband and the natural provider for her children, released from sentence of indefinite earthly banishment from her family through government pension.[3]

Public representations of the policy emphasized the social value of keeping families together and the public economy achieved by aiding the "worthy" poor. The portrayals that romanticized mothers in poverty also obscured the political dissension behind the program's public face.

The significance of the events surrounding the implementation of mothers' pensions rests in what it reveals about the reorganization of political life in the early twentieth century and the shift in the distribution of public resources from parties to bureaucracies. General support for the ideals of the program did not forestall local resistance to the measure. Distinct interests quickly emerged and the policy became a site of struggle between politicians, local charities, and reform women. The County Board sought to control and to limit pensions when its privilege to control the jobs and funds associated with public aid was directly challenged by the placement of the mothers' pension program within the juvenile court. Social workers involved in social justice reforms played an important role in research, advocacy, and legislative reform. They began to forge a new route to political authority in the name of enhanced social provision for poor women and their families. Working with predominately white clubwomen in the years following suffrage, they operated as an interest group to forward an agenda of "social politics" in Chicago. The expansion of public resources directed toward mother-only families should not be viewed in isolation, however. Divided political interests, entrenched political systems, and resistance to an emerging agenda of liberalism limited the scope of the plan.[4]

This chapter begins with an account of the political conflict that quickly arose around the mothers' pension program from its inception in 1911 to the first major revision in 1913. The conflict between the Chicago Juvenile Court and the Board of County Commissioners initially presented itself as a struggle for control over administration and jobs. But the election of progressive reformer A. A. McCormick as president of the County Board in 1912 made clear another arena of political opposition in the form of fiscal control. This resistance as well as the influence of private charity agencies resulted in major restrictions to the program. During the second stage of implementation, women emerged as a political force that greatly influenced the program's expansion. Public visibility on issues of municipal welfare and the organization of women voters followed the 1914 partial franchise. At the same time, Edith Abbott and

Sophonisba Breckinridge conducted the research that would be used to expand eligibility and create a tax base for the policy. Support from clubwomen proved a vital part of that success as the policy entered a period of consolidation in its third stage during the 1920s. The chapter concludes with an examination of the interest-group politics played by Chicago's clubwomen, particularly in expanding eligibility and in ensuring appropriations, in a context defined by the loss of suffrage unity and conservatism.

THE COUNTY ADMINISTRATION
VERSUS THE JUVENILE COURT

In contrast to the warm reception given mothers' pensions by the press, county administrators balked at the new program and expressed alarm at its public cost. Peter Bartzen, president of the Board of County Commissioners, introduced the new policy by telling the commissioners that the law would be tested for its constitutionality. In particular, he challenged the state legislature's ability to pass laws that placed financial burdens upon localities. The board made a small appropriation for the policy until this issue could be resolved. Meanwhile, county agent Joseph Meyer, who oversaw distribution of county relief, expressed alarm at the enormous potential costs of the program, estimating that it would cost between $3 million and $5 million annually. "Women have been flocking in, telephoning, and writing," since the county began distributing pensions, he told the *Chicago Daily Tribune*. "All want to know how they can get a pension. . . . It is my guess we will be swamped within a short time."[5] He also warned against possible abuses of the new policy in his annual report. "The benefits of the law are readily recognized[;] and fairly and justly administered the law will result in undoubted benefit to many worthy families," he noted, "but an abuse of its provisions will result in great harm, not only in the waste of the county's money but in the encouragement of sloth and idleness."[6] Meyer pressed for a revision in the law that would limit eligibility and limit the amount of the grant.

Meyer's prediction of bankruptcy for the county was called "groundless" by others. "If blundering and demagogical, or dishonest and grafting politicians had to pass on applications the situation might in truth be serious. But the juvenile court sifts, scrutinizes and passes on them, and that puts a very different face on the case. Abuse can and will be prevented," a *Record-Herald* editorial stated.[7] The president of the Cook County Civil Service Commission, Ballard Dunn, estimated that 20,000 women would receive mothers' pensions, at a cost to the taxpayers of approximately $1 million. But, he added, the county could pay $2 million to $3 million without creating problems.[8] The ethnic papers of Chicago that covered the new policy generally applauded the state's action to aid poor families. One Polish newspaper called the mothers' pension program "the first great step on the part of society" to eliminate the "poverty . . . which torments our brave sons of labor." The same paper dismissed the county agent's fears of costs and called the estimate of $5 million a "trifle" that should be raised from corporate taxes, specifically, the Chicago meatpacking industry, "which exploits these unfortunate people."[9]

Juvenile court judge Merritt Pinckney defended the policy and argued that the stipend for pensions entailed no greater expense than that already paid to institutions for the care of dependents. While he realized that the legislation would need some adjustment, particularly in limiting who received the pensions, he believed it was "right in fundamentals" with its preference for family care over institutionalization.[10] Furthermore, Pinckney defended the new program to the public by emphasizing that great care would be taken in the "proper administration" of this program to ensure that only those in need would be included.[11] Self-sufficiency would be maintained in pensioned families. "Women will not be encouraged to give up jobs, neglect opportunities and depend wholly on the county," Pinckney told the press.[12] Such public reassurances reveal the improbability of universal maternal provision from its earliest days. The court immediately felt the pressure to mediate political criticism and allay taxpayers' fears in order to preserve the policy.[13]

The court took immediate steps to establish a plan of operation for the pension program. Pinckney enjoyed close relations with the Chicago Woman's Club, settlements, and charities. These groups played a significant role in the creation of the court and in financing probation officers during the early years. Pinckney realized the court did not have the preparation to do the work of social agencies and he called upon his associates in the private sector to assist him. He also understood that the program's success depended upon the support of these groups. "There are troubles ahead," he said in the early weeks of the program, "troubles that might result in the repealing of the law."[14] In early December, he invited representatives of the city's private agencies and select organizations to form a citizen's committee for mothers' pensions. Pinckney asked the committee to set up the program's administration, including a hiring procedure, methods of operation, and criteria for eligibility. He hoped the committee would provide a safeguard against political interference in the distribution of pension funds and he used his legal authority to dispatch the administrative work of the court to the probation staff. Edith Abbott praised Pinckney's reliance on social-work expertise and called him "a judge who is not only conspicuously honest and disinterested, but, what is more rare, genuinely open-minded and eager to accept suggestions and advice from those experienced in social work." Within a few weeks, a committee formed that represented the city's welfare agencies. It selected an executive committee and recommended five social workers to staff the new division. Julia Lathrop was among the six executive committee members.[15]

The selection of "experts" outside political appointment angered those in the county administration. County Agent Meyer objected to Pinckney's inclusion of private relief agencies in the court's work. He argued that his department's investigations were satisfactory and that such a move only led to "favoritism" on the part of private groups who "want to turn county funds to their own advantage." Meyer's objections reflected a growing concern about private-sector interference with public provision. Although both public and private agencies had served the poor in Chicago, the direct invitation to determine policy and staff positions for poor relief seemed inappropriate to county officials. Meyer had no authority over the pension program itself, but his vocal opposition would influence the actions of the citizen's committee.[16]

One of the committee's first acts established "extralegal qualifications" to limit the number of applicants. These criteria followed long-established poor relief policies. They excluded women who had relatives able to provide them with support, did not meet a one-year residency requirement, were deserted for less than two years, owned property, or were assessed to be "physically, mentally, and morally" unfit. In addition, only children under the legal working age (fourteen years at that time) could receive aid.[17] Recognizing the fragile political viability of the new policy, the citizen's committee made concessions to county administrators' fears of wildly expanded costs. Scrutiny at the local level by the county agent, an ever-increasing national spotlight on the Chicago "experiment," and a privileging of charity methods led the committee to move cautiously forward.

In January 1912, Pinckney made two administrative decisions for the policy. The Funds to Parents law created significantly more work for the court's probation department, and Pinckney created a Mothers' Pension Division to handle all these cases. The staff consisted of a director, five probation officers specifically assigned to handle pension cases, and six clerical workers to keep up with the paperwork generated by case reports. Within two years, dietitian Florence Nesbitt joined the staff. Her work on family budgets provided the data that advocates used to lobby for higher pension stipends. Those employed in the Mothers' Pension Division, like the juvenile court in general, frequently received training at the Chicago School of Civics and Philanthropy. This was the case for Emma Quinlan, director of the Mothers' Pension Division, and her supervisor, chief probation officer Joseph Moss. In addition, many students worked as probation officers in the court upon graduation. The original staff of thirteen expanded to twenty-one by 1921.[18] Pinckney also established a second committee, called the Conference Committee, to review and recommend cases for funding. This committee reviewed investigation reports and decided either to dismiss or approve the pensions. The original members included the chief probation officer and his assistant, the county agent, and representatives from five relief organizations. Later, the director of the Mothers' Pensions Division joined the committee. By April 1913, the private agency members had been phased out.[19]

The tensions surrounding pension implementation and its challenge to the political control of jobs and public funding developed into a full-blown attack on the juvenile court by the president of the County Board. The passage of the new law in June 1911 provided an opportunity for political opponents on the Cook County Board to renew their attack on the court.[20] Bartzen's campaign against the juvenile court was at its core a conflict over the control of public jobs. Seventy-five to 100 jobs went to probation officers of the juvenile court in the years 1910 to 1912. That figure swelled to 148 positions by 1913.[21] Bartzen wanted to fill the positions as temporary appointments, but the juvenile court and its supporters wanted to fill the positions with trained professionals, preferably those who passed civil service examinations. Aided by the Hearst press, Bartzen attacked the court on its performance and its competence in handling dependent care cases, and chose chief probation officer John Witter as the target for his campaign.

In July 1911, *Chicago Examiner* columnist Winifred Black wrote a series of sensational articles criticizing the work of the court and the School of Civics and Philanthropy. Black criticized the "scientific reformers," "professional philanthropists," and "theoretical mothers" whose work for the juvenile court, she said, lacked common sense and a mother's "heart full of knowledge." She raised questions and complaints about the legitimacy of state intervention in family issues, a charge that had troubled the court from its inception. But Black saved the powerful issue of race to discredit the probation work of the court. As an example of the misguided actions of the court, she criticized the placement of an African American woman, Joanna Snowden, as a probation officer in an Irish neighborhood. "Why then do you put an officer of one race or even of one nationality in authority over people of quite another color or even just belonging to another nation?" Black asked her readers. This error, just the latest in a long series of blunders, according to the columnist, should raise doubts about the court and its programs. Joanna Snowden refuted Black's assertions privately and called them "grievously wrong and unjust." She realized that her position as a black social worker in a white district was a "peculiar one," but nevertheless the quality of her work remained high and people in her district had written to say so. Nevertheless, these articles captured two points about which Americans shared great anxiety—the social relations of sex and race—and wove them into a public criticism of the activist state.[22]

While the *Chicago Examiner* articles raised doubts about the court's work among its readers, two public committees investigated the case. The county commissioners appointed a committee to examine the charges of wrongdoing. Bartzen initially appointed Henry Neil as the sole investigator for the board, but the commissioners expanded the committee to five nonpartisan citizens charged with evaluating the administration of the court and the child-caring institutions. Their report, submitted in January 1912, provided useful criticisms of the court's work, but found no evidence for censure of Witter.[23] Bartzen had not waited to hear their findings, however. In September, he suspended John Witter for failure to properly advise workers under him about the mothers' pension law and filed charges of "neglect of duty, incompetency, and lack of executive ability" with the Civil Service Commission.[24] This body formed the second investigative committee and its hearing resulted in Witter's firing despite the fact that it operated improperly.[25]

According to John Witter, Bartzen's dispute with him had more to do with filling jobs in the court with "temporary appointments," positions outside civil service regulation, than with public provision for dependent children. Witter said Bartzen had asked him to relieve some of the probation officers so that the president might make some new appointments. When he refused, Bartzen sent members of the Civil Service Commission into the field to find charges against the probation officers. The Civil Service Commission complied with Bartzen's request because his appointees had a majority on the commission. Bartzen had filled five Civil Service Commission seats in two years.[26] Ballard Dunn, who had been fired as the president of the Civil Service Commission by Bartzen, told the *Chicago Tribune* that Bartzen wanted to frame Witter so that he could fill his position. This may explain why Julia Lathrop refused to provide Henry Neil the information he requested for the commission.[27]

The conclusion of this episode took place in the courts. Witter took his case to the circuit court and in April 1912 the judge found that neither Bartzen nor the Civil Service Commission had the authority to discharge an officer of the juvenile court because the law granting authority to the civil service position was unconstitutional. The State Supreme Court upheld this decision and determined that the court held appointive powers. The decision contained an ironic twist, however. The county commissioners lost their battle to control juvenile court jobs, but reformers lost the civil service hiring provision.[28]

The second arena of conflict between the County Board and the juvenile court revolved around the increase in expenditures created by the new mothers' pension legislation. This conflict did not become partisan, as did control over jobs, but arose as a problem for both parties. At issue was the control of county expenditures and the countervailing pressure to expand the pension program. Mothers' pensions became law in June, yet the county commissioners did not consider funding for the program until October. With only a short time left in the fiscal year, the commissioners appropriated $2,000 from the Miscellaneous Purposes Fund to pay for pensions and placed them under the fiscal control of the county agent.[29] The Board authorized $75,000 from the general budget for 1912, the first full year of pension funding, as no separate tax fund had been established.[30] The amount was very small, just one-half of 1 percent of the entire county budget and only one-quarter of the amount appropriated for poor relief supplies. If the funding had been set at the maximum authorized in forthcoming (1913) legislation, it would have reached $274,768, more than three and one-half times the amount granted. All these figures were a far cry from the $3 million to $5 million originally estimated by the county agent as the cost of the program. The funding limitations set by the county commissioners exerted pressure upon the juvenile court to limit this policy.

WELFARE POLITICS IN THE 1912 CAMPAIGN FOR COUNTY BOARD PRESIDENT

The national election of 1912 and the Progressive Party's reform platform energized many Chicagoans, but local politics also drew significant attention. The campaign for president of the Cook County Board resounded with the rhetoric of welfare reform, and the issues of county funds and public jobs made the headlines. Peter Bartzen, the incumbent, received the support of the Hearst-Harrison faction of the Democratic Party and the endorsement of Hearst's *Chicago Examiner*. The challenger, Alexander A. McCormick, received the endorsements of the *Chicago Daily Tribune* and the *Record Herald*. He was an editor, Republican progressive, director of the Immigrants' Protective League, and friend of Hull House residents. Both candidates presented themselves as "friends of the poor" and characterized the opponent as a puppet of corporate interests. The incumbent was vulnerable to attacks on his policies. Headlines announced "Bartzen's Swollen County Payrolls Cut into the Food and Coal Fund

Voted for the Poor" and "Protect the Poor! Deliver the Helpless from Bartzen!"[31] Bartzen's attacks on the juvenile court and his lack of financial support for mothers' pensions gave McCormick two more points with which to galvanize members of the reform community.

Many of Chicago's white reform women lined up behind McCormick. Although women could not yet vote, both parties recognized that suffrage would soon pass and appealed to organized women. McCormick targeted the well-organized group of women reformers for whom public welfare and municipal housekeeping had been central issues. Louise de Koven Bowen sent a letter to women's club members soliciting their support for the reform candidate. In it she promised that McCormick would prevent the juvenile court from being used as a "partisan football." At a mass meeting of clubwomen for McCormick, Mrs. George Bass, president of the Chicago Woman's Club, charged Bartzen with undoing all the humanitarian work of the last ten years. Sophonisba Breckinridge and Hannah Soloman, both Democrats, also spoke against Bartzen because of his partisanship in county welfare matters.[32] Two days before the election, pro-McCormick forces held a rally at which they scourged Bartzen for dismantling the welfare institutions of the county while simultaneously increasing the number of public employees and raising salary costs threefold.[33] Louise de Koven Bowen said Bartzen made a joke of county government. He was "incapable and incompetent," jeopardized services, and hurt the county's poor and dependent population. Bowen wondered about the future of the new mothers' pension law under his administration. The policy was currently administered well by Judge Pinckney, but she feared that Bartzen waited for an opportunity "to build up a great political machine in the poor neighborhoods" through this new source of funds.[34]

Bartzen distinguished himself from his opponent by allying with the working people. He called McCormick "a 'highbrow' picked by Jane Addams and backed by the corporations to ride over the wishes of the working-men."[35] At a pre-election rally, he told the audience "I want to be elected by the votes of the laborer, the tradesmen, and the small businessman. I do not want the aid of the moneyed interests, and I couldn't have such aid if I wanted it." Bartzen also made special appeals to women. His campaign material claimed he supported mothers' pensions and fought against the separation of children from poor parents.[36] He also arranged a gathering of women as part of his campaign strategy. Winifred Black, a Bartzen supporter and the *Chicago Examiner* columnist who had written a series critical of the juvenile court, organized a "Mothers' Meeting" to demonstrate that some women in Chicago supported the Democratic candidate. Her newspaper account of that meeting described the women in attendance and their reasons for supporting the candidate.

> They came from the West Side and from the South Side . . . from the stockyards and from the river wards. . . . some there were who came wrapped from head to foot in shawls of ancient pattern. . . . And nearly every woman of them held a little child by the hand and most of them carried babies besides. . . . all of them come to testify for Peter Bartzen . . . and you could not have kept them away if the heavens had broken loose and flooded the whole of the downtown district.[37]

These women supported Bartzen because he had given aid to their families when they were desperate, the columnist claimed. Food, a bag of coal, and medical care were the benefits distributed by Bartzen individually to these indigent women. She praised Bartzen, who addressed the crowd "simply, directly, kindly, like a father talking to his big family of daughters," and she challenged the clubwomen to join the poorer women who had shown up to support "their friend." Black's account illustrated no self-awareness of her paternalist portrayal of Bartzen. Neither did she hesitate to applaud his use of public welfare services for personal political gain. Apparently unconsciously, Black's reportage substantiated reformers' claims that public welfare funds would be used for spoils under Bartzen, but she also made clear that she found no wrongdoing in it.[38]

Did the Democrats sponsor this bill for impoverished families? If Bartzen's campaign speeches can be taken at face value, it would be possible that Henry Neil had joined forces with Bartzen to promote aid to workingmen's widows. By his own admission, Bartzen recognized this as an opportunity to help constituents as well as consolidate his own power with additional patronage. But several flaws exist in this account. First, Bartzen never welcomed the policy. He challenged its constitutionality and made no attempt to fund it in a significant way. Second, poor relief supplies offered a marginal means of patronage compared to jobs. They held tremendous symbolic meaning, but relatively meager real benefits. Finally, Bartzen viewed women's political support as a defensive measure against similar strategies by Republicans. He responded like a benevolent patriarch to the widows whom he had helped. Most politicians understood that controlling the structure of provision provided the greatest gains. The challenges posed by reformers focused on control of that structure.

McCormick won the election by a slim margin of 393 votes. The majority of his support came from the country towns, and those commissioners became his most active supporters on the board.[39] His narrow victory left him in a weak position, however, and provided him little political leverage to accomplish his agenda. He spent much of his administration fighting over the budget, which had a devastating impact on the fledgling mothers' pension program.

"AID TO MOTHERS WITH CHILDREN": THE 1913 REVISION

As the new president of the County Board, McCormick began his term of office with a commitment to reduce the costs of county government. He attributed the county's deficit to the careless fiscal operations of the previous administration and the additional financial burdens of new state programs such as mothers' pensions. Within the first month of McCormick's administration, deputy comptroller Frank S. Ryan recommended that one of the county attorneys be appointed to watch the state legislature to avoid additional legislation that would increase county expenditures.[40] McCormick reappointed Joseph Meyer as county agent with the specific goal of reducing costs within the relief department. He was not disappointed. Meyer reported that $80,000 had been saved by cutting thirty-two temporary appointments and by eliminating "cheats" from the public rolls.[41] McCormick moved next to cut the costs of mothers' pensions. In early January, he held a meeting of interested parties to discuss the Funds to Parents law and its impact upon the budget. He was particularly concerned about a report produced by the Russell Sage Foundation on the Illinois law which cautioned that such aid would reduce individual initiative and family responsibilities. Chicago's status as a pioneer in the implementation of mothers' pensions made it the focus of several national discussions. Opponents saw it as "an insidious attack upon the family . . . illustrating all that is most objectionable in state Socialism." Charity administrators raised alarms about the consequences of supporting deserted families, the drain on public funds, and the "dissolution" of private responsibilities. The latter point, made again by C. C. Carstens in the Russell Sage Report, emphasized the old view on pauperism, that all private resources should be extracted from relatives before any public funds were made available.[42] McCormick criticized the ambiguity of the law, saying that it left "the county wide open to obligations unlimited" and called for a committee to work with Judge Pinckney to revise the law.[43]

As soon as they heard about it, Henry Neil and McKenzie Cleland defended the legislation and attacked McCormick and the private charities for their cautious attitude toward pensions. "The very purpose of the law is to prevent churches, relatives and other people from going in and feeding deserving people one meal a week, when twenty-one are needed."[44] Their views were quickly marginalized.

From February through March, budget battles filled the meeting agendas of the County Board. In February, McCormick vetoed specific items in the budget, calling the appropriation a "riot of extravagance" and "wasteful and criminal expenditures of the taxpayers' money." McCormick urged the Finance Committee to cut the mothers' pension appropriation from $250,000 to $150,000, arguing that if it was not changed "the major portion of the county's money this year might have to go to pay these pensions." In March, the budget stalemate threatened payments of pensions when the absence of a quorum almost prevented the allocation of funds from being made. The final budget compromise included a pension appropriation of $165,000.[45]

While McCormick worked on the budget with the county commissioners, Pinckney worked with the citizen's advisory committee to write a new law. The proposed legislation, "Aid to Mothers and Children," was not an amendment to the previous act, but rather an entirely new piece of legislation. It put into effect one of the most severely restrictive sets of eligibility requirements existent in pension legislation at the time. It defined specific conditions under which mothers could work but made pensions mandatory for all counties. The new law left administrative control to the juvenile court, but it clarified the process of application and investigation, the role of probationary officers, and specific grant amounts. Finally, it provided a tax revenue plan to fund the policy. On 25 March 1913, Senate Bill 300 was submitted to the state senate. County agent Joseph Meyer actively lobbied for the bill's passage in Springfield. In Chicago, McCormick brought the issue of mothers' pensions to the county commissioners again. This time he sought and received their endorsement for the proposed restrictions to the policy. With significant support from both the court and commissioners, the legislation passed both houses of the state legislature in June.[46]

The new eligibility standards of the 1913 Mothers' Aid law allowed only widows or wives of permanently disabled men to apply. They could receive "partial support" if they had children under fourteen years of age living at home. Approximately 16 percent of the women lost their aid because they were either divorced or deserted. The judge justified the exclusion of deserted women as a precaution against "the desertion microbe" which set "indifferent husbands" to abandon their families.[47] The greatest number of people lost benefits because of the new citizenship requirement. The severity of the restriction on immigrants may be attributed to the influence of County Agent Meyer's virulent anti-immigration sentiments. He frequently advocated the deportation of dependent immigrants. It was an odd position for McCormick to sponsor, however. Aside from his position as president of the County Board, he had been president of the Immigrants' Protective League and remained closely associated with it. Finally, the new law provided revenues for the policy through a tax-based fund. It authorized a county tax of up to "three-tenths of one mill on the dollar annually on all taxable property" to be collected with the general taxes and set aside specifically for the mothers' pension fund.[48] This provision met significant opposition, and it was declared unconstitutional by the Illinois Supreme Court in 1915.

The revised law clearly defined the centrality of wage-earning within the pension program. Pinckney defended the policy in its early days with reassurances that women would keep paid employment when possible and that every measure would be taken to keep families from utter dependency upon the county. These pressures to ensure self-support became institutionalized in the 1913 revision when it specified the wage-work requirements for able-bodied mothers. "She [the mother] may be absent for work a definite number of days each week to be specified in the court's order, when such work, can be done by her without the sacrifice of health or the neglect of home and children," the bill stated.[49] This provision prevented any form of universal entitlement, while it hampered women's ability to earn by promoting limits on the amount of time they worked outside the home.

The support for such a proposal by those in the court who claimed to want a policy for poor mothers must be found in the concessions of the policy process. The new policy had not received the full endorsement of the public. In fact, it had raised fears about ever expanding public costs. Furthermore, no distinct political constituency had lobbied for the initial law. The national social-work community also cast its intense and critical gaze on Chicago. The city had embarked on a risky venture in their eyes and many states watched, discussed, and freely criticized the process. In a context of political opposition, public fears of misused public funds, social workers' concerns for administration, and the absence of any specific political constituency, the court compromised the policy. The revised plan held out the possibility of acceptance in the short term with the potential for expansion later. However, the tenets of control and supervision over indigent women became essential components of the policy's continuation. The court selected families for mothers' pensions who had "less difficult" problems to address. In the words of the county agent,

> This form of relief will fail with mothers who even though they meet all other requirements of the law and willingly accept advice yet through ignorance and incompetency fail to follow it, unless they are visited frequently and very carefully and intelligently supervised in their care of

their children and their expenditure of money . . . [and] with mothers who
. . . are willfully negligent, oppose supervision, reject friendly counsel and
are untrustworthy.[50]

Those families who presented a more complex situation, such as deserted families, felt the brunt of the compromise. While public sympathies might extend a certain generosity to the widow, aid to deserted families implied not only sympathy for the woman and children, but a willingness to relieve the deserting husband of his legal responsibility for their support. Joel Hunter, chief probation officer at the time, told the National Conference of Social Work years later that such concerns had shaped the restrictive legislation of 1913.[51]

The new law not only resulted in a severe reduction in the breadth of support available for single mothers, but it also changed the central concept of provision from one of a minimum standard of living to one that mirrored relief policies. The original Funds to Parents Act authorized the state to provide indigent but otherwise sound parents "the amount of money necessary . . . to properly care for [the] child."[52] This measure of social insurance was replaced with the concept of "partial support" in the Aid to Mothers law. The revision recognized that the state had some responsibility, but it also expected family members, including the mother, to earn wages and contribute to the family's income. The language of relief, which had been entirely absent from the first law, was clearly articulated in the 1913 law. The indigent mother made an "order of relief" to the court, was selected on the basis of need, and was exposed to the punitive and investigative methods of poor relief. The political opposition and private charity influences of the initial period of implementation became imprinted in the law.

The human cost of the revisions are evident from the case history of one family dropped from the rolls because of the father's desertion. Known to us only as "Mrs. R," the mother worked outside the home as a scrubwoman to support her family after her husband left. After she contracted tuberculosis, she eventually received a pension that allowed her to stop earning until she could recover. The 1913 revisions resulted in the cancellation of her pension, however, and she was referred to a private charity. The case history notes that she rejected the referral and returned to work instead.

> Mrs. R began scrubbing again in the county building, where for the next
> two years she earned $60 a month. . . . When the family was visited by the
> investigator, they were living in a dark apartment in a rear tenement,
> crowded in between two higher buildings. The children who were at home
> were frail and delicate, and their mother said they were tubercular. In ver-

ifying this statement at the municipal tuberculosis sanitarium, the records showed that the mother herself was in the second stage of tuberculosis, moderately advanced, two of the children were glandular and in need of treatment; and one girl was in the first stage in need of sanitarium care.

The recorder of Mrs. R's story concluded that in this family "the costs of 'independence' had been too great." [53]

Having watched the politics of the 1913 revision from the sidelines, Breckinridge and Abbott moved quickly to use research to expand the policy. Their work argued for the need to increase women's wages and pointed out the social costs of neglecting to do so. Breckinridge examined the effects of occupational segregation on the wage gap between male and female workers. Minimum wage laws for women would counteract the negative effect of industrial forces when workers' organization was too weak. Abbott's research demonstrated that women's wages were not discretionary income, but made up an essential part of the family income. Improving the value of women's wages would save society money, she argued, because low wages and deteriorating health eventually forced women to leave wage-earning and rely upon public or private relief to support their children.[54]

In the spring and summer of 1913, Abbott published two pieces critical of the mothers' pension program. The major article, published in the *American Economic Review*, responded to C. C. Carstens' report on publicly funded pension programs for single mothers. This was the same report that attracted the attention of McCormick and led to his call for a limitation in the Illinois pension law. In her article, Abbott argued that the provision of aid to indigent single mothers might have been handled best without a new public policy. Since the 1911 law, however, the operation of the policy in Chicago had been superior to that provided by the poor relief office. Abbott defended the social work and training of many students who presently worked in the Mothers' Pension Division of the juvenile court, but she also attacked the "brutality" of the county agent's methods of investigation. Finally, she argued that the policy must be removed from the court to a separate administrative body to avoid "chaos and corruption" in the event that an unsympathetic judge should assume authority over the policy.[55] Abbott's defense of the mothers' pension policy was qualified and revealed her reluctance regarding public aid. She was cautious, yet critical of the duplication of efforts by a public agency (like Cook County's poor relief office) with its untrained workers and vulnerability to political administrations. Her solution revolved around the construction of new administrative structures that she hoped would remain outside the politicians' reach.

Shortly after the passage of the Aid to Mothers law, the School of Civics and Philanthropy organized a study on the effects of the cutbacks. The department of social investigation under the directorship of Breckinridge and Abbott worked with the Mothers' Pension Division of the juvenile court to evaluate 1,115 families whose pension applications were denied owing to the provisions of the new law. One of the main purposes of the study was to provide sufficient information to support an expansionary revision of the new law.[56] The survey documented the drastic effect of the new law on previously pensioned families. The new law hit children hardest, eliminating 79 percent of them from the rolls because their mothers no longer met the qualifications. Children of unnaturalized immigrants made up two-thirds of this number. At the time, a married woman's citizenship followed that of her husband, a law that remained in effect until the Cable Act of 1922.[57] All of the families received referrals to county poor relief as well as private charity organizations, but only half of the previously pensioned families replaced that aid with another source. Eighteen percent made their own arrangements, 20 percent used a combination of relief and self-support. Families were broken up and children institutionalized in 4 percent of the homes.[58] The survey made clear that the withdrawal of pension funds as a result of the 1913 law was comparable to the crisis experienced in a family after the death of the father. Family income declined severely and it was frequently accompanied by the worsening health and overwork of the mother, as was evident in the case of "Mrs. R."

Abbott and Breckinridge used these findings to lobby for the expansion of the Mothers' Aid law in 1915. They encouraged Julia Lathrop to use the resources of the Children's Bureau to generate studies on the new policy. As the first chief of the new federal bureau, Lathrop directed the bureau's research toward anti–child labor laws and maternal-infant health care. She authorized the compilation of information on mothers' pension legislation nationally and internationally, the formation of a clearinghouse on information about states' mothers' pension bills, and the production of materials on the expansion of mothers' pension eligibility and standards.[59] In addition, the Children's Bureau sponsored state-level research on working mothers and juvenile courts which produced supportive documentation for those who advocated higher standards in pension legislation. Lathrop maintained her professional and personal relationships with colleagues at the Chicago School of Civics and Philanthropy through frequent contracts for bureau research.

The dissension between the county administration and the juvenile court exposed the contest for authority over mothers' pensions and the larger battle over the distribution of public resources. Regardless of party affiliation, "machine" or "reform" status, the presidents of the Board of County Commissioners moved to limit the mothers' pension policy quickly. Bartzen attempted to discredit the court and acquire the privilege of making job appointments. McCormick used his alliances with the court and the reform community to negotiate a reduction in the eligibility of the policy. The juvenile court succeeded in obtaining control over the operation of the program and jobs, but the county officials captured a larger prize when they succeeded in having a new restrictive law written. Within this context, support for enlarging the policy came from social researchers interested in obtaining equity for women in work opportunities and protection in social provision. This agenda complemented their other agenda to dislodge politicians' control over public aid. Edith Abbott and Sophonisba Breckinridge followed the policy closely, conducted research on the effects of the 1913 revision, and solicited their colleague Julia Lathrop to collect data on mothers' pension policies nationally. The tensions of the early years would continue, but the emergence of women as a new force in Chicago politics helped to expand the benefits of the policy.

§

High unemployment and labor unrest rocked Chicago in 1915. The year began with a March of the Unemployed and ended with a prolonged strike by garment workers. Unemployed workers held a meeting in January to plan a march to call attention to the needs of those out of work. The meeting's featured speaker was Lucy Parsons, widow of Albert Parsons, who was hanged for his involvement in the Haymarket Riot. Following the meeting, 1,800 unemployed men, women, and children marched onto Halsted Street carrying signs that read: "We want work, not charity," "We Have Neither Food, nor Shelter," and "We Refuse to Starve." They were met and stopped by police. According to one participant, "shots were fired, clothes were torn, eyes blackened, and heads cracked while clubs, blackjacks, and revolver butts were used with bruising effect on heads, arms, and knuckles." Twenty-one people went to jail for what the police described as "incendiary" activities. Sophonisba Breckinridge attended the meeting but she heard nothing in the speeches or the subsequent march to provoke violence. She accompanied Jane Addams to the jail to assist in securing the release of the marchers.[60]

Deteriorating economic conditions continued to produce tremendous stress for workers' families through the spring. Mayor William "Big Bill" Thompson referred to the problems of the unemployed and underpaid in his inaugural mayoral address in April 1915, but he was unwilling to intervene between workers and management when garment workers went out on strike in November of that year.[61] The desperate situation of young working girls was made uncomfortably clear by Grace Abbott when she noted that they received their wages—as little as thirteen cents a day—in pay envelopes printed with the inscription "save a dollar of your pay each week."[62]

Women reformers argued that the solution to economic and social problems rested in the expansion of the franchise. Illinois women won partial suffrage in 1913 and full voting rights in 1920; thus the era of pension implementation offers a clear demonstration of the impact of women's voting power. Initially, women's reform organizations promoted the election of the "right people" for political office as well as a social legislative agenda. It did not take long, however, for the diverse political interests of women to become visible and for different paths to be chosen. The following section focuses on the divergent allegiances that emerged among Chicago's middle-class women reformers. The new political culture shaped mothers' pensions in two ways. Organized women became a more visible and vocal advocacy group for the expansion of the mothers' pension law, particularly after 1918. And some advocates of nonpartisan politics pursued an alternative route to political authority using new administrative capacities.

"A New Force in Chicago Politics"

The state legislature passed a limited woman suffrage bill in June 1913.[63] In anticipation of their new political power, Chicago clubwomen ran massive registration campaigns, conducted voter education programs, and promoted women for public office. Eight women filed petitions for "alderwomanic" positions, including Sophonisba Breckinridge, Mary McDowell, and Marion Drake.[64] The Republican, Democratic, and Progressive parties placed women candidates on their tickets for county commissioner seats in 1914. The Woman's City Club endorsed Mary McDowell and Harriet Vittum for the county positions.[65] The County Board presented a logical entry into officeholding in that it fit within the turn-of-the-century framework of middle-class women's political ideology, one that identified the city as an extension of the home. The constituency served by the County Board included the aged, ill, indigent, and children. "Woman's place in the home has been that of nurse and comforter," candidate Harriet Vittum stated. "She can just as well be a public welfare nurse and comforter."[66] Male allies also used gender symbols in speeches about the place of women in public life. Alexander McCormick told Progressive Party supporters, for example, that "the refining influence[s] of women members are needed on that [County] board."[67] The newly enfranchised women claimed these offices as their domain. The excitement of this pioneering election can be seen in Vittum and McDowell's election committee. Grace Abbott directed the committee, which included some of the city's most distinguished women reformers, such as Jane Addams, Sophonisba P. Breckinridge, Anna Wilmarth, Ida B. Wells-Barnett, Fannie Barrier Williams and Agnes Nestor.[68]

Many of these women wanted to win public office so they could challenge the power structure of political parties. If elected, they wanted to reduce the ability of party bosses to make patronage appointments. As Mary McDowell wrote, "We may have to use machinery at hand to make a new and better kind of machinery that shall be possessed and fed by an intelligent public opinion, and not be owned and run *by* a Party *of* a Party and *for* a Party, but by the People, of the People and for the People." McDowell's statement assumed that "the people" had harmonious interests and she overlooked conflicting social and political agendas. Yet, her words indicate how these women hoped to use their new political positions to reshape local politics.[69]

McDowell and Vittum were the only women to win in the primaries. This early victory for women reformers lasted briefly. The next month, the Supreme Court excluded County Board offices from the 1913 suffrage.[70] Despite this limitation upon voting, these reformers turned their attention to a campaign for better social legislation. In January 1915, the Woman's Legislative Congress, a coalition of representatives from women's organizations across the state, assembled in Chicago to discuss "bills for social betterment" to be submitted to the state legislature that winter. The roster included sixteen bills that addressed wages and hours, child labor, education, and the support of abandoned families or children born outside marriage.[71] The next challenge for the social agenda came from within the body of mobilized women rather than outside.

In the spring of 1915, Chicago women had their first opportunity to vote for mayor. William Thompson and Judge Harry Olson faced each other in the Republican primary. Louise de Koven Bowen appealed to the Woman's City Club members to vote in the upcoming election. The Woman's City Club had organized in 1910 "to bring together women interested in promoting the welfare of the city," and it described its work as "a constructive fight" that would challenge the spoils system, elevate home life, and call women to their "civic patriotism."[72] The woman who failed to take her first opportunity to vote for Chicago's mayor, Bowen said, would "put herself on record as a poor housekeeper, a poor mother, and a poor citizen."[73] The progressive settlement workers and many among the Woman's City Club membership backed Olson. But African American women reformers viewed the contest between Olson and Thompson quite differently.

For several years, African Americans in the Second and Third Wards worked with the political parties for greater representation in local and state politics. Both factions of the Republican organization solicited African Americans' political support, but black voters increasingly wanted their own man in the city council. "The Jew has a representative, the Irish has a representative, the Italian has a representative, the Polack has a representative. Why not the Negro?" the *Defender* asked its readers.[74] Representation in municipal government would bring public resources to the predominantly black wards. In addition to playgrounds, parks, streets, and sanitation, a "race man" in the city council would protect the constituents' interests in schools and public jobs. In the spring of 1914, the first election in which women could vote, William Randolph Cowan ran independently in the primary as the race candidate from the Second Ward. His campaign appealed to women voters and raised the important issue of local services to the community. Support for Cowan would "Protect Your Home, Your Children, Your Property," a *Defender* article advised. Cowan lost to the ward organization candidate by only 167 votes.[75]

The campaigns of 1915 held greater promise. Oscar DePriest received the support of the Second Ward Republican organization and won in the primaries. According to Ida B. Wells-Barnett's autobiography, William Thompson needed the labor vote and the black vote to win the mayoral campaign. He promised the African American community that his administration would not discriminate in appointments and that he would build a well-equipped school in the area.[76] Wells-Barnett organized the Alpha Suffrage Club in 1913 to win the vote for women, to promote African American candidates, and to defeat discriminatory national legislation.[77] That club campaigned for Cowan's challenge in 1914 and endorsed DePriest for alderman and Thompson for mayor.[78] Wells-Barnett actively worked for Thompson for six months until the regular Republican organization put Harry Olson on the primary ballot. Olson had appointed her a probation officer, a position she used to enhance the work of the Negro Fellowship League. She stopped campaigning three weeks before the election, an action which she later wrote lost her influence in Thompson's administration.[79]

DePriest and Thompson won. The outcome, which disappointed so many white women reformers, was seen initially as a major triumph by many within the black community. Thompson appointed DePriest to committees for schools, police, fire, and public health; and he appointed Edward H. Wright as assistant corporation council over the objections of others. According to the *Defender*, DePriest and Thompson passed, as one of the first acts of the new administration, a resolution making August 23 a holiday in honor of emancipation.[80] Wells-Barnett found the election a missed blessing. African American politicians would experience greater recognition in the Thompson administration, but the community never saw the full benefits of public services promised in the campaign. As James Grossman has argued, black citizens continued to receive limited public resources and symbolic patronage.[81]

Edith Abbott's analysis of the women's vote in 1915 and 1916 attempted to highlight gender differences and made no mention of race or ethnic interests in the campaigns. The greatest difference in voting behavior appeared in the primary and on bond issues where women voted for "good government," she said. As for the general election, over one-half of the women voters supported Thompson in the general election across the city. Nearly 70 percent of the women who voted in the Second Ward voted for Thompson, and nearly 64 percent did so in the Third Ward. In his reelection campaign of 1919, Thompson again carried the Second Ward, with 74 percent of women voters. Abbott wrote that Thompson's election placed Chicago "in the hands of spoilsmen" and "one of the most vicious political machines that ever controlled the administration of a great city." The division in voting patterns also appeared in the presidential election of 1916, when the majority of Illinois women supported Charles Hughes over Woodrow Wilson. The *New York Evening Post* noted that "the drift to Wilson among clubwomen, the social workers, and the leading peace advocates did not materially affect the great majority of the non-club and non-political women." Even among Chicago's politically active, reform-minded clubwomen, the election illustrated the different agendas of the new voters.[82]

About one year after the 1915 mayoral election, the Woman's City Club organized a mass meeting to protest the actions of the Thompson administration and to rejuvenate the women's reform agenda. The 3,000 women who attended the meeting were read a Woman's Municipal Platform, a plan of action on municipal problems ranging from civil service to public welfare to housing.[83] In what the *Record Herald* called "an impressive demonstration of the new force in Chicago politics," the women criticized the mayor for backsliding on civil service, reducing the effectiveness of the Department of Public Welfare, and politicizing the Board of Education. Despite the assertion of the organizers that the platform stood for "principles, not men," the meeting had the distinct air of an election rally designed to inform and agitate forces against the Thompson machine.[84] Throughout the winter of 1916–1917, the Woman's City Club continued to discuss plans to generate a broader base of support throughout the city in an attempt to rectify the lack of cohesion in the women's vote. Jane Addams appealed to the members to get outside their own group and make links with other women around the city. The president of the Chicago Equal Suffrage Association, Mrs. James Morrison, called upon members to extend their network. "We are all dependent on each other," she said; "we have all got to stand or fall together."[85]

The Aid to Mothers law was revised several times over the next few years. The legislature discussed several liberalizing amendments to the mothers' pension law during the 1915 session. The House passed a series of amendments that would include women who had been deserted two or more years, had applied for their first papers of citizenship, and had dower's rights not exceeding $1,000. In addition, the House raised the minimum stipend for families from $50 to $60 a month. The Senate deleted the provisions for deserted women and those with property interests. It restricted the benefits to noncitizen families by limiting aid to the American-born children. The House approved the Senate amendments, leaving only a moderate expansion of the policy. The property provision passed during the next session of the legislature in 1917, but deserted women remained ineligible until 1923 (see Appendix).[86] Nevertheless, the new amendments had an immediate effect. The number of grants in Cook County increased 58 percent during the first six months.

The most troubling problem for local politicians, the funding of pensions, remained unresolved. The State Supreme Court declared the 1913 tax provision unconstitutional in 1915. That decision left full discretion for the appropriation of funds to the County Board. The juvenile court did not hesitate to spend more than was authorized, however, overspending by $20,000 to $30,000 in 1915 and 1916. Frustrations over the imprecise funding mechanisms led County Board president Peter Reinberg to ask the court and the county to appeal to the state legislature, or stay within the appropriated budget.[87]

Such an appeal was not made to the legislature in 1917 and families who would have benefited from mothers' pensions experienced increasing economic pressures.[88] The juvenile court began to keep a waiting list of families who applied for pensions but for whom funding was unavailable. By the end of 1917, the waiting list had 400 families on it. The insufficient appropriations also adversely affected those receiving pensions. Inflation eroded the real value of the pension and the likelihood of stipend increases remained small. Representatives of the Woman's City Club lobbied the county and succeeded in getting county commissioner Thomas Kasperski to request a $75,000 increase in the mothers' pension budget for 1918. The previous year's appropriation had proven "so far inadequate that no new pensions have been granted during the last six months," Kasperski argued.[89] Even with additional funding, no new applicants were accepted between June 1918 and the end of the year. Those who had previously received aid were readmitted only when another grant was cancelled. County Board President Reinberg depicted a bleak environment for workers' families in his annual address, as he noted the impact of industrial conditions from the dislocation of World War I on the increase in demand for relief in general. "This condition goes to show that the increase in wages has not kept pace with the growing cost of living and that hundreds of families who have hitherto been able to live on their earnings during spring and summer months were last season unable to do so."[90] The court asked private agencies to provide supplemental aid, but some hesitated because they considered such action politically dangerous. Covering the costs of public agencies "would relieve the tension on public officials . . . and would hinder rather than promote additional legislation needed to make such relief adequate." In December, 900 applicants waited for aid.[91]

The funding problem received more concerted effort in the next legislative session. Reinberg again asked all interested parties from both the public and private sectors to draft a measure for the legislature that could produce needed revenues. The county agent followed through, soliciting advice and support from county commissioners, the juvenile court judge, the state's attorney, and representatives of private organizations.[92] The chief probation officer appealed to maternalist sentiments to gain public sympathy for new funding. Quoting English sociologist L. T. Hobhouse, the court revived the ideal of a maternal endowment.

> If we take in earnest all that we say of the duties and responsibilities of motherhood, we shall recognize that the mother of young children is doing better service to the community and one more worthy of pecuniary remuneration, when she stays at home and minds her children than when she goes out charing and leaves them to the chances of the street or to the care of the neighbor. In proportion as we realize the force of these arguments, we reverse our views as to the nature of public assistance in such a case. We no longer consider it advisable to drive the mother out to her charing work, nor do we consider her degraded by receiving public money. We cease in fact to regard the public money as a dole; we treat it as a payment for civic service and the condition that we are trying to exact is precisely that she should not endeavor to add to it by earning wages but rather that she should keep her home respectable and bring up her children in health and happiness.[93]

On a practical level, the court proposed a property tax to be collected with general taxes but held in a separate fund specifically for pensions.[94]

A tax-based plan for funding the mothers' pension policy finally received Supreme Court approval in June 1919. A tax rate of four-fifteenths of a mill in counties with a population over 300,000 succeeded over other more generous proposals. From this point on, it was not a matter of how the revenue would be raised, but rather what millage would be politically acceptable. Women reformers seeking to expand the tax base in 1921 succeeded in raising the allotment to four-tenths of a mill, a compromise from their original request for six-tenths. This rate remained in effect until 1927. During that legislative session, organized clubwomen again tried to raise the millage to six-tenths. The House approved it in June but several counterproposals in the Senate led to the passage of an alternate bill in July, one that actually decreased the tax rate to three-tenths of a mill.[95]

"A NEW FORM OF STATE AID"

Between 1916 and 1919, Abbott and Breckinridge undertook a series of teaching and research projects that promoted an expanded role for government in social provision. Their course, "Social Politics," exposed students to the "modern methods of social insurance" that included mothers' pensions, workmen's compensation, and old-age pensions. Students in the department of social investigation worked on several studies concerning the juvenile court and social policy. The most significant of these projects relative to mothers' pensions was the major review of the Illinois' Aid to Mothers Law requested by the Children's Bureau. Although the Children's Bureau had developed several comparative studies of pension legislation and administration in specific localities, this provided the first in-depth study of the policy for an individual state.[96]

Julia Lathrop wrote Graham Taylor in 1915 to ask if the School of Civics and Philanthropy would undertake the state-wide study and specifically requested that Abbott and Breckinridge direct it. They agreed and within the month Lathrop had secured the support of Judge Pinckney and the State Charities Commission.[97] Abbott and Breckinridge used the 1917 court records for families on mothers' pensions as well as the 1913 research that measured the impact of the law's change. Their conclusions indicted the system for "irresponsible local administration" and promoted the "new principle of State control." Left to localities, the law remained unenforced or illegally operated. Even their praise for the Cook County program was qualified by their dismay that these gains could be rapidly erased by a change in the assignment of the juvenile court judge.[98]

The study proposed three changes to make public aid more effective: centralized administration, trained professional employees, and state funding for operations. For the program to operate as it was intended, it must be organized and administered at the state level. Central coordination could ensure that counties provided funds to families and practiced consistent methods. The centralized program would be effective, however, only if trained social service professionals conducted the operations. Pursuing their challenge to politicians' control over jobs, the plan suggested that a merit process be used to hire a professional staff. Finally, the state must provide funds to counties for the program. Revenue pooling and the central distribution of funds would equalize benefits across the counties regardless of individual differences in wealth. "If the State wants its mothers' pension law to be properly administered, State aid must be provided in some form, a pooling of resources so that the rich counties can help the poorer and more backward counties."[99] State subsidies to counties would end the damaging budget cuts by "parsimonious county boards" whose restrictions severely affected the economic health of families and stalled the benefits of policies. Abbott and Breckinridge's attempt to expand legislation in 1915 and the subsequent restrictions by the county commissioners no doubt influenced their thinking on this point. Furthermore, Abbott and Breckinridge recommended that if the state legislature expanded the program it must assist counties with a method to finance those additional increases. "Legislation increasing the number of beneficiaries must be accompanied by legislation guaranteeing a State subsidy or support from State funds to provide the new pensions," they said, "or the statute will remain, in its neglect of provisions for enforcement, an official mockery of the needs of the poor."[100] The proposals for change in the mothers' pension program had obvious benefits for the authors. As founders of the field of social work, they were creating a niche for their students and colleagues. However, this need not overshadow the political dimensions of their proposals. The ideas of centralization, cost-sharing, and equalized redistribution of services were components of a restructured politics. It was the most ambitious articulation of state activism to date in their work.

Abbott and Breckinridge had the improvement of the mothers' pension policy in mind with these recommendations, but their agenda went beyond one specific policy. Their report suggested that a well-organized mothers' pension policy contained "the nucleus of a new form of State aid vastly superior to any form of public assistance which our American States have known, and capable of being very considerably extended."[101] The obvious place to work for this provision would have been within the social insurance movement, yet mothers'

pensions found little support there. Furthermore, Abbott and Breckinridge
found fault with contemporary social insurance plans developed by the American Association for Labor Legislation on two counts. They objected to the de-
duction of workers' wages to provide a significant share of the costs. They
found that the plans ignored pertinent issues of working women—not only
young single women, but older women who were in the workforce to support
their families. In contrast to other social insurance advocates, Abbott, in particular, used the mothers' pension policy, without its means test, as a model for a
new form of noncontributory social provision.[102]

Abbott reiterated the recommendations of the Illinois mothers' pension
study in an address to the National Conference of Social Work in 1917. The
problems of social welfare could not be addressed by the juvenile court system,
she said, because the majority of judges lacked the "social intelligence" to administer the policy. Mothers' pensions were originally placed in the juvenile
court to eliminate the poor relief machinery, but the courts and private agencies
had subverted that goal and made it relief once again. Social justice could be
achieved only with "a new public assistance authority that would give adequate
care to all." Only the state could support the scope of such a project. Illinois had
already created the foundation for such a structure with the recently formed Illinois State Department of Welfare, yet the proposal put forth by Abbott and
Breckinridge was far more ambitious.[103]

Abbott and Breckinridge put their policy recommendations into legal
form in 1919 when they proposed two amendments to the mothers' aid law.
Ernst Freund drafted the amendments that would place program supervision
under the Department of Public Welfare and authorize state subsidies for the
policy, sections 15-A and 17, respectively. Breckinridge thought that Morton D.
Hull would introduce the legislation and wrote chief probation officer Joseph
Moss for his support. However, judge Victor Arnold of the juvenile court did
not support the propositions, which may account for their lack of success at
that time. Abbott and Breckinridge continued to work with the chief probation
officer and women's organizations to apply pressure for the expansion of
the policy.[104]

Many women's clubs had directed their energies toward civil defense
work during the war; but, following the Armistice they returned to social problems and the government's role in solving them. The Women's Committees of
the State Council of Defense were encouraged to continue their work but to focus on social service programs. The war had increased the numbers of deser-
tions, and more public services were needed to help mother-only families. Cities
needed a new revenue system to meet the current debt crises and to shrink bud-

get deficits. "It is important to develop public opinion throughout the state on these problems," one newspaper reported. "Public opinion should insist on adequate appropriations for city, county and state work and the enforcement of social legislation." Among the endorsed social policies was the expansion of the mothers' pension program. Clubs like the Chicago Woman's Club and the Woman's City Club that had been unusually silent on this policy despite their interest in larger welfare issues began to work energetically for pensions after the war.[105]

The first direct measure came from the Woman's City Club. Harriet Vittum, chair of the Committee on Cook County Affairs, began to study the appropriations for the mothers' pension program in December. Vittum personally attended the county commissioner's meetings and those of its finance committee during the budget-making process to represent the club members' interests in regard to mothers' pension funds. In response to the 900 eligible families who remained unable to receive pensions because of funding shortages, Vittum submitted a resolution to the Woman's City Club that the appropriation be no less that $330,000 for the year. The county appropriated $320,000 for 1919. The figure fell short of the request, but it nevertheless amounted to a 23 percent gain over the previous year.[106]

In December 1918, the 300 delegates who attended the annual meeting of the Women's Legislative Congress supported a proposal that "mothers should receive a compensation for the profession of motherhood," a clear reference to pensions. In addition, they endorsed day nurseries to aid working mothers and a shorter work week "so the father can give personal care to the child."[107] Within a few months, the Woman's City Club endorsed Senate Bill 26, which would increase the tax millage for the mothers' pension fund. Although the millage was significantly reduced before passage, these endorsements provide examples of Chicago clubwomen's support for the pensions.[108]

As diverse patterns of political participation developed during the 1910s, Abbott and Breckinridge aligned themselves with a nonpartisan political strategy advocating that women develop political power outside the mainstream parties. More important for the development of mothers' pensions, they advocated the formation of centralized public welfare services, which they hoped would remove the patronage from social policy. These nonelectoral strategies became increasingly important as women's voting patterns made it clear that the social welfare agenda would not direct the "women's vote." The 1919 mayoral campaign replayed the lessons of 1915. The Woman's City Club and Hull House reformers supported University of Chicago professor Charles Merriam's bid against incumbent William Thompson and lost. A Chicago-based newspaper called the *Women's Press* derisively characterized those in the Woman's City Club who supported Charles Merriam's failed bid. "This same group of women has been assuming for years that they always 'spoke for the women of Chicago.' Perhaps they did in matters of reform, but practical politics is something else. This one election proves conclusively that this group of women wields very little power in politics." The newspaper reported that its lack of support for Merriam as a candidate was due largely to its dissatisfaction with this type of organization. "We must remember that the great mass of women do not like the militant type of American womanhood that eternally tries to arrange the affairs of the world and is eternally injecting her own personality into hazy reform movements."[109]

Dissension also arose within the Woman's City Club. Edith Abbott recounted the debate that took place within the club immediately after the federal suffrage victory, between those who favored a nonpartisan strategy and those who advocated party participation.

> After the amendment had given all women the right to vote, the question about what to do with the old suffrage organizations was one about which there were differences of opinion. Many of the long-time suffragists were anxious that the women should continue to work together on a non-partisan basis for good government and a plan for a new organization that came to be called the League of Women Voters was widely supported. Other suffragists, and Mrs. [Ruth Hanna] McCormick was one of this group, thought that the old women's suffrage associations that were no longer needed should be disbanded and the women should in the future work in their political parties.[110]

Advocates for nonpartisanship won that round within the Woman's City Club, but the strategy did not galvanize women voters across the city.

African American women found themselves on the defensive in an increasingly hostile environment in the late 1910s. Race tensions increased steadily in Chicago with the migration of southerners to the city and the increased political visibility of African Americans within the Thompson administration. Tensions exploded in late July 1919 in a race riot that lasted several days, but evidence of violence had preceded that eruption and would continue for years after. In just less than three years, fifty-eight bombs were exploded in African American homes in Chicago.[111] In addition, clubwomen engaged in local battles against the Ku Klux Klan to protest the film presentation of *Birth of a Nation*. This political context set African American reformers on a different path from the nonpartisan reform agenda advocated by white reformers like

Abbott.[112] Nevertheless, African American clubwomen worked in conjunction with the Woman's City Club, the Illinois League of Women Voters, the Federation of Colored Women's Clubs, and the Chicago and Northern District Association of Clubwomen on political education and reform issues.[113]

"Good laws are dust and ashes if administered in bad faith, in stupidity," Julia Lathrop told an audience of newly enfranchised women. "Whenever and wherever offices are used to pay political purposes, the primary duty of the official becomes not his duty to the public but to that power which gave him his office."[114] In this speech, Julia Lathrop restated an old theme that Hull House reformers had voiced from the time they challenged alderman Johnny Powers. As long as "the wrong" people were in office, whether elected or appointed, the reform agenda would suffer. But Lathrop also pointed to state-building in her speech. The administration of public services, including welfare, must be outside of political patronage and administered by professionals. The welfare functions of the state should be organized and funded through a central state agency whose director and workers were hired by merit, not placed by political appointment. The mothers' pension program was the test case for this vision of the activist state. Interest-group tactics had already proved successful as a counterpressure to county politics. During the 1920s, an era characterized by its decline in social policies, the Chicago and Northern District Association of Clubwomen continued to draw upon the mobilization of women's voluntary organizations. In particular, the Woman's City Club and the League of Women Voters applied pressure to the political system and enlarged the policy for "dependent mothers."

§

The decade of the 1920s began with great optimism for politically active women. Ratification of woman suffrage and the passage of federal maternal-infant protection held the promise of success for major social legislation of the 1910s. But the decade also contained elements of radical conservatism, intensifying racist, anti-immigration, and anti-labor sentiments. In contrast to the decade's popular image of robust economic health, the economy experienced a severe postwar depression and weakness toward the end of the decade which sent large numbers of Chicagoans to seek public aid. These events set the context for the last phase of mothers' pensions implementation in Chicago. Representatives of the city's major women's clubs picked up their lobbying efforts and won broader eligibility, higher stipends, and an expanded revenue base. Abbott and Breckinridge and their colleagues continued to move toward greater state centralization of public provision. These political efforts took place, however, in the face of increasing opposition.

The postwar depression produced wide-spread unemployment in Chicago, as elsewhere across the nation. An estimated 50,000 unemployed men lived in Chicago in March 1921 and added greatly to the demand for private and public aid. The United Charities of Chicago recorded a 63 percent increase in cases between 1920 and 1921. The county agent also noted a sharp increase in public relief cases, which began in December 1920 but continued into April 1922. Not all of these cases were the direct result of men's unemployment; they frequently reflected the loss of wages of other family earners, specifically women and children.[115]

The number of mothers' pension families rose sharply in the postwar years, with an annual increase of 33 percent and 25 percent in 1919 and 1920 respectively. The additional appropriations of 1919 temporarily relieved the strain on the program; but by the summer of 1920, the court once again stopped adding families to keep within its budget. In the spring of 1921, the legislature increased the allotment per child, which benefited families, but increased the overall fiscal pressures. Between October 1921 and the spring of 1922, the mothers' pension fund once again suffered a deficit and developed a waiting list of 868 women.[116]

In the midst of these demands on budgets, the United Charities of Chicago notified the county commissioners that it would no longer provide supplemental aid to pensioned families. Nor would it continue to carry families placed on the mothers' pension waiting list. These duties clearly belonged to the county, the charity board stated. This threat, similar to an action taken in 1918, was intended to pressure the county commissioners to seek redress in the legislature and increase the sources of public revenue.[117]

Pressure to increase public resources for mothers' pensions came from the coordinated efforts of Lathrop, Abbott, and Breckinridge and some of the city's clubwomen. Lathrop retired as Children's Bureau director in 1921 and returned to her home in Rockford, Illinois. She assumed an active role in the state and national League of Women Voters and frequently spoke to women's organizations about the necessity of increasing the public provisions of social welfare. "The drive against poverty will go on with increasing momentum, as the public is educated to the importance of abolishing it through state action. This is a move based upon economics, and not upon sentiment." Women, she said, were no longer interested in the "friendly visiting" of an earlier era.[118] Citizenship for women involved being informed on all matters of politics and government and should include a thorough understanding of the tax system.

> [Women] come into politics from a different experience in life from man's experience. They see first of all, the need of humanitarian and social betterment making for the protection of the home and child. Of course, these things cost money and they are constantly met by the reproach that they are inexperienced, that they are spenders and not earners of money, that the things for which they want money are frills and that the taxes and revenues of the state will not permit such extravagances as they desire. They can only meet this argument when they themselves understand taxation and revenue.[119]

This advice would soon be put to use as clubwomen, particularly those in the Woman's City Club, lobbied for an expansion of the pension policy.

Abbott and Breckinridge moved their program of social-work education from the School of Civics and Philanthropy to the University of Chicago in 1920. Edith Abbott announced that the school would continue to emphasize the close relationship between research and social reform, and credited Julia Lathrop with this guiding philosophy. She wrote of her colleague:

> To Miss Lathrop we owe our staunch belief in the importance of social research as a sound means of social reform. She supported us in rejecting the academic theory that social work could only be "scientific" if it had no regard to the finding of socially useful results and no interest in the human beings whose lives were being studied.[120]

The school's students produced a generation of research on public welfare and filled positions in social-work administration in Chicago and across the nation. As Robyn Muncy has noted, many graduates worked for the Children's Bureau and shared a positive view on the activist state.[121]

The relationship between unemployment, poor work opportunities, and women's poverty continued to absorb Abbott and Breckinridge's research time. In the fall of 1921, Breckinridge wrote to Grace Abbott about a Children's Bureau study on the effects of unemployment upon women and children. "It seems to me that one of the biggest things Miss Lathrop did was to tie up in people's minds the [ideas] of low father income and high infant death-rate." Looking ahead to the impact of the unemployment study, Breckinridge continued, "I wish we could get regularity of income fixed as an essential in the same way and to a greater extent. It has been so hideously confined to the men, and [as] though the women and children did not count."[122] Breckinridge attempted to do just that in an article published in 1923, in which she criticized the common view that male workers were the only parents who had "burdens in the support of dependents." Women also had dependent children, as well as the inequity of industrial opportunities with which to contend. "In such cases," Breckinridge wrote, "the doctrine of dependents with which men bolster their claims [for a family wage] would certainly apply to them [single mothers]." Breckinridge's work continued to analyze the interplay of women's employment, family responsibilities, and legal equality.[123]

Breckinridge used her position on the Illinois Department of Public Welfare Sub-Committee on Family Relief to reiterate several points made in the Children's Bureau mothers' pension study. The 1921 report submitted by the committee blamed local administration for "indiscriminate and unskilled" handling of mothers' pensions, and for failure to meet the original intention of the law. Despite the legislation's purpose "to provide dependent mothers with sufficient means so that they could stay at home and *be real mothers* to their children" (emphasis mine), the stipend to families had been increased only once since its inception. The committee suggested that all relief and pension work be coordinated under one official in each county who would be accountable to the county commissioners and the State Department of Welfare. "Neither industrial nor political organization is strictly local now," and neither should public aid remain local. As in the Children's Bureau study, the committee recommended that jobs be filled through civil service appointments and state financial assistance be provided for administration.[124]

The problems for the state's dependent African American children proved more difficult. The state's Sub-Committee on Colored Children convened in 1921 and found fewer resources available to African American children despite indications of greater need. For example, mothers and children more often worked for wages, a situation that reformers like Breckinridge, who chaired the committee, wished to improve. After at least a decade of attention to the topic, little had changed. Racial discrimination still shaped public and private services for dependent children, and tremendous animosity lay just beneath the surface of these discussions. As has been pointed out elsewhere, the state institutions accepted few if any African American children; and the city's private agencies for child care (from day nurseries to orphanages to foster home placements) restricted services by race (as they did by religion) with few exceptions. The county's Juvenile Detention Home accepted blacks; in fact, they were overrepresented there because of few placements elsewhere. The black community created several voluntary efforts aimed at dependent children. For example, the Illinois Federation of Colored Women's Clubs sponsored a series of homes during these years. During the 1920s, more black nurses and social workers received training and jobs in social service work. The *Defender* noted that thirty-one African American social workers were employed as health, school, or probation officers by the decade's end.[125] But little dialogue between the races appears to have taken place on child welfare issues, and the issue of the public's role in providing care found no resolution. Few representatives of the black community were invited to the White House conference in 1909 and none participated on the Chicago Juvenile Court committee despite the fact that the National Association of Colored Women played an active role in relief work at the national and local levels.[126]

The state's Committee on Family Relief acted upon its own recommendations and wrote an amendment to the Mothers' Aid law in the spring of 1921. House Bill no. 294 proposed an increase in the pension stipend, and dower and homestead rights, as well as an increase in taxes to raise revenues for pensions. A grant ceiling had been placed on families in 1913 providing the first child an allotment up to $15 per month and additional children aid up to $10 each until the family grant reached a monthly limit of $50. This amount was raised to $60 in 1915 in part because of the documentation of budget studies provided by the Chicago Juvenile Court. The 1921 proposal requested a stipend increase to $35 and $15 respectively with no family limit. The higher grants were necessary "to enable them [pensioned mothers] to bring up their children properly in their own homes and such mothers and their children shall not be deemed to be paupers by reason of receiving aid." This time juvenile court judge Victor Arnold sponsored the bill and the Woman's City Club endorsed it. During the session, House Bill 294 was replaced by House Bill 847, which succeeded in raising the stipend amounts for each child to $25 and $15 respectively and in removing the family maximum. This level of benefit remained constant throughout the 1920s. The tax millage rate was increased to four-tenths of a mill, but supporters did not get the full increase they had wanted (see Appendix). A second child welfare measure that would have placed mothers' pensions under state supervision also received the Woman's City Club's endorsement but failed to pass.[127]

The Woman's City Club pressed for full appropriations for the program once the measure was approved. The club *Bulletin* told members to contact their commissioners and inform them of their support for the pension policy. Citing competition for funds, the *Bulletin* noted that "it is possible that they will not appropriate the maximum amount for mothers' pensions unless they feel that the public is sufficiently interested in the widows and orphans of the county to demand the full appropriations."[128] Harriet Vittum continued her work as chair of the Cook County Affairs Committee and recommended a $650,000 appropria-

tion for mothers' pensions for 1922.[129] That amount, an increase of 44 percent
over the previous year, passed the County Board. The Woman's City Club's
support for mothers' pensions also included campaigning for candidates who
were supportive of the policy. In 1921, the club *Bulletin* covered the race for circuit court judges and reminded its members that the juvenile court judge was selected from this pool. "Do you want the poor mothers and little children of
Cook County to be exploited by a political machine[?]" the *Bulletin* asked.[130]
The Woman's City Club endorsed the presiding judge, Victor Arnold, and
made no pretense about its election goal to unseat judicial appointees of the
Thompson machine.

Eligibility changed minimally after World War I, with each expansion of
the policy hard-won and cautiously limited. Advocates won the inclusion of deserted women in 1923 after ten years and multiple attempts; yet the final legislation contained restrictive measures. The abandonment had to occur within the
state and a warrant must be issued for the man. The Chicago court went further
and stated that the desertion must have been for at least one year. The age of dependency was increased to sixteen years in 1923, but the court tended to extend
the pension beyond that only in cases where school records indicated particular
ability on the part of the child.[131]

The pace of local reform reflected a larger shift in political opportunities
during the 1920s. Several reforms of the previous decade hit major judicial and
political obstacles. The Supreme Court rejected the minimum wage argument
for women workers in *Adkins v. Children's Hospital* in 1923. The Sheppard-
Towner Act, the first major federal policy success of women's suffrage, came
under attack during the extension of its appropriation in 1926. Not even child
labor legislation could pass the Supreme Court. The antisocialist sentiments
that followed World War I and created a hostile environment for social reform
also hit hard at the coalition of national women's organizations. The release of
the Spider Web chart in 1923 established a connection, alleged and not proven,
between international socialism and the country's major women's organizations, from the National Congress of Mothers to the National Consumers'
League. Despite the absence of credible documentation for such a claim, the al-
legations sent a chill through women's groups.

The red scare shaped and limited the broader political context, but the
equal rights amendment highlighted dynamic divisions between women's
rights supporters.[132] In 1924, the *Congressional Digest* published opposing and
supportive views of the impact of the equal rights amendment on mothers' pension laws.[133] Speaking on behalf of the ERA, Mrs. Harvey W. Wiley of the Na-

tional Woman's Party found no conflict between the two because mothers' pensions were child-welfare measures, not provisions specific to women. Equity legislation would not alter their distribution, Wiley argued. Sophonisba Breckinridge disagreed. Presenting the opposing view, she argued that the "Blanket Amendment" would negatively affect mothers' pensions in two ways. Her years of experience tracking the administration of the program led her to believe that local opposition to this policy would seize upon equal rights legislation as a tool to stall, if not end, the program. Furthermore, she argued that the bill would negatively impact wage structures. If the law allowed single fathers to accept aid, it would in effect be subsidizing male wages, and pensions should not be used to subsidize industry for either men or women. Already in a defensive position, Breckinridge predicted that rather than improve the social and economic conditions for poor women, the ERA would create the opportunity for opponents to block the policy, resulting in a policy vacuum.

By mid-decade, advocacy for pensions, as for most social policies, became increasingly difficult in Illinois. The mood in the legislature had turned negative for social legislation. Bills like the child labor amendment, maternity and infant health, the eight-hour law for women workers, and increased revenue for mothers' pensions had a difficult time.[134] The political climate of the United States was characterized by fear, Jane Addams wrote, and it shaped the field of social work. "Throughout the decade this fear of change, this tendency to play safe, was registered most conspicuously in the field of politics, but it spread over into other fields as well. There is little doubt that social workers exhibited many symptoms of this panic and with a kind of protective instinct carefully avoided any identification with the phraseology of social reform."[135] In 1925 the Woman's City Club and the Illinois League of Women Voters pushed a bill to significantly increase the tax rate for mothers' pensions from four-tenths mill to two-thirds mill, but it failed to receive the legislature's support. One observer noted that the failed bill had been "condemned by Cook County officials."[136] The county commissioners did appropriate the full amount authorized in the law for pensions, $760,000, but even with this increase applicants spent one year on a waiting list. In December 1925, 1,576 women on the waiting list could not be considered until another family's aid was cancelled. The demand for mothers' pensions far outpaced the resources of local government.[137]

During this same period, efforts to centralize welfare services took a major step forward. The state legislature approved the consolidation of county public services to dependents under one Bureau of Public Welfare. The new, centralized plan intended to consolidate social work, place it on a professional basis, and remove it from patronage politics. These goals had been proposed since 1917 in Abbott and Breckinridge's work. Sophonisba Breckinridge, Harriet Vittum, Mary McDowell, Edith Abbott, and Joel Hunter were appointed to a committee and charged with establishing a plan for the new bureau.[138] During the preliminary stages, Breckinridge had solicited information from a number of associates on the best form of state centralization. A Boston colleague, Ada Sheffield, warned Breckinridge that a centralized plan would not necessarily end political interference.[139] The pattern that Sheffield had noticed in Boston occurred in Chicago. Elected officials filled one-third of the positions with temporary appointments when the new administration was fully implemented in 1927. By 1931, the Democrats had built a machine under Mayor Anton Cermak and exercised significant control over government agencies. A contemporary observer noted, however, that the field of social service had been the most effective in limiting political interference.[140] Breckinridge lamented the continuation of "dishonest and corrupt practices" within the new system of social services even at the state level. Despite the introduction of advisory bodies, civil service, and new state structures, the patronage system remained healthy and active in state public welfare. Nevertheless, Breckinridge continued to hope that moving the administration of public welfare to the federal level, as had been done with health and education, could eliminate such practices.[141]

By the decade's end, instability in the local economy produced greater numbers of unemployed and transients, who placed greater pressures upon municipal welfare services. From December 1927 through 1928, unemployment reached high levels in Chicago. Homeless men numbered 75,000 by conservative estimates and the director of the Department of Public Welfare noted that "not since 1921 has there been a year when the ratio of the number of men seeking work has been so consistently unfavorable to the number of jobs open." Lodging houses were overfilled, employment bureaus had one job for every 200 applicants, and relief requests were high. The situation was exacerbated for Chicago's African Americans. The municipal lodging houses served predominantly homeless white men. A lodging house specifically for black men which opened in 1927 lasted only three months and was closed because of overcrowding. The Chicago Urban League worked to find jobs for unemployed black men but were limited in what they were able to achieve.[142]

Mothers' pension advocates pressured the county commissioners to increase the appropriation, and in 1927 the amount of $1,050,000 was set aside to meet the rising numbers of families applying for aid. The increase enabled the department to process those on the waiting list; but as quickly as those families were given aid, more applied. By September 1928, nearly 1,500 women remained on the waiting list.[143] Fiscal relief should have come in 1929 as the last measure of the state centralization plan went into effect. The state began making subsidies to counties to help cover the costs of pensions. The full effect of the law was never felt as the economic crisis of the depression intervened. The state contributed approximately $200,000 to Cook County, but the total budget for mothers' pensions in 1932, for example, reached $1,175,000. A significant portion remained for the county to pay and it was simply unable to supply the revenue for the program's continuation during the depression. The county made late payments, offered temporary relief supplies, and helped some families to ward off evictions. The fiscal crisis that limited the distribution of mothers' pensions in Cook County by the end of the 1920s highlighted the problems of a social policy that continued to use predominantly local funding and poor relief practices.[144]

§

Chicago's experiment with mothers' pensions reveals several layers of conflict that emerged within the first two decades and carried serious consequences for the families involved. One of the most immediate conflicts pertained to the definition of direct services. Would the policy provide a minimum standard of living for families or would it put a new face on poor relief practices? The early legislative revision produced a law that, while an improvement over poor relief, more closely resembled relief than social insurance. This chapter has suggested several reasons why this occurred. No social group or political constituency emerged to provide sufficient political pressure to counteract the institutions that existed before 1918. In Chicago, that vacuum was filled by social workers intent on using their research as a vehicle to shape public opinion and revise legislation. Women's organizations rose to the challenge later and deserve credit for the incremental expansions of the policy. This analysis is at odds with Theda Skocpol's studies on the influence of mass women's organizations on the passage of laws through state legislatures. However, as Skocpol acknowledges, passing the law and putting it into effect required different political strategies. We know less about the role played by mass organizations during the latter stage. Several groups did have an interest in public subsidies for dependent families, and these actors, frequently associated with charity institutions, courts, or settlements, moved to the fore. In Chicago, the juvenile court, private charities, and social workers wrested administration of the policy from the poor relief office and county commissioners. This coalition had great differences among themselves, yet they responded to preserve the policy against intense criticism directed not only by local politicians, but also by the national social-work community. This defensive posture led to the inclusion of a charity ethos in pension policy; that is, wage-earning requirements for able-bodied mothers and regulation of behavior through casework methods. After this reactionary phase of implementation which produced the 1913 law, social justice feminists could recapture elements of the original intent only through incremental legislative change. To be effective, these changes needed a political constituency willing to support expansionary proposals. Edith Abbott and Sophonisba Breckinridge worked successfully with women's civic reform organizations to play that role, but by the mid-1920s opposition became increasingly great.

How then did the politics of welfare reform result in a reorganization of political life, and how significant were those changes? Over the last decade, the literature on gender and the welfare state has led scholars to inquire how women, once they obtained political authority and positions of power, could have produced such an ineffective policy. The Chicago case complicates that question somewhat by introducing a number of political and institutional factors. Even if the coalition of supporters had agreed on the role of state provision for mother-only families (and they did not); and even if they had lobbied for a social insurance provision inclusive of all women (and many clubwomen objected to deserted or unmarried mothers being included), the opposition of politicians and charities would have defeated it. Too much apprehension existed about state support for families. One only needs to examine the successful debates surrounding the social insurance measures to understand the level of resistance to public provision in the United States in the early twentieth century. At the same time, too little support existed for the principle that wives and mothers should be socially insured against the inequities of industry regardless of their means.

The limits of the program have overshadowed one of the most significant aspects of this policy—the way in which it expanded public resources for mother-only families. The structures of public aid expanded with mothers' pensions and the fiscal revenues of the program grew dramatically. This expansion is hardly apparent from research that focuses on individual pensioned families, but it is important from the perspective of tax dollars directed toward this constituency. Supporters managed to change the public distribution of resources for a time. Furthermore, the policy initiated a new bureaucratic administration of social welfare, thus creating an intermediary between citizen and political party. Breckinridge did not achieve her goal of patronage-free social services.

However, new administrative capacities did create the potential for greater distributive benefits in the future.

The most significant failure of this experiment was the disappearance of the dialogue on the value and location of women's work. The policy gained national attention and advocates because of its promise to recognize the work women performed in child-rearing. Yet the various implementation schemes reduced the level of support from the ideal of an endowment, as in the ill-fated Funds to Parents Act, to a partial subsidy. The subject of support also shifted from women as mothers to their children. A pensioned family could keep young children out of the labor force, but able-bodied mothers must earn. The result once again devalued women's work at home. At the same time, the fervent activism surrounding women's wages and workforce opportunities which had sought to adjust the value of women's workplace labor had declined by the mid-1920s. The Supreme Court's rejection of minimum wages for women in *Adkins v. Children's Hospital* left the progress on women's labor conditions stalled. Within the larger context of the women's movement, labor organizing, and shifts in public provision, poor single mothers' labor value did not change. Neither arena of their work, the home or the marketplace, had been radically changed by the advent of mothers' pension legislation or the debates surrounding it.

This chapter's evaluation of the political forces that shaped the policy has said little about the women and children who received mothers' aid. The politics of welfare reform left a clear imprint on the families with its emphasis on self-support. The following chapter explores the internal dynamics of the policy.

Pension Mothers Receiving Their Allotments

Ideas about the value of the mother's work in the family competed with demands for self-support in the mothers' pension program. Chicago Historical Society.

The Economies of Mothers' Pensions

The "social experiment" in public provision for poor, mother-only families presented a conundrum for women's rights supporters as well as social workers: how to foster the independence of women while acknowledging and protecting families with dependent children. Those proponents of mothers' pensions who wanted an endowment or a form of social insurance wanted to end requirements for mothers to earn, but they failed to shift the majority opinion to this form of entitlement. In the process of implementing mothers' pensions, other concerns about private responsibilities, public costs, and the role of the government entered the debate and reshaped the program's methods and goals. As this chapter will illustrate, the program evolved into one that insisted upon earning for the majority of pensioned women. Scholars have been slow to examine closely the relationship between wage-earning and mothers' pensions, or the growth of this policy in its local context. And yet in both language and practice, the relationship between families, markets, and social policy was being contested through this early welfare policy. In this phase of public support for impoverished families, the demands for individual self-support in a laissez-faire political economy took precedence.[1]

The evidence presented in this chapter demonstrates that women's potential to earn (and that of their older children) played a much greater role than historians have previously recognized in their explanations of the mothers' pension program. An analysis of the reasons for the initial denial of aid, as well as explanations for the cancellation of pensions, reveals the prominence of earning criteria.[2] With few exceptions, those involved in planning and administration recognized the value of women's domestic work in child-rearing; but they balanced this against competing demands for self-support and fiscal responsibility. Furthermore, racial and moral systems became conflated with social workers' ideas about those mothers who had the "ability to earn"—a distinction that led to the exclusion of groups of mothers. African American women, deserted women, and mothers with one child were denied mothers' pensions and directed to other programs that relied heavily on earning. As Linda Gordon and Regina Kunzel have shown for other cases, the attitudes of social workers had an extraordinary impact on the treatment and services that families received.[3]

The chapter also explores the public economy of pensions; that is, the growth of the program in comparison to other forms of public aid. The Chicago mothers' pension program expanded tremendously during the years considered in this study, particularly in comparison to poor relief, in large part owing to the political activities discussed in the previous chapter. Yet the deliberations of the program administrators reveal the shift in policy to *assist* but not entirely support poor mothers. I shall begin with a discussion of the characteristics of pensioned families, and then explore the relationship between public funds and private resources for pensioned families.

§

Cook County had the largest mothers' pension program in the state and one of the largest in the country. It expanded from a small program serving 51 families in 1911 to one providing aid to 1,689 families in 1927. Between 1915 and 1927, years for which there are comparable records, the number of families on the program increased twofold and appropriations increased 437 percent when adjusted for inflation. The number of families covered by the mothers' pension program also expanded relative to the overall number of Chicagoans, although pensioned families remained a small portion of the population.[4]

Women learned about the availability of pensions in a number of ways, but records indicate that the majority came from referrals. Through contact with a charity, settlement house, health agency, or even the public schools a woman could receive a referral to the court to apply for a pension. Social workers or visiting nurses had a great opportunity to relay this information to families, and the absence of services in some communities had corresponding negative effects, as discussed below. In some cases, friends or neighbors might advise the court of a family's need. Other families found out about the program only when other problems brought them into the courts. If a woman wanted to apply for a pension, she did so at the juvenile court. This application requested information about the immediate family members such as their age, level of education, race, and previous marriages. It also asked for the size and condition of their home, a list of relatives, and details on their financial resources, including insurance policies or contributions from mutual aid societies. Finally, the applicant listed the occupations and wages of all family members.

Two separate investigations followed the application—the first conducted by the Mothers' Pension Division of the juvenile court and the second conducted by the Cook County Poor Relief Agent's office. The investigation began when the Mothers' Pension Division assigned a probation officer to determine whether the family received assistance from other social agencies. If this was the case, the department requested the agencies to send information about the family to the court. The second step of the investigation pursued the provisions of the Pauper Act and determined whether relatives could assist the family. If the relatives had resources but refused to assist, the mothers' pension applicant could be asked to prosecute them for nonsupport before the application could move forward. If the applicant refused to prosecute her relatives, the case was dismissed. The third step verified the applicant's information with that of other sources such as churches, unions, and schools. With the investigation complete, the probation officer submitted a report to the Conference Committee, whose members made the decision to recommend or reject the application. The committee evaluated the resources and eligibility of the family compared to the estimated need as determined by a family budget. Their decision went directly to the juvenile court and to the county poor relief agent. The county agent conducted a second investigation of the family because that office, which actually disbursed the funds, felt it necessary to maintain rigorous checks on "abuses." In the event of a disagreement about eligibility, both sides took their evidence to the judge, who made the final decision. Shortly thereafter, the mother received notification of a court hearing by a summons. She attended the hearing along with the director of the Mothers' Pension Division, a representative from the county agent's office, and the investigating probation officer. If approved, the family received a pension once a month at the county agent's office and a probation officer supervised their progress.[5]

Unlike the entitlement characteristics of other pensions, this policy relied heavily on values and methods of supervision and rehabilitation similar to those employed in poor relief. It disrupted the family's privacy, and applicants frequently objected to the "needless prying into their private affairs" and the "great hardship" imposed by a detailed accounting of expenditures. In contrast to the language of rights and entitlements used to pass the laws, the policy assumed standards of charities, once implemented. Ironically, this concession saved the program, but irrevocably changed it.[6]

The administrators of the Mothers' Pension Division determined that impoverished women needed both financial assistance and "constructive social services" to get through their crisis. The probation officer played a major role in setting the conditions for the benefits a family might receive and was encouraged to visit families more than once a month. A field supervisor made periodic visits to the home to suggest methods of improving "domestic skills." They kept track of children's progress in school and the family's need for child care arrangements. These highly regulatory features of casework which were intrusive and demeaning could also connect families with needed resources and provide positive interventions, as Linda Gordon has observed. For example, if a family needed additional social services, the probation officer had the opportunity to make hospital referrals or assist in locating better housing.[7]

The interplay between rehabilitation and public aid is evident in the history of one American-born family known to us only as "the B family." The husband had been a Teamster and when he died without insurance, his union raised funeral expenses. With no other aid, the family turned to county poor relief. They had used charity in the past when the father had been too ill to work "and the children were begging from house to house." When Mrs. B applied for a pension she was thirty-five years old, "sick practically all the time" and "looked frail, slovenly, and discouraged." Her home was described as "filthy, damp, and dark." The following segment of the case history approvingly records the diligence of caseworkers with the family.

> In all there were eight probation officers on this case, but each one seems to have given herself to the problems in hand with energy and determination, and gradually the standards of living were raised, and the mother's health began to show a decided improvement. The family was moved from time to time to more desirable rooms. Medical treatment for Mrs. B was secured, and regular dispensary treatment was insisted upon. The diet and buying of the family was carefully supervised, and Mrs. B instructed in the art of keeping a clean home.[8]

The administrators of mothers' pensions operated from the position that the success of the program depended upon the rehabilitative work of the probation officers and the close cooperation of the pensioned woman. This dynamic had an impact on the selection of families through both legal and extralegal eligibility requirements.

FAMILY CHARACTERISTICS

The popular image of a mothers' pension family presented in Chicago's newspapers and in the pages of the *Charity Service Reports* followed closely that of the "worthy poor." The mother was portrayed as a widow, often an immigrant, who now had the full responsibility for several young children. The *Chicago Daily Tribune* ran a photograph of such a family with an article about pensions around Thanksgiving in 1911. Four children stood at their tenement window and waited for their mother to return home with groceries purchased with the pension check. Widows did in fact receive the greater share of pensions. They made up 84 percent of all the cases throughout the period of this study. But they were also the largest group of mother-only families in the population at the time. Many of the women had lost their husbands at an early age. Almost half of the women (44 percent) included in a 1917 study had lost a husband when he was between thirty and thirty-nine years of age. Illness alone claimed nearly 70 percent of the men. Such families lost their primary wage-earners not only during their peak earning years, but also at a time when young children were likely to be present. While widows were the largest group of recipients, they were by no means the only women eligible. Only five states with mothers' pension laws restricted this aid to widows by 1926.[9]

Deserted women and two-parent families also received pensions. Approximately 10 percent of the pensions went to deserted women in the first year of the program; however, the 1913 revision revoked their eligibility out of fear that the policy would encourage husbands to desert. During the years of ineligibility, private agencies aided families while the Court of Domestic Relations attempted to locate the fathers. Despite the legal prohibition against aiding deserted mothers, a few cases continued to receive mothers' pensions. The court considered cases of desertion when the husband had been absent for over two years and consistently granted pensions when he had been absent seven years, the period of time in which he could be declared legally dead. This figure amounted to less than 1 percent of all families, however. Persistent efforts by civic groups to expand eligibility to include deserted women were successful in 1923. From 1925 to 1927 deserted women received 9 to 12 percent of all pensions. Two-parent families could also receive aid if the husband was totally incapacitated and unable to work. Between 1911 and 1927, 13 percent of the pensioned families included a father who had been either institutionalized or disabled through illness or injury.[10]

Unmarried mothers faced the greatest barriers to eligibility. They could not receive pensions for the first several years of the Chicago program because they were categorized as "morally unfit" mothers and administrators opposed their eligibility for public aid on the basis that it would be interpreted as public acceptance of immoral behavior. These children and their mothers, while few in number, received discriminatory treatment across the United States. In 1926, only three states specifically allowed mothers' pensions for children of unmarried parents. Some social welfare progressives criticized the unequal treatment of children born to unwed parents and worked for their rights. The Chicago Juvenile Court exercised a limited expansion of the policy in 1917 in that it allowed the "legitimate" children in the family to receive aid.[11]

The image of the immigrant mother, head covered with a shawl and children tugging at her knees, frequently represented the program to the public. In fact, the foreign-born predominated in the program throughout the period of the study. They received the hardest blow in the revision of the program in 1913 which made citizenship a requirement of eligibility. The exclusion of noncitizens was lessened only slightly in 1915 as American-born children of mothers who had taken their first steps toward citizenship could again be eligible. Table 9 includes the major groups that participated in the program by nativity. Irish and German families had high rates of participation during the first years of the pension policy. Together, they made up 10 percent of Chicago's families, but received 21 percent of poor relief and 42 percent of mothers' pensions in 1911. With declining rates of immigration during the 1910s and 1920s, these two groups made up a smaller part of the general population. (They accounted for 6 percent of the metropolitan families in 1920.) While still overrepresented on relief and mothers' pensions, their proportion continued to decline over the next decade. Other European immigrant groups followed the opposite pattern.[12]

Italians and Poles increased their use of public aid while maintaining their population ratios. Italians made up 2 percent of Chicago's families in 1911, but received 8 percent of both pensions and relief. While their population ratio remained stable through 1930, Italians became the second-largest pension recipient group among the foreign-born. They expanded their receipt of pensions in 1918 and continuously made up about 10 percent of the pension group throughout the 1920s. Polish participation in poor relief and mothers' pensions remained well above their ratio in the population. During the years 1918 to 1921, years of tremendous dislocation due to war and depression, the Polish became the largest group among the foreign-born receiving mothers' pensions. By 1927, Polish families received 21 percent of all pensions.

Native-born European Americans made up the largest segment of pension recipients of any national group after 1915. Of course, this category includes all second-generation families. In 1910, native-born European Americans made up 62 percent of Chicago families, received 20 percent of relief and 14 percent of pensions the first year (1911). By 1930, they still comprised two-thirds of the metropolitan population, but their proportion on relief and mothers' pensions had increased to 30 percent and 26 percent respectively.

Like some foreign-born groups, African Americans' rates of poor-relief use were several times greater than their ratio in the population. However, unlike the immigrant poor, African Americans received no mothers' pensions un-

TABLE 9 Percentage of Families in the General Population, on Poor Relief, and Receiving Mothers' Pensions, by Race and Nativity, 1910–1930

Group	1910			1920			1930		
	P	R	MP	P	R	MP	P	R	MP
European American	62	20	14	66	24	26	67	30	26
African American	2	6	0	4	8	3	7	31	5
Total native-born	64	26	14	70	32	29	74	61	31
German	7	11	20	4	8	6	3	4	6
Irish	3	10	22	2	5	5	2	2	4
Italian	2	8	8	2	11	9	2	8	10
Polish	6	19	14	5	19	17	4	11	21
Other	18	26	22	17	25	34	15	14	28
Total foreign-born	36	74	86	30	68	71	26	39	69
Total	100	100	100	100	100	100	100	100	100

Sources: Chicago population figures: *Thirteenth Census, 1910: Population; Fourteenth Census, 1920: Population; Fifteenth Census, 1930: Population.* Data on foreign-born families came from the *Fourteenth Census of the United States, 1920,* vol. 2: 739. Relief data came from the Cook County, IL, Board of County Commissioners, *Charity Service Reports,* 1910, 1920, 1927; and mothers' pension figures from the Cook County, IL, Board of County Commissioners, *Proceedings,* County Agent, 1911; and *Charity Service Reports,* Juvenile Court, Mothers' Pension Department, 1920, 1927.

Notes: P = Population; R = Poor Relief; MP = Mothers' pensions. Mothers' pensions figures are for the years 1911, 1920, 1927; poor relief figures for 1927 were used.

til 1913 and were underrepresented in the pension program throughout the period. In 1920, for example, when African Americans made up 4 percent of the
population and 8 percent of the families on relief, they received only 3 percent
of the mothers' pensions. In addition, the African American community in
Chicago had a higher proportion of families headed by women in their childbearing years. One-half of all African American mother-only families were
headed by women between 15 and 44 years of age in 1910, compared to 18 percent of all foreign-born mother-only families. Higher rates of female headship
also meant higher rates of employment. The majority of African American
women worked in service jobs during the early twentieth century. These low-
wage jobs and the presence of children would predict a high degree of economic
need, a situation that highlights their underrepresentation on mothers' pensions
even more than population ratios. A 1931 Children's Bureau report on mothers'
pension programs in thirty-eight states found the provisions for African American families to be extremely limited when compared to their need or their ratio
in the population. Some areas excluded these families entirely despite the fact
that they made up 20 to 45 percent of a county's population.[13]

Ida B. Wells-Barnett thought that the lack of participation in the mothers'
pension program had a direct connection to the lack of political representation
in local government. The small numbers of African American social workers
and public health nurses also limited resources. In 1915, Sophie Boaz, a social
worker at the Wendell Phillips settlement, told the Alpha Suffrage Club that
much work needed to be done to inform African American mothers of the availability of mothers' pensions because they were underserved by the program.[14]
Changes in political representation and social work training might explain part
of the change during the 1920s. African American families became a larger portion of those families receiving public aid. This extended to mothers' pensions
as well. Despite their underrepresentation overall, African American mothers
made gains in their portion of new mothers' pension cases, increasing from 2.7
percent in 1916 to 5.4 percent in 1922 and 11.4 percent in 1927.

The statistics confirm the characterization of women on pensions as
foreign-born widows, but two additional generalizations are not borne out by
the figures. While generally portrayed as families with many children, the majority of mothers' pension families had three or fewer children. Between 1913
and 1926, 25 percent had two children and 30 percent had three. Families with
four children made up only 21 percent of all cases. A second study conducted by
the Mothers' Pension Division of the juvenile court for the years 1913 to 1915
confirmed that families with three children were most common. Mothers with

TABLE 10 Total Monthly Family Earnings at Time
of Application for a Mothers' Pension

Amount	Number	Percent
Less than $20	236	62.0
$20–29	84	22.5
$30–39	35	9.4
$40–49	15	4.0
$50 and above	3	.9

Source: Cook County, IL, Board of County Commissioners, *Charity Service Reports*, Juvenile Court (1917), 266.

only one child could be denied pensions based on the assumption that they could become self-supporting. As one might expect given the purpose of the program, the majority of children in mothers' pension families were under the age of fourteen.[15]

A second erroneous generalization referred to the program as a benefit for skilled workers' families, a predecessor to Social Security Survivors' Benefits. Although nearly one-third of the families reported that the father had worked in a trained or skilled occupation, the larger portion represented more economically marginal families. Unskilled laborers had previously headed 44 percent of the families who subsequently received pensions, and an additional 8 percent had worked in personal service. One report noted that while "a great number of the men were unskilled laborers, working with pick and shovel, driving teams, working in the stockyards, etc. . . . a not inconsiderable number were doing work requiring some degree of training or experience . . . [and] a smaller group was doing work of a clerical or professional nature."[16] Regardless of the previous income, these families experienced a significant decline in income between the death of the male breadwinner and the time of application for a pension (see table 10).

The family offered the main recourse when crisis hit, but a growing segment of working-class and immigrant families could not assume this responsibility. As Edith Abbott frequently pointed out, poor people's relatives were also poor. A wide array of self-help associations, including churches, benevolent societies, and fraternal organizations, provided some help, but in most cases these funds paid for the immediate costs of a burial and expenses for a few weeks or months. Insurance provided slightly longer benefits (approximately half a year) for those fortunate enough to have it. Half of the women who applied for pensions had no insurance, yet they did not turn immediately to public aid.

Slightly over 40 percent waited from six months to over three years before making an application. At the point of application for a pension, 62 percent of the families had combined family earnings of less than twenty dollars a month. Over 8 percent of those families had experienced a 50 percent drop in their family income.[17] Consider the example of Mrs. C, recorded in the case records of the juvenile court and published as an example of a "success" among pensioned families.

> In June, 1913, Mrs. C, a Polish woman, applied for a pension for her two children aged 8 and 5 years because she found it impossible to earn enough to support them. Her husband had died of heart disease in 1909, leaving some insurance; but the money had been used for paying funeral bills, debts, and living expenses. The family had been compelled to ask help from the county agent and the united charities a number of times during the four years following the death of the father. A stepson had gone to work at the age of 14, but Mrs. C found him so unmanageable that in 1911 she sent him to his uncle in Tennessee. Mrs. C had been earning only $10 a month by sweeping in a school.
>
> The family budget was estimated at $34, and in October, 1913, the court granted a pension of $10 for each of the two children. With the mothers' earnings of about $10 a month, the income of the family was brought up to within $4 of their estimated needs. It was found that the dust raised by sweeping in the school was very bad for the mother, as it caused her to cough so much that she could not sleep. Her work was changed to cleaning in a bank, where she earned $3 a week instead of $10 a month.[18]

The onset of unemployment, illness, or loss of the father destabilized the family. The majority of pensioned families had lived on a basic standard of living before the loss of the father. Whether the father was a skilled or unskilled worker, the loss of his income sent the family into a precipitous decline which led to public assistance.

Many pension applicants sought additional assistance from public and private agencies. Nearly 95 percent of mothers' pension applicants between 1913 and 1915 had requested aid from other relief agencies at the time of their application and received aid from more than two agencies. In addition to the United Charities of Chicago, which supplied the majority of private aid, and the Cook County Poor Relief office, which supplied additional public aid, health services were provided by the Municipal Tuberculosis Sanitarium, the Visiting Nurses Association, and the Cook County Hospital. Public and private relief agencies shared responsibilities during the early twentieth century, but pressure existed from the private sector for public agencies to assume more of the costs of long-term cases.[19]

The policy may be described as well by who was denied mothers' pension benefits. Although the literature on mothers' pensions has focused on moral regulation, an examination of the reasons given for denying aid or cancelling pensions point to the centrality of economics. Between the years 1911 and 1927, the Conference Committee listed over thirty reasons for dismissed applications. I have arranged these reasons into four main categories in the order of their significance: economic sufficiency (49 percent), legal ineligibility (37 percent), lack of cooperation (8 percent), and fitness or moral standards (4 percent). A family could be dropped for economic reasons if the investigator found resources available or estimated that the woman could be "self-supporting." Legal ineligibility included cases where applications were withdrawn, where there were no children under age fourteen, or where the woman had remarried. A lack of cooperation referred to an applicant's unwillingness to disclose fully her economic situation or to comply with the investigations. Fitness standards included physical and mental capability as well as moral behavior.

Economic reasons accounted for nearly one-half of the dismissed cases. In the first year of implementation, 73 percent of the families had their applications denied because the committee estimated that they had actual or potential resources sufficient for a basic standard of living. These same economic reasons explained over 40 percent of the dismissals through World War I, 50 percent of dismissals for the first half of the 1920s, and 40 percent for the remainder of the decade.[20] Of all the economic reasons given for rejecting an applicant, "sufficient income" was most frequently cited. Sufficient income could include hard economic resources or the potential earnings of family members. Consider for example, the case of one African American woman who received a pension for five children until the 1913 revisions made her ineligible. She managed the situation by giving her fifteen-year old daughter the home responsibilities while she went out to work. Two years later a revised law made her eligible once again and she reapplied for a pension. Her case was denied, however, on the basis that she was "a good wage earner."[21] Children's wages also held particular weight in considerations of which families would get by without public aid. A study of families denied pensions during the 1920s found that children's earnings frequently took the family over the line and into a minimum standard-of-living budget. The report cited a family with four children in which "the oldest works, earning $90 a month and the mother works part time." Other families included "two older children who evidently are supporting the family," and one in which the "mother decided that she could get along until the oldest boy went to work in June, after graduating from the 8th grade."[22] Additional economic reasons for the denial of a pension included the possession of property or financial interests (37 percent), self-support (10 percent) and assistance of relatives (1.8 percent). These applicants would frequently reapply within months when temporary savings were depleted and be admitted to the program.

A woman's legal ineligibility accounted for the second most common explanation for a denial. This category fluctuated with legislative changes, but for a large part of the period under study it applied to families of imprisoned fathers, institutionalized mothers, deserted women, and those for whom the application had been withdrawn. Citizenship was a category of legal eligibility for the first decade of the program.

Women who resisted the intrusive methods of social workers had their applications denied for failure to cooperate or to disclose their finances. These families made up an average of 8 percent of all cases over the period. Lack of cooperation had a variety of meanings to the caseworkers of the Mothers' Pension Division. It could mean that a woman did not account for her expenditures to the satisfaction of the caseworker, or that she refused to reveal the addresses of relatives so that the department could approach them for support of the family. Lack of cooperation could also mean that an ill parent refused to see a doctor or be placed in a sanitarium. A family's unwillingness to comply with the program of rehabilitation, be it in thrift, health, or familial responsibility, jeopardized its access to this subsidy.

The concept of "fitness" was also a factor in restricting access to mothers' pensions. The original Funds to Parents Act defined the criteria for parents as "proper guardians," but the 1913 revision explicitly clarified that a mother would receive a pension only under the condition that she was "in the judgement of the court, a proper person, physically, mentally and morally fit, to bring up her children."[23] Physical and mental fitness might be readily defined by records of health, but the criteria for moral fitness remained ambiguous. Caseworkers pointed to criteria such as "no proof of marriage," "male roomers" and "woman never married" as well as an unspecified characterization of "unfitness." By 1918, when fitness had been explicitly described as either mental, physical, or moral, only a minute portion of the applications were denied for this reason. Over the entire period from 1911 to 1927, fitness and moral criteria accounted for only 4.4 percent of the reasons for dismissing a pension application. Caseworkers used these reasons most frequently in the first five years of the policy, when they made up between 8 and 10 percent of denials, but by World War I and throughout the 1920s, only 1 to 5 percent of the applications were thrown out for reasons of morality. Furthermore, not all women found to be unfit were treated alike. The lack of clarity in the policy can be seen in the following example. Some mothers who were judged morally unfit (4 percent) had petitions filed against them in court to separate them from their children, while other unmarried mothers (1 percent) who could not be served by the pension legislation were referred to charities. The court and caseworkers used the criteria in a discretionary manner. Notions of unfit parenting surely kept many women from ever applying for aid, and this description cannot fully reflect the impact of social regulation. However, the analysis presented here does reveal the overlooked and essential characteristic of a family's ability to earn as a central component in the operations of mothers' pension policy.

THE FAMILY ECONOMY

The early debates on mothers' pensions frequently discussed the social goal of reducing the pressure on poor women to earn. "It is against sound public economy to allow poverty alone to cause the separation of a child from the care of a good mother," Julia Lathrop wrote, "or to allow the mother so to exhaust her powers in earning a living for her children that she can not give them proper home care and protection."[24] Sophonisba Breckinridge added "that mothers of dependent children are not to be forced by economic necessity to assume the responsibilities both of support and of care."[25] But this goal, supported by juvenile court judges, National Congress of Mothers leaders, journalists, and reformers, fell short of its mark in implementation. The legislation that outlined the administration of mothers' pensions in Illinois authorized wage-earning by pensioned women when they were able-bodied. The Chicago Juvenile Court accepted the standard established by the city's social agencies that mothers with three or more children should not take wage work outside the home in recognition of their duties in child care. However, the ceiling on pension benefits produced a family income that frequently fell below even the court's standard budget, with the result that single mothers "practically always [had] to work at least part time."[26]

Studies that examined the operation of the program found mothers earning. A report on 1,115 pensioned families conducted by the Mothers' Pension Division of the Chicago Juvenile Court during the years 1913 to 1915 found that 60 percent of mothers who received pensions also worked. The report noted that the court not only knew of the wage-earning performed by mothers, but played a central role in its practice. "The court considers the first duty of all pensioned mothers to care for their children. However, if a mother is physically able to work and her children can be properly cared for in her absence she is asked to work a certain amount." The Children's Bureau survey of Illinois mothers' pensions noted that the court viewed the policy as a *supplement* to the mother's income; but the Bureau argued against this practice because of the inability of some mothers to earn. A third study that focused on Chicago cases between 1917 and 1925 found that the work requirement continued through the 1920s.[27] The insistence on earning was not peculiar to Chicago. The Children's Bureau studied nine diverse communities across the country and found that shortfalls in fiscal revenues led to budget constraints for pensioned families. In many cases, a mother's wages made up the difference.

> Some mothers were working because there was no other way to get an adequate income for the family, although the physical strain of work in addition to the care of the house and children was probably more than they could long endure. The work, of the other mothers was leaving the children too much to their own resources or with oversight of doubtful character. In many instances, however, it was believed that some money-earning occupation on the part of the mother was a wholesome influence in the family life.[28]

Over one-half of the mothers surveyed in this 1923 report contributed to the family income through wage-earning.

The emphasis on wage-earning came into play when the Chicago mothers' pension Conference Committee compared family resources to the standard budget for a minimum standard of living. They considered the "potential earnings" of able-bodied family members of working age as well as savings, property, and contributions by relatives. The tension between family needs, court budgets, and women's earnings emerges from the story of the "A" family. Mr. A had been an American-born woodworker. He supported his wife and four children on approximately $48 per month. He had a small insurance policy that allowed Mrs. A to pay the funeral costs and family debts after his death. She managed for three years, adding money made from home sewing to the remaining insurance money. The case record picks up the family's history three years past the father's death.

> She managed to keep the family together without charitable assistance but was doing it at the expense of her health, and the family was not being adequately fed. It was at this time, in January, 1913, that the municipal tuberculosis sanitarium referred the family to the court for a pension. The mother had been found to be tubercular, the three boys had tubercular glands, the children were all undernourished, and the physical condition

of the whole family seemed to be going down very rapidly. The doctors said that Mrs. A ought not to work any longer. When this pension of $10 per child was granted she promised to "sew up" what she then had on hand and to stop work until her condition was improved. This $40 a month was the maximum pension that the court was willing to grant at that time; but, as it was not sufficient in view of the tubercular condition of four members of the family, the White Cross League was asked to contribute. It furnished special diet of milk and eggs for nine months. The condition of Mrs. A improved so much that at the end of this period she was able to earn about $7 a month without detriment to her health.[29]

As soon as family members could work (for example, when Mrs. A restored her health or when the children reached the legal working age), the court adjusted the pension.[30]

Most of the women worked in domestic service jobs. One would expect working mothers to earn wages in the home more often than outside it, since the goal to provide support for women to stay at home became part of the policy. However, only one-third of the 360 jobs listed by pensioned women were located inside the home, including washing, sewing, and taking boarders. Fourteen percent of pensioned mothers earned income by keeping boarders, although prohibitions existed against male boarders who were not relatives.[31] The studies do not indicate the amount of time devoted to each type of job, but such proportions suggest that only a minority of women who received pensions could look after their children while earning at home. Washing outside the home occupied 61 percent of the women. Cleaning, home laundry, home sewing, and keeping boarders followed as major areas of employment. The higher-paid factory and restaurant jobs accounted for only 5 percent of their employment. Furthermore, 70 percent of the women had more than one job. All together, the average monthly earnings amounted to $12.60.[32]

Pensioned women in other communities found similar occupational limitations, with the exception that factory work occupied a larger portion of women in the national study than in Chicago. Certain localities adjusted the amount of work required in recognition of the home responsibilities faced by women. For example, Denver and some Pennsylvania counties placed a limit of three days of full-time work on pensioned mothers. Despite this limit, 13 percent of pensioned women in a Children's Bureau study worked six or seven days a week. The study also found that administrators encouraged women to work "short hours" jobs while their children were in school. About one-quarter of the women did choose part-time wage-earning, but many of them worked between six and seven days a week.[33] In Chicago, women also faced limits on the number of hours of employment and penalties for taking night work.

Child labor supplied an important part of the family income. Case records are peppered with the contributions of older children and the corresponding reduction of mothers' pension grants, such as the following. "The pension for this family has been gradually reduced from $40 to only $24, as the children have become old enough to go to work. Both girls have good positions, one as a stenographer, and the other working for the telephone company. In another year one of the boys will be able to go to work."[34] One-quarter of pensioned families had at least one child who had reached the legal age to work, and 43 percent of children who were legally eligible to work did so. This would be the equivalent of 10 percent of pensioned families having working children. Sons' and daughters' contributions to the family income varied: boys could make an average weekly wage of $5.69, while girls would make $5.39. But the greatest difference in the children's contribution had to do with the length of time they continued to help the family. When a son matured, he moved out of the house earlier than a daughter and thus ended or reduced his direct contribution to the family economy. A Cook County study found that a son's contribution to the family declined by half for every two years of age. On the other hand, the daughters remained at home longer and contributed to the family economy longer than did sons.[35]

Women and older children in pensioned families continued to earn, as did other families among the unskilled poor. Some observers expressed concern that subsidizing mother-only families, while also insisting on their workforce participation, could have the effect of depressing women's employment opportunities and wages. A more sound policy, they argued, would include minimum wages for women workers and outright social insurance for mother-only families. These policy options, while supported by some women's organizations, remained peripheral to the social insurance cause. While a few social workers continued to frame mothers' pensions as a new form of public aid, local administrators applied old relief rules in practice.[36]

FAMILY BUDGETS AND PENSION STIPENDS

Nearly every report on mothers' pensions written during these years addressed the inadequacy of pension grants. Mothers' pensions, after all, were to have made an improvement over other types of aid by providing regular and sufficient payments to meet the family's needs. The discussion of adequate budgets in mothers' pension grants was part of a larger discourse on guaranteeing an adequate living standard for American families. The fact that pension grants deteriorated into relief practice has obscured this early motive. In Chicago, social workers developed a standard budget based upon cost-of-living studies of working families. The budget estimated the current costs of clothing, food, heating, rent, and household supplies to determine the lowest level of family income that would still permit "full growth, training and development of children." Pensions supplied between 25 and 75 percent of the budget estimate, the remainder to be met by wages or in some cases contributions by private agencies.[37] While initially designed as a tool to raise family standards of living, the budget ended up being used to both expand and contract public payments.

As parsimonious as the family budget seems, advocates used those figures to argue for and win stipend increases. The Welfare Council of Metropolitan Chicago (formerly the Chicago Central Council of Social Agencies), in particular, used the budget as a vehicle to gain greater benefits. Formed in 1914 to provide planning for welfare services, the Welfare Council included representatives from both the public and private sectors. In addition to Edith Abbott and Sophonisba Breckinridge, its Committee on Family Welfare had as members University of Chicago sociologist E. W. Burgess, United Charities director Joel D. Hunter, family budget specialist Florence Nesbitt, and juvenile court chief probation officer Joseph Moss. The office of the chief probation officer of the juvenile court frequently advocated an expansion of the pension program, unlike the county agent or the county commissioners. For example, in 1916 the chief probation officer asked Florence Nesbitt to document the gap between real family expenses and pension benefits by producing a budget study. This documentation contributed to the successful increase of stipends in 1917.[38]

Chicago's budget studies provided an important source of statistical evidence for stipend increases as inflation increasingly eroded the value of the pension after World War I. The Welfare Council sponsored Nesbitt in updating her study on living costs in 1919 and 1920 to reflect the cost-of-living increases.[39] Table 11 illustrates the gap between purchasing power and the actual stipend. The average monthly grant appeared to have increased, yet when adjusted for inflation the stipend's value diminished to 50 or 60 percent of the original amount for much of the period. Recognizing the serious deficit in aid, the Welfare Council persuaded the juvenile court to ascertain an amount that might be contributed from private agencies. The Committee on Family Welfare even requested that Nesbitt readjust the budget figures upward to justify enlarged grants. This research played a part in the 1921 legislative revision that removed ceilings on grants to families.[40]

The attention paid to family budgets by Chicago's social workers fit within a larger national discussion on a minimum standard of living. The Na-

TABLE 11 Comparison of Average Monthly Grant Stipend
and Inflation-adjusted Value

Year	Amount	Adjusted	Ratio	Year	Amount	Adjusted	Ratio
1915	22.29	22.74	1.02	1921	35.73	20.19	.57
1916	26.73	24.98	.93	1922	48.28	29.26	.61
1917	31.41	24.34	.77	1923	50.57	30.10	.60
1918	29.64	18.88	.63	1924	50.04	29.61	.59
1919	31.81	17.87	.56	1925	53.50	30.92	.58
1920	35.08	17.03	.49	1926	52.58	30.22	.57

Sources: Douglas' Index of Relative Living Costs (1914 = 100). Paul H. Douglas, *Real Wages in the United States, 1890–1926* (Boston: Houghton Mifflin, Co., 1930), 40–42, 60–61. "Statistics of the Aid to Mothers and Children Division of the Juvenile Court," and "Total Expenditures by the County for Mothers' Pensions, Number of Families and Average Amount per Family," *Charity Service Reports* (1915–1926). Comparable figures were not available for the years 1911–1915 because of irregular record-keeping.

tional Conference of Social Work and the Children's Bureau took up the topic of budget studies and minimum standards in mothers' pension policies at a national conference on mothers' pensions in 1922. Nesbitt's research on Chicago and her larger study for the Children's Bureau provided one model for developing minimum standards of aid to dependent children.[41] The national attention to the issue and the corresponding research remained entirely advisory, however. For example, during the summer of 1923 the Welfare Council became aware that juvenile court judge Victor Arnold reduced pension stipends when he found that private agencies supplemented aid above the minimum set by the court. Welfare Council members had little success getting Judge Arnold to retreat from this practice.[42]

The following year the Welfare Council found itself in a situation in which it advocated a family budget for mothers' pensions that surpassed the average working-class family income. The committee's standard budget for 1924 established an income "substantially above the wages of the average laborer, head of a family, in Illinois."[43] The larger problem, of course, was that workers' wages did not meet minimum standards of living and that families dealt with the difference by putting more family members in the labor force. To expose the larger industrial issue, the Welfare Council sponsored a study on families of unskilled workers in conjunction with the University of Chicago's Local Community Research Committee. Leila Houghteling conducted the research under the direction of a subcommittee comprised of Harry Millis, Edith Abbott, Sophonisba Breckinridge, E. W. Burgess, and Florence Nesbitt.[44] Houghteling found that an "analysis of the general living conditions . . . has shown quite clearly that the families living on a lower standard than that provided by the budget estimate are living under conditions that fail utterly to provide a standard of living that will make possible . . . the full physical and mental growth and development of children."[45] The results justified the Welfare Council's position and they decided to maintain their recommendation of a higher mothers' pension budget. This position placed them at odds with critics who maintained that public aid should never rise above the potential earnings of a worker.[46]

Budgets could be used to raise a family's standard of living, as the Welfare Council actions illustrated, but they could also be used to justify cuts in grants and to eliminate grants totally when fiscal pressures dictated. This second scenario is best illustrated with a description of the public finance environment of mothers' pensions.

THE FISCAL ECONOMY OF MOTHERS' PENSIONS

An account of the fiscal growth of the mothers' pension policy is as important as a description of the families who received it. It is difficult in fact to understand the program's operation without understanding the fiscal politics under which it developed. It was, on one hand, a tremendous financial success. The budget for mothers' pensions surpassed that of other public welfare in Chicago by the mid-1920s. On the national level, James Patterson found that mothers' pension programs exceeded those for the aged in that they existed in four times as many states, covered 932 times more people, and cost 152 times more in public expenditures. By 1924, local and state funds across the nation had paid $13 million for pensions. Cook County appropriated nearly 6 percent of that amount, or $750,000.[47]

Mothers' pension appropriations increased in Cook County over the years of this study with the exception of two years. The appropriations doubled in 1913, then dropped by 26 percent in 1915, but regained its loss over the next two years. Between 1916 and 1918, appropriations increased 40.5 percent and grew in each subsequent year. Inflation eroded these gains, however. Between 1912 and 1926, the appropriations for mothers' pensions increased 940 percent in current value and 473 percent when adjusted for inflation (see table 12). In addition, mothers' pensions appropriations far outpaced those for general relief and the Cook County budget. The relief budget declined in real value by 34 percent, and the County Board's appropriations gained 37.5 percent during the same years. Pension appropriations did as well as they did because the state policy authorized a separate tax to support the pension fund.

This comparison between the budgets of mothers' pensions and relief highlights the range of public resources available to single-mother families relative to their marital status. While widows might receive a share of an ever enlarged budget, women who were separated from their husbands, deserted, or

TABLE 12 Comparative Appropriations of Public Expenditures

Category	1912	1914	1916	1918	1920	1922	1924	1926
Appropriations in thousands of dollars								
Mothers' pensions	75.0	—	185.0	260.0	450.0	650.0	750.0	780.0
Relief supplies	274.5	—	240.0	235.9	200.0	247.0	175.0	325.0
Appropriations per 100 residents								
Mothers' pension								
Current	3.3	—	7.4	9.9	16.5	22.9	25.5	24.9
Inflation-adjusted	3.4	—	6.9	6.3	8.0	13.9	15.1	14.3
Relief supplies								
Current	11.9	—	9.5	9.0	7.3	8.7	5.9	10.4
Inflation-adjusted	12.4	—	8.9	5.7	3.6	5.3	3.5	6.0
County budget								
Current	549.3	—	468.4	408.0	665.7	719.1	598.6	938.5
Inflation-adjusted	572.2	—	437.8	259.9	323.1	435.8	354.2	539.3

Note: No data were available for 1914. Appropriations are in thousands of dollars, except in population comparisons.

Sources: Douglas' Index of Relative Living Costs (1914 = 100). Paul Douglas, *Real Wages in the United States, 1890–1926* (Boston: Houghton Mifflin, Co., 1930), 40–42, 60–61. Cook County, IL, Country Board of Commissioners, *Charity Service Reports* (1911–1927).

never married received referrals to poor relief or the Court of Domestic Relations division of nonsupport. These divisions did not provide regular cash stipends and consequently placed more weight on the women's ability to earn as well as on financial support from relatives (see table 13). This had a great impact upon African American women, who had higher rates of separation and desertion. As the public sector expanded, this focus on marital status created an inequality in the distribution of resources by race.

Increased demands for aid erased the visible signs of expanding public resources directed at single-mother families. The juvenile court frequently faced a situation in which hundreds of families who needed aid could not receive it because of insufficient appropriations. The court responded to the situation with three strategies: waiting lists, lowered stipends, and the removal of families from public aid as soon as the court determined that they were able to earn. The importance of a family's earnings in the court's decision to grant aid has been discussed. Here, I want to emphasize the interrelationship between public appropriations and the percentage of positive recommendations for pensions. Approximately 30 to 40 percent of applications were approved by the committee over the years of this study, but variations occurred annually. There could be very low years, as in the first year when only 19 percent of the cases received

TABLE 13 Variations in Monthly Aid between Public
and Private Agencies, Chicago 1928

Cook County Mothers' Pension Department	$53.07
Cook County Bureau of Public Welfare	7.27
Jewish Social Service Bureau	47.23
United Charities of Chicago	30.14

Source: Helen R. Jeter and A. W. McMillen, "Some Statistics of Family Welfare and Relief in Chicago—1928," Social Service Review 3:3 (September 1929): 456.

aid, and in 1918 when the committee approved only 16 percent of the applications. The opposite could also occur. In 1923, 45 percent of pension applications were recommended for funding. The recommendations of the committee went directly to the juvenile court judge, who generally followed the committee's suggestions; but both the judge and the county agent retained the authority to reject or add cases. The judge used such authority in 1921 when the committee put forward 33 percent of the applications but the court granted only 10 percent.

What explains such variations in the court's granting of pensions? Neither moral arguments nor legislative change varied so radically as to account for these differences year to year. A more compelling explanation rests with the fiscal capacity of the court. In the first year of the policy, a year in which fewer than one-fifth of the applicants received grants, the county commissioners made no appropriation until the last month of the fiscal year. In 1917, 59 percent of the applicants were dropped simply because no funds were available. The court faced similar funding shortages relative to pension requests in 1918 and 1921, and long waiting lists developed. Conversely, higher rates of pension acceptance occurred when additional funding existed. This situation occurred in the years 1922 to 1923 when additional revenue became available after a tax increase.[48] The availability of funds also influenced the committee's decisions to cancel pensions.

The emphasis on economic factors, so evident in the initial denial of the pension application, appears in the explanations for moving families off pensions altogether. A close review of the cancelled pensions, called "stays," demonstrates the role fiscal policy played. Once a woman received a pension for her children, the family underwent periodic reviews to maintain their eligibility. The three most common reasons to end a pension—economic, legal, or moral-behavioral causes—closely followed the eligibility criteria. Tremendous variations could occur annually in the percentage of cancelled pensions. For example, only 8 percent of families lost their pensions in 1915, but three years later cancellations reached a high of 35 percent. The postwar period 1920–1922 also witnessed cancellation rates of 20 to 28 percent of families. Can we assume that cancellations increased in concert with a rise in the three areas of ineligibility? Let's consider each cause in the order of its increased importance.[49]

Pensions cancelled for reasons of "fitness" or resistance to casework methods (moral-behavioral) occurred most frequently in the first few years of the pension program. According to the Children's Bureau study that examined the administration of pensions in Illinois, moral reasons accounted for 17 percent of the cancellations in Cook County. An internal study of the Mothers' Pension Division for the years 1913 to 1915 show that 10 percent of pension cases were dropped because mothers failed to cooperate or made false statements to the investigator. An additional 10 percent lost their pensions because they were deemed morally unfit or kept male boarders. From the viewpoint of pension administrators, the work of rehabilitating families could be seriously disrupted by such clients.

> The woman's refusal to cooperate means that she is unwilling to take those steps which in the judgment of the officer and of the conference committee are essential to the proper care of her children. She may refuse to move from an insanitary house or a demoralizing neighborhood, she may insist on keeping male boarders or lodgers, or the husband may be the victim of an infectious disease, dangerous to the members of his family, and may refuse to leave the home. The court may become convinced that not even with an allowance can the home be kept at that level for which the county is willing to be responsible.[50]

After 1915, a sharp decline in the use of moral-behavioral reasons took place. On average they accounted for only 3.3 percent of the cancelled pensions. Resistance or failure to cooperate accounted for 4.2 percent of the reasons. Together, both moral and resistance reasons never made up more than 11 percent of the stayed cases in any year.[51]

Legal ineligibility and remarriage each accounted for approximately 17 percent of the cancelled pensions. In addition to the legal criteria, this category included changes in the woman's status that affected her eligibility—the absence of children from the home, for example. Another change in status was brought about by marriage. The war and postwar period witnessed the greatest rise in remarriage as a reason to end a family's pension. In 1918, remarriage accounted for only 12 percent of cancelled cases, but after the end of World War I it made up 21 and 26 percent of those cases for 1919 and 1921 respectively.[52] Marriage offered a better arrangement for some than the waiting lists and casework supervision of mothers' pensions.

As in the case of denied applications, economic reasons accounted for the largest portion (approximately 58 percent) of all cancellations over the entire time span. Although this figure is significant in itself, the percentage rose closer to 60 and 70 percent in several years. The two largest categories of economic reasons, sufficient income of a family and a child reaching the legal working age of fourteen, made up 52 percent and 30 percent respectively.[53]

Fiscal politics best explain the variations year to year in the cancellation of pensions. The fitness criteria showed no correlation to periods of increased cancellations. The law expanded eligibility after 1915 and consequently would also have no correspondence to cancellations. Remarriage on the other hand could account for a part of the rise in the postwar years as one-fifth to one-quarter of the closed cases ended as a result of remarriage. Economic explanations also do not offer a clear pattern. One could argue that an expansionary economic climate accounted for the closed pensions in 1918, but what about the remaining years of the 1920s? Did general economic prosperity lead to higher rates of cancellations as families moved into jobs and off pensions? This question cannot be completely answered, although indications from the discussion of budget appropriations would argue that some manipulation of the caseload occurred. In 1918, when one-third of the families who lost their pensions did so for reasons of self-sufficiency, the juvenile court also reported a substantial waiting list of 900 families. In 1920–1921, when 20 percent of the cases were closed for sufficient income, Chicago was in the midst of a postwar depression and public and private charities were taxed beyond their limits. In the fall of 1928, facing tremendous economic pressure and a waiting list of 1,500 women, the juvenile court took unprecedented action and rebudgeted families. That is, it reduced the amount of a family's estimated need to justify a reduction in their stipend. It is conceivable that the court took this path to provide aid to a greater number of families, even though this type of action had been firmly rejected as unsound social policy in the past. The view advocated by social justice feminists as well as many on the Welfare Council had been to increase funding rather than reduce benefits. Family budgets, which previously had been used as a statistical vehicle to lobby for higher stipends, were reduced to a shuffle of numbers by the juvenile court to manage administrative budgets. The logic of pension cancellations, like that of denied applications, needs to be understood as more than a

result of behavioral regulation. It included the fiscal politics of welfare reform—that is, the administrators' need to manage demands for public aid with
expanding but nevertheless inadequate appropriations.

In the Children's Bureau's assessment of mothers' pension programs
across the nation in 1931, the author restated one of the primary purposes of the
program—that it provide the family "a reasonable standard of living without
the necessity of outside employment of the mother." The report recognized,
however, that with few exceptions localities provided such low stipends to families that the provision had in effect been nullified. Family budgets received wide
administrative approval across the country, and while these were used to measure individual family need against local standards of living, the 1931 report
found that in only a few cities did the maximum allowable grant come close to
the established level of need.[54] Chicago may have differed from other major
cities in its organization, but it shared an important characteristic with them. It
relied upon individual earning, and it subsidized, not supported, mothers' pension families. This contrasted with the goals of the earliest proponents of the
policy who claimed the right to an endowment; that voice had been lost in the
difficulties of local politics. It also contrasted with the efforts to provide what
would be called an American standard of living for all citizens regardless of
means or family status.

§

The entitlement language and rhetoric of maternal provision so evident in the
national movement for passage of mothers' pensions virtually disappeared in
the actual operation of the program. The private economy of individual family
resources and the public economy of taxes and appropriations played a much
greater role in determining the substance of the policy than scholars have previously recognized. Those who have examined the mothers' pension movement
have drawn from the goals of pension advocates to argue that the policy created
a maternalist form of social provision that recognized and supported the social
value of child-rearing, or that it replicated unequal power relations through a
family wage ideal that kept women at home to rear children. These analyses il-
luminate new forms of political activity by women as well as important changes
in the relationship between states and families during the Progressive Era.
However, mothers' pensions also involved an important connection between
families and labor markets. Contemporaries remarked on the interrelationships
between pensioned families and wage-earning. One cannot examine the actual
operation of the program without seeing the connection. I am not suggesting

that welfare colluded with local labor markets, for I could find no clear evidence of this in Chicago during these years. The public economy record is very clear, however. A woman's "ability to earn" became a way to exclude families from mothers' pensions, move families off benefits, or reduce the size of public aid when fiscal resources declined. A family's ability to produce income, whether it be from a mother's part-time wages or from those of working-age children, took precedence over the values of either maternalism or social justice articulated by mothers' pension advocates.

Insistence on wage-earning did not produce useful employment practices or sound social policy. Instead, the contradictory values discussed here point to a legacy of ambiguous social goals regarding impoverished mothers. The program did validate women's traditional responsibilities in child-rearing to the degree that it subsidized some families. But prescriptions of self-support could merge with contemporary moral and racial ideologies. That is, concerns about the negative impact of a mother's job upon the children of an unmarried mother or one separated from her husband did not surmount objections to their inclusion in the mothers' pension program. Overall, the program maintained women's unskilled labor force participation. Finally, the insistence on earning for impoverished families, while couched in terms that many Americans would value—self-support, independence, and personal responsibility—obscured a competing agenda by politicians and program administrators to regulate public expenditures. The first decades of mothers' pensions demonstrate the fragility of this early social experiment in public provision and the political decision to refuse a guarantee of support for single mothers.

African American family with the visiting nurse. Chicago Historical Society.

Conclusion

"Women are becoming self-conscious and irritable," wrote Edith Abbott and Sophonisba Breckinridge in the early years of the twentieth century. Although they used these words to describe the feelings of women wage-earners about the resistance they faced in the workforce, their observations would apply equally well to other areas. The movements for woman suffrage, civil rights, and industrial democracy that engaged so many American women involved them in debates about equality and independence as well as older ideas about women's place. While great differences existed between them, women nevertheless came together self-consciously as women to promote their agendas as citizens, workers, and mothers. They looked to the government to aid them in their goals. The emergence of this "new force in politics" took place within a changing political environment, particularly evident in the nation's cities. An expansion of public capacities created new opportunities for political authority for reformers and new arenas for political conflict with existing powers. The expansion of public provision through mothers' pensions provides an important example of the diverse political strategies used by organized women who succeeded in directing a significant portion of public funds toward poor women. The infrastructure they helped to develop signaled a reorganization of public welfare within the local state from political parties to state agencies.[1]

Middle-class women reformers had often made poor women and children the objects of their charity and reform. That avenue of reform continued while another emerged. Some reformers looked for ways to extend the legal, economic, and social benefits of citizenship to working-class women through practical policies. Cross-class alliances of women built labor organizations and promoted labor legislation. Their campaigns for wage reforms used arguments of sexual difference as well as the need for a living wage for women workers. However, the unskilled women workers with intermittent hours and low wages, particularly that group with young children and no husbands, posed a more difficult problem. Women's wage campaigns rarely promised wages to support more than one person, let alone a family. The nineteenth-century methods of charity and self-support had failed to provide any measure of adequate care and they diminished the value of a woman's contribution to the family. Employment measures alone would not achieve economic security for the majority of mother-only families. The original idea of a maternal subsidy offered a significant change over existing measures and a new form of economic security for families. It would end the charity practices of separating children from a mother and enforcing her labor. At the same time, it promised to remunerate women's child-rearing work. Mothers' pensions could keep families intact and subsidize the family economy.

The movement for mothers' pensions unfolded quite differently in the United States than the movement for maternal endowments in Great Britain or child allowances in other industrialized nations. Supporters in the United States followed the progress of these policies closely, largely through the Children's Bureau, but the U.S. political context produced a different form of provision. In addition to having less well-developed administrative capacities and local political parties, social groups mobilized around different interests in the United States. Organized women played a larger role than either trade unionists or social insurance advocates. The gender-conscious political mobilization of women succeeded in advancing not only woman suffrage, but labor laws and social provision such as mothers' pensions. However, by the 1920s the solidarity that had united various groups dissipated and left a weakened political base less able to negotiate for public benefits.

By 1930, Chicago's social provision for mothers in poverty had expanded both in the amount of public funds made available to families and in the expansion of new state agencies. Thirty years earlier, families headed by women who fell into extreme poverty had limited options. They frequently moved older children out of school and into the workforce, the mother assumed some level of wage-earning, and they sought the aid of their families and communities. Some placed their children into orphanages or child-caring institutions. These actions still did not prevent destitution for some families and they turned to the only available social provision—the poorhouse or charity. During the intervening years, local government developed two new programs to ameliorate the poverty of mother-only families: mothers' pensions and the nonsupport division of the Court of Domestic Relations. The mothers' pension policy, while selective in its eligibility and thus in its coverage, represented a major commitment of public funds to impoverished families. During the 1920s, when other social reforms experienced restrictions, the mothers' pension policy continued to expand in its fiscal appropriations and in the number of families it served in Cook County. Furthermore, the development of new administrative agencies created an intermediary between politicians and social benefits. This restructuring of the disbursement of public resources would have been inconceivable two decades earlier.

Yet, virtually from the beginning of implementation, the initial promise of mothers' pensions disappeared. The issues of economic security for poor families, the government's role in providing that security, and the powerful ideologies of race and morality complicated the once simple adage of "support for mothers." Americans shared tremendous uncertainty about the degree to which government should intervene in family life, more frequently condoning such action for punishment and regulation than for expansion of social benefits. If government appropriated the role of providing the husband's support, some feared this would destabilize family relations and encourage men to reject their duty. Elected officials questioned the expansion of public agencies not directly under their political control. The ideals of the program did not translate clearly into the political context of early-twentieth-century urban politics.

Of all the arguments for this new social policy, the maternalist claim for a pension for service had the broadest appeal. It complemented turn-of-the-century essentialist ideas of sexual difference and "women's nature," and it promoted an ideal of social order premised on stable family life. Using a model parallel to men's military service, maternalists argued that the work performed by mothers in child-rearing provided as valuable a service to the state as that offered by the soldier. But the maternalists' claim of universal provision floundered quickly. They had in mind a particular kind of service, one that met specific criteria. A mother's entitlement rested not solely with the condition of being a mother, but rather upon the achievement of certain standards. The maternal claims for universal aid shrank almost immediately as proponents backtracked on aid to deserted families or children born to unmarried parents. They failed to extend their rights of motherhood to African American mothers and instead let local race relations dictate outcomes. They recoiled in the face of opposition to the rising costs of pension programs.

African American women's organizations developed measures other than publicly funded subsidies to support impoverished mothers. Unlike the white reform community or the majority of child welfare associations, African American women's organizations rarely used the term "dependent motherhood" to describe impoverished single mothers. In its place, reformers and clubwomen recognized that single mothers were working mothers in the black community and they raised funds to provide support services like day nurseries, homes for working women, and facilities for dependent children. Clubwomen and reformers appealed to various levels of their government to intervene in civil

rights issues, but on the issue of relief from poverty for single mothers, their resources went into education, jobs, and services as well as charity.

Feminists promoted economic independence for women. Some, like
Crystal Eastman, supported a European-style maternal endowment as a means
to eradicate the persistent economic dependency of mothers and homemakers.
In general, feminists pursued independence through equity legislation, most
notably the equal rights amendment, introduced in 1923. Unlike the African
American community, no broad-based support for day nurseries, education, or
training for poor women arose from feminist circles. This form of support
would wait until the second wave of feminism in the 1960s.

Few alternatives for provision for "dependent mothers" existed outside
the context of women's reform activism. Social insurance and trade unionists
responded to the problem with an agenda for workingmen's families. Higher
wages for male workers would lift the family's standard of living. The worker
and his family would be protected from poverty in the case of accident, illness,
or death by workmen's compensation or personal insurance. Unemployment
insurance could reduce the insecurity produced by irregular business cycles.
Trade unionists worked for these goals through increased bargaining power in
the workplace, and reform organizations such as the American Association for
Labor Legislation worked through state legislation. But these policies had little
effect on those who worked in uncovered occupational areas and, by extension,
they offered little aid for the women and children in those families. Similarly,
they did not address the issue of nonsupport for women who had been deserted,
divorced, or never married. Supporters of workingmen's insurance defended
this omission by arguing that the problems of economic insecurity for the majority of poor mothers would eventually be solved by providing for the male
worker.

Another proposal, situated between the independence of feminism, the
protection of maternalism, and the exclusion of social insurance, emerged. Social justice feminists, such as Edith Abbott and Sophonisba Breckinridge, used
economic evidence and legal constructions to argue that economic means
should not disenfranchise women and their children from the protection of law.
The obligations of support ensured in contracts of marriage and guardianship
of children should apply equally to women of the working class and to those of
the middle class. If society endorsed the economic relationship undertaken
through the marriage contract, society had an obligation to support a wife's
claims for support when the contract failed; that is, when the husband failed to
economically support his family. A pension would provide such security. Their

claim attempted to combine women's rights with a practical policy for support and intended not to restrict women's right to earn, but rather to provide a safety net of security. Certainly, these well-educated professional women of the middle class brought their own assumptions into the debate. As others have observed, they devised these arguments without the consultation of working-class women and with an emphasis on behavioral regulation. While willing to challenge political and economic relations, they did not challenge social relations within the family. Their arguments, like those for the maternal endowment, never succeeded in gaining majority support. By World War I, Abbott and Breckinridge shifted their arguments toward a rationale for child welfare and concentrated on building the profession of social work. The point of separating this position from maternalist discourse is to highlight the women's rights agenda that rested at the center of their early plans.

The mothers' pension, or its successor Aid to Dependent Children, proved a poor vehicle in which to advance women's rights, however. The family wage ideal ascended as the framework that shaped social policy. It institutionalized a gender system that recognized the location of women's labor in the home and a system of social insurance that based its benefits upon contributions made predominantly from primary-sector jobs. Many workers fell outside this entitlement system when it became federalized in the New Deal's Social Security Act. In a system increasingly defined by wage labor participation, the official standard of the family wage eclipsed women's labor at home and effectively made women's wage-earning invisible.

The ascendance and institutionalization of the family-wage ideal also obscured the way in which welfare and wage-earning interacted for single mothers. The policy subsidized some mother-only families in recognition of the value of their "mothering" or of the difficulties of self-support owing to women's low wages. Yet the policy insisted upon self-support from those who were able-bodied even when they received a pension, and it indirectly enforced wage-earning for the women who were denied pension grants. Although historians have analyzed maternalist politics, the value of women's domestic labor, and the inequities of women's wage labor, few have discussed the integration of women's dual roles as earner and caretaker in the development of social provision for poor women. The persistent characterization of women on welfare as non-wage-earners has contributed to the invisibility of their dual roles.

Mothers' pensions developed within a fragmented system of public provision that particularly marginalized African Americans despite the dramatic growth in programs by 1930. Isolated from many public programs and excluded from the majority of white private charities, impoverished families relied on family, church, and community. In the old poor relief system, African Americans had gained in their proportion of those using relief, but they did so at a time when the relief budget declined. Consequently, they received a larger share of a smaller pie. In the newer programs directed at mothers with young children, African American women remained underrepresented on mothers' pensions while overrepresented in cases of nonsupport. Their participation in the expanded services of the local state was restricted to the programs that provided the fewest benefits. Social Security continued the system of differentiated benefits with its family wage framework and contributory plan. The wage labor of African Americans remained hidden within the benefit structure of the emerging welfare state.

How did an agenda driven by gender-specific ideals and supported by coalitions that included some of the largest women's organizations produce a policy that perpetuated gender-status difference and contributed to the invisibility of women's labor? While others have focused on class interests or professional motives to answer this question, political opportunities provide another part of the answer. The Chicago case makes clear the importance of a unified agenda. The political self-consciousness of women described by Abbott and Breckinridge played a vital role in the politics of welfare reform. Unlike in other states, clubwomen in Illinois did not organize actively on behalf of mothers' pensions. Despite their belated support for the policy, reform women demonstrated their capacity to operate as an interest group and they used successful political strategies to achieve gains for poor families through the mid-1920s. Women had gained the vote and by mid-decade were beginning to gain seats in elected office. Working in conjunction with policy activists and representatives of the juvenile court, members of the Woman's City Club in particular proved a consistent advocate for policy expansion during the 1920s and, perhaps more important, a watchdog over the county commissioners' appropriation process. They understood the necessity of advocates' pressure to ensure full appropriations. The moment to actualize the "women's welfare agenda" in at least one policy—mothers' pensions—was at hand.

An examination of the diverse views of organized women makes clear that the unified vision necessary to implement the policy did not exist. Progressive reformers such as Abbott, Breckinridge, and Lathrop shared tremendous faith in the transformative and positive powers of the state; but others remained skeptical. The majority of organized women recognized the problems created by the "dual burden," but some sought solutions based on private responsibility, others in equalizing employment opportunities, and others in universalized social provision. A large sector of organized women attached their claims to the stability of family life. Consequently, they backed away from the notion of a universal entitlement to poor women when it conflicted with other values such as male responsibility for family support. Similarly, some women's organizations supported poor women's rights to remain heads of their families only to the extent that they conformed with particular standards of mothering. Even motherhood, the central unifying theme of women's political rhetoric, signified very different meanings to different groups of women. The absence of political unity among organized women contributed to a negotiated and renegotiated incremental policy more similar to relief than social insurance—a policy that did not resolve the dual roles of women in mother-only families.

Other political factors contributed to the policy's limitations. The influence of private charities can be seen in the degree of regulation inscribed in the policy, particularly as the court sought to justify the law after it received so much national attention and criticism in 1912. Pressure exerted by the county commissioners on appropriations shaped the actions taken by Chicago's juvenile court. Responding to both demand and limitations in the amount of funding, the court restricted or expanded its caseload.

After World War I, political conservatism and fiscal deficits plagued reformers' goals for social legislation. These factors influenced the strategies of those promoting pensions as they changed their justification for the program. Just a few years earlier supporters called for mothers' pensions "Not as a Charity but as a Right—As Justice Due Mothers."[2] By the 1920s, advocates increasingly shifted the arguments for the policy to terminology that focused on child welfare. In a letter to Julia Lathrop, Ben Lindsey wrote that the experimental stage of mothers' pensions had proved to him that the "fundamental idea" needed to be "the duty of the State to care for the child, and the use of the mother in the process should be more on the theory that she too is an agent of the State in dispensing its funds."[3] Lindsey advocated the shift in terms of the justification of the policy as a political strategy. The same letter advised Lathrop that the organized women of Colorado had defeated a series of child welfare measures because of the confusion over the focus. "The whole conservative, privileged political group were united in their determination to defeat the legislation," he wrote.[4] In the face of growing opposition to centralized, publicly funded policies that were increasingly called socialist, and within the context of the demise of suffrage unity, many mothers' pensions advocates left aside the discussion of wage equity or equitable social rights for poor widows in order to salvage the social measure.[5]

By the late 1920s, fiscal weaknesses became evident in the mothers' pension program in Cook County. The appropriations constantly fell behind the burgeoning demand from women who sought assistance. The onset of the depression made this situation worse. Tax revenues declined, employment opportunities lessened, and the auxiliary sources of private aid shrank severely. Cook County did what municipalities frequently do under such conditions. It limited aid, reduced benefits, and created waiting lists of families. Across the country, states and localities reneged on their responsibility to support dependent families.[6]

In 1934, when President Roosevelt told Congress that he wanted to create a system that would provide economic security for all Americans—men, women, and children—to alleviate the crisis of the depression, he referred to the lessons learned through state experiments with social insurance as well as models from Western European countries. But the political context for policy formation had changed. Roosevelt appointed several cabinet members to the Committee on Economic Security (CES) in 1934 and drew from national experts as well as government officials to form the Advisory Council to the CES. An assortment of subadvisory councils reviewed social research on specific issues during the initial stages of policy formation and submitted their recommendations in a report to the CES. Only a few members of the women's reform network held these positions. The goal of achieving a uniform system of security for all Americans failed to materialize from these deliberations. Congress passed the Social Security Act, which has been characterized as a piecemeal package of social legislation with two distinctly different areas of provision—categorical aid and social insurance.

Contemporary accounts of the formation of the Social Security Act agree that aid to dependent children had a very low profile in the writing of the legislation. The impetus for any policy came from the Children's Bureau. Edwin Witte, executive secretary of the Committee on Economic Security, wrote Edith Abbott that child welfare provisions would have fallen by the side if not for the efforts of her sister.[7] Grace Abbott received an appointment to the Advisory Council to the Committee on Economic Security in 1934. She worked with Katherine Lenroot, then director of the Children's Bureau, and Martha Eliot, a Children's Bureau staffer, to formulate a plan for child welfare. The authors focused on three areas of need in the recommendations: dependent children in mother-only homes, services for neglected and delinquent children, and maternal and child health services. On the topic of dependent children, their report drew upon the state-level experiences with mothers' pensions. It estimated that over one million mother-only families with minor-age children existed in the United States in 1930, and 40 percent (431,424) of those families had children under ten years of age.[8] Although the report found it impossible to determine the economic status of these families, it estimated that "a very considerable percentage" were impoverished. In 1935, children receiving benefits under state mothers' pension laws numbered 280,565, but many more eligible families relied on relief. Employment would not solve the problems of these families, because women could not earn enough to support their families. The report called for 50 percent federal matching grants to the states and estimated the federal government's cost for an expanded program to fall between $25 million and $50 million a year.[9]

By the time the CES submitted the economic security bill to Congress, the language and content of the recommendations had changed again. Political opposition in Congress would further revise them. A clear division existed between provisions for social insurance and needs-based programs such as ADC. To garner support for funding for aid to children in their own homes, advocates turned to Progressive Era arguments of the social benefits of mothering. In her testimony before congressional committees, Grace Abbott used a familiar argument on the great social cost of a policy that made lower-income women carry the dual role. "The mother's services are worth more in the home than they are in the outside labor market," Abbott said; "consequently she should be enabled to stay home and take care of the children, and we expect she will have to do so until the children reach working age." Abbott acknowledged that the public hesitated to support families in which the father was able to work, but reported that states had greater success with programs that subsidized mother-only families. She knew she faced an uphill battle. State policies in practice had failed to provide a subsidy sufficient to prevent wage-earning on the mother's part.[10] In the context of the depression, as Witte noted, benefits to mother-only families were a low priority for Congress and the Committee on Economic Security. The discourse and political context had shifted considerably since "the woman's moment" of the 1910s. Employment and security for the politically mobilized working man drove Social Security initiatives.[11]

In the last revision of the report, the Children's Bureau lost three of its objectives. First, the bureau lost control over the program. It was transferred to the Federal Emergency Relief Administration to be administered under the public assistance agency initially, but the House Ways and Means Committee rejected this placement and moved it to the Social Security Board. The Senate briefly discussed returning Aid to Dependent Children to the Children's Bureau, but never proposed an amendment. Second, the Children's Bureau lost its recommendations on grants to families. Planners established a stipend based on the amount paid to children of veterans; no one noticed, however, that the veteran's benefit included an additional amount for the mother. Since ADC had no grant for mothers, the prorated figure actually paid less than a veteran's benefit, and came to slightly more than one-half the amount paid in an old-age grant. "There was so little interest on the part of any of the members in the aid to dependent children," Witte noted, "that no one thereafter made a motion to strike out the restriction." Secretary of Labor Frances Perkins took up the issue of the low grant with the Senate Finance Committee, but committee members never brought the issue to a formal vote. Finally, the Children's Bureau's recommendation of 50 percent federal funding was reduced to one-third.[12]

Title IV of the Social Security Act created a federal program for Aid to Dependent Children (ADC). Far from the ideas of a maternal endowment that aimed to provide for women's economic security, the policy categorized mother-only families on a needs basis along with the aged and disabled. At the federal level, planners wanted to discourage mothers from earning and at times referred to them as "unemployables." At the state and local levels an entirely different scenario could exist. Administrators wanted to manage budgets by adjusting caseloads and maintaining work requirements. ADC perpetuated the ambiguity regarding women's dual roles which had existed in mothers' pensions. The entitlement framework of social insurance excluded them, yet they had great difficulty earning enough to support the family.

At the state level, the process of implementing ADC revealed the problems of the new policy. ADC improved upon mothers' pension policy in that states that received federal funds agreed to make the policy available throughout the state, share costs with counties, and coordinate the program through one centralized agency. On the other hand, states retained control over eligibility criteria, which allowed some states to sidestep the broader objectives of adequate standards of living and social provision for impoverished Americans. States stalled in the implementation of necessary provisions that would bring in federal aid. Ten states, including Illinois, had not met the federal standards as late as January 1938. Those states that did adopt the cost-sharing program did not make full use of it. Jane Hoey, director of the Bureau of Public Assistance of the Social Security Board, attributed the slow progress of the policy to "hampering opinions and attitudes" in some localities.[13] Edith Abbott repeatedly criticized the placement of ADC under relief provisions rather than social insurance, particularly when mothers' pensions and workmen's compensation had provided such great examples of noncontributory social insurance, she said. Abbott campaigned to abolish the means test and "all surviving remnants of the old poor laws" to be replaced with insurance for children and the aged.[14]

The 1939 Social Security Amendment for Survivors' Insurance for Widows of Workingmen secured social insurance benefits for one group of mothers—the wives of workers in particular job categories. Citing the precedent of mothers' pension legislation and the superiority of social insurance over relief in "meeting childhood dependency," the Advisory Council on Social Security recommended that widows of workers receive benefits if they had dependent children. Survivors' insurance differed from all previous public aid in that it included a stipend for the woman which allowed her to stay at home. This form of insurance built upon other core benefits of social security and provided the "counterpart of the protection of the wage-earner and his aged wife or widow."[15]

This amendment to the Social Security Act institutionalized a division of public funding for mother-only families. Widows of industrial workers could receive a survivors' benefit sufficient to maintain the family without means tests, periodic inspections of the home, or behavioral regulation. Justification for the grant came entirely from the male earner's contributions and it was viewed as an entitlement, an extension of the social insurance package received by predominantly white male workers in the country's primary-tier jobs. The second group of mother-only families received benefits for their children only from the categorical relief program of ADC. If her husband had worked in agriculture, service, or trades that remained outside the umbrella of social insurance, a woman received no survivor's benefits in the event of death. If a woman's husband divorced, deserted, or separated from her or if she had never married, any state had the right to determine her ineligible for benefits. Furthermore, some state governments and local administrators would use state work rules to continue the close relationship between welfare and wage-earning over the subsequent decades.

Between 1935 and the early 1960s, state governments challenged and changed the meaning of "parental support" in Aid to Dependent Children. The original provision intended to aid children whose fathers had died, deserted, or suffered from long-term disabilities. Consequently, the language of the act defined eligible children as those who had "been deprived of parental support or care." To the authors of the Social Security Act, this phrase meant that fathers would provide the income and mothers would provide the care. However at the local level, parental support meant a mother would assume both roles, as the pattern of mixing relief and wage-earning continued in some locations during the

1940s and 1950s. Louisiana adopted the first "employable mother" rule in 1943, only eight years after the passage of the SSA. The state maintained that all capable women with children over the age of seven years who received public aid could be denied assistance when field work was available. Georgia implemented a similar rule in 1952 but lowered the age of the child to three years.[16] Having been given the leeway to set limits on aid, states used criteria such as family size or structure, residency, and "employable mother" rules to reduce public costs and address local political demands. Local control over eligibility also gave governing bodies the flexibility to address taxpayers' complaints and to retain "customary" practices of race relations. The federal Bureau of Public Assistance did not support compulsory earning by mothers, but the agency proved unable or politically unwilling to challenge the many and varied state departures from federal rules. It has been estimated that "two-thirds of eligible dependent children" remained uncovered by ADC in 1940.[17]

Federal welfare reform proposals began to openly discuss work incentives for women receiving Aid to Families of Dependent Children (AFDC) in 1962.[18] Thirty-three states already had work requirements in their state welfare codes by that time. Over the next thirty years, continuing to the contemporary debates on welfare reform, the central premise of these revisions has been to increase women's wage-earning contribution. The Kennedy administration initiated federal funding for services that would enhance both parents' efforts to become self-supporting. This plan recognized that women needed child care to work outside the home and promoted the reimbursement of these expenses; however the amount appropriated by Congress remained too small to be meaningful. By the mid-1960s, the growing number of families receiving AFDC, many of whom were never-married mothers, and the increased costs to localities created what academic and popular commentators referred to as a "welfare crisis." The War on Poverty programs made efforts to expand job and training programs, but they solicited primarily unemployed men and teenagers. Neither proved effective in moving people into self-supporting jobs. In 1967 and again in 1971, Congress implemented more stringent work requirements for those receiving AFDC. The new rules reduced a family's grant in relation to the amount earned by the working parent. In many cases, the costs associated with the job, and the reduction in supplementary aid, were greater than the benefits. Disincentives replaced incentives for self-support. While Congress responded to political and fiscal imperatives to increase work requirements, it left the details to the states. Congress and the courts justified the need for states to have flexibility in the administration of their welfare programs and the means to manage their costs. This included a state's right to make eligibility for AFDC contingent upon accepting work.

Much has changed in social provision over the twentieth century. Most notably, the growth in the public sector from local-level policies during the Progressive Era to the much expanded federal programs of the New Deal and Great Society that have created the modern welfare state. Far more expansive than programs for the poor, the welfare state today comprises a myriad of publicly subsidized programs that service many constituencies, from corporations to the middle class. Civil rights campaigns also changed the political context of the late twentieth century by raising expectations of legal and political protections for Americans. Finally, transitions in the national economy have created tremendous changes in social relations and the structure of families across class lines.

Despite these important differences, several persistent themes emerge from this study of mothers' pensions which continue to influence public welfare. The perception that mothers on welfare do not work has obscured the work women do in both family and market economies. Ambiguity toward the earning and caretaking roles of impoverished mothers, reflected in contradictory policy goals, negatively influenced our ability to reduce poverty among these families. The women reformers of the early twentieth century displayed considerable rhetorical consensus on the need to support women at home, but they disagreed on the details of a maternal subsidy. Contemporary welfare debates, for the most part, have left aside the privileging of mother-work and issues of women's rights, but they have their own set of contradictory agendas for welfare policy. Is the goal self-support for parents, control over public spending, or economic security for young children? Each necessitates a different strategy, and those who would answer the above question by saying "all three" find that the strategies conflict with each other.

Little progress has been made in addressing the relationship between welfare and wage-earning. The assumptions of self-support that shaped welfare policy for most men during the early twentieth century, as well as for some groups of mothers, now apply more broadly. Yet, the suggestion that families can simply replace welfare with wages ignores the overwhelming evidence that work in the low-wage job sector does not pay enough to keep unskilled workers' families above the poverty line. Although job creation has been great in this area since 1979, the low level of wages has reduced the likelihood of self-support. The problem is magnified for women, who on average receive less in wages and have greater needs for child care. Furthermore, significant gaps exist between the number and location of available jobs and the women who need them, and between the level of training required and the number of recipients with those skills. In the 1910s, proponents focused solely on caregiving and obscured the labor force participation of working mothers. Contemporary policy discourse gives little support for the goals of caregiving and instead focuses on earning. Social policy for mother-only families continues to need a plan that will bring together both areas of work undertaken by mothers. Such a plan cannot rely solely on economic growth to reduce poverty.[19]

Diverse political objectives, ranging from behavioral reform to fiscal politics, continue to set entitlement provisions aside for cost-cutting measures. The absence of a clear political constituency in support of social provision for mother-only families has contributed to the policy's weak status. Politicians have had an investment in the direction of this policy since its inception, but the political activism of social organizations has vacillated. The Progressive Era provided a context for political opportunity, not only with women voters, but also in the expansion of state capacities. The social mobilization of organized women made a difference in the expansion of the policy during those years. By comparison, despite the position of women reformers within the New Deal administration and a major transition in the historical expansion of social provision, the economic security of mother-only families became marginalized as workingmen's insurance moved toward the center. At the end of the twentieth century, the strongest political mobilization rests with those seeking to end welfare as an entitlement.[20] As the new federalism seeks to move the policy to the states, the experiences of the Chicago case may again be instructive. Local programs have a history of providing less standardized care and narrower coverage. States that seek to end child poverty will be challenged to do so without reducing benefits or eligibility.

At the end of World War II, Edith Abbott prioritized economic security as her goal for Americans and challenged policy makers to expand the benefits of social security. She wanted them to include not only those workers with stable jobs, but also the poor who could not earn their own support. She advocated the creation of a children's allowance to guarantee each American child a minimum standard of living and to replace the means-tested Aid to Dependent Children.[21] The period of economic growth and public-sector expansion that defined the postwar era seems quite distant from the economic restructuring and federal government downsizing of the late twentieth century. The opportunities to expand social insurance, in the face of significant political opposition and without mass public support, would appear to be few. While the problems of economic security for mother-only families cannot be solved outside the context of these larger transitions in our political economy, opportunities exist to find universal solutions. Single-mother families share many of the same problems as working-poor families. Policies directed at those areas of shared need would have a greater chance for political support. Americans are unlikely to reduce their expectations of their government, but how far the public will go to expand social provision for the poor remains to be seen.

Legislative and Judicial Changes in the Illinois' Aid to Mothers' Law

1911   The Funds to Parents Act passed the Illinois State Legislature. Although a statewide provision, it remained optional, at the discretion of counties. It authorized public funds to support children in their own homes. Eligibility, grant amounts, funding, and procedures were not defined.

1913   The Aid to Mothers and Children Act replaced the 1911 law. Eligibility criteria limited aid to citizens who met residency requirements and successfully completed application procedures. Only widows and women with permanently disabled husbands could apply. The new law limited stipend amounts to $50 per month and the age of children to fourteen years and younger. It also authorized "visitors" to supervise and oversee the case. Counties could establish a separate county tax of three-tenths of a mill to fund the program.

1915   An amendment modified the citizenship requirement to allow women who had taken out their first papers for citizenship to apply. Only their American-born children could receive funds, however. The grant ceiling increased to $60. The legislature defeated provisions to extend pensions to deserted women and women with $1,000 in property. The courts found the funding provision of 1913 to be unconstitutional.

1917   Women with a dower right in real estate or a homestead entitlement up to $1,000 could apply for mothers' pensions. Additional residency requirements limited eligibility to those who lived in Illinois at the time of the husband's death or disability.

1919   The court established the constitutionality of taxes to fund mothers' pensions. A tax of four-fifteenths of a mill in Cook County (two-thirds of a mill in counties with a population under 300,000) on "all taxable property" passed.

1921   An amendment increased Cook County's tax rate to four-tenths of a mill. The amount per child rose to $25 for the first child and $15 for additional children. Amendments to extend eligibility to deserted women or women with institutionalized husbands failed to pass.

1923   Deserted women became eligible for the first time since 1913. The age limit on children's benefits was raised to 16 years.

1925   The legislature maintained the tax rate at four-tenths of a mill for Cook County.

1927   The tax rate was reduced to three-tenths of a mill in counties with more than 300,000 population. A bill to make abandoned and nonsupported mothers eligible failed.

1929   The state began to reimburse counties for the cost of mothers' aid up to 50 percent.

Notes

NOTE TO THE FOREWORD

1. The phrase is from May Sarton's 1953 poem "Letter from Chicago."

NOTES TO THE INTRODUCTION

1. *Chicago News*, 12 June 1913, Scrapbooks of the political campaigns of A. A. McCormick, 1912–1915, Newberry Library, Chicago, IL; hereafter cited as the Alexander A. McCormick Scrapbooks.

2. *Chicago Daily Tribune*, 13 October 1914, Alexander A. McCormick Scrapbooks.

3. *Chicago American*, 21 November 1913, Louise Haddock de Koven Bowen Scrapbooks, vol. 1, Chicago Historical Society, Chicago, IL.

4. The family's name has been changed from the original source to protect confidentiality. "Study of Americanization," box 1, folder 16, Sophonisba P. Breckinridge Papers, Department of Special Collections, University of Chicago Library, Chicago, IL.

5. Discussions of the restructuring of American politics include Richard L. McCormick, *The Party Period and Public Policy: American Politics from the Age of Jackson to the Progressive Era* (New York: Oxford University Press, 1986); Stephen Skowronek, *Building a New American State: The Expansion of National Administrative Capacities, 1877–1920* (Cambridge: Cambridge University Press, 1982); Morton Keller, *Affairs of State: Public Life in Late Nineteenth Century America* (Cambridge: Harvard University Press, 1977); Terrence J. McDonald, *The Parameters of Urban Fiscal Policy: Socioeconomic Change and Political Culture in San Francisco, 1860–1906* (Berkeley: University of California Press, 1986); and Theda Skocpol, *Protecting Soldiers and Mothers: The Political Origins of Social Policy in the United States* (Cambridge: Belknap Press of Harvard University Press, 1992). See also Steve Fraser and Gary Gerstle, eds., *The Rise and Fall of the New Deal Order, 1930–1980* (Princeton: Princeton University Press, 1989), ix–xxv. Among the many syntheses of the Progressive Era, see William L. O'Neill, *The Progressive Years: America Comes of Age* (New York: Dodd, Mead, 1975); and Robert Wiebe, *The Search for Order, 1877–1920* (New York: Hill and Wang, 1967). For the debate surrounding the meaning of progressivism, see John D. Buenker, John C. Burham, Robert M. Cruden, *Progressivism* (Cambridge: Schenkman Publishing Co., 1977). On the expansion of public welfare before the New Deal, see Michael B. Katz, *In the Shadow of the Poorhouse: A Social History of Welfare in America* (New York: Basic Books, 1986); James T. Patterson, *America's Struggle Against Poverty, 1900–1985* (Cambridge: Harvard University Press, 1986); Ann Vandepol, "Dependent Children, Child Custody, and the Mothers' Pensions: The Transformation of State-Family Relations in the Early Twentieth Century," *Social Problems* 29:3 (February 1982): 221–235; and Susan Tiffin, *In Whose Best Interest? Child Welfare Reform in the Progressive Era* (Westport, CT: Greenwood Press, 1982).

6. Paula Baker, "The Domestication of Politics: Women and American Political Society, 1780–1920," *American Historical Review* 89 (June 1984): 620–647; and Kathryn Kish Sklar, "The Historical Foundation of Women's Power in the Creation of the American Welfare State,

1830–1930," in *Mothers of a New World: Maternalist Politics and the Origins of Welfare States*, ed. Seth Koven and Sonya Michel (New York: Routledge, 1993), 68, 44. Both Sklar and Theda Skocpol argue that in the United States organizations of middle-class women played the pivotal role of garnering early political support for social provision that the working class played in Europe. See Theda Skocpol, *Protecting Soldiers and Mothers*, 50–54.

Two of the many works that discuss the important role of women's voluntarist politics include Anne Firor Scott, *Natural Allies: Women's Associations in American History* (Urbana: University of Illinois Press, 1991); and Dorothy Salem, *To Better Our World: Black Women in Organized Reform, 1890–1920* (Brooklyn, NY: Carlson Publishing Co., 1990).

For international comparisons of gender and the origins of welfare state policies, see Seth Koven and Sonya Michel, eds., *Mothers of a New World;* Susan Pedersen, *Family, Dependence, and the Origins of the Welfare State: Britain and France, 1914–1945* (New York: Cambridge University Press, 1993); Alisa Klaus, *Every Child a Lion: The Origins of Maternal and Infant Health Policy in the United States and France, 1890–1920* (Ithaca: Cornell University Press, 1993); and Miriam Cohen and Michael Hanagan, "The Politics of Gender and the Making of the Welfare State, 1900–1940: A Comparative Perspective," *Journal of Social History* 24:3 (Spring 1991): 469–484.

7. The extensive literature on differences among American reform women includes Noralee Frankel and Nancy S. Dye, eds., *Gender, Class, Race, and Reform in the Progressive Era* (Lexington: University Press of Kentucky, 1991); and Louise A. Tilly and Patricia Gurin, eds., *Women, Politics, and Change* (New York: Russell Sage Foundation, 1990). For two analytical frameworks that assess early-twentieth-century differences, see Nancy Cott, *The Grounding of Modern Feminism* (New Haven: Yale University Press, 1987); and Wendy Sarvasy, "Beyond the Difference Versus Equality Policy Debate: Post-Suffrage Feminism, Citizenship, and the Quest for a Feminist Welfare State," *Signs* 17:2 (Winter 1992): 329–362.

Several studies explore the voluntary social service work of African American reform women and the ways in which it differed from the work of white women reformers. In addition to Dorothy Salem (noted above), see Stephanie Shaw, *What a Woman Ought to Be and to Do: Black Professional Women Workers During the Jim Crow Era* (Chicago: University of Chicago Press, 1996); Evelyn Brooks Higginbotham, *Righteous Discontent: The Women's Movement in the Black Baptist Church, 1880–1920* (Cambridge: Harvard University Press, 1993); and Jacqueline Anne Rouse, *Lugenia Burns Hope, Black Southern Reformer* (Athens: University of Georgia Press, 1989). See also n. 24, below.

8. Private agencies and public agencies historically worked together for local welfare provision; however, this study focuses on the expansion of public aid to mother-only families.

For an overview of the research on gender and the U.S. welfare state, see Linda Gordon, "The New Feminist Scholarship on the Welfare State," in *Women, the State, and Welfare* (Madison: University of Wisconsin Press, 1990), 9–35; idem, *Pitied But Not Entitled: Single Mothers and the History of Welfare, 1890–1935* (New York: Free Press, 1994); Virginia Sapiro, "The Gender Basis of American Social Policy," in *Political Science Quarterly* 101:2 (1986): 221–238; Theda Skocpol, *Protecting Soldiers and Mothers;* and Molly Ladd-Taylor, *Mother-Work: Women, Child Welfare, and the State, 1890–1930* (Urbana: University of Illinois Press, 1994). Gordon and Skocpol have laid out their disagreements on the extent to which society-centered or polity-centered politics shaped early social provision. See *Contention* 2:3 (Spring 1993): 139–156.

9. Until recently, the scholarship discussed mothers' pensions solely within the context of

child welfare. The aspects of the policy that focus on problems of women as distinct from those of children are difficult to separate out because the maternal role provided the basis for arguments for special protective legislation. Despite the difficulties, retrieving the arguments that attempted to highlight women's rights within the context of social reproduction provides a full and more complex discussion of the issue. For an analysis of the shortcomings of the "children first" strategy, see Linda Gordon, "Putting Children First: Women, Maternalism, and Welfare in the Early Twentieth Century," in *U.S. History as Women's History: New Feminist Essays*, ed. Linda K. Kerber, Alice Kessler-Harris, and Kathryn Kish Sklar (Chapel Hill: University of North Carolina Press, 1995), 63–86.

10. Nancy Fraser and Linda Gordon, "A Genealogy of Dependency: Tracing a Keyword of the U.S. Welfare State," *Signs* (Winter 1994): 309–336; Barbara J. Nelson, "Women's Poverty and Women's Citizenship: Some Political Consequences of Economic Marginality," *Signs* 10:2 (1984): 209–231; and Linda Kerber, *Women of the Republic: Intellect and Ideology in Revolutionary America* (Chapel Hill: University of North Carolina Press, 1980).

11. The most comprehensive account of the passage of pension legislation in the states, written by Theda Skocpol, found that the network of women's organizations like the General Federation of Women's Clubs had far more impact in the passage of legislation than settlement workers or organizations like the National Consumers' League. This study of Chicago found little involvement by these traditionalist women's clubs, relatively speaking, and significant involvement by settlement workers. On the origins of the movement nationwide, see Mark H. Leff, "Consensus for Reform: The Mothers' Pension Movement in the Progressive Era," *Social Service Review* 47 (1973): 397–417; and Theda Skocpol, *Protecting Soldiers and Mothers*, 424–479.

12. Theda Skocpol, *Protecting Soldiers and Mothers*, 477. This point is also made by Linda Gordon, *Pitied But Not Entitled*, 51. Local studies will enable us to better evaluate the politics of implementation. For example, Sherry Katz's study of California argues that socialist women played the most important role in advocating an inclusive mothers' aid law. Conservative women favored a more restrictive provision and were largely responsible for the state's limited measure passed in 1913. See Sherry Katz, "Socialist Women and Progressive Reform," in *California Progressivism Revisited*, ed. William Deverell and Tom Sitton (Berkeley: University of California Press, 1994), 117–143.

13. The stance of activist state proponents is of course not neutral. Self-interest as well as paternalist ideas of what constituted "positive" change have been detailed by Progressive Era revisionists and those exploring the expansion of middle-class prerogatives in state reorganization.

My purpose in focusing on Abbott, Breckinridge, and Lathrop is twofold. First of all, they were indisputably important in the development of mothers' pensions in Chicago, but they also had a national influence through their work with the Children's Bureau. Secondly, they serve as representatives of a larger cohort of women activists who used research and politics to expand liberalism, women's rights, and redistributive policies.

14. Hundreds of women wrote to the Children's Bureau seeking help for their families. Children's Bureau Records, Central Files, 1914–1940, record group 102, National Archives, Washington, D.C. See Barbara J. Nelson, "Help-Seeking From Public Authorities: Who Arrives at the Agency Door?" *Policy Sciences* 12 (1980): 175–192.

The voice of women who received mothers' pensions is unavoidably underrepresented in this study. The juvenile court case histories are nonexistent and other juvenile court records offer the barest details of family life. Early in this project, I decided to use the reports of the Mothers' Pension Division of the juvenile court published in the *Charity Service Reports* as my primary source. What this approach lacks in personal detail it makes up in consistent data on patterns over time, something that is unobtainable from selected case histories.

15. Notable exceptions exist. Beverly Stadum's case study of Minneapolis provides a clearly documented example of the interaction between wage-earning and charity. Beverly Stadum, *Poor Women and Their Families: Hard Working Charity Cases, 1900–1930* (Albany: State University of New York Press, 1992). Barbara Nelson's early work on gendered social policies recognized that mothers' pensions had the capacity to "subsidize low wages" of beneficiaries, but pursued it no further. Barbara J. Nelson, "The Gender, Race and Class Origins of Early Welfare Policy and the Welfare State: A Comparison of Workmen's Compensation and Mothers' Aid," in *Women, Politics, and Change*, ed. Louise A. Tilly and Patricia Gurin (New York: Russell Sage Foundation, 1990), 413–435. Mimi Abramovitz draws this connection for the decades after World War II, but not the early years. Mimi Abramovitz, *Regulating the Lives of Women: Social Welfare Policy from Colonial Times to the Present* (Boston: South End Press, 1988).

16. Linda Gordon, "Social Insurance and Public Assistance: The Influence of Gender in Welfare Thought in the United States, 1890–1935," *American Historical Review* 97 (February 1992): 19–54. In *Pitied But Not Entitled*, Gordon argued that both mothers' pensions and Aid to Dependent Children were formulated on the family wage ideal. For a debate on the relative significance of family regulation and labor force regulation, see Linda Gordon, "What Does Welfare Regulate?" *Social Research* 55:4 (Winter 1988): 609–630; and Frances Fox Piven and Richard Cloward, "Welfare Doesn't Shore Up Traditional Family Roles: A Reply to Linda Gordon," *Social Research* 55:4 (Winter 1988): 631–647. On the socially constructed differences in wages, see Alice Kessler-Harris, *A Woman's Wage: Historical Meanings and Social Consequences* (Lexington: University Press of Kentucky, 1990).

17. See William L. O'Neill, *Everyone Was Brave: A History of Feminism in America* (Chicago: Quadrangle Books, 1971); J. Stanley Lemons, *The Woman Citizen: Social Feminism in the 1920s* (Urbana: University of Illinois Press, 1973); Wendy Sarvasy, "Beyond the Difference versus Equality Policy Debate"; Kathryn Kish Sklar, *Florence Kelley and the Nation's Work, The Rise of Women's Political Culture, 1830–1900* (New Haven: Yale University Press, 1995), xiii–xvi; and Nancy A. Hewitt and Suzanne Lebsock, eds., *Visible Women: New Essays on American Activism* (Urbana: University of Illinois Press, 1993).

18. Nancy F. Cott, "What's in a Name? The Limits of 'Social Feminism'; or, Expanding the Vocabulary of Women's History," *Journal of American History* 76 (December 1989): 825; idem, *The Grounding of Modern Feminism*, 4–5; Linda Gordon, *Pitied But Not Entitled*, 324–325, n. 2; and Karen Offen, "Defining Feminism: A Comparative Historical Approach," *Signs* 14 (Autumn 1988): 119–157.

Different types of "gender-conscious" politics are explored in Elsa Barkley Brown, "Womanist Consciousness: Maggie Lena Walker and the Independent Order of St. Luke," in *Unequal Sisters*, ed. Vicki L. Ruiz and Ellen Carol DuBois (New York: Routledge, 1994), 268–283; Nancy Cott, "What's in a Name?" 827–828; Kathryn Kish Sklar, "The Historical Foundations of Women's Power," 43–93; and Hewitt and Lebsock, *Visible Women*.

19. For discussions of maternalism, see Molly Ladd-Taylor, *Mother-Work;* Seth Koven and Sonya Michel, eds., *Mothers of a New World*, 1–42; and "Maternalism as a Paradigm," *Journal of Women's History* 5:2 (Fall 1993): 96–131. For an assessment of the shortcomings of maternalism,

see Alice Kessler-Harris, "Women and Welfare: Public Interventions in Private Lives," *Radical History Review* 56 (1993): 134.

20. The terms come from Molly Ladd-Taylor's *Mother-Work*, 43–66, 75; and Linda Gordon, *Pitied But Not Entitled*, 325, n. 2.

21. Wendy Sarvasy, "Beyond the Difference versus Equality Policy Debate," 330; Ellen Fitzpatrick, *Endless Crusade: Women Social Scientists and Progressive Reform* (New York: Oxford University Press, 1990); and Robyn L. Muncy, *Creating a Female Dominion in American Reform, 1890–1930* (New York: Oxford University Press, 1991).

22. Abbott and Breckinridge did not refer to themselves as either feminists or maternalists.

23. "Race" is used here to compare African Americans and European Americans. During the early twentieth century, the word "race" more typically referred to the national or cultural differences of people. See Gwendolyn Mink, *The Wages of Motherhood: Inequality in the Welfare State, 1917–1942* (Ithaca: Cornell University Press, 1995).

24. Works that include an analysis of race in the development of welfare include Darlene Clark Hine, "'We Specialize in the Wholly Impossible': The Philanthropic Work of Black Women," in *Lady Bountiful Revisited: Women, Philanthropy, and Power,* ed. Kathleen D. McCarthy (New Brunswick: Rutgers University Press, 1990), 70–93; Linda Gordon, "Black and White Visions of Welfare: Women's Welfare Activism, 1890–1945," *Journal of American History* 78 (September 1991): 559–590; and Eileen Boris, "The Power of Motherhood: Black and White Activist Women Redefine the 'Political,'" in *Mothers of a New World* (New York: Routledge, 1993), 213–245.

25. For example, see Alice Kessler-Harris, *A Woman's Wage,* 9; Eileen Boris, *Home to Work: Motherhood and the Politics of Industrial Homework in the United States* (New York: Cambridge University Press, 1994); and Elizabeth Faue, *Community of Suffering and Struggle: Women, Men, and the Labor Movement in Minneapolis, 1915–1945* (Chapel Hill: University of North Carolina Press, 1991).

26. Several areas had experimented with aid to mother-only families. Jewish private agencies in several cities reported success in subsidizing these families with pensions. New York and California attempted variations on the idea and other states had related programs like school scholarships (as discussed in chapter 1). Missouri passed the first law in March 1911, but its provisions covered only Kansas City and Jackson County. A case study offers the opportunity to test program goals against outcomes and to evaluate several aspects of political action. This study examines the presence of private-sector groups and their relative resources, the level of development of administrative structure, and the political context in which the policy developed.

27. The exact figures from the census are 1,698,575 (1900) and 3,376,438 (1930). U.S. Department of the Interior, Bureau of the Census, *Twelfth Census of the United States, 1900: Population* (Washington, DC: Government Printing Office, 1901); idem, *Fifteenth Census of the United States, 1930: Population* (Washington, DC: Government Printing Office, 1931).

28. Jane Addams, "The Objective Value of a Social Settlement" (1892), reprinted in *The Social Thought of Jane Addams,* ed. Christopher Lasch (New York: Bobbs-Merrill Co., 1965), 44–61.

29. Allan H. Spear, *Black Chicago: The Making of a Negro Ghetto, 1890–1920* (Chicago: University of Chicago Press, 1967); James R. Grossman, *Land of Hope: Chicago, Black Southerners, and the Great Migration* (Chicago: University of Chicago Press, 1989); and E. Franklin Frazier, *The Negro Family in Chicago* (Chicago: University of Chicago Press, 1932), 99–116.

30. Bessie Louise Pierce, *A History of Chicago*, vol. 3, *The Rise of a Modern City, 1871–1893* (New York: Alfred A. Knopf, 1957), 53.

31. Jane Addams, "The Objective Value of a Social Settlement," 61.

32. Cohen's discussion of self-help among ethnic and racial groups in Chicago after 1919 reveals the diverse array of mutual aid groups that existed. She dates the transition to public aid in the 1930s. "In short, foreign-born Chicagoans received little substantial help during the 1920s from welfare agencies outside their own communities." Evidence in chapters 2 and 5 documents high rates of participation by the foreign-born in both general relief and mothers' pensions between 1900 and 1930. The difference may revolve around Cohen's stipulation of "substantial help." Poor relief provided meager benefits for short periods. Lizabeth Cohen, *Making a New Deal: Industrial Workers in Chicago, 1919–1939* (New York: Cambridge University Press, 1990), 62.

33. For a more detailed account of the Chicago Relief and Aid Society, see Kathleen D. McCarthy, *Noblesse Oblige: Charity and Cultural Philanthropy in Chicago, 1849–1929* (Chicago: University of Chicago Press, 1982), 70–71, 129–131. For a contemporary account, see Jane Addams, *Twenty Years at Hull House* (New York: New American Library, 1910), 133–134, 154–164.

34. On the accomplishments of this settlement, see Martin Bulmer, Kevin Bales, and Kathryn Kish Sklar, eds., *The Social Survey in Historical Perspective, 1880–1940* (New York: Cambridge University Press, 1991); and Allen F. Davis, *Spearheads for Reform: The Social Settlements and the Progressive Movement, 1890–1914* (New York: Oxford University Press, 1967), 24. For an analysis of settlements that played a more conservative role, see Ruth Hutchinson Crocker, *Social Work and Social Order: The Settlement Movement in Two Industrial Cities, 1889–1930* (Urbana: University of Illinois Press, 1992).

35. Ellen Fitzpatrick, *Endless Crusade;* Lela B. Costin, *Two Sisters for Social Justice: A Biography of Grace and Edith Abbott* (Urbana: University of Illinois Press, 1983); Steven J. Diner, *A City and Its Universities: Public Policy in Chicago, 1892–1919* (Chapel Hill: University of North Carolina Press, 1980). For the influence of these reform women in the national arena, see Robyn L. Muncy, *Creating a Female Dominion in American Reform*.

36. Ellen Fitzpatrick discusses several reform campaigns in *Endless Crusade*. For intellectuals, see James T. Kloppenberg, *Uncertain Victory: Social Democracy and Progressivism in European and American Thought, 1870–1920* (New York: Oxford University Press, 1986). Allen Davis discussed the participation of settlement workers in party politics and reform movements in *Spearheads for Reform*.

37. Maureen A. Flanagan, "Gender and Urban Political Reform: The City Club and the Woman's City Club of Chicago in the Progressive Era," *American Historical Review* 95:4 (October 1990): 1032–1050.

38. Robyn L. Muncy, *Creating a Female Dominion in American Reform;* Susan Ware, *Beyond Suffrage: Women in the New Deal* (Cambridge: Harvard University Press, 1981); J. Stanley Lemons, *The Woman Citizen;* and Robert Wiebe, *The Search for Order, 1877–1920*.

39. Elizabeth Lindsay Davis, *The Story of the Illinois Federation of Colored Women's Clubs, 1900–1922* (Chicago: [n.p.], 1922), 5; Alfreda M. Duster, ed. *Crusader for Justice: The Autobiography of Ida B. Wells* (Chicago: University of Chicago Press, 1970); and Fannie Barrier Williams, "Social Bonds in the 'Black Belt' of Chicago: Negro Organizations and the New Spirit Pervading Them," *Charities* 15 (7 October 1905), 40–44, 64–65. Anne Meis Knupfer found that over 160 women's clubs existed in Chicago by 1930, but not all joined the Federation. See Anne

Meis Knupfer, "'Toward a Tenderer Humanity and a Nobler Womanhood': African-American Women's Clubs in Chicago, 1890–1920," *Journal of Women's History* 7:3 (Fall 1995): 58–76.

NOTES TO CHAPTER ONE

1. Hastings H. Hart, "The Economic Aspect of the Child Problem," *Proceedings of the National Conference of Charities and Correction at the Nineteenth Annual Session held in Denver, Colorado, June 23 to 29, 1892* (Boston: George H. Ellis Press, 1892), 192; Mrs. G. H. Robertson, "The State's Duty to Fatherless Children," *Child Welfare Magazine*, January 1912, 158; and Jane Addams, "Charity and Social Justice," *Proceedings of the National Conference of Charities and Correction at the Thirty-seventh Annual Session held in the City of St. Louis, Missouri, May 19 to 26, 1910*, edited by Alexander Johnson (Fort Wayne, IN: Archer Printing Co., 1910), 6. See also Nancy Fraser and Linda Gordon, "A Genealogy of Dependency: Tracing a Keyword of the U.S. Welfare State," *Signs* 19:2 (Winter 1994): 309–336.

2. Molly Ladd-Taylor describes three groups of actors: sentimental maternalists, progressive maternalists, and feminists. This study uses the term "social justice feminist," rather than "maternalist," in recognition of the commitment of those individuals to both equity between the sexes and social justice. Molly Ladd-Taylor, *Mother-Work: Women, Child Welfare, and the State, 1890–1930* (Urbana: University of Illinois Press, 1994).

3. Several scholars have noted the way in which race and gender have been used to construct the ideal worker-citizen as white and male. This citizen is politically and economically independent and entitled to provisions of the state. Conversely, workers outside this constructed ideal had their work characterized as nonproductive and as dependent. Nancy Fraser and Linda Gordon developed this framework using examples of the colonial native or the American slave to illustrate the invisibility of the work performed by these people. A similar analysis explains the value of work produced by women, whether in the home or in industry. Those perceived to be nonworkers might in fact work, but receive fewer resources from either public or private sectors. On dependency, see Fraser and Gordon, "A Genealogy of Dependency." On the gendered and racially constructed meaning of wages in the United States, see Alice Kessler-Harris, *A Woman's Wage: Historical Meanings and Social Consequences* (Lexington: University Press of Kentucky, 1990); and Lawrence Glickman, "Inventing the 'American Standard of Living': Gender, Race and Working-Class Identity, 1880–1925," *Labor History* 34:2–3 (Spring-Summer 1993): 221–235.

4. During the early twentieth century, the word "race" referred to the national or cultural differences of people. Wendy Mink uses the term "racial-ethnic" to refer to racialized thinking. See Gwendolyn Mink, *The Wages of Motherhood: Inequality in the Welfare State, 1917–1942* (Ithaca: Cornell University Press, 1995). For a discussion of the separation of services by race in Chicago, see James R. Grossman, *Land of Hope: Chicago, Black Southerners, and the Great Migration* (Chicago: University of Chicago Press, 1989), 171–173, 186, 260. Grossman notes that the opposition expressed by Edith Abbott, Sophonisba Breckinridge, Jane Addams, and Mary McDowell to segregated facilities positioned them as a "vanguard" of white social workers, but had little impact on black social services. A more detailed description of the de facto segregation of social services which shares Grossman's view of progressive white reformers on race may be found in Thomas Lee Philpott, *The Slum and the Ghetto: Neighborhood Deterioration and Middle-Class Reform, Chicago, 1880–1930* (New York: Oxford University Press, 1978), 293–301, 323–341.

5. The idea to provide public funds for support of dependent families was not unique to the United States. Western European countries, Australia, and New Zealand devised a variety of programs. The cross-national comparisons are instructive in understanding the matrix of political factors in the creation of social policy and their outcomes. For example, see Marilyn Lake, "A Revolution in the Family: The Challenge and Contradictions of Maternal Citizenship in Australia," in *Mothers of a New World: Maternalist Politics and the Origins of Welfare States,* ed. Seth Koven and Sonya Michel (New York: Routledge, 1993), 378–395; and Susan Pedersen, "Catholicism, Feminism, and the Politics of the Family during the Late Third Republic," in *Mothers of a New World,* 246–276. The Children's Bureau served as a clearinghouse for national and international developments. See U.S. Department of Labor, Children's Bureau, *Laws Relating to 'Mothers' Pensions' in the United States, Denmark, and New Zealand,* Bureau Publication no. 7 (Washington, DC: Government Printing Office, 1914).

This book uses the term "mothers' pensions" uniformly. The most comprehensive histories of the movement to gain mothers' pensions are Theda Skocpol, *Protecting Soldiers and Mothers: The Political Origins of Social Policy in the United States* (Cambridge: Belknap Press of Harvard University Press, 1992); and Mark H. Leff, "Consensus for Reform: The Mothers' Pension Movement in the Progressive Era," *Social Service Review* 47 (1973): 397–417. A diverse range of interpretations of the policy may be found in Linda Gordon, *Pitied But Not Entitled: Single Mothers and the History of Welfare, 1890–1935* (New York: Free Press, 1994); Mimi Abramovitz, *Regulating the Lives of Women: Social Welfare Policy from Colonial Times to the Present* (Boston: South End Press, 1988); Molly Ladd-Taylor, *Mother-Work;* Barbara Nelson, "The Gender, Race, and Class Origins of Early Welfare Policy and the Welfare State: A Comparison of Workmen's Compensation and Mothers' Aid," in *Women, Politics, and Change,* ed. Louise A. Tilly and Patricia Gurin (New York: Russell Sage Foundation, 1990), 413–435; Ann Vandepol, "Dependent Children, Child Custody, and the Mothers' Pensions: The Transformation of State-Family Relations in the Early Twentieth Century," *Social Problems* 29:3 (February 1982): 221–235; Christopher Howard, "Sowing the Seeds of 'Welfare': The Transformation of Mothers' Pensions, 1900–1940," *Journal of Policy History* 4:2 (1992): 188–227; Roy Lubove, *The Struggle for Social Security, 1900–1935* (Cambridge: Harvard University Press, 1968), 91–112; and Muriel W. Pumphrey and Ralph E. Pumphrey, "The Widows' Pension Movement, 1900–1930: Preventive Child-Saving or Social Control?" in *Social Welfare or Social Control? Some Historical Reflections on "Regulating the Poor,"* ed. Walter I. Trattner (Knoxville: University of Tennessee Press, 1983), 51–66. Important unpublished studies include Libba Gage Moore, "Mothers' Pensions: The Origins of the Relationship between Women and the Welfare State" (Ph.D. diss., University of Massachusetts, 1986); and Janet Marie Wedel, "The Origins of State Patriarchy during the Progressive Era: A Sociologic Study of the Mothers' Aid Movement" (Ph.D. diss., Washington University, 1975).

Other summary treatments are included in Michael B. Katz, *In the Shadow of the Poorhouse: A Social History of Welfare in America* (New York: Basic Books, 1986), 127–129, 208; Walter Trattner, *From Poor Law to Welfare State: A History of Social Welfare in America* (New York: Free Press, 1974), 187–190; Frank J. Bruno, *Trends in Social Work, 1874–1956: A History Based on the Proceedings of the National Conference of Social Work* (New York: Columbia University Press, 1957), 177–182; Susan Tiffin, *In Whose Best Interest? Child Welfare Reform in the Progressive Era* (Westport, CT: Greenwood Press, 1982); Hace Tishler, *Self-Reliance and Social Security, 1870–1917* (Port Washington, NY: National University Publications, 1971).

For a history of Aid to Dependent Children, later Aid to Families with Dependent Children, see Linda Gordon, *Pitied But Not Entitled;* Mimi Abramovitz, *Regulating the Lives of Women;* James T. Patterson, *America's Struggle Against Poverty, 1900–1985* (Boston: Harvard University Press, 1986); Frances Fox Piven and Richard A. Cloward, *Regulating the Poor: The Functions of Public Welfare* (New York: Pantheon Books, 1971); and Winifred Bell, *Aid to Dependent Children* (New York: Columbia University Press, 1965).

6. Public charities were represented by members of the State Boards of Public Charity, as in the case of Illinois, and by officials of the public agencies. Private relief agencies, including charity organization societies, settlements, and ethnic and religious associations, were always a significant part of the conference.

7. Some private agencies, primarily in urban areas, subsidized families of widows; but the practice was heatedly debated. Some agencies that aligned with the charity organization societies resolutely opposed any policy of "outdoor" relief (aid given outside an institution), because they believed it corrupted families and contributed to pauperization. On the other hand, the Jewish Charities (in selected cities) made a policy of supporting widows sufficiently so they would not need to supplement their incomes with wage work. The Improved Order of Red Men taxed members in order to provide a stipend for the mothers or other relatives of members' dependent children. See White House Conference, 1909, *Proceedings of the Conference on the Care of Dependent Children Held at Washington, D.C., January 25–26, 1909* (Washington, DC: Government Printing Office, 1909), 54. For California, see Grace Abbott, *The Child and the State, Select Documents* (Chicago: University of Chicago Press, 1938), vol. 1: 107–108; for Massachusetts, see *Proceedings of the National Conference of Charities and Correction, 1890*, cited in Pumphrey and Pumphrey, "The Widows' Pension Movement," 55; for New York, Oklahoma, and Michigan, see Mark Leff, "Consensus for Reform," 399.

8. Report of the Child-Saving Committee, *Proceedings of the National Conference of Charities and Correction at the Twenty-fourth Annual Session held in Toronto, Ontario, July 7–14, 1897* (Boston: George H. Ellis, 1898), 87–88.

9. Discussion of the session "The Child Problem in Cities," *Proceedings of the National Conference of Charities and Correction, at the Eighteenth Annual Session held in Indianapolis, Indiana, May 13–20, 1891* (Boston: George H. Ellis Press, 1891), 326–327.

10. John H. Finley, "The Child Problem in Cities," *Proceedings of the National Conference of Charities and Correction, 1891*, 129.

11. Ibid., 132.

12. Reverend S. S. Craig, "The Abolition of Poverty," *Proceedings of the National Conference of Charities and Correction, 1897*, 272–273.

13. Reverend J. A. Ryan, "The Standard of Living and the Problem of Dependency," *Proceedings of the National Conference of Charities and Correction at the Thirty-fourth Annual Session held in the City of Indianapolis, Indiana, 1907* (Indianapolis: William B. Burford, 1907), 342–343.

14. Marion I. Moore, "Discussions," *Proceedings of the National Conference of Charities and Correction at the Twenty-eighth Annual Session held at the city of Washington, D.C., May 9–15, 1901* (Boston: George H. Ellis, 1901), 391.

15. *Proceedings of the National Conference of Charities and Correction at the Thirty-second Annual Session held in the City of Portland, Oregon, July 15–21, 1905*, ed. Alexander Johnson ([n.p.]: Fred J. Heer, 1905), 598.

16. *Proceedings of the National Conference of Charities and Correction at the Twenty-ninth Annual Session held in the City of Detroit, Michigan, 1902*, 378. The NCCC did not generate much discussion on African Americans until after the Great Migration. Between 1915 and 1930, the vast majority of speakers reflected the de facto segregation of welfare institutions and policies. For a discussion of the NCCC and its attention to issues of African Americans, see Pauline Lide, "The National Conference on Social Welfare and the Black Historical Perspective," *Social Service Review* (June 1973): 171–183.

17. Sherman C. Kingsley, "Public Dependents and the State," *Proceedings of the National Conference of Charities and Correction, 1905*, 396. See also 149, 411. Julian Mack, a lawyer, settled in Chicago in 1890 and became the secretary of Chicago's Jewish Charities. He worked with Hull House reformers on a number of projects. In 1903, he chose to serve on the juvenile court after being elected to the Cook County Circuit Court. For biographical information on Mack, see Edward T. James, ed., *Dictionary of American Biography,* suppl. 3, 1941–1945 (New York: Charles Scribner's Sons, 1973). Florence Kelley moved to Hull House in 1891 and served as the State of Illinois chief factory inspector. For biographical information on Kelley, see Kathryn Kish Sklar, *Florence Kelley and the Nation's Work: The Rise of Women's Political Culture, 1830–1900* (New Haven: Yale University Press, 1995).

18. Reverend J. A. Ryan, "The Standard of Living and the Problem of Dependency," 342–343.

19. Edward T. James, Janet Wilson James, and Paul S. Boyer, eds., *Notable American Women, 1607–1950: A Biographical Dictionary* (Cambridge: Harvard University Press, 1971), vol. 1: 147–148, s.v. "Alice Josephine McLellan Birney"; ibid., vol. 3: 237–239, s.v. "Hannah Kent Schoff." According to Ladd-Taylor, the National Congress of Mothers popularized the theories of child development and parent education of the period. Ladd-Taylor, *Mother-Work*, 50–51.

Members believed that women could develop their natural abilities for mothering through self-education available in mothers' clubs and school programs on child development. For example, see National Congress of Mothers, Board Minutes, 10 June 1910, 261, National Congress of Parents and Teachers Records, Special Collections, University Library, University of Illinois at Chicago; *National Congress of Mothers Magazine*, 12 May 1906, [n.p.]. (This newsletter ran under a series of titles: the *Clubwoman*, the *National Congress of Mothers Magazine*, the *Child Welfare Magazine*, and the *Parent Teacher Association*).

20. Ladd-Taylor, *Mother-Work*, 49.

21. Judge Ben Lindsey, National Congress of Mothers, Board Minutes, 10 June 1910, 261; National Congress of Mothers, "Address by Theodore Roosevelt," in *The Child in Home, School, and State: Report of the National Congress of Mothers Annual Meeting held in the City of Washington, D.C., March 10–17, 1905* (Washington, DC: National Congress of Mothers, 1905), 78.

22. *National Congress of Mothers Magazine*, November 1906, 2–3.

23. Josephine Hart was the third wife of Hastings Hart, director of the Illinois Children's Home and Aid Society. In 1903, the executive board called for specialized training of all probation officers who worked with dependent or delinquent children and the board requested that the universities of Chicago, Columbia, Pennsylvania, and California take steps to provide professional training for these jobs. National Congress of Mothers, *Legislation History, 1899–1958*, vol. 1: 3; National Congress of Mothers, Executive Board Minutes, 14 January 1903, 89.

24. National Congress of Mothers, *Legislation History, 1899–1958*, vol. 1: 7.

25. Mrs. G. H. Robertson, "The State's Duty to Fatherless Children," *Child Welfare Magazine*, January 1912, 156.

26. National Congress of Mothers, "Address by Theodore Roosevelt," *The Child in Home*, 1905, 67, 78–79.

27. National Congress of Mothers, *Legislation History, 1899–1958*, vol. 1: 11.

28. National Congress of Mothers, *The Child in Home*, 1905, 12.

29. National Congress of Mothers, Board Minutes, 10 June 1908, 183. Molly Ladd-Taylor explores the race and culture-specific assumptions of the National Congress of Mothers in *Mother-Work*, 50–56.

30. William Edward Burghardt Du Bois, "The Black Mother," *Crisis* (December 1912): 78; Darlene Clark Hine, "'We Specialize in the Wholly Impossible': The Philanthropic Work of Black Women," in *Lady Bountiful Revisited: Women, Philanthropy, and Power*, ed. Kathleen D. McCarthy (New Brunswick, NJ: Rutgers University Press, 1990), 70–93, quotation on 71. See also Gerda Lerner, *Black Women in White America* (New York: Pantheon, 1972), 441, 451–453; and Dorothy Salem, *To Better Our World: Black Women in Organized Reform, 1890–1920*, vol. 14, *Black Women in United States History*, ed. Darlene Clark Hine (Brooklyn, NY: Carlson Publishing, 1990). I am grateful to Nancy Marie Robertson, who shared her bibliography on race and reform with me at the beginning of my research.

31. A discussion of the NACW may be found in several works, including Stephanie Shaw, "Black Club Women and the Creation of the National Association of Colored Women," *Journal of Women's History* 3:2 (Fall 1991): 10–25; Deborah Gray White, "The Cost of Club Work, the Price of Black Feminism," in *Visible Women: New Essays on American Activism*, ed. Nancy A. Hewitt and Suzanne Lebsock (Urbana: University of Illinois Press, 1993), 247–269; Paula Giddings, *When and Where I Enter: The Impact of Black Women on Race and Sex in America* (New York: William Morrow, 1984); and Gerda Lerner, *Black Women in White America*. For a history written by the organization's own historian, see Elizabeth Lindsay Davis, *Lifting as They Climb: The National Association of Colored Women* (Washington, DC: National Association of Colored Women, 1933). The organization's papers are available in a microfilm edition, *Records of the National Association of Colored Women's Clubs, 1895–1992, Part 1: Minutes of National Conventions, Publications, and President's Office Correspondence* (Bethesda, MD: University Publications of America, 1994); hereafter cited as the *Records of the NACW*. An illustration of the platform may be found on the cover of *National Notes* 28:12 (September-October 1926), *Records of the NACW*, reel 24, frame 145.

32. Dorothy Salem, *To Better Our World*, 30.

33. "Women's Work—Where Does It Begin?" *National Notes* 3:7 (January 1900), *Records of the NACW*, reel 23, frame 334.

34. "Importance of Mothers' Unions," *National Notes* 7:11 (July 1904): 18, *Records of the NACW*, reel 23, frame 427.

35. *National Notes* 19:4 (January 1917): 11, *Records of the NACW*, reel 23, frame 694.

36. Mary Church Terrell, "First Presidential Address to the National Association of Colored Women," reprinted in Beverly Washington Jones, *Quest for Equality: The Life and Writings of Mary Eliza Church Terrell, 1863–1954*, vol. 13 of *Black Women in United States History*, ed. Darlene Clark Hine (Brooklyn, New York: Carlson Publishing, 1990), 133–138.

37. Mary Church Terrell, "The Duty of the National Association of Colored Women to the Race," *AME Church Review* (January 1900), 340–354; reprinted in Jones, *Quest for Equality*, 146–147.

38. Fannie Barrier Williams, "The Club Movement among Colored Women in America," *Voice* 1 (March 1904): 101, cited in Salem, *To Better Our World*, 31. Maternalism in club work is also discussed in Paula Giddings, *When and Where I Enter*.

39. Evelyn Brooks Higginbotham, *Righteous Discontent: The Women's Movement in the Black Baptist Church, 1880–1920* (Cambridge: Harvard University Press, 1993), 199.

40. Evelyn Brooks Higginbotham, *Righteous Discontent*, 202.

41. Mary Church Terrell, "First Presidential Address," 137.

42. "What Can We Do to Advance the Industrial Interests of Our Women and Children?" *National Notes* (September 1898): [n.p.], *Records of the NACW*, reel 23, frame 265.

43. "Co-operation Needed in Club Effort to Reach the Unfortunate," *National Notes* (April 1899): [n.p.], *Records of the NACW*, reel 23, frames 285–289.

44. Mary Church Terrell, "Club Work of Colored Women," *Southern Workman* 30 (August 1901): 437. Fannie Barrier Williams also testified on her efforts to overcome the color line in employment. Fannie Barrier Williams, "A Northern Negro's Autobiography," *Independent* 57 (14 July 1905): 91–96.

45. Laura Drake Gill, "A Creed of Work for Women," *National Notes* 18:2 (November 1915): [n.p.], *Records of the NACW*, reel 23, frame 624.

46. *National Notes* (January 1931): 7, *Records of the NACW*, reel 24, frames 572–575. Eileen Boris argues that the overlap between the language of maternalism and an insistence on work opportunities destabilizes the equality/difference paradigm used to define women's reform activism. Eileen Boris, "The Power of Motherhood: Black and White Activist Women Redefine the 'Political,'" in *Mothers of a New World*, ed. Seth Koven and Sonya Michel, 213–245, especially 217–220.

47. Several convention reports document the range of programs. For example, see NACW *Convention Reports* (1897), Nashville, Tennessee; (1899), Chicago, Illinois, *Records of the NACW*, reel 1, frames 84–260. Du Bois noted the range of charity activities in his summary of club work. See W. E. B. Du Bois, *Efforts for Social Betterment among Negro Americans*, Atlanta University Publications no. 14 (Atlanta: Atlanta University Press, 1909), 47–64. African American newspapers in Chicago, the papers of the Chicago Urban League, and coverage of the activities of African American social workers confirm that local clubs gave these measures priority. Concern about the dependency of children and social work services for "family rehabilitation" evolved during the 1920s with casework and social work training.

48. Mary Church Terrell, "The Duty of the National Association of Colored Women to the Race," *AME Church Review* (January 1900): 340–354; reprinted in Jones, *Quest for Equality*, 142.

49. W. E. B. Du Bois, *Efforts for Social Betterment among Negro Americans*, 133.

50. Higginbotham argues that by laying a claim to moral respectability, women participated in an act of self-definition while offering a defensive response to racist assumptions. Evelyn Brooks Higginbotham, *Righteous Discontent*, 187–192.

51. "How Can We as Women Advance the Standing of the Race?" *National Notes* 7:11 (July 1904), 9–13, *Records of the NACW*, reel 23, frames 410–423. Fannie Barrier Williams found the church, secret orders, and settlements to be among the most important institutions for Chicago's

black community. Fannie Barrier Williams, "Social Bonds in the 'Black Belt' of Chicago," *Charities* (October 1905), 40–44.

52. Various interpretations exist on the positive or negative results of state action. For example, see Rosalyn Terborg-Penn, "African-American Women's Networks in the Anti-Lynching Crusade," in *Gender, Class, Race, and Reform in the Progressive Era*, ed. Noralee Frankel and Nancy S. Dye (Lexington: University Press of Kentucky, 1991), 148, 154. The public-sector support of African American social services is covered in Jacqueline Anne Rouse, *Lugenia Burns Hope: Black Southern Reformer* (Athens: University of Georgia Press, 1989), 71; and Stephanie Shaw, "Black Club Women," 218–222. See also Linda Gordon, "Black and White Visions of Welfare: Women's Welfare Activism, 1890–1945," *Journal of American History* 78 (September 1991): 559–590; and Eileen Boris, "The Power of Motherhood," 213–245.

53. Mary Church Terrell, "Club Work of Colored Women," 438.

54. *Proceedings of the Conference on the Care of Dependent Children* (1909), 113–117, 136–138. Booker T. Washington spoke in general terms about dependency and poverty, but by his own admission knew little about the situation of blacks and charities.

55. *Proceedings of the Conference on the Care of Dependent Children* (1909), 5, 9–10. A 1904 Census Bureau study reported that 93,000 dependent children lived in orphanages or children's homes and that an additional 50,000 were placed in private child-caring homes. In Roosevelt's words, each of these children represented "destructive forces" if left without proper guidance and rearing. See U.S. Department of Commerce, Bureau of the Census, *Benevolent Institutions* (Washington, DC: Government Printing Office, 1905).

56. *Proceedings of the Conference on the Care of Dependent Children* (1909), 93, 90.

57. Ibid., 51, 71, 217–218.

58. Several sources on the charity organization society position in the debate over mothers' pensions may be found in the 1912 and 1914 *Proceedings of the National Conference of Charities and Correction;* and in Edna D. Bullock, ed., *Selected Articles on Mothers' Pensions* (New York: H. W. Wilson Co., 1915). The popular literature and suffrage magazines reflected the sides of the debate.

59. European discussions of social policy, particularly British, influenced American thought. Katharine Anthony wrote the preface to a British plan for a universal maternal endowment that combined opportunities for working women with supports for women who preferred to stay home. Eleanor F. Rathbone et al., *Endowment for Motherhood*, with preface by Katharine Anthony (New York: B. W. Huebsch, 1920). Edith Abbott and Sophonisba Breckinridge followed the welfare and social provision writings of Sidney Webb and Beatrice Webb. See n. 5, above.

For a discussion of the position of National Woman's Party feminists, see Nancy F. Cott, *The Grounding of Modern Feminism* (New Haven: Yale University Press, 1987), 117–129; Molly Ladd-Taylor, *Mother-Work*, 104–127; and Linda Gordon, *Pitied But Not Entitled*, 57–60.

60. Charlotte Perkins Gilman, *Women and Economics: A Study of the Economic Relation Between Men and Women as a Factor in Social Evolution* (1898; reprint edited by Carl N. Degler, New York: Harper & Row, 1966), 5–22. For biographical treatments of Gilman, see Ann J. Lane, *To Herland and Beyond: The Life and Work of Charlotte Perkins Gilman* (New York: Pantheon Books, 1990); and Mary A. Hill, *Charlotte Perkins Gilman: The Making of a Radical Feminist, 1860–1896* (Philadelphia: Temple University Press, 1980).

61. See Charlotte Perkins Gilman, "Paid Motherhood," *Independent* 62 (10 January 1907): 77; idem, "Does a Man Support His Wife?" leaflet printed by the National American Woman Suf-

frage Association, 1912; reprinted in *History of Women* (Woodbridge, CT: Research Publications, 1977), reel 935, frame 7972 (microfilm); idem, "On Ellen Key and the Woman Movement," *Forerunner* 4 (February 1913): 35–38; and idem, "Education for Motherhood," *Forerunner* 4 (October 1913): 259–262; reprinted in Larry Ceplair, ed., *Charlotte Perkins Gilman: A Nonfiction Reader* (New York: Columbia University Press, 1991), 234–249.

62. For the trans-Atlantic discussion on the maternal endowment and its influence on the feminist critique of family wage theory, see Linda Gordon, *Pitied But Not Entitled*, 55–58; and Molly Ladd-Taylor, *Mother-Work*, 105–118.

63. H. G. Wells, "Socialism and the Family," *Independent* 61 (1 November 1906): 1025–1028; idem, *New York Herald*, November 4, 1906, cited in Charlotte Perkins Gilman, "Paid Motherhood," *Independent* 62 (10 January 1907): 76. Other socialist discussions of dependent motherhood explored European models of maternity insurance, municipal child care, and pensions for poor mothers and their children as future directions for U.S. policy. For example, John Spargo criticized industrial conditions that placed such hardships on working mothers that ill health, infant mortality, and premature births resulted. He encouraged socialists to support equality between the sexes without discounting the different liabilities faced by women who had children, and endorsed a plan to keep mothers at home to raise their children. John Spargo, *The Bitter Cry of the Children*, with an introduction by Walter I. Trattner and an introduction to the original 1906 edition by Robert Hunter (Chicago: Quadrangle Paperbacks, 1968), 227, 231; and John Spargo, *Socialism and Motherhood* (New York: B. W. Huebsch, 1914).

64. Charlotte Perkins Gilman, "Paid Motherhood," *Independent* 62 (10 January 1907): 75–78.

65. Blanche Wiesen Cook, ed. *Crystal Eastman on Women & Revolution* (New York: Oxford University Press, 1978), 57.

66. For example, see Eleanor F. Rathbone et al., *Endowment for Motherhood*, 17–19.

67. Sherry Katz, "Socialist Women and Progressive Reform," in *California Progressivism Revisited*, ed. William Deverell and Tom Sitton (Berkeley: University of California Press, 1994), 117–143. Katz's characterization of socialist women's views are nearly identical to those articulated by Edith Abbott and Sophonisba Breckinridge in later chapters of this book. They would never identify themselves as socialists, which raises the difficulty of drawing precise lines between advocates of feminist reforms before the 1920s.

68. Sherry Katz, "Socialist Women and Progressive Reform," 140, n. 24.

69. National Congress of Mothers, Board Minutes, 8 April 1916, 148. Both Ladd-Taylor and Skocpol credit the National Congress of Mothers and the General Federation of Women's Clubs for the swift passage of laws in state legislatures. See Ladd-Taylor, *Mother-Work*, 140–141; Skocpol, *Protecting Soldiers and Mothers*, 439–465.

70. Edwin D. Solenberger, "Placing Out Work for Children," *National Congress of Mothers Magazine*, February 1909, 178.

71. Mrs. G. H. Robertson, "The State's Duty to Fatherless Children," *Child Welfare Magazine*, January 1912, 156–160; *Child Welfare Magazine*, June 1911, 194–196. Other articles mentioned the broad coverage of a pension policy endorsed by the National Congress of Mothers. For example, Agnes Downing, "A Wider Pension Move," *Child Welfare Magazine*, October 1912, 59.

72. "Editorial Comment on the Congress of Mothers," *North American;* reprinted in the *Child Welfare Magazine*, September 1911, 30–31.

73. *Child Welfare Magazine*, June 1914, 432; *National Congress of Mothers Magazine*, May 1913, 410; Hannah Schoff, "The Evolution of the Mother's Pension," *Child Welfare Magazine*, December 1914, 113–117.

74. Ben Lindsey to Mrs. Frederic Schoff, 3 November 1913, box 43, Benjamin Lindsey Papers, Library of Congress, cited in Janet Marie Wedel, "The Origins of State Patriarchy," 343–344.

75. Mrs. Frederick Schoff to Ben Lindsey, 10 November 1913, cited in Wedel, "The Origins of State Patriarchy," 344.

76. Several progressive settlement workers, including Edith Abbott and Sophonisba Breckinridge, were influenced by the release of the minority report of Great Britain's Poor Law Commission, which recognized not only the special needs of mother-only families, but the importance of publicly funded aid. Great Britain, Royal Commission on Poor Laws and Relief of Distress, *The Minority Report of the Poor Law Commission*, edited with an introduction by Sidney Webb and Beatrice Webb (London: Longmans, Green, 1909; reprint Clifton, NJ: A. M. Kelley, 1974).

77. Edith Abbott, *Women in Industry: A Study in American Economic History* (New York: D. Appleton & Co., 1910), 8, 322–323; Sophonisba P. Breckinridge, "Neglected Widowhood in the Juvenile Court," *American Journal of Sociology* (July 1910): 53–87; and Jane Addams, "Charity and Social Justice," *Proceedings of the National Conference of Charities and Correction at the Thirty-seventh Annual Session held in the City of St. Louis, Mo., May 19 to 26, 1910*, ed. Alexander Johnson (Fort Wayne, IN: Archer Printing Co., 1910, 6–7). Florence Kelley criticized policy makers' frequent use of maternal rhetoric and glorification of the home when labor conditions like low wages and homework contradicted the public's claim to honor motherhood and family. Florence Kelley, "The Family and the Woman's Wage," *Proceedings of the National Conference of Charities and Correction at the Thirty-sixth Annual Session held in the City of Buffalo, New York, June 9–16, 1909*, ed. Alexander Johnson (Fort Wayne, IN: Fort Wayne Printing Co., 1909), 118–121.

78. Margaret Dreier Robins, "Need of a National Training School for Women Organizers, the Minimum Wage, and Industrial Education," Presidential Address to the Fourth Biennial Convention, National Women's Trade Union League, St. Louis, June 2, 1913, pp. 3–8, *History of Women*, reel 946, frame 8782 (microfilm). The WTUL discussed a living wage for women workers earlier. For example, see *Hull House Year Book* (1 September 1906–1 September 1907), 46–47. For a general history of the WTUL, see Elizabeth Anne Payne, *Reform, Labor, and Feminism: Margaret Dreier Robins and the Women's Trade Union League* (Urbana: University of Illinois Press, 1988); Nancy Schrom Dye, *As Equals and as Sisters: Feminism, the Labor Movement, and the Women's Trade Union League of New York* (Columbia: University of Missouri Press, 1980). Several good studies of wage and hour legislation include Alice Kessler-Harris, *Out to Work;* Vivien Hart, *Bound by Our Constitution: Women, Workers, and Minimum Wage Laws in the United States and Britain* (Princeton: Princeton University Press, 1994); Susan Lehrer, *Origins of Protective Labor Legislation for Women, 1905–1925* (Albany: State University of New York Press, 1987), 63–94; and Sybil Lipschultz, "Social Feminism and Legal Discourse, 1908–1923," *Yale Journal of Law and Feminism* 2:1 (Fall 1989): 131–160. Florence Kelley's role in gaining minimum wage laws, as leader of the National Consumers' League, is covered in Kathryn Kish Sklar, "Two Political Cultures in the Progressive Era: The National Consumers' League and the American Association for Labor Legislation," in *U.S. History as Women's His-*

tory, ed. Linda Kerber, Alice Kessler-Harris, and Kathryn Kish Sklar, 36–62 (Chapel Hill: University of North Carolina Press, 1995).

79. Alice Kessler-Harris argues that assigning "a woman's wage" for a job, rather than "a rate for the job" precluded equality in wage structures and "symbolized the limits of political citizenship." On the development of separate wage strategies for male and female workers in the United States, see Alice Kessler-Harris, *Out to Work*, 180–214; idem, *A Woman's Wage*, 32.

80. Irene Osgood Andrews, "The Relation of Irregular Employment to the Living Wage for Women," *American Labor Legislation Review* 5:2 (1915): 287–379. Although many working-class women supported minimum wage laws, some women recognized that they might serve as a wage ceiling, and consequently rejected sex-based laws. For example, the members of the New York WTUL voted not to support the 1912 New York minimum wage bill. See Kathryn Kish Sklar, "Two Political Cultures in the Progressive Era," 59, n. 87.

81. Two important legal analyses that discuss the impact of sociological jurisprudence and legal formalism on feminists' options, and which complicate the oppositional framework of equality or difference, are Joan G. Zimmerman, "The Jurisprudence of Equality: The Women's Minimum Wage, the First Equal Rights Amendment, and *Adkins v. Children's Hospital*, 1905–1923," *Journal of American History* 78:1 (June 1991): 188–225; and Sybil Lipschultz, "Social Feminism and Legal Discourse." Minimum wage and maximum hours laws did not apply to both male and female workers until the passage of the Fair Labor Standards Act in 1938. The U.S. Supreme Court found these provisions constitutional in 1942.

82. For studies published during the policy debates, see Mary Richmond, *A Study of 985 Widows Known to Certain Charity Organization Societies in 1910* (New York: Russell Sage Foundation, 1913); Massachusetts House, *Report of the Commission on the Support of Dependent Minor Children of Widowed Mothers*, House Document 2075 (Boston: [n.p.], 1913); Katharine Anthony, *Mothers Who Must Earn* (New York: Russell Sage Foundation, Survey Research Association, 1914); New York, *Report of the New York State Commission on Relief for Widowed Mothers Transmitted to the Legislature March 27, 1914* (Albany: J. B. Lyon Co. Printers, 1914); Wisconsin State Board of Control, *Recommendations and Conclusions Based on Its Investigation into the Question of State Aid to Mothers with Dependent Children* (Madison: [n.p.], 1915). The United States Children's Bureau published several studies on mothers' pensions from the 1910s through the 1930s. U.S. Department of Labor, Children's Bureau, *Laws Relating to 'Mothers' Pensions' in the United States, Denmark, and New Zealand*, Bureau Publication no. 7 (Washington, DC: Government Printing Office, 1914); idem, *Laws Relating to 'Mothers' Pensions' in the United States, Canada, Denmark, and New Zealand*, Publication no. 63 (Washington, DC: Government Printing Office, 1919); idem, *The Administration of the Aid-to-Mothers Law in Illinois*, by Edith Abbott and Sophonisba P. Breckinridge, Publication no. 82 (Washington, DC: Government Printing Office, 1921); idem, *Children of Wage-Earning Mothers: A Study of a Selected Group in Chicago*, by Helen Russell Wright, Publication no. 102 (Washington, DC: Government Printing Office, 1922); idem, *Proceedings of Conference on Mothers' Pensions, Providence, Rhode Island, June 28, 1922*, Publication no. 109 (Washington, DC: Government Printing Office, 1922); idem, *Standards of Public Aid to Children in Their Own Homes*, by Florence Nesbitt, Publication no. 118 (Washington, DC: Government Printing Office, 1923); idem, *Laws Relating to Mothers' Pensions in the United States, Passed during the Years 1920 to 1923, inclusive* (Washington, DC: Government Printing Office, 1924); idem, *Public Aid to Mothers with Dependent Children*, by Emma O. Lundberg, Publication

no. 162 (Washington, DC: Government Printing Office, 1928); idem, *Administration of Mothers' Aid in Ten Localities*, Publication no. 184 (Washington, DC: Government Printing Office, 1928); idem, *Mothers' Aid, 1931*, Publication no. 220 (Washington, DC: Government Printing Office, 1933).

83. New York, *Report of the New York State Commission on Relief for Widowed Mothers*, 43.

84. Alice L. Higgins and Florence Windom, "Helping Widows to Bring Up Citizens," *Proceedings of the National Conference of Charities and Correction*, 1910, 138–144.

85. Anna Garlin Spencer, "What Machine-Dominated Industry Means in Relation to Woman's Work: The Need of New Training and Apprenticeship for Girls," *Proceedings of the National Conference of Charities and Correction*, 1910, 202.

86. New York, *Report of the New York State Commission on Relief for Widowed Mothers*, 42.

87. Edith Abbott and Sophonisba P. Breckinridge, "Employment of Women in Industries: Twelfth Census Statistics," *Journal of Political Economy* (February 1906): 14–40.

88. Marion I. Moore, *Proceedings of the National Conference of Charities and Correction*, 1901, 391.

89. L. B. S., Montana, to the Children's Bureau, 27 December 1919, file 7–3–4–6, Children's Bureau Records, Central Files, 1914–1940, record group 102, National Archives, Washington, DC; hereafter cited as Children's Bureau Records; A. C. to [Children's Bureau], 23 January 1927, file 7–3–2–4, Children's Bureau Records; J. H. B., Florida, 22 August 1924, file 7–3–2–6, Children's Bureau Records.

90. New York, *Report of the New York State Commission on Relief for Widowed Mothers*, 40.

91. Sophonisba P. Breckinridge, "The Home Responsibilities of Women Workers and the 'Equal Wage,'" *Journal of Political Economy* (August 1923): 534; Leila Houghteling, "Charity and Women's Wages," *Social Service Review* (September 1927): 391.

92. Isaac M. Rubinow, *Social Insurance with Special Reference to American Conditions* (New York: Henry Holt & Co., 1913; reprint, New York: Arno Press, 1969), 19, 432–434. For a criticism of the social insurance provisions of the Social Security Act, see Abraham Epstein, *Insecurity, A Challenge to America: A Study of Social Insurance in the United States and Abroad*, 2d rev. ed. (New York: Agathon Press, 1968). For limitations in workmen's compensation benefits, see U.S. Bureau of Labor Statistics, *Effect of Workmen's Compensation Laws in Diminishing the Necessity of Industrial Employment of Women and Children*, by Mary K. Conynton, Bulletin of the whole no. 217 (Washington, DC: Superintendent of Documents, 1918). For a gender analysis of social insurance and welfare, see Linda Gordon, "Social Insurance and Public Assistance: The Influence of Gender in Welfare Thought in the United States, 1890–1935," *American Historical Review* 97 (February 1992): 19–54.

93. Judge Julian Mack, "Presidential Address," *Proceedings of the National Conference of Charities and Correction*, 1912, 7; Frank Tucker, "Presidential Address," *Proceedings of the National Conference of Charities and Correction*, 1913, 9–11; Graham Taylor, "Presidential Address," *Proceedings of the National Conference of Charities and Correction*, 1914, 1–7.

94. Sklar compares the National Consumers' League (working in cooperation with mass women's organizations like the General Federation of Women's Clubs and trade unions like the WTUL) to the AALL, which viewed itself as an information distribution organization. The AALL did not see itself as a mass organization, and a brief experiment with state groups proved to consume more time than the leadership warranted necessary. Despite its desire to remain out-

side partisan politics, the organization found it difficult to do so in the world of labor legislation. Sklar writes that the AALL did not view "government as a democratic extension of the popular will," but as "a vehicle of enlightened administration." Kathryn Kish Sklar, "Two Political Cultures," 51, 54.

95. Theda Skocpol, *Protecting Soldiers and Mothers*, 160–203; Michael Katz, *In the Shadow of the Poorhouse*, 191–195; James Patterson, *America's Struggle Against Poverty*, 26–27; Kathryn Kish Sklar, "Two Political Cultures," 36–62; Henry Rogers Seager, *Social Insurance: A Program of Reform* (New York: Macmillan, 1910); Roy Lubove, *The Struggle for Social Security;* Edward D. Berkowitz and Kim McQuaid, *Creating the Welfare State: The Political Economy of Twentieth-Century Reform* (New York: Praeger Publishers, 1980).

96. The AALL established a Committee on Social Insurance after its 1912 annual meeting. The members included Charles Richmond Henderson, University of Chicago sociology professor; Henry Rogers Seager of Columbia University; Isaac Max Rubinow, author of *Social Insurance;* John Andrews; and Edward T. Devine of the New York School of Philanthropy. *Survey* 29:24 (15 March 1913): 827.

97. For contemporary critiques of mothers' pensions, see Rubinow, *Social Insurance*, 433–438; and Edward T. Devine, "Pensions for Mothers," *American Labor Legislation Review* 3:2 (June 1913): 191–201. For shifts in AALL policy, see *Survey* (15 March 1913): 827; U.S. Bureau of Labor Statistics, "Maternity Insurance and Benefit Systems," by Henry J. Harris, *Proceedings of the Conference on Social Insurance*, Bulletin no. 212 (Washington, DC: Government Printing Office, 1917), 780–793.

98. William Hard, "General Discussion of Pensions for Mothers," *American Labor Legislation Review* 3:2 (June 1913): 229–234.

99. U.S. Bureau of Labor Statistics, "The Theory and Development of the Mothers Pension Movement," by Sherman C. Kingsley, *Proceedings of the Conference on Social Insurance*, Bulletin no. 212, 834. Rather than promote a sexual division of labor and reinforce gender-typing, plans for a universal form of aid to mother-only families sought to provide a safety net of provision. The exclusion of plans for these families from social insurance severely limited the policy options.

100. Conynton was referring to Isaac Rubinow. *New Republic* (6 May 1916): 5–6; U.S. Bureau of Labor Statistics, "The Theory and Development of the Mothers Pension Movement," *Proceedings of the Conference on Social Insurance*, Bulletin no. 212; and Edith Abbott, unpublished biography of Grace Abbott, pp. 13–15, Grace and Edith Abbott Papers, Department of Special Collections, University of Chicago Library, Chicago, IL, Addenda, box 9, folder 14. See also Beatrix Hoffman, "Endless Defeat: Health Insurance and the Making of the American Welfare State" (Ph.D. diss., Rutgers University, 1996).

NOTES TO CHAPTER TWO

1. Carroll D. Wright, *The Slums of Baltimore, Chicago, New York, and Philadelphia: prepared in compliance with a joint resolution of the Congress of the United States approved July 20, 1892, by Carroll D. Wright, Commissioner of Labor* (Washington, DC: Government Printing Office, 1894); Hull House Residents, *Hull House Maps and Papers: A Presentation of Nationalities and Wages in a Congested District of Chicago* (New York: Thomas Y. Crowell & Co., 1895; reprint, New York: Arno Press, 1970), 3; and Kathryn Kish Sklar, "Hull House Maps and Papers: Social Science as Women's Work in the 1890s," in *The Social Survey in Historical Perspective, 1880–1940*, ed.

Martin Bulmer, Kevin Bales, and Kathryn Kish Sklar (New York: Cambridge University Press, 1991), 111–147.

The motivations behind this new attention to poverty have been variously interpreted by historians as a need to control new threats to social order, an expansion of democratic principles, and part of a larger reorganization of American society in the industrial era. Two of many notable examples include James T. Patterson, *America's Struggle Against Poverty, 1900–1985* (Cambridge: Harvard University Press, 1986); and Michael B. Katz, *In the Shadow of the Poorhouse: A Social History of Welfare in America* (New York: Basic Books, 1986).

2. Hull House Residents, *Hull House Maps and Papers*, 5.

3. For a discussion of the family wage ideology and its impact upon social welfare development for mother-only families, see Linda Gordon, "What Does Welfare Regulate?" *Social Research* 55:4 (Winter 1988): 610–630; Mimi Abramovitz, *Regulating the Lives of Women: Social Welfare Policy from Colonial Times to the Present* (Boston: South End Press, 1988); and Martha May, "The Historical Problem of the Family Wage: The Ford Motor Company and the Five Dollar Day," *Feminist Studies* 8:2 (Summer 1982): 399–423.

4. Robert Hunter wrote a major treatise on the extent of poverty in the United States in which he acknowledged that "the working woman and the mother are left almost entirely out of consideration." See Robert Hunter, *Poverty* (New York: Macmillan Co., 1904), vii. Hunter held the office of the organizational secretary of the Chicago Board of Charities from 1896 to 1902 and worked with Julia Lathrop. He also resided at Hull House for the last three years of that tenure. During the 1910s, Edith Abbott and Sophonisba Breckinridge updated his work on Chicago housing, *Tenement Conditions in Chicago* (Chicago: City Homes Association, 1901).

5. Hull House Residents, *Hull House Maps and Papers*, 21.

6. Julia C. Lathrop, "The Cook County Charities," in Hull House Residents, *Hull House Maps and Papers*, 143–144.

7. Kenneth Cmiel referred to progressive reformers' efforts to change Chicago's welfare system as the creation of a "counter establishment." In so doing he acknowledges both the entrenched power of the older charity establishment and the extensive efforts on the part of reformers to make changes in the existing system. See Kenneth Cmiel, *A Home of Another Kind: One Chicago Orphanage and the Tangle of Child Welfare* (Chicago: University of Chicago Press, 1995), 207, n. 11. See also Kathleen D. McCarthy, *Noblesse Oblige: Charity and Cultural Philanthropy in Chicago, 1849–1929* (Chicago: University of Chicago Press, 1982).

8. These institutions included the Cook County Hospital, Dunning Institutions, the Chicago Juvenile Court, Juvenile Detention Home, the Municipal Tuberculosis Sanitarium, and the County Agent Poor Relief Department. The poorhouse was among the Dunning Institutions.

Public and private agencies provided an array of health-care services, but this area fell beyond the scope or focus of my study. For private charities and health care, see Emily K. Abel, "Proper Care," transcript in the author's possession. For the debates surrounding health insurance, see Beatrix Hoffman, "Endless Defeat: Health Insurance and the Making of the American Welfare State" (Ph.D. diss., Rutgers University, 1996).

9. For information on the predominance of single men and the aged in the Cook County poorhouse, see Sophonisba P. Breckinridge, *Family Welfare Work in a Metropolitan Community: Selected Case Records* (Chicago: University of Chicago Press, 1924), 855–856; and Cook County, IL, Board of County Commissioners, *Charity Service Reports;* hereafter cited as *Charity Service*

Reports, Infirmary (1903–1918). This constituency of poorhouse residents was also noted by Michael B. Katz, *In the Shadow of the Poorhouse,* 86–98; and Ann Shola Orloff, *The Politics of Pensions: A Comparative Analysis of Britain, Canada, and the United States, 1880–1940* (Madison: University of Wisconsin Press, 1993).

10. *Proceedings of the First Annual Meeting of the Illinois State Conference of Charities and Correction* (Springfield: Phillips Bros., State Printers, 1897), 62.

11. On the origins of the Chicago Juvenile Court, see Henrietta Greenbaum Frank and Amalie Hofer Jerome, *Annals of the Chicago Woman's Club for the First Forty Years of Its Organization, 1876–1916* (Chicago: Chicago Woman's Club, 1916), 179–190; U.S. Department of Labor, Children's Bureau, *The Chicago Juvenile Court,* by Helen Rankin Jeter, Bureau Publication no. 104 (Washington, DC: Government Printing Office, 1922), 1–10; and Victoria Lynn Getis, "A Disciplined Society: The Juvenile Court, Reform, and the Social Sciences in Chicago, 1890–1930" (Ph.D. diss., University of Michigan, 1994).

12. The delineation of causes of dependency became more elaborate as the court developed. For example, in 1907 the major cause "lack of care" accounted for 45 percent of cases, but by 1912 that assessment accounted for only 6 percent of the cases and more detailed causes were included.

13. The county agent annually reported the poor relief services and expenditures to the Cook County Board of Commissioners in the *Charity Service Reports.* The data on relief have been taken from those reports which provide the most complete information about these early public welfare programs. Sophonisba P. Breckinridge, *The Illinois Poor Law and Its Administration* (Chicago: University of Chicago Press, 1939). For a general history of early public aid, see James Brown, *The History of Public Assistance in Chicago, 1833 to 1893* (Chicago: University of Chicago Press, 1941), 45–46, 102–104.

14. In 1893, the county agent had a staff of thirty-three located in two offices across the city. Women were included on the staff for the first time that year. Julia Lathrop, Hull House resident and first director of the U.S. Children's Bureau, was one of the first two women appointed by the agent. Julia C. Lathrop, "The Cook County Charities," in Hull House Residents, *Hull House Maps and Papers,* 158.

15. The standard of care for impoverished families in the nineteenth century involved placing children in orphanages or asylums, which enabled the parent to earn. Parents paid a part of their earnings for the care of their children. Opposition to the policy of splitting up families simply because of poverty led to a call for mothers' pensions. Kenneth Cmiel found that mothers' pensions and other foster care developments did not reduce the number of children in orphanages but added more resources for the provision of dependent children. For a description of the development of private and public institutions for dependent children in Chicago, see Kenneth Cmiel, *A Home of Another Kind,* 9–15, 95. On the other hand, a comparison of juvenile court figures through 1920 demonstrates a marked decline in the number of dependent children institutionalized and a corresponding increase in children granted pensions. For example, see Cook County, IL, Juvenile Court and Juvenile Detention Home, *Annual Report* (1920), 28–29, Municipal Reference Collection, Chicago Public Library, Chicago, IL.

16. Cook County, IL, Board of County Commissioners, *Proceedings,* County Agent Report (1905–1906), 29–31.

17. The population of Cook County grew from 1,838,735 in 1900 to 3,982,123 in 1930 as reported in the decennial census. An annual tabulation can be found in *Report of the Department of*

Health of the City of Chicago for the Years 1926 to 1930 Inclusive (Chicago: Chicago Department of Health, 1931), [n.p.]. The great majority of the population lived in Chicago. Ninety percent of the county's population resided within the city limits in 1910. Although the percentage decreased with each decennial census, 85 percent of the county population still lived within the city by 1930. Population totals for Cook County were derived from U.S. Bureau of the Census, *Twelfth Census of the United States, 1900: Population* (Washington, DC: Government Printing Office, 1901), vol. 1: 16; Idem, *Thirteenth Census of the United States, 1910: Population* (Washington, DC: Government Printing Office, 1913), vol. 2: 486; Idem, *Fourteenth Census of the United States, 1920: Population* (Washington, DC: Government Printing Office, 1922), vol. 3: 252; Idem, *Fifteenth Census of the United States, 1930: Population* (Washington, DC: Government Printing Office, 1932), vol. 3, pt. 1: 601. Population totals for the City of Chicago were derived from *Twelfth Census, 1900: Population*, vol. 2: 314; *Thirteenth Census, 1910: Population*, vol. 1: 79; *Fourteenth Census, 1920: Population*, vol. 2: 47; and *Fifteenth Census, 1930: Population*, vol. 3, pt. 1: 601. Census data were also drawn from Ernest W. Burgess and Charles Newcomb, *Census Data of the City of Chicago, 1930* (Chicago: University of Chicago Press, 1933), xv.

18. Aggregate ethnicity data came from the following sources: *Twelfth Census, 1900: Population*, vol. 1: 651; *Fourteenth Census, 1920: Population*, vol. 2: 47, 739; Ernest W. Burgess and Charles Newcomb, *Census Data*, xv. Specific data on nationalities selected from the *Fourteenth Census, 1920: Population*, vol. 2: 739. Changes in national territories accounted for an underrepresentation of Polish in the 1900 census.

19. St. Clair Drake and Horace R. Cayton, *Black Metropolis: A Study of Negro Life in a Northern City* (New York: Harcourt, Brace and Co., 1945; reprint, Chicago: University of Chicago Press, 1993), 58, 76; James Grossman, *Land of Hope: Chicago, Black Southerners, and the Great Migration* (Chicago: University of Chicago Press, 1989), 4; Julia C. Lathrop, "The Cook County Charities," in Hull House Residents, *Hull House Maps and Papers*, 143–144.

20. My purpose is to provide an overview of those who used public relief and the impact upon the growth of new programs. A thorough correlation between race, nativity, and access to public provisions would need to compare the availability of private sources, level of economic need, access to public sources, and links to political patronage for each group. This is not within the bounds of this study and data are not available in some areas.

21. Between 1908 and 1919, a separate category in the nationality charts listed "Negroes." By 1920, figures for African Americans were included within national categories, but this figure as well as one for Jewish families were separately noted. I have assumed that African American families were native-born and their numbers included among the category "American." No data were compiled for African Americans on relief for 1918 and 1919.

The data on families have inconsistencies. From 1900 to 1920, the census defined a family as either a group of individuals who occupied a dwelling or part of a dwelling, or as an individual. In 1930, the census changed its definition of a family to specify those related by marriage or by parentage. This study utilized the specific family data provided by the fifteenth census comparing 1920 and 1930, and then estimated family figures by dividing the entire population figure by the average number per family for 1900 and 1910. This procedure demonstrates a trend in the population of families over time. Decennial family totals are from the *Twelfth Census, 1900: Population*, vol. 2: 618; *Thirteenth Census, 1910: Population*, vol. 1: 1289; *Fourteenth Census, 1920: Population*, vol. 3: 274; and Ernest W. Burgess and Charles Newcomb, *Census Data*, xvi. Estimates of ethnic family size for 1900 and 1910 are based on total population figures divided by average family size. This last figure is from the *Thirteenth Census, 1910: Population*, vol. 1: 1289.

22. Ratios of relief use to population are based on census figures (see nn. 17 and 18 above) and aggregate figures for relief. The Germans and Irish were early immigrants to Chicago, and were prominent national groups listed in the relief statistics between 1836 and 1871. For example, in 1870 the Irish made up 13.4 percent of the general population but 48.6 percent of those receiving outdoor relief. Similarly, Germans made up 17.5 percent of the general population and 21 percent of those on outdoor relief. See James Brown, *The History of Public Assistance in Chicago*, 13–14.

23. St. Clair Drake and Horace R. Cayton, *Black Metropolis*, 78.

24. For indications of high rates of layoffs, see Chicago *Defender*, 24 March 1928, pt. 1, p. 2. For sources on the separate system of social services, see James R. Grossman, *Land of Hope*, 139–150, 172–174; Thomas Lee Philpott, *The Slum and the Ghetto: Neighborhood Deterioration and Middle-Class Reform, Chicago, 1880–1930* (New York: Oxford University Press, 1978); Allan H. Spear, *Black Chicago: The Making of a Negro Ghetto, 1890–1920* (Chicago: University of Chicago Press, 1967); Arvarh E. Strickland, *History of the Chicago Urban League* (Urbana: University of Illinois Press, 1966); Alfreda M. Duster, ed., *Crusade for Justice: The Autobiography of Ida B. Wells* (Chicago: University of Chicago Press, 1970); Elizabeth Lindsay Davis, *The Story of the Illinois Federation of Colored Women's Clubs, 1900–1922* (Chicago: [n.p.], 1922); Philip Jackson, "Black Charity in Progressive Era Chicago," *Social Service Review* 52:3 (September 1978): 400–417; Alvin B. Kogut, "The Negro and the Charitable Organization Society in the Progressive Era," *Social Service Review* 44:1 (March 1970): 11–21; Steven J. Diner, "Chicago Social Workers and Blacks in the Progressive Era," *Social Service Review* 44:4 (December 1970): 393–410; Memorandum in Regard to Facilities for Care of Colored Dependent Children, [circa 20 August 1913], Children's Home and Aid Society of Illinois Records, box 30, folder 6, Special Collections, University Library, University of Illinois at Chicago; Charlotte Ashby Crowley, "Dependent Negro Children in Chicago in 1926" (M.A. thesis, University of Chicago, 1927); and "Six Months of South Side Survey" (1 July–30 December 1930), Julius Rosenwald Papers, box 12, folder 2, Department of Special Collections, University of Chicago Library.

25. County Poor Relief had an office on the South Side, and United Charities of Chicago, a citywide private charity, had offices in neighborhoods with black residents. The Chicago *Defender* referred to the United Charities as an organization that served all people of Chicago without reference to race or religion. Chicago *Defender*, 22 March 1913, p. 1. For the social welfare efforts of African American clubwomen in Chicago, see Elizabeth Lindsay Davis, *The Story of the Illinois Federation of Colored Women's Clubs;* and Anne Meis Knupfer, *Toward A Tenderer Humanity and a Nobler Womanhood: African American Women's Clubs in Turn-of-the-Century Chicago* (New York: New York University Press, 1997).

26. Chicago Urban League, *Annual Report* (1917), 4; (1923), cover; (1928), [n.p.].

27. The county agent listed families as married, widowed, deserted, divorced, widower, or single. Married families could include families in which the husband was permanently disabled or ill. Female-headed families included all women who were widows, deserted, or divorced, with or without children. The category "other" included those listed as single or widowers. The population figures are from *Report of the Department of Health of the City of Chicago for the Years 1926 to 1930 Inclusive* (Chicago: Chicago Department of Health, 1931), [n.p.].

28. *Charity Service Reports* (1908), 18; (1915), 10–11; *Chicago Defender*, 9 January 1915, [n.p.];*Charity Service Reports* (1918), 12; idem, *Proceedings* (1920–1921), 241; *Charity Service Reports* (1927), 263.

29. Sophonisba P. Breckinridge, *Family Welfare Work*, 826–828.

30. For the protests of the 1910s, see Cook County, IL, Board of County Commissioners, *Proceedings*, 26 January 1914, 313; 9 January 1914, 231, 313; 26 April 1915, 4; *Charity Service Reports* (1915), 89; *Chicago Daily Tribune*, 18 January 1915.

31. United Charities of Chicago, *Minute Book*, vol. 2 (1915–1922), 28 April 1921, 3, United Charities of Chicago Records, Chicago Historical Society, Chicago, IL.

32. *Charity Service Reports* (1908), 18, 44; (1909), 18; (1913), 18. Local measures also included the establishment of lodging houses for transient, unemployed male workers. Their history in Chicago was erratic, as administrations opened and closed them depending on pressing need and partisan priorities. African Americans and Mexicans were underrepresented in the municipal lodging houses, and the Chicago Urban League opened facilities periodically to serve Chicago's unemployed black men.

33. Chicago, IL, Municipal Markets Commission, *Report to the Mayor and Aldermen on a Practical Plan for Relieving Destitution and Unemployment in the City of Chicago* (Chicago: [n.p.], 1914), 6, 22, 48, 63. After five years of experimentation with employment bureaus in relief offices, administrators viewed the idea as unsatisfactory because it encouraged casual labor.

Several years prior to this report, Edith Abbott sharply criticized unemployment policies that excluded women. Citing her experience in London, she berated policies that perpetuated the "industrial dependence" of women. Edith Abbott, "Municipal Employment of Unemployed Women in London," *Journal of Political Economy* (November 1907): 513–530.

34. United Charities of Chicago, *Minute Book*, 3 March 1921, 2; and 26 May 1921, 3.

35. Cook County, IL, Board of County Commissioners, *Proceedings* (1903–1904), 1054. Female-headed families comprised 96 percent of all families who listed low wages as their reason for seeking aid in 1906. They remained a significant proportion of those claiming low wages as a reason for relief throughout the period: 89 percent (1908), 78 percent (1910), 77 percent (1919), 68 percent (1921), and 56 percent (1927). *Charity Service Reports*, "Table Showing Cause of Distress" (1906–1927).

36. The figures on the length of time a woman would support her children came from an analysis of 1920 census data in which only white families were included. On average, mother-only families had 3.2 members. See Day Monroe, *Chicago Families: A Study of Unpublished Census Data* (Chicago: University of Chicago Press, 1932; reprint New York: Arno Press, 1972), 86, 98, 133. For the high incidence of mother-only families on relief, compared to male-headed unemployed families, for an earlier period, see James Brown, *The History of Public Assistance in Chicago*, 43. This pattern is also discussed by Linda Gordon, *Pitied But Not Entitled: Single Mothers and the History of Welfare, 1890–1935* (New York: Free Press, 1994); and Beverly Stadum, *Poor Women and Their Families: Hard Working Charity Cases, 1900–1930* (Albany: State University of New York Press, 1992). For the importance of children's wages to family incomes, see Susan J. Kleinberg, *The Shadow of the Mills: Working Class Families in Pittsburgh, 1870–1917* (Pittsburgh: Pittsburgh University Press, 1989). The Children's Bureau also produced several studies that traced the incidence of child labor in needy families. For example, see U.S. Department of Labor, Chil-

dren's Bureau, *Children of Wage-Earning Mothers: A Study of a Selected Group in Chicago*, by Helen Russell Wright, Publication no. 102 (Washington, DC: Government Publication Office, 1922).

37. Sophonisba P. Breckinridge, *Family Welfare Work*, 446–461.

38. Mary E. McDowell, "For a National Investigation of Women," *Independent* (3 January 1907): 24–25.

39. U.S. Department of Labor, *Report on the Conditions of Woman and Child Wage Earners in the United States*, 61st Cong., 2d sess., S. Doc. 645 (Washington, DC: Government Printing Office, 1910–1913). For an account of the formation of the study, see Allen F. Davis, *Spearheads for Reform: The Social Settlements and the Progressive Movement, 1890–1914* (New York: Oxford University Press, 1967), 133–134.

40. *Hull House Year Book* (1 September 1906–1 September 1907), 46–47. The Children's Bureau and Women's Bureau led in the support of research on the problems of working mothers and low wages. For government publications on working mothers, see U.S. Department of Labor, Children's Bureau, *Children of Working Mothers in Philadelphia*, Publication no. 204, pt. 1, by Clara Beyer (Washington, DC: Government Printing Office, 1931); U.S. Department of Labor, Women's Bureau, *Family Status of Breadwinning Women*, Bulletin no. 23 (Washington, DC: Government Printing Office, 1922); U.S. Department of Labor, Women's Bureau, *The Share of Wage-Earning Women in Family Support*, Bulletin no. 30 (Washington, DC: Government Printing Office, 1923). For a contemporary analysis of wages, see Paul H. Douglas, *Wages and the Family* (Chicago: University of Chicago Press, 1925), 199–203. The reports of state-appointed minimum wage commissions during the 1910s also provide state-level documentation of this proposal. Selected studies on the subject include Alice Kessler-Harris, *A Woman's Wage: Historical Meanings and Social Consequences* (Lexington: University Press of Kentucky, 1990); Sybil Lipschultz, "Social Feminism and Legal Discourse: 1908–1923," *Yale Journal of Law and Feminism* 2:1 (Fall 1989): 131–160; and Susan Lehrer, *Origins of Protective Labor Legislation for Women, 1905–1925* (Albany: State University of New York Press, 1987).

41. "Day Nursery Service in Chicago," Welfare Council of Metropolitan Chicago Records, box 159, folder 159–3, Chicago Historical Society. The *Social Service Directory* provided a listing of most day nurseries—approximately thirty-two to thirty-seven during the decades of the study. However, this figure does not include some of the centers that operated within the African American neighborhoods. Chicago, Department of Public Welfare, *Social Service Directory* (1915), 18–23; and Elizabeth Lindsay Davis, *The Story of the Illinois Federation of Colored Women's Clubs*, 62. Katherine Parkin recorded seventy-four day nurseries in Chicago between 1890 and 1930. See Katherine Parkin, "Day Nurseries in Chicago, 1890–1930" (Senior Thesis, Lake Forest College, 1993). See also Elizabeth R. Rose, "Maternal Work: Day Care in Philadelphia, 1890–1960" (Ph.D. diss., Rutgers University, 1994).

42. Illinois, State Board of Administrators, *Institution Quarterly* 4:3 (30 September 1913), 91–110; Chicago, Department of Public Welfare, *Annual Report* (1928–1929), 17.

43. Chicago, Department of Public Welfare, *Bulletin* (September 1916), 6–7; Chicago Urban League, *Annual Report* (1923), 9; (1926), 12; (1928), [n.p.]. For articles on African American women's work situation in Chicago, see Louise de Koven Bowen, *The Colored People of Chicago: An Investigation Made for the Juvenile Protective Association* (Chicago: Juvenile Protective Association, 1913); Helen B. Sayre, "Negro Women in Industry," *Opportunity* 2:20 (August 1924): 242–244; Myra Hill Colson, "Negro Home Workers in Chicago," *Social Service Review* 2 (September 1928): 385–413;

and Irene J. Graham, "Family Support and Dependency among Chicago Negroes: A Study of Unpublished Census Data," *Social Service Review* 3:4 (December 1929): 541–562.

44. The state legislature approved the Illinois Workmen's Compensation Law in June 1911 and it went into effect two years later. The law authorized compensation for wives and children of injured, ill, or deceased workers in covered industries. The amount of coverage could be four times the average salary of the worker, but limitations on covered industries kept the program small. For a comparison between workmen's compensation and mothers' pension laws, see Theda Skocpol, *Protecting Soldiers and Mothers: The Political Origins of Social Policy in the United States* (Cambridge: Belknap Press of Harvard University Press, 1992), 293–302; and Barbara Nelson, "The Origins of the Two-Channel Welfare State: Workmen's Compensation and Mothers' Aid," in *Women, the State, and Welfare*, ed. Linda Gordon (Madison: University of Wisconsin Press, 1990), 123–151.

45. The census notation for marital status provides statistics for mother-only families; a few problems exist with this source, however. Enumerators could choose to mark a woman married, widowed, or divorced during this period. The categories "deserted" and "separated," two areas of major importance to relief, remained undocumented. Women who were separated, willingly or unwillingly, from their husbands would have claimed themselves as married or widowed. The census noted this potential for error in its discussion of the discrepancy between married men and women. Effects of migration and emigration accounted for some of the difference, but women also "misrepresented" their marital status when no accurate category was presented. This imprecision in the census would contribute to an underrepresentation of mother-only families if they included themselves as married. This may be most significant for African American women, who had higher rates of separation. *Thirteenth Census, 1910: Population*, vol. 1: 507.

46. The census did not provide figures for foreign-born national groups, nor figures for separated or divorced mothers. This study selected the subset of women aged 15 to 44 years as a conservative measure of families likely to have young children. A study of untabulated Chicago census data found that the greatest majority of white women with dependent children were between the ages 25 and 45 years. See Day Monroe, *Chicago Families*, 120–121. These findings are supported by other historical studies of female-headship within the black community. See Elizabeth Pleck, *Black Migration and Poverty, Boston 1865–1900* (New York: Academic Press, 1979); and Frank Furstenberg, Theodore Hershberg, and John Modell, "The Origins of the Female-Headed Black Family: The Impact of the Urban Experience," *Journal of Interdisciplinary History* 6:2 (Autumn 1975): 211–233.

47. Hull House Residents, *Hull House Maps and Papers*, 144; Cook County, IL, Board of County Commissioners, *Proceedings*, County Agent Report (1903–1904), 1057; Earle Eubank, *A Study of Family Desertion* (Chicago: Department of Public Welfare, 1916); and E. Franklin Frazier, *The Negro Family in Chicago* (Chicago: University of Chicago Press, 1932), 119, 147–148, 257. See also Martha May, "The 'Problem of Duty': Family Desertion in the Progressive Era," *Social Service Review* (March 1988): 40–60. A comparison of deserted families on welfare and in the general population is impossible because the census did not record this status.

48. Cook County, IL, Board of County Commissioners, *Proceedings*, County Agent Report (1903–1904), 1057.

49. United Charities of Chicago, *Sixty-six Years of Service* (Chicago: United Charities of Chicago, 1923), 18.

50. Historians Michael Katz and James Patterson are notable exceptions. Their studies discuss fiscal matters, although neither examines welfare services in their component parts. Katz found that charity expenditures surpassed general budgets in large cities between 1912 and 1930, but he did not specifically address the differences between the programs included in the charity category. Michael B. Katz, *In the Shadow of the Poorhouse*, 154; and James Patterson, *America's Struggle Against Poverty*, 27–28.

51. The data in this section have been drawn from Cook County, IL, Board of County Commissioners, *Proceedings*, "Comptroller's Annual Report for County Appropriations"; and the data on relief, from idem, *Charity Service Reports*. The consumer price index (CPI) used in this study is from Paul Douglas, *Real Wages in the United States, 1890–1926* (Boston: Houghton Mifflin, Co., 1930), 60. This CPI is also one of three listed in U.S. Bureau of the Census, *Historical Statistics of the United States, Colonial Times to 1970* (Washington, DC: Government Printing Office, 1975), pt. 1, 212.

52. *Charity Service Reports* (1905), 17; (1907), 33–34; (1913), 28–29; (1918), 11; (1930), 12.

53. The factors influencing the expansion and contraction of relief budgets are discussed in Cook County, IL, Board of County Commissioners, Bureau of Public Welfare, *Annual Report* (1927); and Helen R. Jeter and A. W. McMillen, "Some Statistics of Family Welfare and Relief in Chicago—1928," *Social Service Review* 3:3 (September 1929): 448–459. For a comparison to other cities, see Michael B. Katz, *In the Shadow of the Poorhouse*, 43–46, 154–155.

54. Public funds covered about 25 percent of the cases because public agencies accepted long-term welfare cases, many of which were mother-only families, while private agencies handled minor-care, or temporary requests. The United Charities of Chicago noted this trend in 1922. The report stated that United Charities had fewer major-care cases owing to the creation of new public welfare units that delivered progressive social legislation. See United Charities of Chicago, *Sixty-six Years of Service*, 12. Michael Katz also noted that public spending on welfare exceeded private spending by a ratio of three to one. Michael B. Katz, *In the Shadow of the Poorhouse*, 154.

One study of public assistance in the nineteenth century argued that public relief carried the major portion of expense for outdoor relief during that period as well. From 1875 to 1893, the county provided an average of 72.8 percent of the expense of outdoor relief. However, the poor relief office periodically reduced its expenditures by shifting families to private agencies. Periods of intense unemployment also led public officials to demand that private agencies direct more of their resources to poor families. During the nineteenth century, Brown argues, the two groups did not coordinate these efforts, but more often engaged in power struggles. James Brown, *The History of Public Assistance in Chicago*, viii, 40–41, 112–116, 121, 124–126.

NOTES TO CHAPTER THREE

1. For a discussion of the intellectual foundations of social democratic and progressive ideas, see James T. Kloppenberg, *Uncertain Victory: Social Democracy and Progressivism in European and American Thought, 1870–1920* (New York: Oxford University Press, 1986). For the origins and divisions within the social sciences, see Dorothy Ross, *The Origins of American Social Science* (New York: Cambridge University Press, 1991); Thomas L. Haskell, *The Emergence of Professional Social Science: The American Social Science Association and the Nineteenth-century Crisis of Authority* (Urbana: University of Illinois Press, 1977); and Mary O. Furner, *Advocacy and Objec-*

tivity: A Crisis in the Professionalization of American Social Science, 1865–1905 (Lexington: University Press of Kentucky, 1975). See also Leon Fink, "'Intellectuals' versus 'workers': Academic Requirements and the Creation of Labor History," *American Historical Review* 96:2 (April 1991): 395–421; and Ellen Fitzpatrick, "Rethinking the Intellectual Origins of American Labor History," *American Historical Review* 96:2 (April 1991): 422–431.

Abbott and Breckinridge have been portrayed as maternalists because of their failure to critique women's economic dependency within the family wage system. The research presented in this chapter will illustrate the limits of that assessment. Their strategies did not challenge family relations directly, but focused on what they believed to be more practical solutions for expanding economic and political opportunities for women.

2. The centrality of Hull House reformers to the progressive social welfare agenda has been widely discussed, although not on the subject of mothers' pensions. See Kathryn Kish Sklar, *Florence Kelley and the Nation's Work: The Rise of Women's Political Culture, 1830–1900* (New Haven: Yale University Press, 1995); Robyn L. Muncy, *Creating a Female Dominion in American Reform, 1890–1930* (New York: Oxford University Press, 1991); Ellen F. Fitzpatrick, *Endless Crusade: Women Social Scientists and Progressive Reform* (New York: Oxford University Press, 1990); Judith Trolander, *Professionalism and Social Change: From the Settlement House Movement to Neighborhood Centers, 1886 to the Present* (New York: Columbia University Press, 1987); Steven J. Diner, *A City and Its Universities: Public Policy in Chicago, 1892–1919* (Chapel Hill: University of North Carolina Press, 1980); Allen F. Davis, *Spearheads for Reform: The Social Settlements and the Progressive Movement, 1890–1914* (New York: Oxford University Press, 1967). For a more critical view of Hull House, see Rivka Lissak, *Pluralism and Progressives: Hull House and the New Immigrants, 1890–1919* (Chicago: University of Chicago Press, 1989); Mina Carson, *Settlement Folk: Social Thought and the American Settlement Movement, 1885–1930* (Chicago: University of Chicago Press, 1990).

Hull House has come to represent the settlement movement despite the evidence that the majority of settlements had far more socially conservative views. See Ruth Hutchinson Crocker, *Social Work and Social Order: The Settlement Movement in Two Industrial Cities, 1889–1930* (Urbana: University of Illinois Press, 1992); Elisabeth Lasch-Quinn, *Black Neighbors: Race and the Limits of Reform in the American Settlement House Movement, 1890–1945* (Chapel Hill: University of North Carolina Press, 1993).

3. U.S. Bureau of Labor, *The Slums of Baltimore, Chicago, New York, and Philadelphia, prepared in compliace with a joint resolution of the Congress of the United States approved July 20, 1892, by Carroll D. Wright, Commissioner of Labor* (Washington, DC: Government Printing Office, 1894); Hull House Residents, *Hull House Maps and Papers: A Presentation of Nationalities and Wages in a Congested District of Chicago* (New York: Thomas Y. Crowell & Co., 1895). For more information on the survey work of the settlements, see Martin Bulmer, Kevin Bales, and Kathryn Kish Sklar, eds., *The Social Survey in Historical Perspective, 1880–1940* (New York: Cambridge University Press, 1991); Steven J. Diner, *A City and Its Universities; Hull House Bulletin* 7:1 (1905–1906): 22.

4. Martin Bulmer, Kevin Bales, and Kathryn Kish Sklar, *The Social Survey*, 116–117. Jane Addams criticized political parties for their lack of attention to neighborhood conditions and acknowledged that reform efforts had shifted from parties to the courts and legislatures. She argued that government needed women's expertise at this moment of transition "because it is obviously

a perilous business to turn over delicate social experiments to men who have remained quite untouched by social compunctions and who have been elected to their legislative position solely upon the old political issues." Jane Addams, *Newer Ideals of Peace* (Chatauqua, NY: Chatauqua Press, 1907); and idem, "The Larger Aspects of the Women's Movement," 1914; reprinted in Christopher Lasch, ed. *The Social Thought of Jane Addams* (New York: Bobbs-Merrill Co., 1965), 157.

5. Addams is cited in Christopher Lasch, ed. *The Social Thought of Jane Addams*, 131. Addams discussed her political education, the challenge to alderman Johnny Powers, and her analysis of municipal politics in several writings. For example, see Jane Addams, *Twenty Years at Hull House* (1910; reprint New York: New American Library, 1981); idem, "Why the Ward Boss Rules," *Outlook* 58(2 April 1898), 879–882; idem, *Democracy and Social Ethics* (New York: Macmillan Co., 1902). A full account of the campaigns against Powers may be found in Allen Davis, *Spearheads for Reform*, 151–162. He also discusses a successful challenge in the Seventeenth Ward led by Chicago Commons reformers. See also Margaret Dunn, "Jane Addams as a Political Leader" (M.A. Thesis, University of Chicago, 1926), 56, 63, 80–89. An excellent analysis of this characterization of the ward boss may be found in William L. Riordon, *Plunkitt of Tammany Hall: A Series of Very Plain Talks on Very Practical Politics*, edited with an introduction by Terrence J. McDonald (Boston: Bedford Books of St. Martin's Press, 1994).

6. According to Edith Abbott, William Lathrop drew up the bill that admitted women to the Illinois bar. Edith Abbott, unpublished biography of Julia Lathrop, box 57, folder 2, pp. 7, 12, Grace and Edith Abbott Papers, Addenda, Department of Special Collections, University of Chicago Library, Chicago, IL; hereafter cited as Abbott Papers.

7. Jane Addams, *My Friend Julia Lathrop* (New York: Macmillan Co., 1935), 48, 75. Julia Lathrop's personal papers are located at the Rockford College Archives, Rockford, Illinois. Most writings about Lathrop discuss her work as director of the Children's Bureau and her contributions to social work. She also had a lengthy involvement with the League of Women Voters. Additional biographical material may be found in Edward T. James, Janet Wilson James, and Paul S. Boyer, eds., *Notable American Women, 1607–1950: A Biographical Dictionary* (Cambridge: Belknap Press of Harvard University Press, 1971), vol. 2: 370–372, s.v. "Julia Clifford Lathrop." See also Jacqueline K. Parker and Edward M. Carpenter, "Julia Lathrop and the Children's Bureau: The Emergence of an Institution," *Social Service Review* 55:1 (March 1981): 60–77; Emily K. Abel, "Benevolence and Social Control: Advice from the Children's Bureau in the Early Twentieth Century," *Social Service Review* (March 1994): 1–19; and Ada C. Sweet, "The Work of Julia C. Lathrop in Illinois," *Home Education* 1:5 (June 1903), 9–10, in the Julia Lathrop Papers, Rockford College Archives, Rockford, Illinois; hereafter cited as Lathrop Papers.

8. Jane Addams noted that Lathrop had worked for the county agent since the winter of 1890–1891 as a county visitor. She believed that Lathrop's early experiences gave her a unique perspective on welfare policy, one that included the recipients' perspectives. Jane Addams, *Twenty Years at Hull House*, 220.

9. Julia C. Lathrop, "The Cook County Charities," in Hull House Residents, *Hull House Maps and Papers*, 143–161.

10. Ibid., 160.

11. Ibid., 150. Molly Ladd-Taylor refers to Julia Lathrop as a progressive maternalist—one who "assumed that women had a special capacity for nurture by virtue of being women," yet

embraced science, professionalism, social justice, and women's rights. At the same time, Ladd-Taylor recognized that Lathrop's maternalist rhetoric reflected, at least in part, a defensive stance against attacks on women in public life. Molly Ladd-Taylor, *Mother-Work: Women, Child Welfare, and the State, 1890–1930* (Urbana: University of Illinois Press, 1994), 75, 81.

12. Lathrop used the opportunity of the annual state conferences to gain support for the idea. The legislative committee supported the juvenile court legislation in 1898. Lathrop worked with Jenkin Lloyd Jones, another member of the State Board of Charities, to arrange sessions on "Children of the State" at the 1898 Illinois Conference of Charities and Corrections. They invited authorities on child welfare to speak about the need for a separate court for youth. Following the conference, Judge Timothy Hurley drafted the Illinois Juvenile Court Act, and with the support of the Chicago Women's Club, the Chicago Bar Association, and other reform groups the legislation became law on 1 July 1899. Jane Addams, *My Friend Julia Lathrop*, 135–140; U.S. Department of Labor, Children's Bureau, *The Chicago Juvenile Court*, by Helen Rankin Jeter, Publication no. 104 (Washington, DC: Government Printing Office, 1922); Julia Lathrop, "The Development of the Probation System in a Large City," *Charities* 13 (7 January 1905): 344; *Laws of Illinois* (1899), 131.

13. *Charities* 7:7 (17 August 1901): 152–155.

14. Addams, *My Friend Julia Lathrop*, 123.

15. The school's name changed to the Chicago School of Civics and Philanthropy in 1907, and the Russell Sage Foundation provided funds for a department of research and investigation. In 1920, the school joined the University of Chicago as the School of Social Service Administration, owing to the efforts of Edith Abbott and Sophonisba Breckinridge. For the early years, see Graham Taylor, *Pioneering on Social Frontiers* (Chicago: University of Chicago Press, 1930), 306–307; "The Institute of Social Science, Chicago," *Charities* 13(28 January 1905): 393–394; Ellen F. Fitzpatrick, *Endless Crusade*, 173–176, 196–200. Manuscript material about the school may be found in the Graham Taylor Papers, Newberry Library, Chicago, IL; and in the Chicago School of Civics and Philanthropy Records, the School of Social Service Administration Records, and the Grace and Edith Abbott Papers, Department of Special Collections, University of Chicago Library, Chicago, IL. See also Chicago School of Civics and Philanthropy, *Announcements* (Chicago: School of Civics and Philanthropy, 1909/1910–1919/1920).

16. The department of social investigation generated a rich source of social survey data for early policies in Chicago. The School of Civics and Philanthropy contained within one institution the resources to conduct social research on problems and to train a new generation of social workers to implement policies in a developing welfare structure. On the significance of the School of Social Service Administration and its predecessor, the Chicago School of Civics and Philanthropy, see Robyn L. Muncy, *Creating a Female Dominion in American Reform*, 66–92; Ellen F. Fitzpatrick, *Endless Crusade*, 166–200; and Lela B. Costin, *Two Sisters for Social Justice: A Biography of Grace and Edith Abbott* (Urbana: University of Illinois Press, 1983).

17. Breckinridge qualified her father's support of education by writing that while not a suffragist, he did support "the development of separate facilities for the education of women and negroes." Sophonisba Preston Breckinridge, unpublished autobiography, 9, Department of Special Collections, University of Chicago Library, Chicago, IL.

Sophonisba Breckinridge's personal papers are included among the Breckinridge Family Papers at the Library of Congress. A small collection of her papers may be found at the Department of Special Collections, University of Chicago Library. Additional papers are included in the Abbott Papers. For biographical information and her role in social welfare research, see Ellen Fitzpatrick, *Endless Crusade;* Lela B. Costin, *Two Sisters for Social Justice;* Helen R. Wright, "Three Against Time: Edith and Grace Abbott and Sophonisba P. Breckinridge," *Social Service Review* 28:1 (1953): 41–53; and Edward T. James et al., *Notable American Women* (Cambridge: Belknap Press of Harvard University Press, 1971), vol. 1: 233–236, s.v. "Sophonisba Preston Breckinridge."

18. Oscar Kraines, *The World and Ideas of Ernst Freund: The Search for General Principles of Legislation and Administrative Law* ([n.p.]: University of Alabama Press, 1974), 16; Ernst Freund, *The Police Power: Public Policy and Constitutional Rights* (Chicago: Callaghan and Co., 1904); idem, *Standards of American Legislation: An Estimate of Restrictive and Constructive Factors* (Chicago: University of Chicago Press, 1917); and *Dictionary of American Biography* (New York: Charles Scribner's Sons, 1944), supp. 1, vol. 21: 323, s.v. "Ernst Freund."

19. Furner notes that the year Breckinridge began her doctoral work with Laughlin he was embroiled in an ideological and professional battle to keep Edward Bemis from teaching courses on labor in the economics department, and eventually maneuvered Bemis's forced resignation from the university. Mary O. Furner, *Advocacy and Objectivity,* 57, 77, 172, 196.

Sophonisba Preston Breckinridge, "Administration of Justice in Kentucky" (M.A. thesis, University of Chicago, 1897); idem, "Legal Tender: A Study in English and American Monetary History" (Ph.D. diss., University of Chicago, 1901). idem, unpublished autobiography, 14, Sophonisba P. Breckinridge Papers, Department of Special Collections, University of Chicago Library; hereafter cited as Breckinridge Papers. For a more detailed examination of the relationship between Freund and Breckinridge or about her dissertation, see Ellen Fitzpatrick, *Endless Crusade,* 44–52.

20. Sophonisba P. Breckinridge, unpublished autobiography, Breckinridge Papers.

21. Sophonisba P. Breckinridge, "Legislative Control of Women's Work," *Journal of Political Economy* (February 1906): 107.

22. Ibid., 108. For an interpretation that Breckinridge justified state intervention and defended protective legislation based on biology, see Fitzpatrick, *Endless Crusade,* 170.

23. Edith Abbott and Sophonisba P. Breckinridge, "Employment of Women in Industries: Twelfth Census Statistics," *Journal of Political Economy* (February 1906): 16.

24. In particular she criticized the Chicago Municipal Markets Commission on Unemployment (1914), which entirely overlooked the problems of unemployment for women workers. Sophonisba P. Breckinridge, *Women in the Twentieth Century: A Study of Their Political, Social, and Economic Activities* (New York: McGraw-Hill Book Co., 1933), 233.

25. Breckinridge described to Julia Lathrop her recollection of how she became involved with the federal study on woman and child wage-earners. "One night Miss McDowell was asking some questions of Miss Abbott and me; we could not answer them, and she reproached me because I was giving a course on the subject of the industrial position of women. And I told her that nobody could answer them—there were no data on those subjects. . . . At first we did not want to include the children—already the movement for the Children's Bureau was pretty strong, and we were thinking that children were having their day and nobody was saying anything about women. But after a good deal of effort . . . it was decided to combine with those who wanted the conditions of children's work investigated." Sophonisba P. Breckinridge to Julia Lathrop, 30 October 1914, Abbott Papers; Costin, *Two Sisters for Social Justice,* 101.

26. Breckinridge's career included a long history of suffrage and women's rights activism. When Chicago passed partial suffrage she worked on a citizenship education program for the new voters through the Woman's City Club and enjoyed a brief campaign for city alderman in 1914. Breckinridge recognized that political rights were necessary for women's equality. However, she focused her activities on women's economic rights. She worked for the Women's Trade Union League, drafted bills for hours and wages legislation, and exposed the structural barriers to pay equity. Her research also revealed the gap in social policy through which impoverished single mothers fell, and advocated social insurance measures that began to address the dual burdens of working-class women.

27. Costin, *Two Sisters for Social Justice*, 59.

28. Abbott was born in Grand Island, Nebraska, the eldest daughter of Othman and Elizabeth Abbott. Barbara Sicherman and Carol Hurd Green, eds., *Notable American Women, The Modern Period: A Biographical Dictionary* (Cambridge: Belknap Press of Harvard University Press, 1980): 1–3, s.v. "Edith Abbott." Edith Abbott articulated her professional views in over one hundred articles and publications. Her personal and professional papers are in the Grace and Edith Abbott Papers. The most extensive treatment of Edith Abbott's life is in the dual biography of Edith and her sister, Grace, by Lela B. Costin, *Two Sisters for Social Justice*. See also Ellen Fitzpatrick, *Endless Crusade;* and Robyn L. Muncy, *Creating a Female Dominion in American Reform.*

29. Edith Abbott, "The Rights of Women," [biography of Grace Abbott], recopied 10 January 1945, Abbott Papers, Addenda.

30. Sophonisba P. Breckinridge, unpublished autobiography, Breckinridge Papers. Edith Abbott, "A Statistical Study of the Wages of Unskilled Labor in the United States, 1830–1900" (Ph.D. diss., University of Chicago, 1905). Ellen Fitzpatrick argued that this study revealed Abbott's fears about the "threat" to social control posed by unskilled workers. See Fitzpatrick, *Endless Crusade*, 66–69. Robyn Muncy described Abbott as resistant to reformers and intent upon keeping research separate from reform until she arrived at Hull House. See Robyn L. Muncy, *Creating a Female Dominion*, 72; and Lela B. Costin, *Two Sisters for Social Justice*, 31–35.

31. Edith Abbott and Sophonisba P. Breckinridge, "Employment of Women in Industries," 14–40; Edith Abbott, "Employment of Women in Industries: Cigar-making—Its History and Present Tendencies," *Journal of Political Economy* (January 1907): 1–25; idem, "Municipal Employment of Unemployed Women in London," *Journal of Political Economy* (November 1907): 513–530; and idem, "Women in Manufactures: A Supplementary Note," *Journal of Political Economy* (December 1907): 619–624. For a review of *Women in Industry*, see *Sociological Review* 3 (1910): 340.

32. Abbott took Sidney and Beatrice Webb's course, "Methods of Social Investigation." Their use of social research to formulate policy particularly impressed her and she later used this course as a model for her own teaching at the Chicago School of Civics and Philanthropy. See Lela B. Costin, *Two Sisters for Social Justice*, 31; and Ellen Fitzpatrick, *Endless Crusade*, 88–89.

Abbott also noted new principles in public provision established in Webb's minority report: a principle of universal maintenance and the community's obligation to the individual. See Edith Abbott, "English Poor Law Reform," *Journal of Political Economy* (January 1911): 47–59; and Great Britain, Royal Commission on Poor Laws and Relief of Distress, *The Minority Report of the Poor Law Commission*, edited with an introduction by Sidney Webb and Beatrice Webb (London: Longmans, Green, 1909; reprint, Clifton, NJ: A. M. Kelley, 1974). Jane Lewis has called Beatrice Webb's minority report proposals "administrative solutions of profoundly limited vision." This type of criticism has also been lodged against the Social Security provisions for women in the United States. Jane Lewis, "The Place of Social Investigation, Social Theory, and Social Work in the Approach to Late Victorian and Edwardian Social Problems: The Case of Beatrice Webb and Helen Bosanquet," in *The Social Survey in Historical Perspective*, ed. Martin Bulmer, Kevin Bales, and Kathryn Kish Sklar, 148–169, especially 163.

33. Edith Abbott, "Municipal Employment of Unemployed Women in London," 513–530.

Abbott understood the connection between economic and political equality for women and was an interested observer of the British suffrage movement during her time in London. On her return to the United States, she continued to write on suffrage and analyzed women's voting patterns in Chicago. See Edith Abbott, "Woman Suffrage Militant: The New Movement in England," *Independent* 61 (29 November 1906): 1276–1278; Edith Abbott and Sophonisba P. Breckinridge, *The Wage-Earning Woman and the State: A Reply to Miss Minnie Bronson* (Boston: Boston Equal Suffrage Association for Good Government, [1912]); Edith Abbott, "Statistics in Chicago Suffrage," *New Republic* (12 June 1915): 151; idem, "Are Women a Force for Good Government? An Analysis of the Returns in the Recent Municipal Elections in Chicago," *National Municipal Review* 4 (July 1915): 437–447; and idem, "The Woman Voter and the Spoils System in Chicago," *National Municipal Review* (July 1916): 460–465.

34. Edith Abbott, "The Experimental Period of Widows' Pension Legislation," *Proceedings of the National Conference of Social Work* (1917): 164.

35. Edith Abbott, *Public Assistance*, vol. 1, *American Principles and Policies*, cited in Arlien Johnson, "Edith Abbott's Contribution to Public Social Policy," *Social Service Review* (September 1939): 17.

36. Sophonisba P. Breckinridge to Edith Abbott, 28 June 1907, Breckinridge Family Papers, Library of Congress, Washington, DC; hereafter cited as Breckinridge Family Papers.

37. Chicago School of Civics and Philanthropy, "Department of Social Investigation," *Bulletin* 1:7 (January 1911): 192–194; Sophonisba Breckinridge and Edith Abbott to Russell Sage Foundation, 25 November 1910, "Report to the Director of the Russell Sage Foundation Concerning the Work of the Department of Social Investigation in the Chicago School of Civics and Philanthropy," Russell Sage Foundation Reports, Rockefeller Archive Center, Tarrytown, New York. Three major publications came from the three-part study: Sophonisba P. Breckinridge and Edith Abbott, *The Delinquent Child and the Home: A Study of the Delinquent Wards of the Juvenile Court of Chicago* (New York: Russell Sage Foundation, 1917); Edith Abbott and Sophonisba P. Breckinridge, *Truancy and Non-Attendance in the Chicago Schools: A Study of the Social Aspects of the Compulsory Education and Child Labor Legislation in Illinois* (Chicago: University of Chicago Press, 1917); and U.S. Department of Labor, Children's Bureau, *The Administration of the Aid-to-Mothers Law in Illinois*, by Edith Abbott and Sophonisba P. Breckinridge, Publication no. 82 (Washington, DC: Government Printing Office, 1921).

38. The authors noted that many of the crimes were of an economic nature and argued that the pressure upon the child to contribute to the family's support was one factor in the large number of cases among the poor. Edith Abbott and Sophonisba P. Breckinridge, *The Delinquent Child and the Home*, 70–89; Sophonisba P. Breckinridge, "Neglected Widowhood in the Juvenile Court," *American Journal of Sociology* (July 1910): 53–87; Chicago School of Civics and Philanthropy, *Bulletin* 14 (January 1912): 9.

39. Sophonisba P. Breckinridge, "Neglected Widowhood," 54.

40. Ibid.

41. According to Abraham Epstein, in 1910 Europeans had formed policies for mothers and children based on "the right to insurance." The United States in contrast passed mothers' pensions on the basis of woman's role as a "servant of the state in bringing up her children." Abraham Epstein, *Insecurity, A Challenge to America: A Study of Social Insurance in the United States and Abroad*, 2d rev. ed. (New York: Agathon Press, 1968), 621. Grace Abbott completed her M.A. thesis on the subject of married women's rights one year earlier. Grace Abbott, "The Legal Position of Married Women in the United States: A Study of Eighteen Selected States" (M.A. thesis, University of Chicago, 1909), Abbott Papers, Addendum, box 12, folder 6.

42. The study surveyed 14,099 cases generally and 734 cases in detail. Mother-only families made up 15 percent of the larger group, a figure Breckinridge argued was very understated. Edith Abbott and Sophonisba P. Breckinridge, *The Delinquent Child and the Home*, 57, 66–67.

43. Ibid., 75.

44. Ibid., 79.

45. "When . . . the lack of discipline and child care results in some acts on the part of the child, of which the police or possibly an injured neighbor takes note, the mother is summoned with the young offender to the Juvenile Court. It is interesting to ask what problem in particular she then presents, and how far the implications of her presence at the bar of the court are different from those suggested by her presence in the office of the relief society." Sophonisba P. Breckinridge, "Neglected Widowhood," 55.

46. Ibid., 62–73. Evidence exists to suggest that Breckinridge and Abbott thought this subsidy should be handled by private agencies initially. For example, Judge Pinckney wrote Julia Lathrop that Breckinridge "was against this form of relief" until her review of the Chicago Juvenile Court's work. Similarly, Edith Abbott expressed concern about the ability of public agencies to handle relief measures and argued that the "costly new machinery" of pension administration could have been avoided by better coordination between the juvenile court and the United Charities of Chicago. Merritt Pinckney to Julia Lathrop, 18 September 1916, Children's Bureau Records, National Archives, Washington, DC; and Edith Abbott, "Public Pensions to Widows with Children," *American Economic Review* 3 (June 1913): 475.

47. Sophonisba P. Breckinridge, "The Family and the Law," *Proceedings of the National Conference of Social Work* (1925): 296.

48. Julia Lathrop, "Responsibilities of the New Philanthropy," p. 7, 1908, Lathrop Papers.

49. Julia Lathrop, "Newer Needs for Cooperation," p. 3, 1908, Lathrop Papers.

50. Ibid., p. 7.

51. Ibid., p. 9. When asked about democracy years later, Lathrop said, "I have never seen it tried." Catherine Hackett, "Julia Lathrop, Friend at Large," *Woman Citizen* (12 July 1924): 12.

52. Sophonisba P. Breckinridge, "The Treatment of Dependent Children by Public Agencies," reprinted in *Institution Quarterly* 3:1 (31 March 1912): 60, 64. Illinois State Charities Commission, *First Annual Report* ([n.p.]: 1910), 136–137. Henry W. Thurston, former chief probation officer of the juvenile court and then superintendent of the Illinois Children's Home and Aid Society, cited the findings of the juvenile court study in his article "Ten Years of the Juvenile Court in Chicago," *Survey* (5 February 1910): 656–666.

53. Addams, Breckinridge, and Lathrop took positions far in advance of the White House conference of the preceding year in their advocacy of public pensions. Jane Addams, "Charity

and Social Justice," *Proceedings of the National Conference of Charities and Correction at the Thirty-seventh Annual Session held in the City of St. Louis, Mo., May 19th to 26th, 1910,* edited by Alexander Johnson (Fort Wayne, IN: Archer Printing Co., 1910), 6–7; *Chicago Tribune,* 9 May 1910, [n.p.]. Hull House opened a day nursery in 1891. Residents also sponsored a conference on the lack of day nursery facilities in Chicago. See *Hull House Year Book* (1906–1907), 44.

54. Juvenile court judges were appointed from a pool of circuit court judges. The latter were elected by Cook County voters.

55. Judge Julian Mack, "Presidential Address," *Proceedings of the National Conference of Charities and Correction,* 1912, 3.

56. Illinois, General Assembly, *Senate Journal* (21 March 1911): 493; Illinois, *House and Senate Bills,* 47th General Assembly, 1911, SB403; *Illinois State Journal,* 22 March 1911, 3.

57. Under the existing law, the juvenile court could recommend probation and leave the child at home with the supervision of a court officer. In cases where the parent, guardian, or custodian of the child was evaluated as an "unfit or improper guardian" or "unwilling to care for, protect, train, educate or discipline such child," the court had the authority to appoint a guardian, send the child to a state industrial school, place the child in a state-subsidized private institution for dependents, or place the child in a foster home.

The bill was reported from the Judiciary Committee on 29 March and passed by the Senate on 27 April. The only change to the original proposal was the omission of the clause "or to such other person for them as the court may direct." The House passed the bill on 19 May and it was approved by the governor on 5 June. *Laws of Illinois,* 47th General Assembly, 1911, 126.

According to press coverage, this piece of legislation was apparently one in the last group of bills approved in an extended session. It was not actually passed until the early hours of 21 May, and the governor did not actually approve it until after 5 June; the official dates, however, are used in the state documents to conform with the specific deadlines. *Illinois State Journal,* 21 May 1911, 3.

58. The court established maximum grants based on the sum paid to institutions, but no grant allotted more than $40 per month.

59. *Chicago Daily Tribune,* 21 March 1911, p. 1; 26 March 1911, sec. 2, p. 7.

60. *Chicago Daily Tribune,* 22 March 1911, p. 2.

61. *Chicago Daily Tribune,* 27 March 1911, p. 3; 31 March 1911, p. 9.

62. *Dziennik Związkowy Zgoda,* 18 January 1910 (transcript), Foreign Language Press Survey, Chicago Public Library, Omnibus Project, U.S. Works Progress Administration, 1942.

63. N. Sue Weiler, "The Uprising in Chicago: The Men's Garment Workers Strike, 1910–1911," in *A Needle, A Bobbin, A Strike: Women Needleworkers in America,* ed. Joan M. Jensen and Sue Davidson (Philadelphia: Temple University Press, 1984), 114–139. Breckinridge was one of three members of a citizens committee that investigated the workers' complaints. The report, released in November 1911, supported the strikers and endorsed arbitration. See Ellen Fitzpatrick, *Endless Crusade,* 192; and Steven Diner, *A City and Its Universities,* 148–151.

64. *Jewish Courier,* 4 October 1908, Foreign Language Press Survey, Chicago Public Library, Omnibus Project, U.S. Works Progress Administration, 1942.

65. Robert Hunter, "Reformism vs. Marxism," *Chicago Daily Socialist,* 15 August 1910, p. 4.

66. *Chicago Daily Tribune,* 10 May 1912; p. 4; 8 June 1911, p. 8; *Record Herald,* 26 November 1911, sec. 6, p. 1. The Illinois Federation of Women's Clubs published news of club activities in

their *Bulletin,* but the account of the legislative agenda that spring discussed no activity on mothers' pensions. Illinois Federation of Women's Clubs *Bulletin* 2:3 (April 1911).

67. Theda Skocpol has argued that the activities of this organization made the difference in passage of bills across the states. I could find no evidence for that in the club materials or newspapers. The Illinois Congress of Mothers began in 1900 and quickly established 102 clubs across the state, twenty-five in Cook County alone. Several Chicago Woman's Club members were involved in the National Congress of Mothers and were responsible for the state chapter. These included Mrs. William S. Heffernan, Lucy Flower, Josephine Hart, and Mrs. Orville T. Bright. Some, like Josephine Hart, who was chair of the dependent children committee, took voluntary positions that complemented their husbands'. Hastings H. Hart directed the Illinois Children's Home and Aid Society. Little overlap existed between the settlement community and the Illinois Congress of Mothers, although Julia Lathrop and Florence Kelley spoke at state meetings and would lobby the membership on behalf of social legislation. National Congress of Mothers, *The Child in Home, School and State: Report of the National Congress of Mothers Held in the City of Washington, D.C., March 10–17, 1905* (Washington, DC: National Congress of Mothers, 1905), 239, 257.

68. *Chicago Daily Tribune,* 4 May 1910, p. 9; *Child Welfare Magazine,* May 1910, 280.

69. *Chicago Daily Tribune,* 7 May 1911, p. 8.

70. *Child Welfare Magazine,* May 1911, 314–315.

71. Ibid., December 1911, 136. The Illinois Congress of Mothers recognized Henry Neil as the author of the legislation.

72. Ibid., June 1915, 383.

73. Woman's City Club, *Yearbook* (1910–1911), 2, Woman's City Club of Chicago Records, Special Collections, University Library, University of Illinois at Chicago.

74. Illinois, Board of Administration, *Institution Quarterly* (31 March 1915): 197.

75. *Chicago Daily Tribune,* 31 December 1911, sec. 9, p. 1.

76. For news accounts crediting Neil with passage of the Funds to Parents Act, see *Chicago Daily Tribune,* 15 August 1939, p. 25; *Chicago Daily Socialist,* 15 July 1911, p. 6; *Christian Herald,* 25 February 1914, p. 184.

77. Municipal Court Records, box 3, folder 21, Chicago Historical Society, Chicago, IL; *Chicago Daily Socialist,* 18 August 1910, p. 1; McKenzie Cleland to Mr. J. K. Grune, 29 November 1910, Municipal Court Records, Chicago Historical Society, Chicago, IL; *Newer Justice Magazine,* vols. 1–9 (1911–1917). Cleland also claimed to have written the Funds to Parents Act. See Albert Nelson Marquis, ed., *The Book of Chicagoans* (Chicago: A. N. Marquis & Co., 1917), 138, s.v. "McKenzie Cleland." For a description of the adult probation bill that passed and municipal court chief justice Harry Olson's support, see *Chicago Daily Tribune,* 11 May 1911, p. 4.

78. *Chicago Daily Socialist,* 22 November 1911, p. 3.

79. Cook County, IL, Board of County Commissioners, *Charity Service Reports,* Juvenile Court (1910), 143–144.

80. For the accounts of Pinckney's relationship to the early legislation see Frank T. Flynn, "Judge Merritt W. Pinckney and the Early Days of the Juvenile Court in Chicago," *Social Service Review* 28:1 (1954): 20–30; Anthony R. Travis, "The Origin of Mothers' Pensions in Illinois," *Illinois State Historical Society Journal* (1975): 421–428; Merritt W. Pinckney, "Public Pensions to Widows: Experiences and Observations Which Lead Me to Favor Such a Law," in *Selected*

Articles on Mothers' Pensions, comp. Edna D. Bullock (New York: H. W. Wilson Co., 1915), 139. In their report on the Illinois law, Abbott and Breckinridge noted that "the approval of the presiding judge of the Chicago juvenile court is said to have been obtained, and he is said to have examined and indorsed the law as passed; but neither he nor the chief probation officer appeared before the legislature in its behalf." U.S. Department of Labor, Children's Bureau, *The Administration of the Aid-to-Mothers Law in Illinois,* 10, n. 6. The *Survey* also credited Pinckney and the chief probation officer, John Witter, with the legislation, although the juvenile court reports for the period preceding passage do not discuss the idea. *Survey* (19 November 1911): 1238; *Survey* (30 March 1912): 2004. As chief probation officer, Witter oversaw the casework and investigations of all the dependent family cases. Henry Neil credited John Witter for his work on the pension bill. *Chicago Daily Socialist,* 28 August 1911, [n.p.].

81. *Chicago Daily Tribune,* 29 January 1912, p. 3.

82. Ibid., 1 February 1912, p. 3.

83. Ibid., 20 January 1913, p. 7.

84. United Charities of Chicago, *Minute Book,* vol. 1 (1909–1914), 23 January 1913, United Charities of Chicago Collection, Chicago Historical Society, Chicago, IL.

85. *Survey* (1 February 1913): 559; *Survey* (22 March 1913): 891, 849–851. Despite his ostracism from this sector of the welfare community, Neil continued his advocacy of pensions. He traveled widely in midwestern and eastern states promoting pensions. During World War I, he campaigned for aid to dependent children in England. *Chicago Daily Tribune,* 15 August 1939, p. 25.

86. Ruth Newberry, "Origin and Criticism of the Funds to Parents Act" (M.A. thesis, University of Chicago, 1912), 10–12.

87. Grace Abbott to Mr. Meikle, 14 July 1928, memo, file 10–12–2–5, Children's Bureau Records, Central Files, 1914–1940, record group 102, National Archives, Washington, DC.

88. Sophonisba P. Breckinridge, [autobiography], Breckinridge Papers, University of Chicago Library, Chicago IL.

89. *Chicago Daily Tribune,* 12 May 1911, p. 1.

90. For example, see the speeches of Jane Addams, Harriet H. McCormick, and Anita McCormick Blaine. Sophonisba P. Breckinridge, ed., *The Child in the City: A Series of Papers Presented at the Conferences Held during the Chicago Child Welfare Exhibit* (Chicago: Department of Social Investigation, Chicago School of Civics and Philanthropy, 1912), 4–5, 485, 493.

91. *Chicago Daily Socialist,* 12 May 1911, p. 1.

92. *Chicago Daily Tribune,* 12 May 1911, p. 1.

93. Sophonisba P. Breckinridge, ed., *The Child in the City,* 322–323.

94. Merritt W. Pinckney, "Public Pensions to Widows: Experiences and Observations Which Lead Me to Favor Such a Law," in *Selected Articles on Mothers' Pensions,* compiled by Edna D. Bullock (New York: The H. W. Wilson Co., 1915), 139.

95. Ibid., 142.

96. Jane Addams, *My Friend Julia Lathrop,* 144.

97. Catherine Hackett, "Julia Lathrop, Friend at Large," *Woman Citizen* (12 July 1924): 12.

98. Sophonisba P. Breckinridge, *Women in the Twentieth Century,* 101.

99. Sophonisba P. Breckinridge to Grace Abbott, 24 October 1921; Sophonisba P. Breckinridge to Frances Perkins, 7 March 1933, Breckinridge Family Papers.

100. Sophonisba P. Breckinridge to Anna Wilmarth Ickes, Illinois State Representative, March 1933, Breckinridge Family Papers.

101. Sophonisba P. Breckinridge, "Home Economics and the Quest for Economic Security," paper given at the American Home Economic Association Annual Meeting, Chicago, June 23–28, 1935, p. 11.

102. Edith Abbott, *Democracy and Social Progress in England,* University of Chicago War Papers, no. 8 (Chicago: University of Chicago Press, 1918); and idem, "Social Insurance and/or Social Security," *Social Service Review* 8:3 (September 1934): 537–540.

103. Edith Abbott, "The Experimental Period of Widow's Pension Legislation," 155.

104. Ibid., 163. Arlien Johnson, "Edith Abbott's Contribution to Public Social Policy," *Social Service Review* (September 1939): 17.

105. Edith Abbott, "The Hull House of Jane Addams," *Social Service Review* (September 1952): 337.

106. Springfield newspapers noted that the house passed 700 bills in an average session. *Illinois State Journal,* 3 March 1911, 2. Senate Bill no. 403 passed the Senate by a vote of 41 to 0 on 27 April 1911, and passed the House by a vote of 105 to 0 on 19 May 1911. *Illinois State Journal,* 28 March 1911, 3; 21 May 1911, 3.

107. Edith Abbott, "The Experimental Period of Widows' Pension Legislation," 154–155. In contrast, anti–child labor legislation faced significant resistance at the state-level.

NOTES TO CHAPTER FOUR

1. *Record Herald,* 9 October 1911, p. 9.

2. When the policy became fully operative, twenty-one women had their names, addresses, and pension amounts published in the newspaper. *Chicago Daily Tribune,* 19 November 1911, sec. 1, p. 3.

3. *Record Herald,* 26 November 1911, sec. 6, p. 1.

4. The Chicago record illustrates a case in contrast to those who place the emphasis on pre-suffrage efforts to pass legislation by women's mass organizations. Theda Skocpol, et al., "Women's Associations and the Enactment of Mothers' Pensions in the United States," *American Political Science Review* 87:3 (September 1993): 696.

5. *Chicago Daily Tribune,* 24 November 1911, p. 9.

6. Cook County, IL, Board of County Commissioners, *Proceedings* (1910–1911), 1127; idem, *Charity Service Reports* (1911), 28–29; hereafter cited as *Charity Service Reports.*

7. *Record Herald,* 25 November 1911, p. 8.

8. *Chicago Daily Socialist,* 23 November 1911, p. 1.

9. *Dziennik Związkowy Zgoda,* 24 November 1911, Foreign Language Press Survey, Chicago Public Library, Omnibus Project, U.S. Works Progress Administration, 1942.

10. *Record Herald,* 9 October 1911, p. 9.

11. *Chicago Daily Tribune,* 1 December 1911, p. 1.

12. *Record Herald,* 25 November 1911, p. 8.

13. Pinckney continued to defend the policy by emphasizing the mother's vital role in the family and thus the validity of state support. At the same time, he emphasized the need for women to make efforts at self-support. See *Proceedings of the National Conference of Charities and Correction*

at the Thirty-ninth session held in Cleveland, Ohio, June 12–19, 1912 (Fort Wayne, IN: Fort Wayne Printing, 1912), 479, 477.

14. *Chicago Daily Tribune*, 14 December 1911, p. 14.

15. Edith Abbott, "Public Pensions to Widows with Children," *American Economic Review* 3 (June 1913): 477. On the formation of the committee, see U.S. Department of Labor, Children's Bureau, *The Chicago Juvenile Court*, by Helen Rankin Jeter, Publication no. 104 (Washington, DC: Government Printing Office, 1922), 27; Joel Hunter, "Administration of the Funds to Parents Law in Chicago," *Survey* (31 January 1914): 516–518; Merritt W. Pinckney, *Survey* (1914): 473–474. Committee recommendations for the staff may be found in Joseph Moss, "A Short History of the Cook County Juvenile Court," *Charity Service Reports* (1913), 206. The complete list of representatives and organizations included Charles Wacker, United Charities; Sol Sulzbreger, Jewish Aid Societies; Reverend C. J. Quille, Catholic Charities; James F. Kennedy, St. Vincent de Paul Society; Mrs. Arthur T. Aldis, Visiting Nurse Association; Mary H. Wilmarth, Woman's City Club; Dr. Henry Favill, City Club; Julia Lathrop, Federation of Settlements; Gustave Fischer, Industrial Club; A. A. McCormick, Immigrants' Protective League; Louise de Koven Bowen, Juvenile Protective Association; Mrs. L. L. Funk, Children's Day Association; Sherman Kingsley, Elizabeth McCormick Memorial Fund; Adolph Kurtz, Jewish Home-Finding Association; Minnie Low, Bureau of Personal Service; Jane Addams, Hull House. Kingsley, Quille, Kennedy, Low, Funk, and Lathrop were on the executive committee. *Chicago Daily Tribune*, 1 December 1911, pp. 1–2; *Record Herald*, 13 December 1911, [n.p.]

16. *Chicago Daily Socialist*, 13 December 1911, p. 5.

17. U.S. Department of Labor, Children's Bureau, *The Administration of the Aid-to-Mothers Law in Illinois*, by Edith Abbott and Sophonisba P. Breckinridge, Publication no. 82 (Washington, DC: Government Printing Office, 1921), 11–12.

18. On the growth of the program, see *Charity Service Reports*, Juvenile Court (1912), 147–148; U.S. Department of Labor, Children's Bureau, *Chicago Juvenile Court*, 31; and Sherman Kingsley, "The Working of the Funds to Parent Act in Illinois," *Proceedings of the National Conference of Charities and Correction*, 1914, 438. The alumni status of Quinlan and Moss are recorded respectively in *Training for Social Work* (Chicago: School of Civics and Philanthropy, 1910–1911), 161; and *The New Profession and Preparation for It* (Chicago: Chicago School of Civics and Philanthropy, 1910), 180.

19. Edith Abbott recorded the intention to represent Jewish and Catholic agencies in Edith Abbott, "Public Pensions to Widows and Children," 476. No one from the African American community was solicited. The committee comprised Louise de Koven Bowen of the Juvenile Protective Association; Rabbi Emil G. Hirsch of Sinai Temple; Leonora Meder, President of the Federation of Catholic Women's Charities; Reverend C. J. Quille, superintendent of the Working Boys' Home; and Sherman C. Kingsley, director of the McCormick Memorial Fund. Cook County, IL, Board of County Commissioners, *Proceedings* (1912–1913), 123. The extralegal committee ended its work in April 1913. U.S. Department of Labor, Children's Bureau, *The Administration of the Aid-to-Mothers Law in Illinois*, 11; Joel Hunter, "Administration of the Funds to Parents Law in Chicago," 517; and *Charity Service Reports*, County Agent (1915), 43.

20. A serious matter lay beneath the partisan confrontations for control of these court positions. Charges of abuse of young people by their "guardians" and ill-treatment in institutions or child-caring homes occasionally surfaced. The State Board of Charities was aware of problems

with the certification and inspection of institutions and homes, and some members had lobbied for greater centralization of authority, which eventually took place in 1917. This issue was submerged in the local battle, where control over the positions took precedence. In November 1910 in his inauguration speech, Bartzen promised an end to the abuses at the Juvenile Home, including alleged attacks by officers upon their charges. Two months later Judge Pinckney and Louise de Koven Bowen, a member of the Juvenile Court Committee, retired all 195 volunteers in a reform measure. The positions were later filled through a process of application and review. Newspaper clipping, Louise Haddock de Koven Bowen Scrapbooks, vol. 1, Chicago Historical Society, Chicago, IL; *Chicago Daily Tribune*, 1–3 September 1911, 1–3 November 1911; and William Hard, "The Moral Necessity of 'State Funds to Mothers,'" *Survey* (1 March 1913): 769–773.

21. *Charity Service Reports* (1913), 209. This included all the staff from the chief probation officer to clerical workers. There were 125 police and nonpolice probation officers. In 1917, women comprised 80 percent of the 115 probation officers in the court. See *Charity Service Reports* (1917), 207.

22. *Chicago Examiner*, 25 July 1911, [n.p.]; Julia Lathrop Papers, Rockford College Archives, Rockford, IL; hereafter cited as Lathrop Papers. Joanna C. Snowden to Julia C. Lathrop, 25 July 1911, 30 July 1911. Snowden was a pioneer in the field. She became very active in club work, serving as president for the Northwestern Federation of Colored Women's Clubs. See *Records of the National Association of Colored Women's Clubs, 1895–1992*, part 1, *Minutes of National Conventions, Publications, and President's Office Correspondence* (Bethesda, MD: University Publications of America, 1994), microfilm.

23. *Chicago Examiner*, 25 July 1911, Lathrop Papers; Juvenile Court of Cook County, IL, *Report of a Committee Appointed under Resolution of the Board of Commissioners of Cook County*, hearing date August 8, 1911 (Chicago: Citizen's Investigating Committee, 1912).

24. Peter Bartzen to John Witter, 29 September 1911, Lathrop Papers. Witter had also been told that Bartzen suspended him for "taking orders from private corporations." John Witter to Julia Lathrop, 25 September 1911, Lathrop Papers.

25. *Charity Service Reports*, Juvenile Court (1913), 206–208; *Charity Service Reports* (1911), 153–154.

26. *Survey* (11 January 1913): 467. *Charity Service Reports*, Civil Service Commission (1913), 334. Tests for civil service exams were generally accompanied by lists of people whom the county commissioners wanted given a "square deal" on the grading. *Chicago Daily Tribune*, 27 January 1912, sec. 1, p. 7.

27. *Chicago Daily Tribune*, 29 December 1911, p. 1. Correspondence, 26 July 1911, [untitled newspaper clipping], [n.d.], Lathrop Papers.

28. *Witter v. Cook County Commissioners*, 256 Ill. 616 (1912); *Charity Service Reports* (1913), 204–208.

29. Cook County, IL, Board of County Commissioners, *Proceedings* (1910–1911), 1127, 1377, 1439.

30. Ibid., 6 February 1912, Budget Appropriations, 190.

31. McCormick held management positions at the *Evening Post* and the *Record Herald* prior to 1912. *Chicago Daily Tribune*, 28 October 1912, 2 November 1912, Scrapbooks of the political campaigns of A. A. McCormick, 1912–1915, Newberry Library, Chicago, IL; hereafter cited as Alexander A. McCormick Scrapbooks.

32. [Unidentified newspaper clipping], 21 October 1912; *Record Herald*, 24 October 1912, Alexander A. McCormick Scrapbooks. I have used a woman's married name when no other name was provided.

33. Bartzen had fired county agent Joseph Meyer in March on the grounds that too many were receiving poor relief. However, Meyer believed that his firing had more to do with factional politics between the Democrats on the County Board. [Untitled news clipping], 9 March 1912, Alexander A. McCormick Scrapbooks. Bartzen increased salaries 142 percent and employees 117 percent over those of his predecessor. *Herald Examiner*, 9 October 1912, Alexander A. McCormick Scrapbooks.

34. "Report of Meeting Held at the Illinois Theater Sunday Afternoon, November 3, 1912," Cook County Board of Commissioners Records, Chicago Historical Society, Chicago, IL; Louise de Koven Bowen Scrapbooks, vol. 1, Chicago Historical Society.

35. *Chicago Examiner*, 3 October 1912, Alexander A. McCormick Scrapbooks.

36. Ibid., 24 February 1912.

37. Ibid., 3 November 1912.

38. Ibid.

39. *Chicago Daily Tribune*, 7 November 1912; *Record Herald*, 7 November 1912, Alexander A. McCormick Scrapbooks.

40. *Charity Service Reports*, President's Message (1913), 28–29; *Survey* (1 February 1913): 561; *Chicago Herald-Examiner*, 11 December 1912, Alexander A. McCormick Scrapbooks.

41. *Chicago Daily Tribune*, 3 December 1912; *Chicago Post*, 13 October 1913, Alexander A. McCormick Scrapbooks. The discourse on welfare cheats, imposters, and public savings probably reflects more about campaign politics than any specific evidence of relief use. For example, after one year in office, McCormick announced his administration's success in removing "the mass of imposters" from the relief rolls who received county services through their local politicians. With the assistance of his county agent, 2,200 families were removed from county relief. Bartzen had also started his presidency by cleaning house on "welfare cheats." Bartzen announced that 5,000 "unworthy families" who were enjoying the county's welfare services through "favoritism or politics of the prior administration" were cut off the list, saving the county thousands of dollars. See *Charity Service Reports*, President's Message (1911), 12–13.

42. C. C. Carstens, *Public Pensions to Widows with Children: A Study of Their Administration in Several American Cities* (New York: Russell Sage Foundation, 1913). See also *Proceedings of the National Conference of Charities and Correction*, 1912, 473–498; *Survey* (1913): 769–773. Articles on both sides of the debate over mothers' pensions are compiled in Edna D. Bullock, *Selected Articles on Mothers' Pensions* (New York: H. W. Wilson Company, 1915). Grace Abbott, *From Relief to Social Security: The Development of the New Public Welfare Services and Their Administration* (Chicago: University of Chicago Press, 1941), 267–270.

43. *Record Herald*, 3 January 1913, Alexander A. McCormick Scrapbooks. James Mullenbach, chair of the Committee on Social Legislation of the Illinois Conference of Charities and Corrections, verified that "Cook County authorities" concerned about expenditures had started the revision process. Illinois, *Institutional Quarterly* (31 March 1914): 53.

44. *Record Herald*, 3 January 1913, Alexander A. McCormick Scrapbooks.

45. *Survey* (1 February 1913): 561. *Charity Service Reports*, President's Message (1913), 17.

46. Joel Hunter, "Administration of the Funds to Parents Law in Chicago," 516; U.S. Depart-

ment of Labor, Children's Bureau, *The Administration of the Aid-to-Mothers Law in Illinois*, 12–17. *Laws of Illinois*, Senate Bill no. 300, 48th General Assembly, 1913. Two years later the Illinois State Charities Commission found that less than one-third of the state's counties complied with the law. Cook County was among those counties that did not levy a separate tax. It drew upon the aggregate tax revenues and made one appropriation. Illinois, *Institution Quarterly* (31 December 1915): 11, 16.

Women's Clubs won a small victory in the middle of McCormick's first term with the appointment of Mary Bartelme, a Chicago lawyer, as assistant to the juvenile court judge. Bartelme was a member of the Chicago Woman's Club and the Woman's City Club. In 1923, she ran successfully for Circuit Court judge and was assigned to the juvenile court. She was re-elected in 1927. *Charity Service Reports* (1913), 208; Adena Miller Rich to Julia Lathrop, 28 July 1923, 4 August 1923, Adena Miller Rich Papers, Special Collections, University Library, University of Illinois at Chicago.

47. Merritt W. Pinckney, "Public Pensions to Widows: Experiences and Observations Which Lead Me to Favor Such a Law," *Proceedings of the National Conference of Charities and Correction*, 1912, 473.

48. *Laws of Illinois*, Senate Bill no. 300, 48th General Assembly, 1913, 130.

49. Ibid., 129.

50. *Charity Service Reports* (1913), 264–265.

51. Joel D. Hunter, "Administration of the Funds to Parents Law in Chicago," *Survey* (31 January 1914): 518; idem, "Desertion and Non-support by Fathers in Mothers' Aid Cases," *Proceedings of the National Conference of Social Work* (1919): 208. Grace Abbott concurred. Years later, she wrote "leaders in Illinois agreed too readily that the Funds to Parents Act was too inclusive," referring to fears raised about public support for deserted and unmarried mothers. Grace Abbott, *From Relief to Social Security*, 271.

52. *Laws of Illinois*, Senate Bill no. 403, 47th General Assembly, 1911, 126.

53. U.S. Department of Labor, Children's Bureau, *The Administration of the Aid-to-Mothers Law in Illinois*, 110.

54. Lathrop served on the executive committee of the citizen's committee to the court which made suggestions about implementation, but she left Chicago to assume her post as director of the federal Children's Bureau in 1912. Sophonisba P. Breckinridge, "Political Equality for Women and Women's Wages," *Annals of the American Academy of Political and Social Science* 56 (November 1914): 122–123. Breckinridge published on a broad range of social welfare issues, including race bias in housing, sex discrimination in employment, the necessity for a minimum wage, and political equality. Edith Abbott, "Women's Wages in Chicago: Some Notes on Available Data," *Journal of Political Economy* 21:2 (February 1913): 143–158.

55. Edith Abbott, "Lack of Finality in Funds to Parents Legislation," paper delivered at the Illinois Conference of Charities and Corrections, March 1913, *Institution Quarterly* (31 March 1914): 99; Edith Abbott, "Public Pensions to Widows with Children," 473–478.

56. The study analyzed applications received between 1 August 1913 and 1 March 1915. *Charity Service Reports*, Juvenile Court (1917), 257. The survey was conducted by Emma Quinlan, Mothers' Pension Division director, and Blanche Harvey.

57. U.S. Department of Labor, Children's Bureau, *The Administration of the Aid-to-Mothers Law in Illinois*, 14. For a contemporary discussion of the legal and economic liabilities of married

women's citizenship status, see Sophonisba P. Breckinridge, *Marriage and the Civic Rights of Women: Separate Domicile and Independent Citizenship* (Chicago: University of Chicago Press, 1931).

58. U.S. Department of Labor, Children's Bureau, *The Administration of the Aid-to-Mothers Law in Illinois,* 95–100.

59. Within a year of Lathrop's assuming the directorship, Lillian Wald wrote to ask her to use the resources of the Children's Bureau to compile "expert advice" on public aid to dependent children. Wald was in the early stages of New York's inquiry into the adoption of a pension policy. She had the well-organized opposition of the charity organization society to counteract. Lillian D. Wald to Julia C. Lathrop, 18 January 1913, Grace and Edith Abbott Papers, box 59, folder 1, Department of Special Collections, University of Chicago Library, Chicago, IL; hereafter cited as Abbott Papers; U.S., Department of Labor, Children's Bureau, *Annual Report* (1913), Abbott Papers.

60. *Chicago Daily Tribune,* 18 January 1915, pp. 1–2.

61. *Chicago American,* 18 November 1915, Alexander A. McCormick Scrapbooks.

62. *Chicago Herald,* 1 November 1915, Alexander A. McCormick Scrapbooks.

63. Women were entitled to vote for presidential electors, mayor, aldermen, and municipal propositions. See Steven Buechler, *The Transformation of the Woman Suffrage Movement: The Case of Illinois, 1850–1920* (New Brunswick, NJ: Rutgers University Press, 1986); Joel H. Goldstein, *The Effects of the Adoption of Woman Suffrage: Sex Differences in Voting Behavior—Illinois, 1914–1921* (New York: Praeger, 1984); and Gertrude May Beldon, "A History of the Woman Suffrage Movement in Illinois" (M.A. thesis, University of Chicago, 1913).

64. The *Chicago American* reported that Louise de Koven Bowen, Twenty-first Ward, Mary McDowell, Thirtieth Ward, and Sophonisba P. Breckinridge, Seventh Ward, had filed for "alderwomanic" positions. The candidates listed themselves as Independents, thus announcing that their campaigns were to be run outside the major party lines. Marion Drake was the only woman candidate to run in the general election. She made an unsuccessful bid in the First Ward against "Bathhouse" John Coughlin in April 1914. *Chicago American,* 21 November 1913, Louise de Koven Bowen Scrapbooks, vol. 1, Chicago Historical Society.

65. Local newspapers announced that Jane Addams, Mary Nicholes, and Louise de Koven Bowen were likely to run as Progressive candidates for the County Board. By July, both Bowen and McDowell remained in the race, but by mid-August Bowen dropped out and Harriet Vittum stepped into her place. *Record Herald,* 10 June 1914, 18 July 1914, 15 August 1914, Alexander A. McCormick Scrapbooks.

66. *Record Herald,* 9 October 1914, Alexander A. McCormick Scrapbooks.

67. *Chicago Daily Tribune,* 1 October 1914, Alexander A. McCormick Scrapbooks.

68. *Herald Examiner,* 4 September 1914, Alexander A. McCormick Scrapbooks.

69. Mary McDowell, "Civic Experiences—1914," Mary McDowell Papers, Chicago Historical Society, Chicago, IL. The same women frequently spoke in terms of nonpartisanship as a way to focus on issues regardless of party affiliation. Despite their language, nonpartisan did not mean nonpolitical, as Robyn Muncy and Susan Ware have demonstrated. These reformers wanted to use political systems to forward their agendas and make room for their issues and people. See Robyn L. Muncy, *Creating a Female Dominion in American Reform, 1890–1930* (New York: Oxford University Press, 1991); and Susan Ware, *Beyond Suffrage: Women in the New Deal* (Cambridge: Harvard University Press, 1981).

Political historians have more frequently focused on the centrality of race, ethnicity, or class in Chicago politics. For a description of the significance of these ties to party organization, see John M. Allswang, *A House for All Peoples: Ethnic Politics in Chicago, 1890–1936* (Lexington: University Press of Kentucky, 1971); Harold F. Gosnell, *Machine Politics: Chicago Model* (New York: Greenwood Press, 1968; originally published, Chicago: University of Chicago Press, 1937); idem, *Negro Politicians: The Rise of Negro Politics in Chicago* (Chicago: University of Chicago Press, 1967; originally published, Chicago: University of Chicago Press, 1935); Charles E. Merriam, *Chicago: A More Intimate View of Urban Politics* (New York: Macmillan Co., 1929); St. Clair Drake and Horace R. Cayton, *Black Metropolis: A Study of Negro Life in a Northern City* (New York: Harcourt, Brace and Co., 1945; reprint Chicago: University of Chicago Press, 1993); and Dianne Pinderhughes, *Race and Ethnicity in Chicago Politics: A Reexamination of Pluralist Theory* (Urbana: University of Illinois Press, 1987). Lizabeth Cohen has argued that universal social insurance programs, such as those in the New Deal, remained politically unobtainable until the cultural and ethnic divisions were bridged. Lizabeth Cohen, *Making a New Deal: Industrial Workers in Chicago, 1919–1939* (New York: Cambridge University Press, 1990), 251–261.

The role played by organized women voters and the impact of gender in urban politics do not receive much attention in these works. One notable exception is Maureen Flanagan, "Gender and Urban Political Reform: The City Club and the Woman's City Club of Chicago in the Progressive Era," *American Historical Review* 95:4 (October 1990): 1032–1050.

70. *Daily News*, 8 September 1914, Alexander A. McCormick Scrapbooks.

71. Woman's City Club, *Bulletin* (January 1915): 2–3.

72. *The Woman's City Club: Its Book*, 1 October 1915, Woman's City Club of Chicago Records, Special Collections, University Library, University of Illinois at Chicago, 23. See also Barbara Spencer Spackman, "The Woman's City Club of Chicago: A Civic Pressure Group," (M.A. thesis, University of Chicago, 1930).

73. Woman's City Club, *Bulletin* (March 1915): 1; (May 1915): 1.

74. *Chicago Defender*, 2 April 1910, p. 1.

75. Ibid., 21 February 1914, p. 1; 3 March 1914, p. 1; 4 April 1914, p. 1.

76. Ibid., 13 February 1915, p. 8; 27 February 1915, p. 1; 27 March 1915, p. 2; 1 May 1915, pp. 1–2. Alfreda M. Duster, ed. *Crusade for Justice: The Autobiography of Ida B. Wells* (Chicago: University of Chicago Press, 1970), 345–353. A helpful discussion of the Republican appeals for black votes, and the ethnic and racial divisions engendered by Thompson's inclusion of blacks in his administration, may be found in James R. Grossman, *Land of Hope: Chicago, Black Southerners, and the Great Migration* (Chicago: University of Chicago Press, 1989), 174–178.

77. Wells-Barnett discussed efforts against racist legislation at the national level, such as the African Exclusion Amendment, the intermarriage bill, and a discriminatory streetcar bill. See *Alpha Suffrage Record* 1:1 (18 March 1914), Ida B. Wells Papers, Department of Special Collections, University of Chicago Library, Chicago, IL.

78. Ibid. Wells-Barnett claimed that the Negro Fellowship League worked for the election of a black alderman in the Second Ward in 1915. *Broad Ax*, 18 December 1915, p. 4.

79. "It was understood that if Mr. Thompson won, our reading room and social center [Negro Fellowship League] was to be made an auxiliary of the city, and through our employment agency, colored men were to be given street-cleaning jobs and work in other departments of the city." Wells-Barnett cited in Alfreda M. Duster, *Crusade for Justice*, 349–353 (quotation on 351);

and Harold F. Gosnell, *Negro Politicians*, 50. For a broader discussion of African American women's political leadership, see Evelyn Brooks Higginbotham, "In Politics to Stay: Black Women Leaders and Party Politics in the 1920s," in *Women, Politics, and Change*, ed. Louise A. Tilly and Patricia Gurin (New York: Russell Sage Foundation, 1990), 199–220.

80. *Chicago Defender*, 1 May 1915, pp. 1–2; 29 January 1927, pt. 2, p. 8.

81. James Grossman, *Land of Hope*, 177, 260. See also Manning Marable, "Black Power in Chicago: An Historical Overview of Class Stratification and Electoral Politics in a Black Urban Community," *Review of Radical Political Economics* 17:3 (1985): 157–182.

82. Edith Abbott, "Are Women a Force for Good Government? An Analysis of the Returns in the Recent Municipal Election in Chicago," *National Municipal Review* 4 (July 1915): 437–447; and idem, "The Woman Voter and the Spoils System in Chicago," *National Municipal Review* 5 (July 1916): 460–465, quotation on 460. The *Chicago Daily News Almanac and Yearbook* recorded election results for the previous year. *New York Evening Post*, [n.d.], Alexander A. McCormick Scrapbooks.

83. "Mass Meeting of Women to Protest Against the Spoils System and Adopt a Woman's Municipal Platform," *Report of Proceedings*, 18 March 1916, Woman's City Club Records, Chicago Historical Society, Chicago, IL.

84. *Record Herald*, 19 March 1916, Alexander A. McCormick Scrapbooks; and "Mass Meeting of Women," *Report of Proceedings*, 18 March 1916, Woman's City Club Records.

85. Woman's City Club, Minutes, 29 January 1917, 3–4, 7, Woman's City Club Records, Chicago Historical Society, Chicago, IL; Woman's City Club, *Bulletin* (December 1916): 1.

86. *Laws of Illinois*, 1915, 243; *Senate Journal*, 15 June 1915, 1394–1395; *House Journal*, 19 June 1915, 1338–1339. Abbott and Breckinridge noted that the Chicago court was influential in eliminating the property and deserted-women categories. U.S. Department of Labor, Children's Bureau, *The Administration of the Aid-to-Mothers Law in Illinois*, 14. Florence Nesbitt's work on family budgets for the Chicago Juvenile Court provided the data for the legislature's increase in the monthly stipend.

87. *Charity Service Reports*, President's Address (1916), 12.

88. In 1917, the legislature expanded eligibility to "mothers who are entitled to a homestead . . . or a dower right in real estate" up to $1000. It also applied further residency restrictions by indicating that a man must have been a resident of Illinois when he died or incurred his incapacitating illness for his wife to be eligible. Illinois, *House and Senate Bills*, House Bill no. 537, 50th General Assembly, 1917. The Chicago court added additional restrictions. It defined permanently incapacitated as "totally incapacitated for any work." It excluded women with only one child unless they could show that they were unable to work. Finally, it allowed pensions to the "legitimate" children in families where there was also a child born outside the marriage. U.S. Department of Labor, Children's Bureau, *The Administration of the Aid-to-Mothers Law in Illinois*, 15.

89. Cook County, IL, Board of County Commissioners, *Proceedings* (1916–1917), 1672.

90. *Charity Service Reports*, President's Message (1917–1918), 2. The U.S. entered World War I in April 1917 and the war ended eighteen months later in November 1918.

91. United Charities of Chicago, *Minute Book*, vol. 2, 8 July 1918, United Charities of Chicago Records, Chicago Historical Society, Chicago, IL; *Charity Service Reports*, President's Message (1918), 12.

92. *Charity Service Reports*, President's Message (1918), 11–13; *Charity Service Reports*, County Agent (1919), 7.

93. Cited in *Charity Service Reports*, Chief Probation Officer (1918), 220.

94. Ibid., 223.

95. The original proposal submitted to the Senate in January 1919 was for a one-mill tax. The House amended the bill so that the one-mill rate applied only to counties under 300,000. For Cook County, the only county with a population over 300,000, the House proposed the tax be no more than four-tenths of a mill. The Senate rejected this amendment and a committee was formed to negotiate the differences. After one amendment passed allowing four-tenths mill, a second act passed nine days later reducing it to four-fifteenths mill. The act did separate those funds from other tax-generated revenue. *Laws of Illinois* (1919), 781–782. For revisions, see *Laws of Illinois* (1921), 163; (1927), 197; (1928), 3.

96. The title "social politics" appeared for the first time in 1916–1917, but the course developed from an earlier one on social reform movements. Chicago School of Civics and Philanthropy, *Announcements* (1913–1919). The department of social investigation conducted five studies in 1918–1919 in which students assisted. Two for the Children's Bureau included Helen Wright's study on children of wage-earning mothers (eventually Children's Bureau publication no. 102), and Eva Beldon's compilation of juvenile court laws in the U.S. The remaining research consisted of dietary studies for the Department of Agriculture, a cost-of-living study for the Department of Labor, and a study of homes and family adjustment for the Carnegie Foundation. Chicago School of Civics and Philanthropy, *Announcements* (1918–1919), 18.

The third stage of the juvenile court studies undertaken by the school concerned dependency. Several students, including Wright, were involved in the Illinois pension study for the Children's Bureau. Chicago School of Civics and Philanthropy, *Announcements* (1916–1917), 17. Pennsylvania and Wisconsin also made studies of their programs. Pennsylvania, Mother's Assistance Fund, *Report of the Mothers' Assistance Fund to the General Assembly of Pennsylvania* (Harrisburg: J. L. L. Kuhn, 1920); and Wisconsin, State Board of Control, *The Administration of Aid to Dependent Children Law in Wisconsin* (Madison: The Board), 1921.

97. Julia Lathrop to Graham Taylor, 16 June 1915; Julia Lathrop to A. L. Bowen, 20 July 1915; Sophonisba Breckinridge to Julia Lathrop, 12 July 1916, Children's Bureau Records, record group 102, box 60, folder 7313, National Archives, Washington, DC.

98. U.S. Department of Labor, Children's Bureau, *The Administration of the Aid-to-Mothers Law in Illinois*, 167.

99. Ibid.

100. Ibid., 171.

101. Ibid., 170.

102. Edith Abbott, "Pensions, Insurance, and the State," *Proceedings of the National Conference of Social Work* (1918): 388–389; and idem, "Social Insurance and/or Social Security," *Social Service Review* 8:3 (September 1934): 537–540.

103. Edith Abbott, "The Experimental Period of Widows' Pension Legislation," *Proceedings of the National Conference of Social Work* (1917): 154–165. The Illinois Department of Public Welfare was established in 1917. It oversaw the operations of institutions, foster homes, and mothers' pensions.

104. Sophonisba P. Breckinridge to A. M. Morlock, 28 January 1919, Breckinridge Family

Papers, Library of Congress, Washington, DC; and Sophonisba P. Breckinridge to Joseph Moss, 26 February 1919, 14 March 1919, Breckinridge Family Papers, Library of Congress, Washington, DC.

105. *The Women's Press*, 29 December 1918, 1. I could find no evidence of the Chicago Woman's Club's direct participation in mothers' pensions during the first years of its implementation. However, individual members showed interest in and the club took up the issues of dependency, child welfare, and the wages of working women. In 1911, the club's reform effort focused on the minimum wage. They held a conference on the subject in January 1912, followed by legislation calling for a minimum wage commission and the establishment of minimum wage standards for women. Between 1912 and 1916, the Chicago Woman's Club's reform efforts included state legislation for factory inspection, birth registration, and woman suffrage. At the municipal level, members supported the establishment of a city employment bureau for women and the continuation of the county's Bureau of Public Welfare. They also strongly endorsed the work of Mary Bartelme as assistant to the judge of the juvenile court. See Henrietta Greenbaum Frank and Amalie Hofer Jerome, *Annals of the Chicago Woman's Club for the First Forty Years of Its Organization, 1876–1916* (Chicago: Chicago Woman's Clubs, 1916), 294, 307, 326, 335–336; United Charities of Chicago, *Minute Book*, vol. I, 9 January 1913.

106. Woman's City Club, *Bulletin* (December 1918): 3; (February 1919): 3; (March 1919): 3.

107. *Woman's Press*, 4 January 1919, p. 3; *Chicago Daily Tribune*, 28 December 1918, Alexander A. McCormick Scrapbooks.

108. Woman's City Club, *Bulletin* (February 1919): [enclosure].

109. *Women's Press*, 1 March 1919, pp. 1–2. For divergent views on the state's role in social welfare during the interwar years, see Sonya Michel and Robyn Rosen, "The Paradox of Maternalism: Elizabeth Lowell Putnam and the American Welfare State," *Gender and History* 4:3 (1992): 364–386.

110. "Grace [Abbott] had spoken vigorously and forcefully in support of the plan for holding the women together in a new League of Women Voters when the question came before the Chicago suffragists, and Mrs. McCormick spoke for the other side. But Grace was successful at this meeting in persuading the women who were present to support the plan for remaining together to work in a new organization; and Mrs. McCormick had not taken her defeat gracefully." This incident later threatened Grace Abbott's appointment as director of the Children's Bureau when Ruth Hanna McCormick attempted to influence her husband, Senator Medill McCormick, to block Abbott's appointment. Edith Abbott, unpublished biography of Grace Abbott, 8–9, Abbott Papers, box 9, folder 13.

111. For white ethnic reaction to the Thompson administration's inclusion of blacks, see John M. Allswang, *A House for All Peoples*, 143–152. Grossman discusses the acts of violence, in particular house bombings and personal attacks that preceded and followed the riot. James Grossman, *Land of Hope*, 178–180; Chicago Commission on Race Relations, *The Negro in Chicago: A Study of Race Relations and a Race Riot* (Chicago: University of Chicago Press, 1922), 122–129. Oscar DePriest and Jesse Binga, a real-estate agent and banker, both had their homes bombed. *Chicago Defender*, 4 April 1921; 9 April 1921, p. 1. *The Whip* generally condemned the Thompson administration for its failure to protect Second Ward citizens from bombings. *Chicago Whip*, 9 August 1919, p. 1; 13 March 1920, p. 8.

112. *Broad Ax*, 23 August 1922, p. 3. Many African American clubwomen supported the cam-

paign of Ruth Hanna McCormick, for example. See *Chicago Defender*, 21 November 1925, pt. 1, p. 3.; Scrapbooks, Irene McCoy Gaines Papers, Chicago Historical Society, Chicago, IL.

113. The Douglas League of the League of Women Voters occasionally held joint meetings with the Woman's City Club Second Ward Branch. Throughout the 1920s, the Douglas League sponsored a series of citizenship schools aimed to inform new voters about government, politics, and candidates. Douglas League Records, folder 93, Special Collections, University Library, University of Illinois at Chicago. In 1923, the Illinois League of Women Voters recommended that members organize on the basis of Senatorial districts, not on the basis of race. See Memo from Edith Rockwood, Executive Secretary of the Illinois League of Women Voters, 4 December 1923, Douglas League Records, folder 93, Special Collections, University Library, University of Illinois at Chicago.

114. Julia Lathrop, "Women in Politics," [n.d.], Adena Miller Rich Papers, Special Collections, University Library, University of Illinois at Chicago.

115. United Charities of Chicago, *Minute Book*, vol. 2, 28 April 1921; *Charity Service Reports*, County Agent (1921), 56; (1922), 32.

116. *Charity Service Reports* (1921), 57; (1922), 33.

117. Although the United Charities did reduce supplemental payments, the hardship and "deterioration" within families led them back to a policy of supplementing grants within a few months. United Charities of Chicago, *Minute Book*, vol. 2, 23 October 1919.

118. "Julia Lathrop, Friend at Large," *Woman Citizen*, 12 July 1924, 12.

119. Julia Lathrop, "Women in Politics," [n.d.], Adena Miller Rich Papers, Special Collections, University Library, University of Illinois at Chicago.

120. Edith Abbott, "Julia Lathrop and Professional Education for Social Work," 4, Abbott Papers, box 57, folder 2.

121. For a listing of placements see *Annual Report*, School of Social Service Administration (1924–1926), Abbott Papers, box 19. See also Robyn L. Muncy, *Creating a Female Dominion in American Reform*, 87.

122. Sophonisba P. Breckinridge to Grace Abbott, 24 October 1921, Jane Addams Papers (microfilm), Special Collections, University Library, University of Illinois at Chicago.

123. Sophonisba P. Breckinridge, "The Home Responsibilities of Women Workers and the 'Equal Wage,'" *Journal of Political Economy* 31 (August 1923): 521–543.

124. Illinois, Department of Public Welfare, *Report of the Children's Committee* (Springfield: Illinois State Journal Co., State Printers, 1921), 93, 95, 104–105.

125. *Chicago Defender*, 26 May 1928, sec. 2, p. 8.

126. Illinois, Department of Public Welfare, *Report of the Children's Committee* (Springfield: Illinois State Journal Co., State Printers, 1921), 132–133. The provision of care for dependent children varied somewhat within the black community, because working-class mothers were viewed as independent earners. Consequently, service focused on homes for dependent children and day nurseries for children of working mothers. I am indebted to Anne Knupfer for sharing her information on African American women's involvement in social work at the time. See Anne Meis Knupfer, *Toward a Tender Humanity and a Nobler Womanhood: African American Women's Clubs in Turn of the Century Chicago* (New York: New York University Press, 1997).

Notable exceptions of interracial work existed. See Sandra M. Stehno, "Public Responsibility for Dependent Black Children: The Advocacy of Edith Abbott and Sophonisba Breckinridge," *Social Service Review* 62 (September 1988): 485–503; Steven J. Diner, "Chicago Social Workers and Blacks in the Progressive Era," *Social Service Review* 44:4 (December 1970): 393–410.

127. Woman's City Club, *Bulletin* (April 1921): 3, 5; Illinois, 52d General Assembly, *House Journal* (1921), House Bill no. 294. Two additional house bills attempted to expand eligibility to women whose husbands either had deserted or were institutionalized. These measures failed. Figures are for counties with populations over 300,000, which included only Cook County. After 1921, the law provided lesser amounts for residents in counties with smaller populations. *Laws of Illinois* (1913), 128; (1915), 244; (1921), 162; (1923), 169; (1925), 185.

128. Woman's City Club, *Bulletin* (October 1921): 5.

129. Ibid. (December 1921): 14.

130. Ibid. (June 1921): 2.

131. Another revision that would have granted aid to women whose husbands were institutionalized was cancelled during debate. *Laws of Illinois* (1923), 169. Annette Marie Garrett, "The Administration of the Aid to Mothers Law in Illinois 1917 to 1925" (M.A. thesis, School of Social Service Administration, University of Chicago, 1925), 14–15.

132. Scholars have referred to the division over the ERA in terms of two opposing groups: those who supported women's rights through full legal equality and those who reserved protectionist policies for women based on difference, either sexual or socially constructed. Those who ascribed to the difference category have been too broadly grouped, whereby traditionalist clubwomen have been joined with politically active women's rights advocates.

133. "Could 'Mothers Pensions' Operate under Equal Rights Amendment?" *Congressional Digest* (March 1924): 202.

134. Woman's City Club, *Bulletin* (May 1925): 13–14.

135. Jane Addams, *Jane Addams: A Centennial Reader* (New York: Macmillan Co., 1960), 236–237.

136. Woman's City Club, *Bulletin* (June 1925): 59. The director of the Illinois Congress of Mothers Juvenile Protective Committee, Mrs. Mark Mears, was also the Woman's City Club director of legislation. It is likely that Mears utilized her position in both clubs to garner support for the bill.

137. *Charity Service Reports*, Chief Probation Officer (1925), 273.

138. The law established Bureaus of Public Welfare to provide social services in counties with populations over 500,000. Illinois, *Revised Statutes of the State of Illinois* (Springfield: Chicago Legal News, 1921), chap. 34, p. 67. The new county departments combined the two offices of county agent and chief probation officer. Joseph Moss, who had been the chief probation officer of the juvenile court since 1919, assumed the position of director of the new Cook County Department of Public Welfare. Anna Smith, who had been acting county agent since 1923, became a commissioner of public welfare. Cook County, IL, Board of County Commissioners, *Proceedings* (1924–1925), 1481; Raymond Marcellus Hilliard Papers, Chicago Historical Society; Cook County, IL, Department of Public Welfare, *Annual Report* (1927–1928), 252–253; and Abbott Papers, box 19, folder 6.

139. Ada Sheffield to Sophonisba Breckinridge, 27 January 1922, Jane Addams Papers (microfilm), Special Collections, University of Illinois at Chicago.

140. Harold F. Gosnell, *Machine Politics*, 10–14, 185.

141. Women's City Club, *Bulletin* (February 1928): 508; and Sophonisba P. Breckinridge,

Public Welfare Administration in the United States, Select Documents (Chicago: University of Chicago Press, 1927), 427.

142. Cook County, IL, Department of Public Welfare, *Annual Report* (1927–1928), 18. For the severity of the economic depression on Chicago's African American community, see Arvarh Strickland, *History of the Chicago Urban League* (Urbana: University of Illinois Press, 1966), 83–103; and Chicago Urban League, *Annual Reports* (1928–1930).

143. *Charity Service Reports,* President's Message (1927), 30.

144. The state legislature appropriated half a million dollars for biennium 1929–1931. *Laws of Illinois,* 1929, p. 198; Illinois, *Revised Statutes of the State of Illinois* (Chicago: Burdette J. Smith, 1929), chap. 23, sec. 338a. See *Charity Service Reports,* President's Message (1932), 58. For a description of Chicago's inadequate revenue and administrative systems during the depression, see Harold F. Gosnell, *Machine Politics,* 6–7.

NOTES TO CHAPTER FIVE

1. The intersections of wage-earning and family are addressed in Beverly Stadum, *Poor Women and Their Families: Hard Working Charity Cases, 1900–1930* (Albany: State University of New York Press, 1992). Alice Kessler-Harris argues that the integration of work and family has been far more fluid than historical paradigms acknowledged. See Alice Kessler-Harris, *A Woman's Wage: Historical Meanings and Social Consequences* (Lexington: University Press of Kentucky, 1990), 70. For the overlap between industrial policy and family policy, see Eileen Boris, *Home to Work: Motherhood and the Politics of Industrial Homework in the United States* (New York: Cambridge University Press, 1994).

2. The Mothers' Pension Division of the Chicago Juvenile Court destroyed individual case histories of families. The surviving documents include case files that detail family demographics, published aggregated data, selected case histories in teaching guides, relief agency reports, and private charity records. The material in this chapter came from aggregated data on pensioned families published in the *Charity Service Reports* and from published and unpublished case records preserved as examples of casework. I am grateful to David Tanenhouse, doctoral candidate in history at the University of Chicago, for sharing his information on mothers' pension case records with me.

3. Linda Gordon, *Pitied But Not Entitled: Single Mothers and the History of Welfare, 1890–1935* (New York: Free Press, 1994), 67–108; Regina G. Kunzel, *Fallen Women, Problem Girls: Unmarried Mothers and the Professionalization of Social Work, 1890–1945* (New Haven: Yale University Press, 1993).

4. Cook County, IL, Board of County Commissioners, *Charity Service Reports* (hereafter cited as *Charity Service Reports*), Juvenile Court (1911–1927); and *Report of the Department of Health of the City of Chicago for the Years 1926 to 1930 Inclusive* (Chicago: Chicago Department of Health, 1931), [n.p.].

5. The court received a petition for each child upon completion of both investigations. The petition named the Board of County Commissioners and the mother as respondents. Additional information on the application process may be found in U.S. Department of Labor, Children's Bureau, *The Administration of the Aid-to-Mothers Law in Illinois,* by Edith Abbott and Sophonisba P. Breckinridge, Publication no. 82 (Washington, DC: Government Printing Office, 1921), 19–20. See also U.S. Department of Labor, Children's Bureau, *Laws Relating to 'Mothers' Pen-*

sions' in the United States, Canada, Denmark, and New Zealand, Publication no. 63 (Washington, DC: Government Printing Office, 1919), 24–26.

6. U.S. Department of Labor, Children's Bureau, *The Administration of the Aid-to-Mothers Law in Illinois,* 19–24. The social control aspects of means-tested welfare policies have been described at length. See Michael B. Katz, *In the Shadow of the Poorhouse: A Social History of Welfare in America* (New York: Basic Books, 1986). For a recent example, see Gwendolyn Mink, *The Wages of Motherhood: Inequality in the Welfare State, 1917–1942* (Ithaca, NY: Cornell University Press, 1995).

Roy Lubove was one of the earliest historians to recognize that mothers' pensions continued relief policies in certain aspects. He agreed with Isaac Rubinow's assessment that mothers' pensions differed from other social insurance in the focus on "economic need and moral worth." Roy Lubove, *The Struggle for Social Security, 1900–1935* (Cambridge: Harvard University Press, 1968), 110–111; and Isaac M. Rubinow, *Social Insurance with Special Reference to American Conditions* (New York: Henry Holt and Company, 1913; reprint, New York: Arno Press, 1969), 435–438. Neither, however, addressed the exclusion of impoverished mothers from the social insurance agenda directly. For the persistent, if unsuccessful, argument for providing social insurance for all families with dependent children, see Grace Abbott, *From Relief to Social Security: The Development of the New Public Welfare Services and Their Administration* (Chicago: University of Chicago Press, 1941), 231–233.

For other studies that examine the beneficial as well as social control aspects of social policy, see Linda Gordon, *Pitied But Not Entitled;* and Regina G. Kunzel, *Fallen Women, Problem Girls.*

7. Linda Gordon, *Heroes of Their Own Lives: The Politics and History of Family Violence, Boston 1880–1960* (New York: Viking Press, 1988), 289–299. One example of contested public resources in Chicago is the county agent's refusal to let his staff doctors serve pensioned families, because he felt that poor relief families had so much less than those receiving pensions. U.S. Department of Labor, Children's Bureau, *The Administration of the Aid-to-Mothers Law in Illinois,* 28–32.

8. U.S. Department of Labor, Children's Bureau, *The Administration of the Aid-to-Mothers Law in Illinois,* 35.

9. The information on families came from *Charity Service Reports,* Juvenile Court, Mothers' Pension Division (1911, 1915–1927). In particular, the study of 1,115 families between 1913 and 1915 offers social data not recorded in regular annual reports. See *Charity Service Reports,* Juvenile Court, Mothers' Pension Division (1917), 257–273.

Half of all deaths were attributed to either tuberculosis, pneumonia, or heart disease. Tuberculosis, the single largest cause of death, accounted for 26 percent of the deaths. Accidents accounted for only 11 percent. *Charity Service Reports,* Juvenile Court (1917), 260–262; and U.S. Department of Labor, Children's Bureau, *The Administration of the Aid-to-Mothers Law in Illinois,* 90.

Utah, Texas, Maryland, New Jersey, and Connecticut restricted mothers' pensions solely to widows. U.S. Department of Labor, Children's Bureau, *Public Aid to Mothers with Dependent Children,* by Emma O. Lundberg, Publication no. 162 (Washington, DC: Government Printing Office, 1928), 5.

10. *Charity Service Reports,* County Agent (1911–1917); and *Charity Service Reports,* Juvenile Court, Mothers' Pension Division (1918–1927).

11. U.S. Department of Labor, Children's Bureau, *Public Aid to Mothers with Dependent Children*, 4; and idem, *The Administration of the Aid-to-Mothers Law in Illinois*, 15.

12. The figures on race and ethnicity refer to the cases added in a year. These figures are subject to the same disclaimer as those for relief. Children born in the United States to foreign-born parents, are included in the native-born group. *Charity Service Reports*, County Agent (1911–1917); and *Charity Service Reports*, Juvenile Court, Mothers' Pension Division (1918–1927).

13. U.S. Department of Labor, Children's Bureau, *Mothers' Aid, 1931*, Publication no. 220 (Washington, DC: Government Printing Office, 1933), 13. See table 7 in chapter 2, which compares rates of female headship by groups.

14. *Chicago Defender*, 3 July 1915, p. 6.

15. *Charity Service Reports* (1915–1926); (1917), 267. The 1917 report listed families with four (30 percent) and two children (17 percent) in second and third place respectively. See also Annette Marie Garrett, "The Administration of the Aid to Mothers Law in Illinois 1917 to 1925" (M.A. thesis, School of Social Service Administration, University of Chicago, 1925), 85.

16. U.S. Department of Labor, Children's Bureau, *The Administration of the Aid-to-Mothers Law in Illinois*, 90.

17. *Charity Service Reports*, Juvenile Court (1917), 266, 269.

18. U.S. Department of Labor, Children's Bureau, *The Administration of the Aid-to-Mothers Law in Illinois*, 35–36.

19. *Charity Service Reports*, Juvenile Court (1917), 258–260.

20. The Children's Bureau study of Illinois drew from data collected from the Cook County Mothers' Pension Division study. The figures published in the federal report differ from those in the Cook County reports. Similarly, some county reports record the data by number of children, not families. The percentages differ accordingly, but the trends remain the same. U.S. Department of Labor, Children's Bureau, *The Administration of the Aid-to-Mothers Law in Illinois*, 74.

21. Ibid., 109–110.

22. Annette Marie Garrett, "Aid to Mothers Law, 1917–1925," 77.

23. *Laws of Illinois* (1913), 129.

24. U.S. Department of Labor, Children's Bureau, *The Administration of the Aid-to-Mothers Law in Illinois*, 5.

25. Sophonisba P. Breckinridge, *Women in the Twentieth Century: A Study of Their Political, Social, and Economic Activities* (New York: McGraw-Hill Book Co., 1933), 118–119.

26. Annette Marie Garrett, "Aid to Mothers Law, 1917 to 1925," 15–16.

27. *Laws of Illinois* (1913), 129; *Charity Service Reports* (1917), 273; U.S. Department of Labor, Children's Bureau, *The Administration of the Aid-to-Mothers Law in Illinois*, 69; Annette Marie Garrett, "Aid to Mothers Law, 1917–1925," 15–16.

28. U.S. Department of Labor, Children's Bureau, *Standards of Public Aid to Children in Their Own Homes*, by Florence Nesbitt, Publication no. 118 (Washington, DC: Government Printing Office, 1923), 17.

29. U.S. Department of Labor, Children's Bureau, *The Administration of the Aid-to-Mothers Law in Illinois*, 33.

30. A compelling example of the conflictual interests of families and private charities is raised by Emily Abel in her study of New York charity organization society (COS) medical aid cases.

Women clients refused COS advice to hospitalize or institutionalize family members because they saw their best interests preserved by providing home care themselves. The COS wanted to reduce the economic need of families with ill members. Removing the sick individual "relieved" the woman of caretaking duties and thus freed her to go out to earn. See Emily K. Abel, "Proper Care," typescript in the author's possession.

31. The percentage of women taking boarders is from the 1917 Mothers' Pension Division study. The restriction on boarders may be found in Annette Marie Garrett, "Aid to Mothers Law, 1917 to 1925," 18.

32. *Charity Service Reports*, County Agent (1917), 273. Women listed more than one job in this survey. For the point that women's work in commercial cleaning became more marginalized during the early twentieth century, see Sophonisba P. Breckinridge, *Women in the Twentieth Century*, 133.

33. U.S. Department of Labor, Children's Bureau, *Standards of Public Aid to Children in Their Own Homes*, 18–21.

34. U.S. Department of Labor, Children's Bureau, *Administration of the Aid-to-Mothers Law in Illinois*, 35.

35. The study surveyed 373 families. Of the total, 89 families or 24 percent had children fourteen years or older. At the time of the study, 107 children (43 percent of all children of working age) were working. *Charity Service Reports*, Juvenile Court (1917), 272. For the importance of children's wages in working-class families, see Susan J. Kleinberg, *The Shadow of the Mills: Working Class Families in Pittsburgh, 1870–1917* (Pittsburgh: Pittsburgh University Press, 1989).

36. The link between the minimum-wage movement and the effect of depressing women's wages through forms of relief is discussed in Leila Houghteling, "Charity and Women's Wages," *Social Service Review* (September 1927): 390–405.

37. *Charity Service Reports*, Juvenile Court (1917), 65, 278; and U.S. Department of Labor, Children's Bureau, *The Administration of the Aid-to-Mothers Law in Illinois*, 70. The Jewish Social Service Bureau believed that the mother should remain at home and contributed the amount designated by the court as earnings to the mother so that she could stay out of the workforce.

38. *Charity Service Reports*, Chief Probation Officer (1916), 270–271, 276.

39. Welfare Council, 24 June 1919, 8 June 1920, Welfare Council of Metropolitan Chicago Records, Chicago Historical Society, Chicago, IL; hereafter cited as Welfare Council Records.

40. Welfare Council, 8 January 1920, 3 June 1920, 12 July 1920, Welfare Council Records.

41. U.S. Department of Labor, Children's Bureau, *Proceedings of Conference on Mothers' Pensions, Providence, Rhode Island, June 28, 1922*, Publication no. 109 (Washington, DC: Government Printing Office, 1922); U.S. Department of Labor, Children's Bureau, *Standards of Public Aid to Children in Their Own Homes*, 1923.

42. Welfare Council, 5 July 1923, Welfare Council Records.

43. Ibid., 9 June 1924.

44. Leila Houghteling, "Income and Standard of Living of Families of Unskilled Wage Earners in Chicago"; "Memo for proposed study," 7 November 1924, Grace and Edith Abbott Papers, Department of Special Collections, University of Chicago Library, Chicago, IL; hereafter cited as Abbott Papers.

45. Welfare Council, 5 January 1925, 3 May 1926, 28 March 1927, Welfare Council Records.

46. In addition to working with standard budgets, the Welfare Council served as an advocacy

group for mothers' pensions. It criticized the county agent's office when their investigators harassed families and made unsubstantiated charges of immoral conduct. It pressured the county commissioners to cover eligible families despite insufficient appropriations. Welfare Council, 7 April 1924, 7 February 1927, Welfare Council Records.

47. James T. Patterson, *America's Struggle Against Poverty, 1900–1985* (Cambridge: Harvard University Press, 1986), 29; and Katherine Lenroot, "Section of paper to be given at the Child Welfare Committee of America Conference, May 15–20, 1925," 6 May 1925, file 7-3-4-6, record group 102, Children's Bureau Records, National Archives, Washington, DC.

48. *Charity Service Reports*, "Report of the Conference Committee to the Mothers' Pension Division of the Juvenile Court" (1911–1927); *Charity Service Reports*, County Agent (1917), 60.

49. Information was recorded by family for the years 1911–1915, then by the number of children for the years 1915–1927. Thus the figures for these two periods are not precisely comparable. This study uses the early period to set the context, but relies most heavily on reported statistics from 1915 to 1927. To get an accurate sense of the proportion of cases cancelled within a year, I compared the stays with a sum of all cases present at the beginning of the year, 1 December, and all cases added during the year. This ratio captured the movement on and off pensions. Alternate methods of comparing stayed cases to all new cases or to only those present at the beginning of a year would overestimate the ratio of stayed families by not including those families carried over annually. *Charity Service Reports*, Juvenile Court, Mothers' Pension Division (1915–1927). Information for the period 1913–1915 comes from the report of 1,115 families. Comparable data for 1911 to 1913 do not exist.

50. U.S. Department of Labor, Children's Bureau, *The Administration of the Aid-to-Mothers Law in Illinois*, 40, 43–44.

51. The Children's Bureau study noted that 14 percent of pensioned cases were stayed owing to the "failure" of the mother. Differences between the Children's Bureau study and the Cook County study occurred even though the former is based on the latter. I have used Cook County figures consistently.

Michael Katz has also discussed the tensions between client and agency worker and the risk of losing benefits. He found that mothers' pensions offered families real advantages over private relief policies, even when used as a wage subsidy. See Michael B. Katz, "The History of an Impudent Poor Woman in New York City from 1918 to 1923," in *The Uses of Charity: The Poor on Relief in the Nineteenth-Century Metropolis*, ed. Peter Mandler (Philadelphia: University of Pennsylvania Press, 1990), 227–246.

52. The following reasons were given for cancelled pensions between 1 July 1911 and 30 November 1912 (no appropriations were made until October 1911): 35 percent for economic reasons, 27 percent for legal reasons, 17 percent due to remarriage, and 17 percent for moral-behavioral reasons. Five percent of the cancelled cases were reinstated. See U.S. Department of Labor, Children's Bureau, *The Administration of the Aid-to-Mothers Law in Illinois*, 43–44. The percentages for the period 1 August 1913 to 1 March 1915 were as follows: 58 percent for economic reasons, 13 percent for legal reasons, 7 percent due to remarriage, and 20 percent for moral reasons. Two percent of the cases gave no reason. *Charity Service Reports* (1917), 271.

53. The years were 1918, 1923, 1924, 1926, and 1927.

54. U.S. Department of Labor, Children's Bureau, *Mothers' Aid, 1931*, 1, 18.

Notes to the Conclusion

1. Edith Abbott and Sophonisba P. Breckinridge, "Employment of Women in Industries: Twelfth Census Statistics," *Journal of Political Economy* (February 1906): 16.

2. Edna Annette Beveridge to Julia Lathrop, 10 June 1916, file 10,441.6–10,441.54, box 121, record group 102, Children's Bureau Records, National Archives, Washington, DC.

3. Ben Lindsey to Julia Lathrop, 25 June 1921, file 7–3–4–0, record group 102, Children's Bureau Records, National Archives, Washington, DC.

4. Ibid.

5. Veronica Strong-Boag noted a similar shift in the Canadian movement for mothers' allowances during the 1920s. The initial recognition of "the mother as a paid representative of the state" changed to focus on the needs of children, insuring, as Strong-Boag argues, "that the women's predicament . . . went largely ignored." Veronica Strong-Boag, "Wages for Housework: Mothers' Allowances and the Beginning of Social Security in Canada," *Journal of Canadian Studies* 14:1 (Spring 1979): 31–32.

6. In January 1935, Cook County had 1,434 families receiving aid through the mothers' pension policy, but the waiting list contained an additional 7,942 women, and the relief office had yet another 3,870 women who were eligible for mothers' aid. Many of the eligible families were transferred to relief rolls after federal and state funds became available. Grace Abbott, *From Relief to Social Security: The Development of the New Public Welfare Services and Their Administration* (Chicago: University of Chicago Press, 1941), 209.

7. Edwin E. Witte to Edith Abbott, 18 October 1939, box 54, folder 11, Grace and Edith Abbott Papers, Department of Special Collections, University of Chicago Library, Chicago, IL; hereafter cited as Abbott Papers. Edwin E. Witte, *The Development of the Social Security Act* (Madison: University of Wisconsin Press, 1963), 14–16, 164–165. See also "Edith Abbott's Contribution to Public Social Policy," *Social Service Review* 13:3 (September 1939): 353; and Lela B. Costin, *Two Sisters for Social Justice: A Biography of Grace and Edith Abbott* (Urbana: University of Illinois Press, 1983), 220–226.

Edith Abbott participated as a member of the Advisory Committee on Public Employment and Public Assistance and took part in two preliminary conferences on social insurance sponsored by the Social Science Research Council which developed studies for the CES. Breckinridge worked on the child welfare provisions in the Social Security Act.

8. "Security for Children: Summary Recommendations of the U.S. Children's Bureau, prepared at the request of the Committee on Economic Security, in cooperation with the Advisory Committee on Child Welfare," 1 December 1934, pp. 1–2, box 12, folder 7, Abbott Papers.

9. Ibid. See also *Supplement to Report to the President of the Committee on Economic Security* (Washington, DC: Government Printing Office, 1935), 15.

Robyn Muncy credits the Children's Bureau leadership with carrying out some of the provisions of the progressive welfare agenda in the Social Security Act. While critical of its limitations, Muncy recognized the significant achievements within the political context. Linda Gordon finds the efforts of Children's Bureau reformers far more limited. Their own commitment to casework and the family wage ideal led them to a position in which "they saw no problem in grounding women's social rights in their dependent position." Robyn L. Muncy, *Creating a Female Dominion in American Reform, 1890–1935* (New York: Oxford University Press, 1991), 151–157; and

Linda Gordon, *Pitied But Not Entitled: Single Mothers and the History of Welfare, 1890–1935* (New York: Free Press, 1994), 254–258.

10. Grace Abbott, *From Relief to Social Security,* 211, 277.

11. Edwin E. Witte to Edith Abbott, 18 October 1939, box 54, folder 11, Abbott Papers.

12. Edwin E. Witte, *The Development of the Social Security Act,* 163–164.

13. Jane M. Hoey, "Aid to Families with Dependent Children," *Annals of the American Academy of Political and Social Sciences,* 211 (March 1939): 74–78, cited in Robert H. Bremner et al., eds., *Children and Youth in America: A Documentary History,* vol. 3, pt. 3 (Cambridge: Harvard University Press, 1970–1974), 538–541. See also Linda Gordon, *Pitied But Not Entitled,* 265–280. For delays in state qualifications for ADC, see Grace Abbott, *From Relief to Social Security,* 283.

14. Edith Abbott, "Abolish the Means Test for Public Assistance," box 3, folder 10, Abbott Papers, Addenda. For social insurance critiques of the Social Security Act by I. M. Rubinow and Abraham Epstein, see Roy Lubove, *The Struggle For Social Security, 1900–1935* (Cambridge: Harvard University Press, 1968), 175–180.

15. "Final Report of the Advisory Council on Social Security," p. 30, box 11, folder 10, Abbott Papers, Addenda. Another 1939 revision increased the portion of federal matching funds for ADC to one-half the amount incurred by the states. The Children's Bureau initially proposed this figure in 1935.

16. Winifred Bell, *Aid to Dependent Children* (New York: Columbia University Press, 1965), 46. For employable-mother rules and the continuation of work policies, see Joanne Goodwin, "'Employable Mothers' and 'Suitable Work': A Re-evaluation of Welfare and Wage-Earning for Women in the Twentieth-Century United States," *Journal of Social History* 29:2 (Winter 1995): 253–274.

17. Scholars disagree on explanations for the bureau's ineffectiveness. For a labor regulation argument, see Frances Fox Piven and Richard A. Cloward, *Regulating the Poor: The Functions of Public Welfare* (New York: Pantheon Books, 1971), 128–130. James Patterson argued that the federal bureau was unable to act alone without the presence of lobbies or poor people's organizations. See James T. Patterson, *America's Struggle Against Poverty, 1900–1985* (Cambridge: Harvard University Press, 1986), 68, 87.

18. The name of the policy changed to Aid to Families with Dependent Children in 1962.

19. On the disparity of wages over the last two decades and women's relative standing, see Sheldon H. Danziger, Gary D. Sandefur, and Daniel H. Weinberg, eds., *Confronting Poverty: Prescriptions for Change* (Cambridge: Harvard University Press, 1994); David Ellwood, *Poor Support: Poverty in the American Family* (New York: Basic Books, 1988). On the combination of welfare and wages, see Roberta Spalter-Roth, Beverly Burr, Heidi Hartmann, and Lois B. Shaw, "Welfare That Works: The Working Lives of AFDC Recipients," A Report to the Ford Foundation by the Institute for Women's Policy Research (1995); Kathryn Edin, *There's a Lot of Month Left at the End of the Money: How AFDC Recipients Make Ends Meet in Chicago* (New York: Garland Press, 1993).

20. President Clinton signed a welfare reform bill on 22 August 1996 which ended AFDC. The new law grants states greater authority in their welfare provision and ends the federal entitlement for poor children. The theme of moving people from welfare to work drew both support and criticism. *New York Times,* 23 August 1996, p. 1.

21. Edith Abbott, "Abolish the Means Test for Public Assistance," box 3, folder 10, Abbott Papers.

Bibliography

P R I M A R Y   S O U R C E S

M A N U S C R I P T   C O L L E C T I O N S

Ann Arbor, MI. Jane Addams, *The Jane Addams Papers*, ed. Mary Lynn McCree Bryan. University Microfilms International, 1985. Microfilm.

Bethesda, MD. National Association of Colored Women's Clubs, *Records of the National Association of Colored Women's Clubs, 1895–1992*, pt. 1, *Minutes of National Conventions, Publications, and President's Office Correspondence*. University Publications of America, 1994. Microfilm.

Chicago, IL. Chicago Historical Society. Archives and Manuscripts Department.
  Chicago Foreign Language Press Survey. Chicago Public Library Omnibus Project, U.S. Works Progress Administration, 1942.
  Chicago Woman's Club Records.
  Cook County Board of Commissioners Records.
  Louise Haddock de Koven Bowen Scrapbooks.
  Raymond Marcellus Hilliard Papers.
  Infant Welfare Society of Chicago Records.
  Irene McCoy Gaines Papers.
  Mary McDowell Papers.
  Municipal Court Records.
  United Charities of Chicago Records.
  Welfare Council of Metropolitan Chicago Records.
  Woman's City Club Records.

Chicago, IL. The Chicago Public Library. Municipal Reference Collection.
  Chicago Department of Public Welfare Records.
  Juvenile Court and Juvenile Detention Home Records.

Chicago, IL. Cook County Circuit Court Archives.
  Juvenile Court Records, 1899–1926.

Chicago, IL. Newberry Library.
  Chicago School of Civics and Philanthropy Records.
  Scrapbooks of the political campaigns of A. A. McCormick, 1912–1915. 5 vols.
  Graham Taylor Papers.

Chicago, IL. University of Chicago Library. Department of Special Collections.
  Grace and Edith Abbott Papers.
  Sophonisba P. Breckinridge Papers.
  Chicago School of Civics and Philanthropy Records.
  Ernst Freund Papers.
  Julius Rosenwald Papers.

School of Social Service Administration Records.
Ida B. Wells Papers.
Chicago, IL. University of Illinois at Chicago. University Library. Special Collections.
Jane Addams Memorial Collection.
Chicago Urban League Records.
Children's Home and Aid Society of Illinois Records.
Hull House Association Records.
Immigrants' Protective League Records.
Juvenile Protective Association of Chicago Records.
National Congress of Parents and Teachers Records.
Adena Miller Rich Papers.
Phyllis Wheatley Association Records.
Woman's City Club of Chicago Records.
Rockford, IL. Rockford College Archives.
Julia Lathrop Papers.
Tarrytown, NY. Rockefeller Archives Center.
Russell Sage Foundation Reports.
Washington, DC. Library of Congress.
Breckinridge Family Papers.
Washington, DC. National Archives.
Children's Bureau Records.

NEWSPAPERS, MAGAZINES, AND SERIALS

Broad Ax (Chicago), 1915–1925.
Chicago Daily Socialist, 1910–1912.
Chicago Daily Tribune, 1909–1929.
Chicago *Defender*, 1909–1928.
Chicago School of Civics and Philanthropy. *Announcements*. Chicago: School of Civics and
     Philanthropy 1909/1910–1919/1920.
Chicago School of Civics and Philanthropy. *Bulletin*, nos. 1–46 (July 1909–January 1920).
Chicago Urban League. *Annual Reports*, 1917–1920, 1923, 1926–1931.
Child, 1912.
Child Welfare Magazine (*The Clubwoman*, *The National Congress of Mothers Magazine*),
     1906–1915.
Hull House. *Hull House Bulletin*.
Illinois Federation of Women's Clubs *Bulletin*, January 1909–March 1920.
Illinois League of Women Voters *Bulletin*, 1924–1925.
Illinois State Federation of Labor, *Weekly Newsletter*, 1925–1927.
Illinois State Journal, 1911, 1921.
Illinois State Register, 1911.
National Conference of Charities and Correction [National Conference of Social Work]. *Pro-
     ceedings*, 1893–1919.
National Notes, 1898–1931.
Newer Justice, vols. 1–9, 1911–1917.

Survey, 1909–1930.
Whip (Chicago), June 1919–December 1922.
The Women's Press, 1919–1920.
Woman's City Club *Bulletin*, 1914–1930.
Woman's City Club *Yearbook*, 1910–1911.

GOVERNMENT DOCUMENTS

Chicago, IL. City Council. *Proceedings* (1910–1915).
Chicago, IL. Commission on Race Relations. *The Negro in Chicago: A Study of Race Relations and a Race Riot*. Chicago: University of Chicago Press, 1922.
Chicago, IL. Department of Public Welfare. *Annual Reports* (1915–1927).
Chicago, IL. Department of Public Welfare. *Bulletin*, vols. 1–11 (August 1916–June 1919).
Chicago, IL. Municipal Markets Commission. *Report to the Mayor and Aldermen on a Practical Plan for Relieving Destitution and Unemployment in the City of Chicago*. 1914.
Cook County, IL. Board of County Commissioners. *Charity Service Reports* (1904–1927).
Cook County, IL. Board of County Commissioners. *Proceedings* (1907/1908–1928/1929).
Cook County, IL. Board of County Commissioners. *A Study of Cook County*, by Alexander A. McCormick, 1914.
Cook County, IL. Juvenile Court. *Report of a Committee Appointed under Resolution of the Board of Commissioners of Cook County, bearing date August 8, 1911*. Chicago: Citizens' Investigating Committee, 1912.
Great Britain. Royal Commission on Poor Laws and Relief of Distress. *The Minority Report of the Poor Law Commission*. Edited with an introduction by Sidney Webb and Beatrice Webb. London: Longmans, Green, 1909. Reprint, Clifton, NJ: A. M. Kelley, 1974.
Illinois. Board of Administration (Department of Public Welfare). *Institution Quarterly*, vols. 1:1–8:4 (May 1910–December 1917). Springfield, IL: Illinois State Journal Co., State Printers.
Illinois. Department of Public Welfare. *Report of the Children's Committee*. Springfield: Illinois State Journal Co., 1921.
Illinois. General Assembly. *House Journal*, 1909–1929.
Illinois. General Assembly. *Senate Journal*, 1909–1929.
Illinois. *House and Senate Bills*, 1911–1929.
Illinois. *Laws of Illinois*, 1907–1929.
Illinois. State Conference of Charities and Corrections. *Reports of Annual Conferences*, 1909–1916.
Massachusetts. *Report of the Commission on the Support of Dependent Minor Children of Widowed Mothers*. H. Doc. 2075. Boston: Wright & Potter Printing Co., 1913.
Massachusetts. *Report of the Special Commission on Social Insurance*. H. Doc. 1850. Boston: Wright and Potter, State Printers, 1917.
New York. *Report of the New York State Commission on Relief for Widowed Mothers Transmitted to the Legislature March 27, 1914*. Albany: J. B. Lyon Co. Printers, 1914.
Pennsylvania. Mothers' Assistance Fund. *Report of the Mothers' Assistance Fund to the General Assembly of Pennsylvania*. Harrisburg: J. L. L. Kuhn, 1920.
U.S. Bureau of Labor. *The Slums of Baltimore, Chicago, New York, and Philadelphia, prepared in*

compliance with a joint resolution of the Congress of the United States approved July 20, 1892, by Carroll D. Wright, Commissioner of Labor. Washington, DC: Government Printing Office, 1894.

U.S. Bureau of Labor Statistics. *Proceedings of the Conference on Social Insurance.* Whole no. 212. Washington, DC: Government Printing Office, 1917.

U.S. Department of Commerce. Bureau of the Census. *Estimates of Population of the United States by States and Cities, 1910–1923.* Washington, DC: Government Printing Office, 1923.

U.S. Department of Commerce. Bureau of the Census. *Thirteenth Census of the United States, 1910: Population.* 4 vols. Washington, DC: Government Printing Office, 1911.

U.S. Department of Commerce. Bureau of the Census. *Fourteenth Census of the United States, 1920: Population.* 4 vols. Washington, DC: Government Printing Office, 1921.

U.S. Department of Commerce. Bureau of the Census. *Fifteenth Census of the United States, 1930: Population.* Washington, DC: Government Printing Office, 1931.

U.S. Department of the Interior. Bureau of the Census. *Twelfth Census of the United States, 1900: Population.* 2 vols. Washington, DC: Government Printing Office, 1901.

U.S. Department of Labor. *Report on the Conditions of Woman and Child Wage Earners in the United States,* 19 vols. 61st Cong., 2nd sess., S. Doc. 645. Washington, DC: Government Printing Office, 1910–1913.

U.S. Department of Labor. Children's Bureau. *The Administration of the Aid-to-Mothers Law in Illinois,* by Edith Abbott and Sophonisba P. Breckinridge. Publication no. 82. Washington, DC: Government Printing Office, 1921.

U.S. Department of Labor. Children's Bureau. *Administration of Mothers' Aid in Ten Localities.* Publication no. 184. Washington, DC: Government Printing Office, 1928.

U.S. Department of Labor. Children's Bureau. *The Chicago Juvenile Court,* by Helen Rankin Jeter. Publication no. 104. Washington, DC: Government Printing Office, 1922.

U.S. Department of Labor. Children's Bureau. *Children of Wage-Earning Mothers: A Study of a Selected Group in Chicago,* by Helen Russell Wright. Publication no. 102. Washington, DC: Government Printing Office, 1922.

U.S. Department of Labor. Children's Bureau. *Children of Working Mothers in Philadelphia,* pt. 1, by Clara Beyer. Publication no. 204. Washington, DC: Government Printing Office, 1931.

U.S. Department of Labor. Children's Bureau. *Laws Relating to 'Mothers' Pensions' in the United States, Denmark, and New Zealand.* Bureau Publication no. 7. Washington, DC: Government Printing Office, 1914.

U.S. Department of Labor. Children's Bureau. *Mothers' Aid, 1931.* Publication no. 220. Washington, DC: Government Printing Office, 1933.

U.S. Department of Labor. Children's Bureau. *Proceedings of Conference on Mothers' Pensions, Providence, Rhode Island, June 28, 1922.* Publication no. 109. Washington, DC: Government Printing Office, 1922.

U.S. Department of Labor. Children's Bureau. *Public Aid to Mothers with Dependent Children,* by Emma O. Lundberg. Publication no. 162. Washington, DC: Government Printing Office, 1928.

U.S. Department of Labor. Children's Bureau. *Standards of Public Aid to Children in Their Own Homes,* by Florence Nesbitt. Publication no. 118. Washington, DC: Government Printing Office, 1923.

U.S. Department of Labor. Children's Bureau. *State Commissions for the Study of Revisions of Child Welfare Laws*, by Emma O. Lundberg. Publication no. 131. Washington, DC: Government Printing Office, 1924.

U.S. Department of Labor. Women's Bureau. *The Family Status of Breadwinning Women*. Bulletin no. 23. Washington, DC: Government Printing Office, 1922.

U.S. Department of Labor. Women's Bureau. *The Share of Wage-Earning Women in Family Support*. Bulletin no. 30. Washington, DC: Government Printing Office, 1923.

White House Conference, 1909. *Proceedings of the Conference on the Care of Dependent Children held at Washington, D.C., January 25–26, 1909*. Washington, DC: Government Printing Office, 1909.

White House Conference, 1930. *Addresses and Abstracts of Committee Reports*. New York: The Century Co., 1931.

Wisconsin. State Board of Control. *Recommendations and Conclusions Based on Its Investigation into the Question of State Aid to Mothers with Dependent Children*. Madison: The Board, 1915.

Wisconsin. State Board of Control. *The Administration of the Aid to Dependent Children Law in Wisconsin*. Madison: The Board, 1921.

ARTICLES, BOOKS, AND REPORTS

Abbott, Edith. "The Administration of the Illinois' Funds to Parents' Law." U.S. Labor Bureau. *Bulletin* 212 (1917): 818–834.

———. "Are Women a Force for Good Government? An Analysis of the Returns in the Recent Municipal Elections in Chicago." *National Municipal Review* 4 (July 1915): 437–447.

———. *Democracy and Social Progress in England*. University of Chicago War Papers, no. 8. Chicago: University of Chicago Press, 1918.

———. "English Poor Law Reform." *Journal of Political Economy* (January 1911): 47–59.

———. "The Experimental Period of Widows' Pension Legislation." *Proceedings of the National Conference of Social Work* (1917): 154–165.

———. "Federal Relief Sold Down the River." *Nation* 142 (18 March 1936): 346.

———. "Is There a Legal Right to Relief?" *Social Service Review* 12:2 (June 1938): 260–275.

———. "Municipal Employment of Unemployed Women in London." *Journal of Political Economy* (November 1907): 513–530.

———. "Pensions, Insurance, and the State." *Proceedings of the National Conference of Social Work* (1918): 388–389.

———. *Public Assistance*. Vol. 1. *American Principles and Policies*. Chicago: University of Chicago Press, 1940.

———. "Public Pensions to Widows with Children." *American Economic Review* 3 (June 1913): 473–478.

———. "Social Insurance and/or Social Security." *Social Service Review* 8:3 (September 1934): 537–540.

———. "Statistics in Chicago Suffrage." *New Republic* (12 June 1915): 151.

———. "Woman Suffrage Militant: The New Movement in England." *Independent* 61 (29 November 1906): 1276–1278.

———. "The Woman Voter and the Spoils System in Chicago." *National Municipal Review* 5 (July 1916): 460–465.

———. *Women in Industry: A Study in American Economic History.* New York: D. Appleton & Co., 1910.

———. "Women's Wages in Chicago: Some Notes on Available Data." *Journal of Political Economy* 21:2 (February 1913): 143–158.

Abbott, Edith, and Sophonisba P. Breckinridge. "Employment of Women in Industries: Twelfth Census Statistics." *Journal of Political Economy* (February 1906): 14–40.

———. *The Tenements of Chicago, 1908–1935.* Chicago: University of Chicago, 1936.

———. *Truancy and Non-Attendance in the Chicago Schools: A Study of the Social Aspects of the Compulsory Education and Child Labor Legislation in Illinois.* Chicago: University of Chicago Press, 1917.

———. *The Wage-Earning Woman and the State: A Reply to Miss Minnie Bronson.* Boston: Boston Equal Suffrage Association for Good Government, [1912].

Abbott, Grace. "After Suffrage-Citizenship." *Survey* (1 September 1920): 655–657.

———. *The Child and the State, Select Documents.* Vol. 1. Chicago: University of Chicago Press, 1938.

———. *From Relief to Social Security: The Development of the New Public Welfare Services and Their Administration.* Chicago: University of Chicago Press, 1941.

———. "The Immigrant and Municipal Politics." *National Conference for Good City Government* (1909): 148–156.

———. "Recent Trends in Mothers' Aid." *Social Service Review* (June 1934): 191–210.

———. "Ten Years' Work for Children." *North American Review* (August 1923): 189–200.

Addams, Jane. *Democracy and Social Ethics.* New York: Macmillan Co., 1902.

———. "Ethical Survivals in Municipal Corruption." *International Journal of Ethics* 8 (April 1898): 273–291.

———. "Lessons of the Election: Discussion Held at the Chicago City Club." *City Club Bulletin* (27 November 1912): 361–364.

———. "Julia Lathrop and Outdoor Relief in Chicago, 1893–1894." *Social Service Review* (March 1935): 24–33.

———. *My Friend Julia Lathrop.* New York: Macmillan Co., 1935.

———. *Twenty Years at Hull House.* 1910. Reprint, New York: New American Library, 1981.

———. "Utilization of Women in City Government," *Newer Ideals of Peace.* Chatauqua, New York: Chatauqua Press, 1907.

Anthony, Katharine. *Mothers Who Must Earn.* New York: Russell Sage Foundation, Survey Research Association, 1914.

Beard, Mary Ritter. "The Legislative Influence of Unenfranchised Women." *Annals of the American Academy of Political and Social Science* 56 (November 1914): 54–61.

———. *Woman's Work in Municipalities.* New York: D. Appleton and Co., 1915.

Bowen, Louise de Koven. *The Colored People of Chicago: An Investigation Made for the Juvenile Protective Association.* Chicago: Juvenile Protective Association, 1913.

Breckinridge, Sophonisba P. "Could 'Mothers' Pensions' Operate under Equal Rights Amendment? Pro and Con." *Congressional Digest* (March 1924): 202.

———. "The Family and the Law." *Proceedings of the National Conference of Social Work* (1925): 290–297.

———. *The Family and the State, Select Documents.* Chicago: University of Chicago, 1934.

————. *Family Welfare Work in a Metropolitan Community: Selected Case Records.* Chicago: University of Chicago Press, 1924.

————. "The Home Responsibilities of Women Workers and the 'Equal Wage.'" *Journal of Political Economy* 31 (August 1923): 521–543.

————. *The Illinois Poor Law and Its Administration* (Chicago: University of Chicago Press, 1939).

————. "Legislative Control of Women's Work." *Journal of Political Economy* (February 1906): 107–109.

————. *Marriage and the Civic Rights of Women: Separate Domicile and Independent Citizenship.* Chicago: University of Chicago Press, 1931.

————. "Neglected Widowhood in the Juvenile Court." *American Journal of Sociology* (July 1910): 53–87.

————. "Political Equality for Women and Women's Wages." *Annals of the American Academy of Political and Social Science* 56 (November 1914): 122–123.

————. *Public Welfare Administration in the United States.* Chicago: University of Chicago Press, 1927.

————. *Women in the Twentieth Century: A Study of Their Political, Social, and Economic Activities.* New York: McGraw-Hill Book Co., 1933.

Breckinridge, Sophonisba P., ed. *The Child in the City: A Series of Papers Presented at the Conferences Held during the Chicago Child Welfare Exhibit.* Chicago: Department of Social Investigation, Chicago School of Civics and Philanthropy, 1912.

Breckinridge, Sophonisba P., and Edith Abbott. *The Delinquent Child and the Home: A Study of the Delinquent Wards of the Juvenile Court of Chicago.* New York: Russell Sage Foundation, 1917.

————, eds. *The Housing Problem in Chicago.* Chicago: University of Chicago Press, 1910–1915.

Brown, James. *The History of Public Assistance in Chicago, 1833 to 1893.* Chicago: University of Chicago Press, 1941.

Bullock, Edna D., ed. *Selected Articles on Mothers' Pensions.* New York: H. W. Wilson Co., 1915.

Burgess, Ernest W., and Charles Newcomb. *Census Data of the City of Chicago, 1920.* Chicago: University of Chicago Press, 1923.

————. *Census Data of the City of Chicago, 1930.* Chicago: University of Chicago Press, 1933.

Carstens, C. C. *Public Pensions to Widows with Children: A Study of Their Administration in Several American Cities.* New York: Russell Sage Foundation, 1913.

Chicago School of Civics and Philanthropy. *Alumni Register, 1903–1913.* Chicago: Chicago School of Civics and Philanthropy, 1912.

Davis, Ada J. "The Evolution of the Institution of Mothers' Pensions in the U.S." *American Journal of Sociology* 35 (January 1930): 573–587.

Davis, Elizabeth Lindsay. *Lifting as They Climb: The National Association of Colored Women.* Washington, DC: National Association of Colored Women, 1933.

————. *The Story of the Illinois Federation of Colored Women's Clubs, 1900–1922.* Chicago: [n.p.], 1922.

Deardorff, R. "Women in Municipal Activities." *Annals of the American Academy of Political and Social Science* 56 (November 1914): 71–77.

Douglas, Paul H. *Real Wages in the United States, 1890–1926.* Boston: Houghton Mifflin, Co., 1930.

———. *Wages and the Family.* Chicago: University of Chicago Press, 1925.

Drake, St. Clair, and Horace R. Cayton. *Black Metropolis: A Study of Negro Life in a Northern City.* New York: Harcourt, Brace and Co., 1945. Reprint, Chicago: University of Chicago Press, 1993.

Du Bois, W. E. B. *Efforts for Social Betterment among Negro Americans.* Atlanta University Publications no. 14. Atlanta: Atlanta University Press, 1909.

Duster, Alfreda M., ed. *Crusade for Justice: The Autobiography of Ida B. Wells.* Chicago: University of Chicago Press, 1970.

Frazier, E. Franklin. *The Negro Family in Chicago.* Chicago: University of Chicago Press, 1932.

Gilman, Charlotte Perkins. *Women and Economics: A Study of the Economic Relation Between Men and Women as a Factor in Social Evolution.* 1898. Reprint, Carl N. Degler, ed. New York: Harper and Row, 1966.

Gosnell, Harold F. *Machine Politics: Chicago Model.* 2d ed. New York: Greenwood Press, 1968. Originally published, Chicago: University of Chicago Press, 1937.

———. *Negro Politicians: The Rise of Negro Politics in Chicago.* Chicago: University of Chicago Press, 1967. Originally published, Chicago: University of Chicago Press, 1935.

Hard, William. "Financing Motherhood." *Delineator* 81 (April 1913): 263, 314–318.

———. "The Moral Necessity of 'State Funds to Mothers.'" *Survey* (1 March 1913): 769–773.

Houghteling, Leila. "Charity and Women's Wages." *Social Service Review* (September 1927): 390–405.

Hughes, Gwendolyn. *Mothers in Industry: Wage-Earning by Mothers in Philadelphia.* New York: New Republic, 1925.

Hull House Residents. *Hull House Maps and Papers: A Presentation of Nationalities and Wages in a Congested District of Chicago.* New York: Thomas Y. Crowell & Co., 1895. Reprint, New York: Arno Press, 1970.

Hunter, Joel. "Administration of the Funds to Parents Law in Chicago." *Survey* (31 January 1914): 516–518.

Hunter, Robert. *Poverty.* New York: Macmillan Co., 1904.

Jeter, Helen R. *Trends of Population in the Region of Chicago.* Chicago: University of Chicago Press, 1927.

Jeter, Helen R., and A. W. McMillen. *Registration of Social Statistics for the Year 1928.* Report submitted to the Joint Committee of the Association of Community Chests and Councils and the Local Community Research Committee of the University of Chicago, 1 October 1929.

———. "Some Statistics of Family Welfare and Relief in Chicago: 1928." *Social Service Review* 3:3 (September 1929): 448–459.

Kelley, Florence. *Modern Industry in Relation to the Family, Health, Education, and Morality.* New York: Longmans, Green & Co., 1914.

———. *Notes of Sixty Years: The Autobiography of Florence Kelley.* Edited and introduced by Kathryn Kish Sklar. Chicago: Charles H. Kerr Publishing Co., 1986.

———. *Some Ethical Gains through Legislation.* New York: Macmillan, 1914.

Key, Ellen. *The Renaissance of Motherhood.* New York: G. P. Putnam's Sons, 1916.

Lundberg, Emma O. "Aid to Mothers with Dependent Children." *Annals of the American Academy of Political and Social Science* (November 1921): 97–105.

————. *Unto the Least of These: Social Services for Children*. New York: Appleton-Century, 1947.

McDowell, Mary E. "For a National Investigation of Women." *Independent* (3 January 1907): 24–25.

Monroe, Day. *Chicago Families: A Study of Unpublished Census Data*. Chicago: University of Chicago Press, 1932. Reprint, New York: Arno Press, 1972.

National Congress of Mothers. *The Child in Home, School, and State: Report of the National Congress of Mothers Held in the City of Washington, D.C., March 10–17, 1905*. Washington, DC: National Congress of Mothers, 1905.

New York Association for Improving the Condition of the Poor. *Shall Widows Be Pensioned?* New York: N.Y.A.I.C.P., 1914.

Odum, Howard W. "Public Welfare Activities." In *Recent Social Trends in the United States*, President's Research Committee on Social Trends, 1224–1273. New York: McGraw-Hill Book Co., 1933.

Rathbone, Eleanor, et al. *Endowment for Motherhood*. With a preface by Katharine Anthony. New York: B. W. Huebsch, 1920.

Richmond, Mary. *A Study of 985 Widows Known to Certain Charity Organization Societies in 1910*. New York: Russell Sage Foundation, 1913.

Riordon, William L. *Plunkitt of Tammany Hall: A Series of Very Plain Talks on Very Practical Politics*. Edited with an introduction by Terrence J. McDonald. Boston: Bedford Books of St. Martin's Press, 1994.

Rubinow, Isaac M. *Social Insurance with Special Reference to American Conditions*. New York: Henry Holt and Co., 1913. Reprint, New York: Arno Press, 1969.

Ryan, John A. "The Standard of Living and the Problem of Dependency." In *Proceedings of the National Conference of Charities and Correction, at the Thirty-fourth Annual Session held in the City of Indianapolis, Indiana, 1907*, 342–347. Indianapolis: William B. Burford, 1907.

Smith, T. V., and Leonard D. White, eds. *Chicago, An Experiment in Social Science Research*. Chicago: University of Chicago Press, 1929.

Spargo, John. *The Bitter Cry of the Children*. 1906. Reprint, Chicago: Quadrangle Paperbacks, 1968.

————. *Socialism and Motherhood*. New York: B. W. Huebsch, 1914.

Terrell, Mary Church. "Club Work of Colored Women." *Southern Workman* 30 (August 1901): 437.

United Charities of Chicago. *Sixty-six Years of Service*. Chicago: United Charities of Chicago, 1923.

Williams, Fannie Barrier. "Social Bonds in the 'Black Belt' of Chicago: Negro Organizations and the New Spirit Pervading Them." *Charities* 15 (7 October 1905): 40–44, 64–65.

THESES AND DISSERTATIONS

Abbott, Edith. "A Statistical Study of the Wages of Unskilled Labor in the United States, 1830–1900." Ph.D. diss., University of Chicago, 1905.

Beldon, Gertrude May. "A History of the Woman Suffrage Movement in Illinois." M.A. thesis, University of Chicago, 1913.

Breckinridge, Sophonisba P. "Legal Tender: A Study in English and American Monetary History." Ph.D. diss., University of Chicago, 1901.

Dunn, Margaret. "Jane Addams as a Political Leader." M.A. thesis, University of Chicago, 1926.

Cade, Harriet Clark. "Statistics of Chicago Relief Agencies." M.A. thesis, University of Chicago, School of Social Service Administration, 1927.

Crowley, Charlotte A. "Dependent Negro Children in Chicago in 1926." M.A. thesis, School of Social Service Administration, University of Chicago, 1927.

Garrett, Annette Marie. "The Administration of the Aid to Mothers Law in Illinois, 1917 to 1925." M.A. thesis, School of Social Service Administration, University of Chicago, 1925.

Powers, Dorothy Edwards. "The Chicago Woman's Club." M.A. thesis, University of Chicago, 1925.

Spackman, Barbara Spencer. "The Woman's City Club of Chicago: A Civic Pressure Group." M.A. thesis, University of Chicago, 1930.

SECONDARY SOURCES

BOOKS AND ARTICLES

Abel, Emily K. "Benevolence and Social Control: Advice from the Children's Bureau in the Early Twentieth Century." *Social Service Review* (March 1994): 1–19.

Abramovitz, Mimi. *Regulating the Lives of Women: Social Welfare Policy from Colonial Times to the Present*. Boston: South End Press, 1988.

Alford, Robert, and Roger Friedland. *Powers of Theory: Capitalism, the State, and Democracy*. New York: Cambridge University Press, 1985.

Allswang, John M. *A House for All Peoples: Ethnic Politics in Chicago, 1890–1936*. Lexington: University Press of Kentucky, 1971.

Ashby, LeRoy. *Saving the Waifs: Reformers and Dependent Children, 1890–1917*. Philadelphia: Temple University Press, 1984.

Baker, Paula. "The Domestication of Politics: Women and American Political Society, 1780–1920." *American Historical Review* 89 (June 1984): 620–647.

———. *The Moral Frameworks of Public Life: Gender, Politics, and the State in Rural New York, 1870–1930*. New York: Oxford University Press, 1991.

Bell, Winifred. *Aid to Dependent Children*. New York: Columbia University Press, 1965.

Berkowitz, Edward D. "History, Public Policy and Reality." *Journal of Social History* 18 (Fall 1984): 78–89.

Berkowitz, Edward D., and Kim McQuaid. *Creating the Welfare State: The Political Economy of Twentieth-Century Reform*. New York: Praeger Publishers, 1980.

Blair, Karen J. *Clubwoman as Feminist: True Womanhood Redefined, 1868–1914*. New York: Holmes & Meier Publishers, 1980.

Boris, Eileen. "Black Women and Paid Labor in the Home: Industrial Homework in Chicago in the 1920s." In *Homework: Historical and Contemporary Perspectives on Paid Labor at Home*, ed. Eileen Boris and Cynthia R. Daniels, 33–52. Urbana: University of Illinois Press, 1989.

———. *Home to Work: Motherhood and the Politics of Industrial Homework in the United States*. New York: Cambridge University Press, 1994.

———. "The Power of Motherhood: Black and White Activist Women Redefine the 'Political.'" In *Mothers of a New World*, ed. Seth Koven and Sonya Michel, 213–245. New York: Routledge, 1993.

———. "Regulating Industrial Homework: The Triumph of 'Sacred Motherhood.'" *Journal of American History* 71 (March 1985): 745–763.

Boris, Eileen, and Peter Bardaglio. "Gender, Race and Class: The Impact of the State on Family and Economy, 1790–1945." In *Families and Work*, ed. Naomi Gerstel and Harriet Gross, 132–151. Philadelphia: Temple University Press, 1987.

Boydston, Jeanne. *Home and Work: Housework, Wages, and the Ideology of Labor in the Early Republic*. New York: Oxford University Press, 1990.

Boyer, Paul. *Urban Masses and Moral Order in America, 1820–1920*. Cambridge: Harvard University Press, 1978.

Brandes, Stuart D. *American Welfare Capitalism, 1880–1940*. Chicago: University of Chicago Press, 1976.

Bremner, Robert H. *From the Depths: The Discovery of Poverty in the United States*. New York: New York University Press, 1956.

Bremner, Robert H., et al., eds. *Children and Youth in America: A Documentary History*. 3 vols. Cambridge: Harvard University Press, 1970–1974.

Breul, Frank R., and Steven J. Diner, eds. *Compassion and Responsibility: Readings in the History of Social Welfare Policy in the United States*. Chicago: University of Chicago Press, 1980.

Brown, Elsa Barkley. "Womanist Consciousness: Maggie Lena Walker and the Independent Order of St. Luke." In *Unequal Sisters*, ed. Vicki L. Ruiz and Ellen Carol DuBois, 268–283. New York: Routledge, 1994.

Bruno, Frank J. *Trends in Social Work, 1874–1956: A History Based on the Proceedings of the National Conference of Social Work*. New York: Columbia University Press, 1957.

Buechler, Steven M. *The Transformation of the Woman Suffrage Movement: The Case of Illinois, 1850–1920*. New Brunswick, NJ: Rutgers University Press, 1986.

Buenker, John D. "The Progressive Era: A Search for Synthesis." *Mid-America* 51 (1969): 175–193.

Bulmer, Martin, Kevin Bales, and Kathryn Kish Sklar, eds. *The Social Survey in Historical Perspective, 1880–1940*. New York: Cambridge University Press, 1991.

Burnham, Walter Dean. *Critical Elections and the Mainsprings of American Politics*. New York: Norton, 1970.

Carnoy, Martin. *The State and Political Theory*. Princeton: Princeton University Press, 1984.

Carson, Mina. *Settlement Folk: Social Thought and the American Settlement Movement, 1885–1930*. Chicago: University of Chicago Press, 1990.

Ceplair, Larry, ed. *Charlotte Perkins Gilman: A Nonfiction Reader*. New York: Columbia University Press, 1991.

Chafe, William. *The American Woman, 1920–1970*. New York: Oxford University Press, 1972.

Chambers, Clarke A. *Seedtime of Reform: American Social Service and Social Action, 1918–1933*. Minneapolis: University of Minnesota Press, 1963.

Clement, Priscilla Ferguson. *Welfare and the Poor in the Nineteenth Century City: Philadelphia, 1800–1854*. Rutherford, NJ: Fairleigh Dickinson University Press, 1985.

Cmiel, Kenneth. *A Home of Another Kind: One Chicago Orphanage and the Tangle of Child Welfare*. Chicago: University of Chicago Press, 1995.

Cohen, Lizabeth. *Making a New Deal: Industrial Workers in Chicago, 1919–1939.* New York: Cambridge University Press, 1990.

Cohen, Miriam, and Michael Hanagan. "The Politics of Gender and the Making of the Welfare State, 1900–1940: A Comparative Perspective." *Journal of Social History* 24:3 (Spring 1991): 469–484.

Cook, Blanche Wiesen, ed. *Crystal Eastman on Women & Revolution.* New York: Oxford University Press, 1978.

Costin, Lela B. *Two Sisters for Social Justice: A Biography of Grace and Edith Abbott.* Urbana: University of Illinois Press, 1983.

Cott, Nancy F. "Feminist Politics in the 1920s: The National Women's Party." *Journal of American History* 71 (June 1984): 43–68.

———. *The Grounding of Modern Feminism.* New Haven: Yale University Press, 1987.

———. "What's in a Name? The Limits of 'Social Feminism'; or, Expanding the Vocabulary of Women's History." *Journal of American History* 76 (December 1989): 809–829.

Crocker, Ruth Hutchinson. *Social Work and Social Order: The Settlement Movement in Two Industrial Cities, 1889–1930.* Urbana: University of Illinois Press, 1992.

Danziger, Sheldon H., and Daniel H. Weinberg. *Fighting Poverty: What Works and What Doesn't.* Cambridge: Harvard University Press, 1986.

Danziger, Sheldon H., et al., eds. *Confronting Poverty: Prescriptions for Change.* New York: Russell Sage Foundation, 1994.

Davis, Allen F. *Spearheads for Reform: The Social Settlements and the Progressive Movement, 1890–1914.* New York: Oxford University Press, 1967.

———. *American Heroine, The Life and Legend of Jane Addams.* New York: Oxford University Press, 1973.

Davis, Allen F., and Mary Lynn McCree, eds. *Eighty Years at Hull House.* Chicago: Quadrangle Books, 1969.

Diner, Steven J. "Chicago Social Workers and Blacks in the Progressive Era." *Social Service Review* 44:4 (December 1970): 393–410.

———. *A City and Its Universities: Public Policy in Chicago, 1892–1919.* Chapel Hill: University of North Carolina Press, 1980.

Dye, Nancy Schrom. *As Equals and as Sisters: Feminism, the Labor Movement, and the Women's Trade Union League of New York.* Columbia: University of Missouri Press, 1980.

Ehrenreich, John H. *The Altruistic Imagination: A History of Social Work and Social Policy in the United States.* Ithaca: Cornell University Press, 1985.

Ellwood, David T. *Poor Support: Poverty in the American Family.* New York: Basic Books, 1988.

Epstein, Abraham. *Insecurity, A Challenge to America: A Study of Social Insurance in the United States and Abroad.* 2d rev. ed. New York: Agathon Press, 1968.

Evans, Peter, Dietrich Rueschemeyer, and Theda Skocpol, eds. *Bringing the State Back In.* Cambridge: Cambridge University Press, 1985.

Faue, Elizabeth. *Community of Suffering and Struggle: Women, Men, and the Labor Movement in Minneapolis, 1915–1945.* Chapel Hill: University of North Carolina Press, 1991.

Filene, Peter. "An Obituary for the Progressive Movement." *American Quarterly* 22 (1970): 20–34.

Fitzpatrick, Ellen F. *Endless Crusade: Women Social Scientists and Progressive Reform.* New York: Oxford University Press, 1990.

Flanagan, Maureen A. "Gender and Urban Political Reform: The City Club and the Woman's City Club of Chicago in the Progressive Era." *American Historical Review* 95:4 (October 1990): 1032–1050.

Frankel, Noralee, and Nancy S. Dye, eds. *Gender, Class, Race, and Reform in the Progressive Era.* Lexington: University Press of Kentucky, 1991.

Fraser, Nancy. *Unruly Practices: Power, Discourse, and Gender in Contemporary Social Theory.* Minneapolis: University of Minnesota Press, 1989.

Fraser, Nancy, and Linda Gordon. "A Genealogy of Dependency: Tracing a Keyword of the U.S. Welfare State." *Signs* 19:2 (Winter 1994): 309–336.

Fraser, Steve, and Gary Gerstle, eds. *The Rise and Fall of the New Deal Order, 1930–1980.* Princeton: Princeton University Press, 1989.

Furner, Mary O. *Advocacy and Objectivity: A Crisis in the Professionalization of American Social Science, 1865–1905.* Lexington: University Press of Kentucky, 1975.

Furstenberg, Frank, Theodore Hershberg, and John Modell. "The Origins of the Female-Headed Black Family: The Impact of the Urban Experience." *Journal of Interdisciplinary History* 6:2 (Autumn 1975): 211–233.

Garfinkel, Irwin, and Sara S. McLanahan. *Single Mothers and Their Children: A New American Dilemma.* Washington, DC: Urban Institute Press, 1986.

Gaylin, Willard, Ira Glasser, Steven Marcus, and David Rothman. *Doing Good: The Limits of Benevolence.* New York: Pantheon, 1978.

Giddings, Paula. *When and Where I Enter: The Impact of Black Women on Race and Sex in America.* New York: William Morrow, 1984.

Ginzberg, Lori D. *Women and the Work of Benevolence: Morality, Politics and Class in the Nineteenth-Century United States.* New Haven: Yale University Press, 1990.

Glickman, Lawrence. "Inventing the 'American Standard of Living': Gender, Race, and Working-Class Identity, 1880–1925." *Labor History* 34:2–3 (Spring-Summer 1993): 221–235.

Goldstein, Joel H. *The Effects of the Adoption of Woman Suffrage: Sex Differences in Voting Behavior—Illinois, 1914–1921.* New York: Praeger, 1984.

Goodwin, Joanne. "An American Experiment in Paid Motherhood: The Implementation of Mothers' Pensions in Early Twentieth Century Chicago." *Gender and History* 4:3 (Autumn 1992): 323–342.

———. "'Employable Mothers' and 'Suitable Work': A Re-evaluation of Welfare and Wage-Earning for Women in the Twentieth-Century United States." *Journal of Social History* 29:2 (Winter 1995): 253–274.

Gordon, Linda. "Black and White Visions of Welfare: Women's Welfare Activism, 1890–1945." *Journal of American History* 78 (September 1991): 559–590.

———. "Family Violence, Feminism, and Social Control." *Feminist Studies* 12:3 (Fall 1986): 453–478.

———. *Heroes of Their Own Lives: The Politics and History of Family Violence, Boston 1880–1960.* New York: Viking, 1988.

———. *Pitied But Not Entitled: Single Mothers and the History of Welfare, 1890–1935.* New York: Free Press, 1994.

———. "What Does Welfare Regulate?" *Social Research* 55:4 (Winter 1988): 609–630.

———, ed. *Women, the State and Welfare.* Madison: University of Wisconsin Press, 1990.

Gordon, Lynn. "Women and the Anti–Child Labor Movement in Illinois, 1890–1920." *Social Service Review* 51 (June 1977): 228–248.

Gough, Ian. *The Political Economy of the Welfare State*. London: Macmillan, 1979.

Grossberg, Michael. *Governing the Hearth: Law and the Family in Nineteenth-Century America*. Chapel Hill: University of North Carolina Press, 1985.

Grossman, James R. *Land of Hope: Chicago, Black Southerners, and the Great Migration*. Chicago: University of Chicago Press, 1989.

Handler, Joel F. *Reforming the Poor: Welfare Policy, Federalism, and Morality*. New York: Basic Books, 1972.

Hart, Vivien. *Bound by Our Constitution: Women, Workers, and Minimum Wage Laws in the United States and Britain*. Princeton: Princeton University Press, 1994.

Haskell, Thomas L. *The Emergence of Professional Social Science: The American Social Science Association and the Nineteenth-Century Crisis of Authority*. Urbana: University of Illinois Press, 1977.

Hays, Samuel. "Politics of Reform in Municipal Government in the Progressive Era." *Pacific Northwest Quarterly* 55 (1964): 157–169.

Helmbold, Lois Rita. "Beyond the Family Economy: Black and White Working-Class Women during the Great Depression." *Feminist Studies* 13 (Fall 1987): 629–655.

Hewitt, Nancy A., and Suzanne Lebsock, eds. *Visible Women: New Essays on American Activism*. Urbana: University of Illinois Press, 1993.

Higginbotham, Evelyn Brooks. *Righteous Discontent: The Women's Movement in the Black Baptist Church, 1880–1920*. Cambridge: Harvard University Press, 1993.

Hill, Mary A. *Charlotte Perkins Gilman: The Making of a Radical Feminist, 1860–1896*. Philadelphia: Temple University Press, 1980.

Hine, Darlene Clark. "'We Specialize in the Wholly Impossible': The Philanthropic Work of Black Women." In *Lady Bountiful Revisited: Women, Philanthropy, and Power*, ed. Kathleen D. McCarthy. New Brunswick: Rutgers University Press, 1990.

Howard, Christopher. "Sowing the Seeds of 'Welfare': The Transformation of Mothers' Pensions, 1900–1940." *Journal of Policy History* 4:2 (1992): 188–227.

Jackson, Philip. "Black Charity in Progressive Era Chicago." *Social Service Review* 52:3 (September 1978): 400–417.

Jones, Beverly Washington. *Quest for Equality: The Life and Writings of Mary Eliza Church Terrell, 1863–1954*. Vol. 13 of *Black Women in United States History*, ed. Darlene Clark Hine. Brooklyn, NY: Carlson Publishing, 1990.

Jones, Jacqueline. *Labor of Love, Labor of Sorrow: Black Women, Work, and the Family from Slavery to the Present*. New York: Basic Books, 1985.

Karl, Barry D. "Philanthropy, Policy Making, and the Bureaucratization of the Democratic Ideal." *Daedalus* 105:4 (Fall 1976): 129–149.

———. *The Uneasy State: The United States from 1915 to 1945*. Chicago: University of Chicago Press, 1983.

Katz, Michael. *In the Shadow of the Poorhouse: A Social History of Welfare in America*. New York: Basic Books, 1986.

———. "Origins of the Institutional State." *Marxist Perspectives* 1:4 (Winter 1978): 6–22.

———. *Poverty and Policy in American History*. Philadelphia: University of Pennsylvania, 1983.

Katz, Sherry. "Socialist Women and Progressive Reform." In *California Progressivism Revisited*, ed. William Deverell and Tom Sitton, 117–143. Berkeley: University of California Press, 1994.

Keller, Morton. *Affairs of State: Public Life in Late Nineteenth Century America*. Cambridge: Harvard University Press, 1977.

Kelly, Joan. *Women, History, and Theory*. Chicago: University of Chicago Press, 1984.

Kerber, Linda K., Alice Kessler-Harris, and Kathryn Kish Sklar, eds. *U.S. History as Women's History: New Feminist Essays*. Chapel Hill: University of North Carolina Press, 1995.

Kessler-Harris, Alice. *Out to Work: A History of Wage-Earning Women in the United States*. New York: Oxford University Press, 1982.

———. *A Woman's Wage: Historical Meanings and Social Consequences*. Lexington: University Press of Kentucky, 1990.

———. "Women and Welfare: Public Interventions in Private Lives." *Radical History Review* 56 (1993): 134.

Keyssar, Alexander. *Out of Work: The First Century of Unemployment in Massachusetts*. New York: Cambridge University Press, 1986.

Kirschner, Don S. "The Ambiguous Legacy: Social Justice and Social Control in the Progressive Era." *Historical Reflections* 2 (February 1975): 69–88.

Kleinberg, Susan J. *The Shadow of the Mills: Working Class Families in Pittsburgh, 1870–1917*. Pittsburgh: Pittsburgh University Press, 1989.

Klaus, Alisa. *Every Child a Lion: The Origins of Maternal and Infant Health Policy in the United States and France, 1890–1920*. Ithaca: Cornell University Press, 1993.

Kloppenberg, James T. *Uncertain Victory: Social Democracy and Progressivism in European and American Thought, 1870–1920*. New York: Oxford University Press, 1986.

Knupfer, Anne Meis. *Toward a Tenderer Humanity and a Nobler Womanhood: African American Women's Clubs in Turn of the Century Chicago*. New York: New York University Press, 1997.

Kogut, Alvin B. "The Negro and the Charitable Organization Society in the Progressive Era." *Social Service Review* 44:1 (March 1970): 11–21.

Koven, Seth, and Sonya Michel, eds. *Mothers of a New World: Maternalist Politics and the Origins of Welfare States*. New York: Routledge, 1993.

Kraditor, Aileen. *The Ideas of the Woman Suffrage Movement, 1890–1920*. New York: Columbia University Press, 1965.

Kraines, Oscar. *The World and Ideas of Ernst Freund: The Search for General Principles of Legislation and Administrative Law*. [N.p.]: University of Alabama Press, 1974.

Kunzel, Regina G. *Fallen Women, Problem Girls: Unmarried Mothers and the Professionalization of Social Work, 1890–1945*. New Haven: Yale University Press, 1993.

Kusmer, Kenneth. "The Functions of Organized Charities in the Progressive Era: Chicago as a Case Study." *Journal of American History* 60:3 (December 1973): 657–678.

Ladd-Taylor, Molly. *Mother-Work: Women, Child Welfare, and the State, 1890–1930*. Urbana: University of Illinois Press, 1994.

———. *Raising a Baby the Government Way*. New Brunswick: Rutgers University Press, 1986.

Lane, Ann J. *To Herland and Beyond: The Life and Work of Charlotte Perkins Gilman*. New York: Pantheon Books, 1990.

Lasch, Christopher, ed. *The Social Thought of Jane Addams*. New York: Bobbs-Merrill Co., 1965.

Lasch-Quinn, Elisabeth. *Black Neighbors: Race and the Limits of Reform in the American Settlement House Movement, 1890–1945*. Chapel Hill: University of North Carolina Press, 1993.

Leff, Mark H. "Consensus for Reform: The Mothers' Pension Movement in the Progressive Era." *Social Service Review* 47 (1973): 397–417.

Lehrer, Susan. *Origins of Protective Labor Legislation for Women, 1905–1925*. Albany: State University of New York Press, 1987.

Leiby, James. *A History of Social Welfare and Social Work in the United States*. New York: Columbia University Press, 1978.

———. "Social Control and Historical Explanation: Historians View the Piven and Cloward Thesis." In *Social Welfare or Social Control? Some Historical Reflections on Regulating the Poor*, ed. Walter Trattner, 90–113. Knoxville: University of Tennessee Press, 1983.

Lemons, J. Stanley. *The Woman Citizen: Social Feminism in the 1920s*. Urbana: University of Illinois Press, 1973.

Lerner, Gerda. *Black Women in White America*. New York: Pantheon, 1972.

Lide, Pauline. "The National Conference on Social Welfare and the Black Historical Perspective." *Social Service Review* (June 1973): 171–183.

Link, Arthur S. "What Happened to the Progressive Movement in the 1920s." *American Historical Review* 64 (1959): 833–851.

Lipschultz, Sybil. "Social Feminism and Legal Discourse, 1908–1923." *Yale Journal of Law and Feminism* 2:1 (Fall 1989): 131–160.

Lissak, Rivka. *Pluralism and Progressives: Hull House and the New Immigrants, 1890–1919*. Chicago: University of Chicago Press, 1989.

Lubove, Roy. *The Professional Altruist: The Emergence of Social Work as a Career, 1880–1930*. Cambridge: Harvard University Press, 1965.

———. *The Struggle for Social Security, 1900–1935*. Cambridge: Harvard University Press, 1968.

"Maternalism as a Paradigm." A symposium in *Journal of Women's History* 5:2 (Fall 1993): 95–131.

May, Martha. "'The Good Managers': Married Working Class Women and Family Budget Studies, 1895–1915." *Labor History* 25 (Summer 1984): 351–372.

———. "The Historical Problem of the Family Wage: The Ford Motor Company and the Five Dollar Day." *Feminist Studies* 8:2 (Summer 1982): 399–423.

———. "The 'Problem of Duty': Family Desertion in the Progressive Era." *Social Service Review* (March 1988): 40–60.

McCarthy, Kathleen D. *Noblesse Oblige: Charity and Cultural Philanthropy in Chicago, 1849–1929*. Chicago: University of Chicago Press, 1982.

McCormick, Richard L. *The Party Period and Public Policy: American Politics from the Age of Jackson to the Progressive Era*. New York: Oxford University Press, 1986.

McDonald, Terrence J. *The Parameters of Urban Fiscal Policy: Socioeconomic Change and Political Culture in San Francisco, 1860–1906*. Berkeley: University of California Press, 1986.

———. "Putting Politics Back into the History of the American City." *American Quarterly* (1982): 200–209.

Meyerowitz, Joanne J. *Women Adrift: Independent Wage Earners in Chicago, 1880–1930.* Chicago: University of Chicago Press, 1988.

Michel, Sonya, and Seth Koven. "Womanly Duties: Maternalist Politics and the Origins of Welfare States in France, Germany, Great Britain, and the United States, 1880–1920." *American Historical Review* 95:4 (October 1990): 1076–1108.

Mink, Gwendolyn. *The Wages of Motherhood: Inequality in the Welfare State, 1917–1942.* Ithaca: Cornell University Press, 1995.

Mohl, Raymond. "Mainstreaming Social Welfare History and Its Problems." *Reviews in American History* 7:4 (December 1979): 469–576.

Muncy, Robyn L. *Creating a Female Dominion in American Reform, 1890–1930.* New York: Oxford University Press, 1991.

Nelson, Barbara. "The Gender, Race, and Class Origins of Early Welfare Policy and the Welfare State: A Comparison of Workmen's Compensation and Mothers' Aid." In *Women, Politics, and Change,* ed. Louise A. Tilly and Patricia Gurin, 413–435. New York: Russell Sage Foundation, 1990.

———. "Women's Poverty and Women's Citizenship: Some Political Consequences of Economic Marginality." *Signs* 10:2 (Winter 1984): 209–231.

Nelson, Daniel. *Unemployment Insurance: The American Experience.* Madison: University of Wisconsin Press, 1969.

O'Connor, James. *The Fiscal Crisis of the State.* New York: St. Martin's Press, 1973.

Odem, Mary E. *Delinquent Daughters: Protecting and Policing Adolescent Female Sexuality in the United States, 1885–1920.* Chapel Hill: University of North Carolina Press, 1995.

Offen, Karen. "Defining Feminism: A Comparative Historical Approach." *Signs* 14 (Autumn 1988): 119–157)

O'Neill, William. *Everyone Was Brave: A History of Feminism in America.* Chicago: Quadrangle Books, 1971.

Orloff, Ann Shola. *The Politics of Pensions: A Comparative Analysis of Britain, Canada, and the United States, 1880–1940.* Madison: University of Wisconsin Press, 1993.

Orloff, Ann Shola, and Theda Skocpol. "Why Not Equal Protection? Explaining the Politics of Public Social Spending in Britain, 1900–1911, and the U.S., 1880s–1920." *American Sociology Review* 49 (December 1984): 726–750.

Parker, Jacqueline K., and Edward M. Carpenter. "Julia Lathrop and the Children's Bureau: The Emergence of an Institution." *Social Service Review* 55:1 (March 1981): 60–77.

Patterson, James T. *America's Struggle Against Poverty, 1900–1985.* Cambridge: Harvard University Press, 1986.

Payne, Elizabeth Anne. *Reform, Labor, and Feminism: Margaret Dreier Robins and the Women's Trade Union League.* Urbana: University of Illinois Press, 1988.

Pedersen, Susan. "The Failure of Feminism in the Making of the British Welfare State." *Radical History Review* (1989): 86–110.

———. *Family, Dependence, and the Origins of the Welfare State: Britain and France, 1914–1945.* New York: Cambridge University Press, 1993.

Philpott, Thomas Lee. *The Slum and the Ghetto: Neighborhood Deterioration and Middle-Class Reform, Chicago, 1880–1930.* New York: Oxford University Press, 1978.

Pierce, Bessie Louise. *A History of Chicago.* Vol. 3, *The Rise of a Modern City, 1871–1893.* New York: Alfred A. Knopf, 1957.

Pinderhughes, Dianne. *Race and Ethnicity in Chicago Politics: A Reexamination of Pluralist Theory.* Urbana: University of Illinois Press, 1987.

Piven, Frances Fox, and Richard A. Cloward. *Poor People's Movements: Why They Succeed, How They Fail.* New York: Pantheon Books, 1977.

———. *Regulating the Poor: The Functions of Public Welfare.* New York: Pantheon Books, 1971.

———. "Welfare Doesn't Shore Up Traditional Family Roles: A Reply to Linda Gordon." *Social Research* 55:4 (Winter 1988): 631–647.

Pleck, Elizabeth. *Black Migration and Poverty, Boston 1865–1900.* New York: Academic Press, 1979.

Pumphrey, Muriel W., and Ralph E. Pumphrey. "The Widows' Pension Movement, 1900–1930: Preventive Child-Saving or Social Control?" In *Social Welfare or Social Control? Some Historical Reflections on "Regulating the Poor,"* ed. Walter I. Trattner, 51–66. Knoxville: University of Tennessee Press, 1983.

Quadagno, Jill S. *The Color of Welfare: How Racism Undermined the War on Poverty.* New York: Oxford University Press, 1994.

———. "Welfare Capitalism and the Social Security Act of 1935." *American Sociology Review* 49 (October 1984): 632–647.

Rochefort, David A. "Progressive and Social Control Perspectives on Social Welfare." *Social Service Review* 55 (December 1981): 568–592.

Ross, Dorothy. *The Origins of American Social Science.* New York: Cambridge University Press, 1991.

Ross, Edyth L., ed. *Black Heritage in Social Welfare, 1860–1930.* Metuchen, NJ: Scarecrow Press, 1978.

Rothman, David. *Conscience and Convenience: The Asylum and Its Alternatives in Progressive America.* Boston: Little Brown, 1980.

Rouse, Jacqueline Anne. *Lugenia Burns Hope: Black Southern Reformer.* Athens: University of Georgia Press, 1989.

Salem, Dorothy. *To Better Our World: Black Women in Organized Reform, 1890–1920.* Brooklyn, NY: Carlson Publishing Co., 1990.

Sapiro, Virginia. "The Gender Basis of American Social Policy." *Political Science Quarterly* 101:2 (1986): 221–238.

Sarvasy, Wendy. "Beyond the Difference Versus Equality Policy Debate: Post-Suffrage Feminism, Citizenship, and the Quest for a Feminist Welfare State." *Signs* 17:2 (Winter 1992): 329–362.

Scott, Anne Firor. *Natural Allies: Women's Associations in American History.* Urbana: University of Illinois Press, 1991.

Scott, Joan W. *Gender and the Politics of History.* New York: Columbia University Press, 1988.

Shaw, Stephanie. "Black Club Women and the Creation of the National Association of Colored Women." *Journal of Women's History* 3:2 (Fall 1991): 10–25.

———. *What a Woman Ought to Be and to Do: Black Professional Women Workers during the Jim Crow Era.* Chicago: University of Chicago Press, 1996.

Sklar, Kathryn Kish. *Florence Kelley and the Nation's Work: The Rise of Women's Political Culture, 1830–1900.* New Haven: Yale University Press, 1995.

———. "The Historical Foundations of Women's Power in the Creation of the American Welfare State, 1830–1930," in *Mothers of a New World: Maternalist Politics and the Origins of Welfare States,* ed. Seth Koven and Sonya Michel, 43–93. New York: Routledge, 1993.

———. "Hull House in the 1890s: A Community of Women Reformers." *Signs* (Summer 1985): 658–677.

———. "Two Political Cultures in the Progressive Era: The National Consumers' League and the American Association for Labor Legislation." In *U.S. History as Women's History: New Feminist Essays,* ed. Linda K. Kerber, Alice Kessler-Harris, Kathryn Kish Sklar. Chapel Hill: University of North Carolina Press, 1995.

Skocpol, Theda. *Protecting Soldiers and Mothers: The Political Origins of Social Policy in the United States.* Cambridge: Belknap Press of Harvard University Press, 1992.

———. ed. *Vision and Method in Historical Sociology.* Cambridge: Cambridge University Press, 1984.

Skocpol, Theda, and Gretchen Ritter. "Gender and the Origins of Modern Social Policies in Britain and the United States." *Studies in American Political Development* 5:1 (1991).

Skocpol, Theda, et al., "Women's Associations and the Enactment of Mothers' Pensions in the United States." *American Political Science Review* 87:3 (September 1993): 696.

Skowronek, Stephen. *Building a New American State: The Expansion of National Administrative Capacities, 1877–1920.* Cambridge: Cambridge University Press, 1982.

Slayton, Robert A. *Back of the Yards: The Making of a Local Democracy.* Chicago: University of Chicago Press, 1986.

Spear, Allan H. *Black Chicago: The Making of a Negro Ghetto, 1890–1920.* Chicago: University of Chicago Press, 1967.

Stadum, Beverly. *Poor Women and Their Families: Hard Working Charity Cases, 1900–1930.* Albany: State University of New York Press, 1992.

Stansell, Christine. *City of Women: Sex and Class in New York, 1789–1860.* New York: Alfred A. Knopf, 1986.

Stehno, Sandra M. "Public Responsibility for Dependent Black Children: The Advocacy of Edith Abbott and Sophonisba Breckinridge." *Social Service Review* 62 (September 1988): 485–503.

Steinberg, Ronnie. *Wages and Hours: Labor and Reform in Twentieth Century America.* New Brunswick, NJ: Rutgers University Press, 1982.

Strickland, Arvarh E. *History of the Chicago Urban League.* Urbana: University of Illinois Press, 1966.

Strong-Boag, Veronica. "'Wages for Housework': Mothers' Allowances and the Beginnings of Social Security in Canada." *Journal of Canadian Studies* (Spring 1979): 24–34.

Terborg-Penn, Rosalyn. "African-American Women's Networks in the Anti-Lynching Crusade." In *Gender, Class, Race, and Reform in the Progressive Era,* ed. Noralee Frankel and Nancy S. Dye, 148–161. Lexington: University Press of Kentucky, 1991.

Thelen, David. "Social Tensions and the Origins of Progressivism." *Journal of American History* 56 (1969): 323–341.

Tiffin, Susan. *In Whose Best Interest? Child Welfare Reform in the Progressive Era.* Westport, CT: Greenwood Press, 1982.

Tilly, Louise A., and Patricia Gurin, eds. *Women, Politics, and Change.* New York: Russell Sage Foundation, 1990.

Tishler, Hace. *Self-Reliance and Social Security, 1870–1917.* Port Washington, NY: National University Publications, 1971.

Trattner, Walter. *Crusade for the Children: A History of the National Child Labor Committee and Child Labor Reform in America.* Chicago: Quadrangle Books, 1970.

———. *From Poor Law to Welfare State: A History of Social Welfare in America.* New York: Free Press, 1974.

———, ed. *Social Welfare or Social Control? Some Historical Reflections on Regulating the Poor.* Knoxville: University of Tennessee Press, 1983.

Vandepol, Ann. "Dependent Children, Child Custody, and the Mothers' Pensions: The Transformation of State-Family Relations in the Early Twentieth Century." *Social Problems* 29:3 (February 1982): 221–235.

Vicinus, Martha. *Independent Women: Work and Community for Single Women, 1850–1920.* Chicago: University of Chicago Press, 1985.

Ware, Susan. *Beyond Suffrage: Women in the New Deal.* Cambridge: Harvard University Press, 1981.

Weiler, N. Sue. "The Uprising in Chicago: The Men's Garment Workers Strike, 1910–1911." In *A Needle, A Bobbin, A Strike: Women Needleworkers in America,* ed. Joan M. Jensen and Sue Davidson, 114–139. Philadelphia: Temple University Press, 1984.

Weinstein, James. *The Corporate Ideal in the Liberal State, 1900–1918.* Boston: Beacon Press, 1968.

Weir, Margaret, Ann Shola Orloff, and Theda Skocpol, eds. *The Politics of Social Policy in the United States.* Princeton: Princeton University Press, 1988.

Wheeler, Adade M., and Marlene Stein Wortman. *The Roads They Made: Women in Illinois History.* Chicago: Charles H. Kerr Publishing Co., 1977.

Wiebe, Robert. *The Search for Order, 1877–1920.* New York: Hill and Wang, 1967.

Witte, Edwin E. *The Development of the Social Security Act.* Madison: University of Wisconsin Press, 1963.

Wilson, William J. *The Truly Disadvantaged: The Inner City, the Underclass, and Public Policy.* Chicago: University of Chicago Press, 1987.

———. *When Work Disappears: The World of the New Urban Poor.* New York: Alfred A. Knopf, 1996.

Zelman, Patricia G. *Women, Work, and National Policy: The Kennedy-Johnson Years.* Ann Arbor, MI.: UMI Research Press, 1982.

Zimmerman, Joan G. "The Jurisprudence of Equality: The Women's Minimum Wage, the First Equal Rights Amendment, and *Adkins v. Children's Hospital,* 1905–1923." *Journal of American History* 78:1 (June 1991): 188–225.

UNPUBLISHED PAPERS AND DISSERTATIONS

Anderson, Paul Gerard. "The Good to Be Done: A History of Juvenile Protective Association of Chicago, 1898–1976." Ph.D. diss., University of Chicago, 1988.

Getis, Victoria Lynn. "A Disciplined Society: The Juvenile Court, Reform, and the Social Sciences in Chicago, 1890–1930." Ph.D. diss., University of Michigan, 1994.

Helmbold, Lois Rita. "Making Choices, Making Do: Black and White Working-Class Women's Lives and Work during the Great Depression." Ph.D. diss., Stanford University, 1983.

Hendricks, Wanda Ann. "The Politics of Race: Black Women in Illinois, 1890–1920." Ph.D. diss., Purdue University, 1990.

Hoffman, Beatrix. "Endless Defeat: Health Insurance and the Making of the American Welfare State." Ph.D. diss., Rutgers University, 1996.

Michel, Sonya A. "Children's Interests/Mothers' Rights: Women, Professionals, and the American Family, 1920–1945." Ph.D. diss., Brown University, 1986.

Moore, Libba Gage. "Mothers' Pensions: The Origins of the Relationship between Women and the Welfare State." Ph.D. diss., University of Massachusetts, 1986.

Parkin, Katherine Joyce. "Day Nurseries in Chicago, 1890–1930." Senior Thesis, Lake Forest College, 1993.

Rose, Elizabeth R. "Maternal Work: Day Care in Philadelphia, 1890–1960." Ph.D. diss., Rutgers University, 1994.

Walsh, Winifred Agnes. "Grace Abbott and Social Action." Ph.D. diss., University of Chicago, School of Social Service Administration, 1966.

Wedel, Janet Marie. "The Origins of State Patriarchy during the Progressive Era: A Sociologic Study of the Mothers' Aid Movement." Ph.D. diss., Washington University, 1975.

Index